D0148444

Practicing Community

PRACTICING COMMUNITY

Class Culture and Power
in an Urban Neighborhood

Rhoda H. Halperin

 UNIVERSITY OF TEXAS PRESS, AUSTIN

Published with the help of the Charles Phelps Taft Memorial Fund, University of Cincinnati.

First edition, 1998

Requests for permission to reproduce material from this work should be sent to Permissions, University of Texas Press, Box 7819, Austin, TX 78713-7819.

☉ The paper used in this publication meets the minimum requirements of American National Standard for Information Sciences—Permanence of Paper for Printed Library Materials, ANSI Z39.48-1984.

Library of Congress Cataloging-in-Publication Data

Halperin, Rhoda H.
    Practicing community : class culture and power in an urban neighborhood / Rhoda H. Halperin. — 1st ed.
        p.   cm.
    Includes bibliographical references and index.
    ISBN 0-292-73118-3 (cloth : alk. paper). — ISBN 0-292-73117-5 (pbk. : alk. paper)
    1. East End (Cincinnati, Ohio)— Social conditions.   2. Cincinnati (Ohio)—Social conditions.   3. Community life—Ohio—Cincinnati.   4. Community development—Ohio—Cincinnati—Citizen participation.   5. Working class—Ohio—Cincinnati.
    I. Title.
HN80.C55H35   1998
306'.09771'78—dc21   97-33917

Some of the owner men were kind because they hated what they had to do, and some of them were angry because they hated to be cruel, and some of them were cold because they had long ago found that one could not be an owner unless one were cold. And all of them were caught in something larger than themselves.

• • •

Sure, cried the tenant men, but it's our land. We measured it and broke it up. We were born on it, and we got killed on it, died on it. Even if it's no good, it's still ours. That's what makes it ours—being born on it, working on it, dying on it. That makes ownership, not a paper with numbers on it.

• • •

The tenant pondered. "Funny thing how it is. If a man owns a little property, that property is him, it's part of him, and it's like him. If he owns property only so he can walk on it and handle it and be sad when it isn't doing well, and feel fine when the rains fall on it, that property is him, and some way he's bigger because he owns it. Even if he isn't successful he's big with his property. That is so."

• • •

And the tenant pondered more. "But let a man get property he doesn't see, or can't take time to get his fingers in, or can't be there to walk on it—why, then the property is the man. He can't do what he wants, he can't think what he wants. The property is the man, stronger than he is. And he is small, not big. Only his possessions are big—and he's the servant of property. That is so, too."

John Steinbeck, *The Grapes of Wrath*

CONTENTS

ILLUSTRATIONS

Maps

Figures

PREFACE

Writing Community

Much has been said about writing culture. This book attempts to write community—to write community within class culture. What does it mean to be writing community?

Writing community mandates writing a text, not for the sake of the text itself, but to reveal to those who do not understand what people do and say, day to day, to keep community—fight for it, revitalize it, honor it, claim community, build it by building institutions, however difficult that process is.

Texts—no matter what sort, are by nature linear. One word follows another.

Community is circular—sometimes spherical with many layers. Community must be understood in the round—in multiple dimensions of ups and downs, of intergenerational ties—of politics personal and bureaucratic, of family, of children and elders, of getting food and the other stuff of livelihood, of home and heritage.

A person must practice community in order to write it. Some East Enders write and practice community. All East Enders practice community. Writing community takes much time—narrative, poetry. Speaking community is also important and must be written down.

For me, thinking and writing are primary—the obligations of academics, a way of giving back to community by documenting, heightening experience, highlighting, explaining, analyzing.

Community is a common, ordinary word. We think we know what it is. We take it for granted. We assume its presence or we lament its absence. We know why we need it; yet we question it at the same time—where is it, what is it?

Identity and community are often linked but in complex ways. The community itself has an integrity—an identity—a set of boundaries, albeit contested ones. People have identities that may or may not be linked to place, to people, to working-class culture because of, or in spite of, the powers that be. People identify with place—especially if it has been home for lifetimes—even generations.

The river is a power, a steady presence, a boundary, a source of identity. "River rats"—said with affection or disdain, depending upon who is talking. A force that can tighten family and community bonds but that can also devastate houses, bring building inspectors, and devastate more houses.

Language, humor—all parts of practicing and writing community. "We have our lingo," an elder East End leader tells me.

So do anthropologists.

The traditions—ethnography, economic history, economic anthropology, social theory—Karl Polanyi spent much of his life working with, teaching, and understanding the British working class.

Polanyi's essential humanism has driven this project. The reality of politics and power also drives this work.

These are politics that matter.

I came into this project by being very sure of what we were doing, and I left feeling very unsure. I am sure, though, that the anthropology here does not just observe or participate. It lives, breathes, and embraces the struggles. This is anthropology that practices daily the tasks of community and then after practicing, doing, extolling, cheering—writes. Writing happens only after the really hard practical community work is done. But the hard work is never done. It is ongoing.

ACKNOWLEDGMENTS

To all East End residents and leaders, especially people who have struggled to maintain this working-class community in the city of Cincinnati, I dedicate this book with heartfelt thanks for sharing life, wisdom, and, most important, heart with me—especially Dorothy, Eileen, Fred, Ruth, John, and Margaret.

Without Michael Maloney, work in the East End would not have been possible. Mike has spent most of his adult life as a researcher, community organizer, and advocate for Appalachian people in the state of Ohio and in the Appalachian region. As the founder of the Urban Appalachian Council (UAC), he has been particularly active in Cincinnati's Appalachian community. He is the person I call in times of community crisis, and he has remained a saintly friend and colleague to me and to all East Enders.

The main ethnographic phase of the East End Study Project (EESP) received funding from Ohio's Urban Policy Action Committee (UPAC) and the Charles Phelps Taft Memorial Fund of the University of Cincinnati. One EESP project, the heritage exhibit entitled *The Life and Times of East End Heritage,* resulted from a wealth of cultural resources (photographs, poems, newspaper clippings, narratives) furnished by East Enders in the course of our team's work. Funding for the exhibit project, which yielded extraordinarily valuable ethnographic material, came principally from the Ohio Humanities Council, the Ohio Joint Program in the Arts and Humanities, and the Ohio Appalachian Arts Initiative. Additional support came from Procter and Gamble, the Murray and

Agnes Seasongood Foundation, the Fine Arts Fund, and the Cinergy Foundation.

Some of my best thinking has happened over many, many cups of coffee served with great warmth and cheer by Carolyn and Bonnie at the Echo Restaurant in Cincinnati. Writing in restaurants has long been a practice of mine, and the Echo is my favorite place of all.

I also want to thank my many colleagues and friends in and outside of the university: Jim Black, Ken Bordwell, Kathy Borman, Ed Burdell, Lynne Coward, Dave Crafts, Duraid Da'as, Nan Ellin, Susan Greenbaum, Pauletta Hansel, Mary Hehemann, Jimmy and Jennie Hirschfeld, Janet Howard, Andy Hofling, Barry Isaac, Ken Kensinger, Jackie McCray, Sally Merry, Pat Mora, Elaine Pennington, Vern Scarborough, John Schreider, Sanjeeb Schrestha, Bonita Singal, Peter Strauss, Joe Tomain, and Bailey Turner.

To my students, I extend a special thanks. Jennifer Reiter has been a wonderful colleague and calming influence. Andrea Zaylor transcribed many of the tapes, as did Lora Anderson. Tom Fugate and Steve McDougal did many chores, especially the kinship charts, the maps, and the bibliography. Matt Purtill also worked on maps. Kathy Lasher and Kristin Quinn did the archival research in local newspapers. Sherry Jared has been with this project from the start. Greg Thompson, Sara Sheets, Judy Trombly, Kelly Mayne, Libby Burnside-Mora, Rachel and Pat Timm, Jonathan Perry, and Margaret Zeigler helped collect the data as a part of the East End Study Project. I would like to thank Lois Allen and Kathleen E. Del Monte for their help with the indexes.

The Charles Phelps Taft Memorial Fund has provided help at various stages of this project. I thank the faculty fellowship committee and the publications committee in particular. Theresa May of the University of Texas Press believed in this project. Carolyn Wylie, also of U.T. Press, took extra care with the manuscript.

To my family, Bill, Sam, Michael, Sidney, and Sylvia, I extend gratitude for their patience with the many years I have spent conducting ethnographic fieldwork and advocacy "at home."

The history of my own involvement in Appalachian culture as a researcher and as an advocate (a long-standing tradition in Appalachian studies) is lengthy. In 1983, I began research in rural northeastern Kentucky, a place that in many ways reminded me of other rural places I had worked in the world—the West Indies, Mexico, Colombia. Northeastern Kentucky is a place where women work alongside men on farms, in marketplaces, in factories. Livelihood patterns are intricately configured and deeply embedded in "the Kentucky way," a regional sense of community and class. I first became involved in research in Kentucky when Deb Williamson, then one of my graduate students—upset with the stereotypes of Appalachians—urged me to investigate the economy of rural Kentucky, especially the Kentucky way of which she was so proud. The Kentucky way has an East End counterpart.

I never intended to become a specialist or "expert" in Appalachian culture (see Batteau 1990). It happened really as an outgrowth of my interest in agrarian systems and systems of social stratification worldwide. But after the results of my work in Kentucky were published as *The Livelihood of Kin* (1990), I automatically became one of the few non-Appalachian specialists on Appalachian culture.

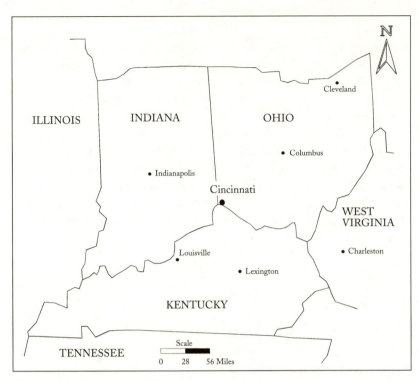

Map 1. Ohio, Indiana, and Kentucky

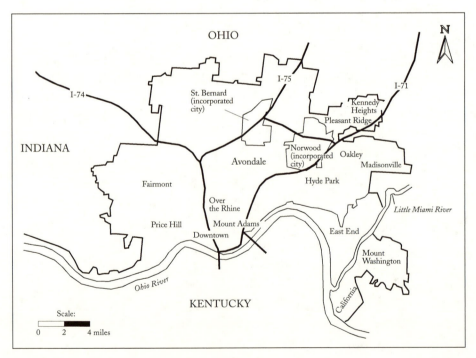

Map 2. Cincinnati Neighborhoods

PROLOGUE

A Historic Enclave

Many Cincinnatians have heard of the East End but don't know where it is. The fact that the East End is a vaguely recognized, but unfamiliar, difficult-to-locate and difficult-to-identify neighborhood in a city that prides itself on its fifty-one discrete and recognizable neighborhoods is probably the most telling fact about the East End. It tells of the marginality, the powerlessness, the contested boundaries, and the hidden and almost mysterious qualities of a geographically large and prominently situated community that begins on the eastern edge of downtown and runs east for eight miles, along the Ohio River out to the suburbs. It does not, however, tell of the strengths, the spirit, or the spirituality of a community that takes pride in calling East End home. Working-class Cincinnatians know exactly where the East End is. Local knowledge varies by class.

To my knowledge, this is the first book-length monograph to be devoted to an urban community within the Appalachian region.[1]

This book is about East Enders working to preserve a community that is embroiled in planning and implementing urban economic development on a valuable strip of riverfront land in Cincinnati, Ohio. The most important words in this sentence are "East Enders" and "community"—working-class people in a working-class community known as the East End.

Practicing Community: Class Culture and Power in an Urban Neighborhood is about the nature of community. As such, it is part of a long tradition of community studies in anthropology in particular and in the social sciences in general. *Practicing Community* is not a traditional community study,[2] however. In this book, I argue for rethinking and re-defining community, not as a geographical and bounded place, not as a set of roads, rivers, dwellings, and geological features, not even as a network of defined and linked relationships. Rather, community is a dynamic, contentious, and changing process that plays out as a series of everyday practices by people who have or have had some link to the East End. Many East Enders have been displaced and no longer live in the East End itself. At the extreme, people may live in Texas or Florida or, more commonly, in another neighborhood in Cincinnati, in a nearby town, in rural Ohio, or in Kentucky. Everyday practices—caring for children and the elderly, providing work, helping in times of crisis, granting favors, passing along information, or lending support—represent the essence of East End life and culture because they are, however tenuously and fleetingly, embedded in specific East End structures that are old and enduring—the extended family, the church, and the neighborhood as a place that confers working-class identity. The practices involved in maintaining these structures take priority over all others. A real East Ender will take a lesser job, quit a job, or drop out of school before denying help or money to family and community members who need support. These structures are working-class structures. Some are being rebuilt; others are being created. Some structures are incipient, in the idea stage or even in the dream stage—a heritage center and a community school, to name two. The practices of institution building require residents and leaders to struggle against existing power structures.

The corollary, or logical extension, of this definition of community, is also practical: to work as a researcher in the East End, a person must become engaged in or at least connected to the everyday practices that work to maintain and rebuild community—meetings, nonprofit boards, informal gatherings. To refrain from becoming engaged represents a failure to comprehend the nature of community. At best, such detachment makes researchers and advocates the targets of criticism from community leaders. At worst, even the most liberal and well intentioned can be ousted from the community entirely.

Class culture is linked to practicing community in distinct working-class styles. Working-class culture, then, is not something that is shared by all people in a given place, not even in a place as small as the East End. Class culture, or the culture of class—in this case, the working class—is a product of the highly unequal power relations in a complex urban economy and society.[3] One of the many ways to express class culture is to engage in practices, both on the political level—the fight for community survival—and on the ordinary, day-to-day level, that resist the power structure or that represent adaptations to inequality. The fight for the heritage center and the struggles for affordable housing are examples of East End practices on the political level. Engagement in the informal economy, everyday practices of trading, sharing, and giving of time, resources, and money, are examples of practices on the ordinary, day-to-day level. These also include withholding information from people in power whenever possible.

Working-class culture is certainly not confined to the East End—indeed, in some general ways, it is a worldwide phenomenon. It is neither shared nor experienced by middle- and upper-class people, however, and is, thus, mysterious. Elites do not understand working-class culture. When people in power do not understand something, they tend to be very critical, judgmental, patronizing, and dismissive.

Practicing Community is based on more than six years of anthropological research and advocacy on the part of a university-based team in this long-lived community of African American and Caucasian Appalachian people. The original goal of the East End Study Project was to gather data that would strengthen the community's voice in the planning process and that would shatter the negative stereotypes about working-class people in general and East Enders in particular. Unlike most research teams that enter communities for periods of a few months to a year, carry out projects, and then exit, members of the EESP have, along with local elites and community volunteers, remained involved in the community—sitting on boards of community nonprofit corporations, advising with technical expertise, and simply participating as friends of the East End. In the process, the lines between researchers and advocates, elites, East Enders, and "university people," have blurred.

A Special Place

East Enders talk about the East End as unique. The East End and East Enders are indeed very special. The East End is not a traditional urban ethnic community, for it is neither urban nor ethnic in the classic senses. With a few exceptions, it is not a community of newcomers, but, rather, of people who have been residents for a half-dozen generations or more. East Enders are difficult to classify. Many people in the East End, black and white, can be said to be Appalachian, but not all.[4] East Enders have "people" (family) who originated in the rural Appalachian parts of Ohio, Kentucky, Tennessee, or West Virginia. Others came directly from Europe, Germany and Ireland, primarily. Still others came from the rural South—North Carolina, Alabama, and Georgia.

Where Appalachia ends and the rural South begins is entirely arbitrary. The Appalachian Regional Commission, which established Appalachia in 1967 by designating certain counties as in or out of the region, had an economic and political agenda. Probably most East Enders would be insulted by the label "Appalachian," since the term is perceived to be equivalent to "hillbilly."

The urban nature of the East End is also problematic, even though it is officially one of Cincinnati's fifty-one urban neighborhoods. In the mid-1970s, it was home to fifteen thousand people in low-density, low-rise buildings and many single-family dwellings. The community has always been small and personal. East Enders see one another frequently on the street and recognize East End ties when they are downtown or in another neighborhood. Resistance to impersonal urbanism and to urban institutions (most notably, large schools, large hospitals, and large bureaucracies) is common among East Enders.

In one sense, the East End is tightly contained; in another, it is permeable. The East End should not be understood to be bounded as commonly understood in traditional community studies. The identity of the East End to East Enders, past and present, is distinct and coherent. At the same time, East End boundaries vis-à-vis non–East Enders are constantly contested. Ties to the region (including rural areas), to the city, to outsiders, all complicate the issue of boundaries and, of course, figure very importantly in the analysis of grassroots efforts to maintain community and class identity. There are branches of the East End in Kentucky, in other neighborhoods of Cincinnati such as Mount Washington, Oakley, Madisonville, Kennedy Heights, Avondale, and Price Hill, and in parts of rural Ohio.

In this context, community identity—as expressed in the phrases "we are East Enders" or he is a "real East Ender"—is a code for class or, as one community leader put it, "the common people." "Real" East Enders are members of the working class. Many East Enders used to work in a large automotive plant in Norwood, an incorporated small city adjacent to Cincinnati, until it closed in 1992. Of eight East End men formerly employed there, only one moved to Florida; everyone else remains in the East End or nearby.

Deindustrialization has hit the East End harder than it has hit many other communities in Cincinnati; East Enders are not dependent on the wage labor economy, however. Long-standing strategies designed to cope with the uncertainties of the wage labor economy are legion. While many people do indeed work for wages, in local factories, downtown, and in neighboring communities (often obtaining jobs through kin and neighborhood ties), East Enders have an elaborate informal economy, which is legal but off the books nonetheless. Odd jobs in the wealthier communities to the north and the east, service jobs in the downtown area to the west, flea markets, and small farms, to the south and southeast, enable East Enders to generate resources in cash and in kind. Going "upriver" is, among other things, a statement about accessing resources from rural areas. The country is also a place of relaxation and fresh air—a respite from the confines of urban life.

People on welfare also work—in flea markets, at odd jobs, or in some other "under the table" fashion. Multiple livelihood strategies are a way of life in the East End. Social scientists call this the informal economy and, in this respect, the rural and Appalachian qualities of the East End must be emphasized, for multiple livelihood strategies historically have been a way of life for all working-class people in the world, rural and urban.

Practicing Community

"Practicing community" is an intentionally active phrase meant to convey the arduous, often grueling, long-term, persistent efforts of East Enders to preserve and revitalize the community as it is changing from an undesirable floodplain to some of the most sought-after property in the region. In order to understand the East End and East Enders, practicing community must be experienced and analyzed as a dynamic, changing, and, at times, tumultuous and dangerous process. At the same time, practicing community must also be understood to confer a sense of peace and well-being on East Enders.

Community is not just a place, although place is very important, but a series of day-to-day, ongoing, often invisible practices. These practices are connected but not confined to place. To maintain the East End community for East Enders requires residents and leaders alike to take community personally. The stakes are high—community, identity, heritage, and survival.

I have written this book to be accessible to a broad audience: East Enders and the working poor, people of varying levels of education, as well as students, educators, scholars, and policymakers. Different readers will interpret the discussions of power, the dialogues, the personal narratives, and the expressions of working-class culture and resistance differently. I write from a perspective that emphasizes classic anthropological holistic approaches to the analysis of culture and community. But this classic holism operates in the context of recent discussions of power and knowledge, colonialism and resistance, hybrid cultures and subaltern studies. The last two are terms that scholars use to refer to what one elderly East End leader calls simply "the people." For example, an updated holistic view of community economic development sees a community center not as an institution controlled by the power structure, but as an institution connected to and controlled by the community for the purpose of building housing, taking care of health, and providing education and jobs, all ideally based locally. A community center such as the Pendleton Heritage Center in the East End, then, is not just a building, but a site for economic development that includes multipurpose spaces for workshops, small businesses, parking, and temporary flea markets. A community center can thus be viewed as a positive social movement that makes building local institutions possible.

In this framework, alternative institutions for ensuring livelihood, health care, housing, and a sense of community can be understood as using the system of market capitalism without succumbing to it. Market and nonmarket mechanisms, formal and informal social and economic activities operate in many combinations and rhythms. The complexity of institutional arrangements needs to be understood and taken seriously before working-class culture can begin to be intelligible to scholars and practitioners, whether the practitioners are social service providers, planners, physicians, teachers, or policymakers. Individual people are important in this book. So, too, are the structures—local, regional, national, and international—within which people live and interact. Class culture is a constantly changing structure; it changes from one generation to the next and from one segment of the neighborhood to the next. A person may feel at home in one part of the neighborhood and completely alone or afraid in another. A woman in her fifties may deny that race matters; a woman in her thirties would never say such a thing.

Historically, the Ohio River bottoms have been located both geographically and politically on the edges of the city.[5] Working-class people of diverse origins, southern blacks and whites plus Germans and Irish, composed the majority of the population.[6] From the moment of arrival, people along the river bottoms experienced poverty and discrimination. In Cincinnati, people who could afford to live on higher ground were, by definition, of higher social class. Stereotypes were formed early on and have been perpetuated and accentuated by the press.[7]

The East End, which in the 1970s had a population of over fifteen thousand and a solid business community, has experienced dramatic changes since then—demographic decline, deteriorating infrastructure, and a series of city-generated community development plans. Many residents say that the decline and deterioration are the result of the city's neglect of the community. This neglect is understood by residents as an intentional strategy designed to decrease property values so that the land in the East End will be attractive as investment for developers.

1 | GUIDEPOSTS

$\mathcal{E}$ast End working-class people, men and women, young and old, black and white, homeowners and tenants, residents and leaders, practice community in an urban neighborhood that is not quite urban and that is under threat of disappearing as a community. The struggles for empowerment, identity, and control of daily life, place, and livelihood are ongoing, often against seemingly relentless and insurmountable odds. I hope this book will strengthen the voices that historically have been silenced or ignored by those in power by examining the systems of oppression that are part of daily life in the East End.

In the 1980s, when I was working in northeastern Kentucky, I found areas that were not quite rural, or at least not *as* rural as others.[1] Small farms and homesteads with gardens lined interstate highways that led to factories, flea markets, shopping malls, and, eventually, to the city. These areas I decided to call "shallow rural" to draw the contrast with "deep rural," or what in Appalachia is called "the country." Geographically, the shallow rural region is located between "the country" and "the city"; conceptually, the shallow rural is "country."

When I say that the East End is not quite urban, I mean that it resembles the "not quite rural" aspects of the shallow rural region. The East End does not fit most of our ordinary definitions of urban areas: large, dense, crowded, dangerous, noisy spaces that bristle with tense activity. The East End has few of these features. For these reasons, I describe the community as shallow urban to emphasize the contrast between East End as a small, spread out enclave and the large, congested inner-city areas such as Over the Rhine. Geographically and culturally, the East End lies between the shallow rural and the city, and East Enders maintain close contact with relatives in rural areas. In short, shallow rural is shallow because of its closeness and accessibility to the city; shallow urban is shallow because of its closeness and accessibility to the country.

When I say that the East End is under threat of disappearing as a community, I think of one leader's 1991 ink drawings of vultures descending on the East End to buy up houses and lots (Figure 1). The sale of the community is the greatest threat to its existence and to its integrity as a community of working-class people. The practice of community, especially the struggles for empowerment, identity, and control, requires daily interaction and confrontation with people in power—landlords, building inspectors, the city, developers. Some outsiders pretend to be insiders the better to control the community.

In order to understand the practice of community, the East End must be understood in the context of the city and, indeed, of the larger global forces that affect work and life in the East End: rural-to-urban migration and return migration, deindustrialization, and intensified marginalization. Market forces (market-rate upscale housing, land speculation, and increased property values) not only are at the East End's door, they have become facts of life in this riverfront community.

It takes hard work to make ends meet in so-called low-income communities. Hard community work (all voluntary and, therefore, unpaid) builds institutions and rebuilds community. Practicing community requires neighborhood people to struggle daily against outside forces that impose themselves on the community; at the same time, East Enders must deal with earning a livelihood and caring for extended family members, especially small children and the elderly. To talk about practicing community is to counter some assumptions commonly held by people of wealth and power about people in the working class, especially about the working poor. To understand these assumptions is to understand the cultural construction of marginality from the point of view of the power structure and from the point of view of "real" East Enders, the grassroots people whose working-class families have lived in the East End for at least three, and often, five, six, or seven generations.

One assumption on the part of the power structure is that the working poor, here, East Enders, don't have an identity, or are not worthy of one. The community and its people are assumed to be deficient, lacking, unstable, and without strengths. Facts about the East End are interpreted, twisted, and used negatively by the power structure. For example, East

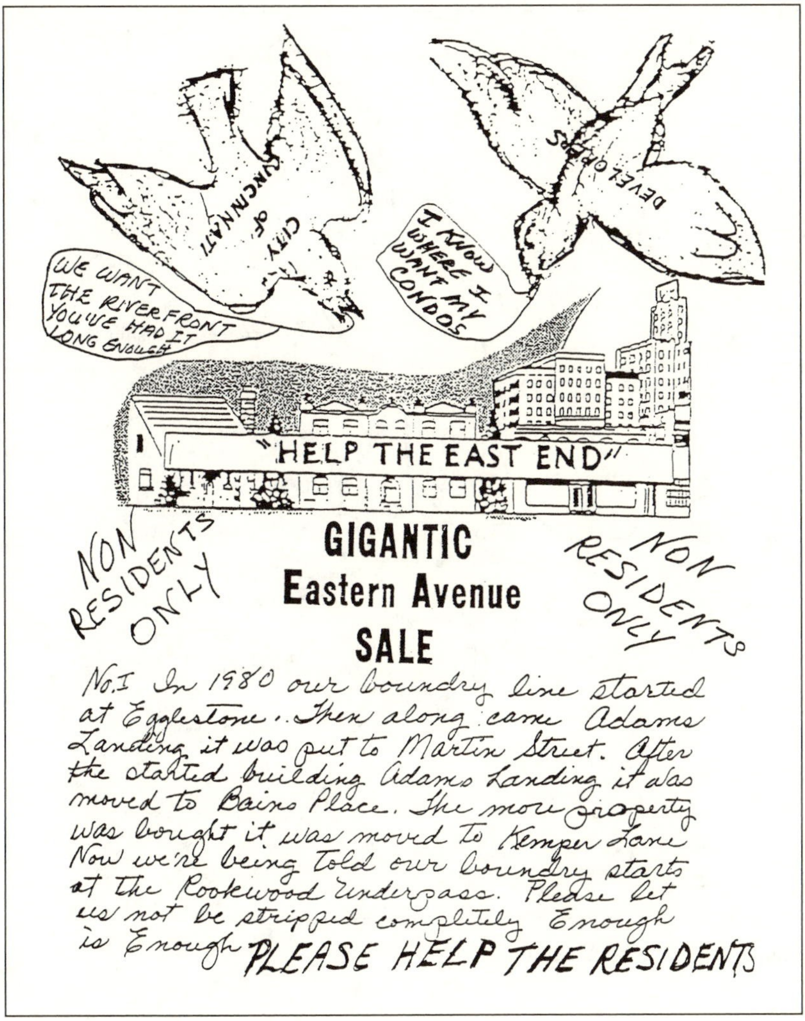

Figure 1. "Gigantic Eastern Avenue Sale" Flyer

End residents are predominantly renters rather than owners of dwellings, and this fact is assumed to be a marker of instability and transience. The very opposite is the case. The majority of East End renters have lived there just as long as the property owners. "Hillbilly" is probably the last stereotype to be still politically acceptable in educated, powerful circles.

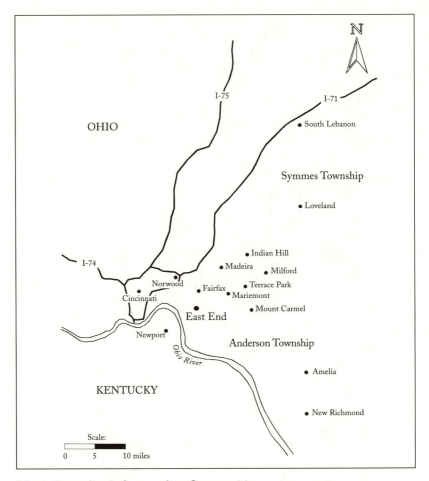

Map 3. Immediately Surrounding Communities

Now that gentrification is well under way, the police have been told "to keep the riffraff out of Columbia Tusculum," a yuppie area of new and newly rehabbed housing that has wedged itself between Upper and Lower East End and that used to be simply part of the East End. The police hassle real East Enders; they ask people standing and talking on the street for identification; they ticket people for failing to wear seat belts. The assumption that working-class people are troublemakers and lawbreakers and are somehow dangerous is part of the hegemonic system's definition of people on the edge of the power structure. The practices of resisting, fighting, and combating these assumptions are part of the assertion of East End identity and are important aspects of practicing community.

There is a Third World quality to the East End that is rather incongruous, given its location in urban Cincinnati. Often, housing is built piecemeal for reasons of time, money, or both. East Enders can afford to fix only a bit at a time. The environment is very much a part of life in the East End. The river periodically floods large parts of the East End—homes, church basements, parks, ball fields. Mud slides down the hillside into East Enders' living rooms. These are acts of nature.

At the same time, urbanity intrudes on East Enders. Traffic noise is constant, as are the dangers of living on an urban east-west artery. Eastern Avenue runs along the river and connects to the wealthy communities of Terrace Park and Mariemont to the east and to downtown Cincinnati to the west. Actually, Eastern Avenue parallels Columbia Parkway, the scenic riverview route to downtown, and became a substitute for it in 1995–1996 while the Parkway was undergoing major reconstruction.

The built, the unbuilt, and the yet-to-be built environments are all important to East Enders who have spent weeks and months participating in community planning as part of a city-generated economic development effort.[2] Can the East End be revitalized without destroying the existing community? Are East Enders only token representatives on city planning groups, or can East End voices be heard in the planning process? To strengthen community voices in the development plan was our research team's original mission in the East End.

East Enders have strong emotional attachments to place—part of the quality and closeness of interpersonal relations both in the most intensely positive and negative senses. People who now live as far away as Florida and Texas come back regularly for East End reunions. But not all of social life is smooth. Conflict, including conflicts over boundaries and definitions of boundaries, is always roughly textured. The power structure assumes anarchy, disorder, disorganization; these assumptions are part of the exoticism and the foreignness of the East End. It has a village quality, not an urban village but a marginal village, an enclave *in* the city but not *of* it.

The East End is geographically accessible to the city but is, in a social and cultural sense, separate and separated. People of higher social class drive in and through the East End but they rarely stop—except to use the ball fields and the Montessori school, which they claim are theirs. The invasion of these facilities by outsiders is another form of margin-

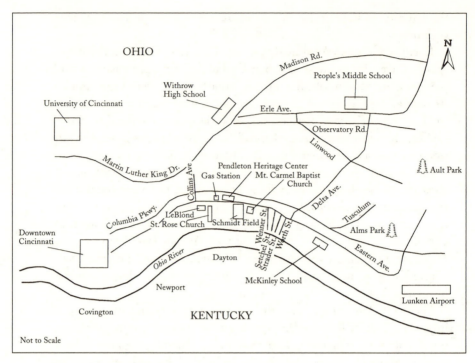

Map 4. The East End

alization. Some years ago, the Montessori school was established by the Junior League as a community project to benefit East End children. Now few East End children attend; some have even been turned away. Labels such as "illiterates," "rednecks," and "unwashed" are still commonly heard.

Practicing Community

Practicing community involves resisting marginality by struggling against neglect, displacement, and isolation. Power relations are strongly entrenched, however. Just getting the city to attend to normal maintenance and repair of city-owned property can involve enormous amounts of red tape. Neglect is almost impossible to fight, since it happens slowly but steadily. Some of the neglect is happening on a citywide basis. The neglect of the public schools hits East End children particularly hard.[3] The city's Department of Recreation facilities in the East End cater to outsiders while community children are left with shortened hours and reduced programs. Police protection is minimal at best. The East End suffers from a paradox and an irony: it is a river community in a river city but has been neglected and ignored and now is being colonized by outsiders.

The identity of East Enders and of the East End as a working-class community is strong yet fragile. While many children are seventh-generation East Enders and have a definite sense of heritage and place, they watch the expensive condominiums being built along prime river-front property and feel very uncertain as to whether there will be a place for them as adults to raise their families in the East End. A fourteen-year-old girl wrote the following in August 1994. The power of her insights contrasts greatly with the powerlessness of the East End's young:

I'm writing on behalf of all the teenagers on Eastern Avenue. We're not gonna ask for much in fact you won't spend a dime! All I'm asking is for our dreams back. You have heard that old saying, kids are our future. If we are the future let us decide if you should tear down buildings or build new condos in East End. You see East End ain't much to you but to us its everything! We love our street just the way it is. We don't need condos. There's people starving in this world and you wanna build condos. If you wanna build something build something we can live in! We ain't got much but what we do have is special and East End is all we got, take that you have nothing no future, just a big place with rich snobby people. I know we don't deserve what I'm asking right now but, please give us another chance. Let our children grow up in a neighborhood they can love and call their own or there will be no future! Take away the East End we have nothing! After all if someone took away your family (all) what would you have? So now do you get my point! East End is our family and you're slowly ripping us apart!

The condos that are being built are symbols of the destruction of her community, which she sees as her family. Uncertainty and insecurity are real feelings—the feelings of instability created by the threat of displacement. Condos also symbolize the unattainable. They are not only market-rate condos, they are high-end market rate; the asking price in 1996–1997 was $325,000.

The line "Take away the East End we have nothing" is very, very important. It tells succinctly of the many levels of meaning conveyed by community and its practice in the East End. Not only is the East End home and a source of identity for East Enders, it is, for real East Enders, common property in the sense that it belongs to all East Enders. The community itself—the houses, the street, the river—provides a sense of richness and abundance for all. Children experience and share the frustrations and struggles of their parents and grandparents as market forces and power dynamics penetrate all aspects of East End life.

Attachment to family is the essence of being a real East Ender and the keystone of working-class culture. Extended families are simultaneously the pillars of and metaphors for community. East End families are very large and complex. They consist of as many as four generations connected by blood, marriage, proximity, necessity, friendship, and combinations of these relationships.[4] Relationships traced through ties of blood and marriage, while certainly the most common form of kinship, are by no means the only forms. Practical kinship ties (what anthropologists used to call "fictive kin" to refer to kin relations that are created outside of ties of blood and marriage) are extremely common. The creation of such ties is part of practicing community.

Intergenerational ties—the intense interactions among and between people of different generations—at home, at community meetings, at City Hall—give children a sense of family stability. But children also learn very early about the fragility of the East End as they have known it and the need for constant struggle to maintain and build community. A two-year-old, on seeing more than three people gathered in one spot, queries in her small voice, "Is this a meeting?" One East End leader wrote the following about the resiliency of East Enders:

> We have weathered the floods and we are going to stand steadfast and unmovable. We've been a forgotten community, but we've earned the right to keep what is rightfully ours. When we were coming up as children, people would ask where do you live? We would say the East End, their reply was oh! You're a "river rat." That comment never bothered us, because we knew who we were and have always been proud of it.

The struggles are about basics, or what should be considered to be basic: housing, programs for children, a community meeting place and heritage center, health care, maintaining the character of the East End while recognizing the need for revitalization.

Community is the source of dreams, the source of a sense of the future, of possibility, of security. To take the East End away from East Enders is to take away the dreams and, therefore, the future. The essence of practicing community in the East End is to claim ownership of the community, not just because the East End is and has been home to seven generations of East Enders, but because, symbolically, the East End is more than a place; it is an identity that confers a sense of belonging whether a person currently lives there or not. The East End symbolizes the culture of working-class East Enders who place family above all else and who see family as the metaphor for community.

Family certainly has to do with ties of blood and marriage, but it extends beyond these to neighbors, friends, even outsiders. Family, in fact, is also a way of incorporating outsiders. A trusted outsider is referred to as "a member of the East End family."

Outline

Here I want to explain the rather unorthodox design of this book, the very different kinds of segments or chapters, and the reasons for their order. As I indicated in the prologue, *Practicing Community* is based on more than six years of ethnographic field research and advocacy by an interdisciplinary team of planners, educators, anthropologists, and students. As the director of the project, I designed the research plan and fieldwork protocols. As an economic anthropologist who for years has studied livelihood, economic processes, and economic development at the margins of states, I must admit that I had little experience with the frustrations, trials, and sheer hard work of community planning and institution building. Community work is grueling; the energy and persistence required to sustain even a small project cannot be appreciated fully until hours of meetings, hearings, and phone calls have become part of one's everyday life. East End leaders take these hours in stride.

The details of the anthropological fieldwork and the methods employed are given in Chapter 5, "Fieldwork at Home: The East End Study Project," after the reader has become familiar with East Enders and the East End as a community (Chapter 2, "Community in Practice") and after the reader thoroughly understands what it means to be a real East Ender (Chapter 3, "Being a Real East Ender: Families and Their Histories") living in a richly textured and complex community (Chapter 4, "East End Textures: Hidden Dimensions of Being a Real East Ender"). This ordering of chapters is an intentional design to immerse the reader in East End life as I have experienced it and as East Enders have portrayed it to me to get right to the heart of community and its practice. I have translated these portrayals into the practice of community before providing the scholarly rationales for and explicit theoretical and practical orientations to the fieldwork and the methods used. Some readers, especially those with an academic orientation and view of the world, may wish to begin with Chapter 5 and go right to the Postscript, which provides much of the theoretical framework for this book. Others may prefer to read the chapters in order.

Chapters 2, 3, and 4 are based on interviews, observations, life and work histories, and narratives written and spoken by East Enders. Chapter 2, "Community in Practice," begins with an overview of topics and practices that highlight some of the essential features of the spirit of East End people and place: nuances of community, the small things one would not notice from merely driving through; the intensity of inter-generational ties, especially the connections between elders and small children; the strength of family and the trust of neighbors; community institutions, monuments, and landmarks (churches and bars alike); uses of space; the role of the East End as a local community in the city and the region; the sense of history and heritage; the development plan and its many contentious elements. The chapter proceeds with a discussion of concepts of class and power in the East End, including a discussion of theories of class and community in the context of urban anthropology and resistance. I reserve the discussion of practice and theory for the Postscript (Chapter 13).

Chapter 3, "Being a Real East Ender: Families and Their Histories," is about authenticity, family, and community, the practices of everyday life. It begins with the words of a fifth-generation East Ender who is wondering anxiously about East Enders' identity. The chapter focuses on different kinds of East End families: large and small, African American and Caucasian, with different compositions and structures, work patterns, feelings about community, worries, and triumphs.

The practices of being an East Ender are all shaped these days by impending economic development and creeping gentrification—all sources of anxiety. The everyday interactions with kin and with neighbors are remarkably consistent, however, even though family structures and resource bases vary. Traditional anthropologists might call this a chapter on East End social organization. Indeed, it is, but with some crucial differences. The kinship charts are there, but the spirit of community and the practice of community put those dull charts in a dynamic context. Most of the families have roots in rural Appalachian America— Ohio, Kentucky, Tennessee, or West Virginia. Embedded in these family and neighborhood ties are nonmarket relationships that involve favors, trades, and gifts—people living rent-free or below the landlord's baseline costs, people selling or renting property to relatives at below market rates. The features of day-to-day life are described in Chapter 3, foreshadowing the discussions in Chapters 6, "The Cultural Economy of the East End," and 8, "Health, Culture, and Practicing Community." Combinations of formal and informal economic processes, the importance of both buying and selling in flea markets (the folk term for marketplaces that are part of a rotating system) are discussed in more detail in Chapter 6. Tensions leading to serious stress and pathology are also discussed in more detail in Chapter 8. At the same time, there are the reliable family and community relationships that (most, but not all, of the time) provide safety nets in times of trouble.

The senses of the East End community—its seasonal rhythms, life-course rhythms, crises punctuating routines—are to me some of its most striking features. These senses, the sounds, sights, smells, are the focus of Chapter 4, "East End Textures." The style and the content of this chapter are unconventional. It is about senses and sensibilities in the East End. To understand these senses of community is to know how to practice community and to know how community is practiced. It takes years to begin to understand, and even when you think you know how things are in the East End, you don't have any greater ability to put together the fragments or soothe the shattered feelings. Chapter 4 is organized according to life course, in part to emphasize the importance of inter-generational ties, in part to indicate that at each point in the life course, different feelings and experiences become heightened and intensified.

East Enders speak eloquently in these initial chapters, as they do throughout the book, in stories, renderings (as I call the short essays), poems, and oral histories. Community voices are honest, rich, and varied; the voices are personal with a mix of happiness and sadness, joy and violence; they are many-layered and changing—powerful in their authenticity and full of triumph and disappointment.

To write about the East End is a great responsibility. Every dialogue, every narrative, every incident will be contested by someone—real East Enders and outsiders alike. All names have been changed in collaboration with a group of East Enders who felt strongly about creating fictional names that were true to East Enders' senses of person, family, and community. Some details associated with people, places, and events have been changed for reasons of confidentiality, although real East Enders and others who have been involved in the East End for many years will no doubt recognize familiar players. Selection, omission, emphasis, editing, striving to maintain the authenticity of voice, these are the tasks of anthropologists in these days of plant closings, welfare reform, downsizings, and postmodernism.

This book could not have been written without the very valuable work and honest words, written and spoken, by East Enders. In part, my intention is to heighten and enhance the importance of East End voices. Many of the writings of East Enders were created to dispel the stereotypes about the illiteracy and ignorance of East Enders. The East Enders' eloquence starkly contrasts with the position of the East End community in relationship to the power structure.

Very few anthropologists spend more than a year to eighteen months in the field. While accessibility is a very positive aspect of doing fieldwork "at home" (Chapter 5) interpretations of events change from week to week, month to month, year to year. An event or even a few words spoken carry different meanings five years after the fact. My view of things changed constantly as the power dynamics shifted within the community and as the position of the East End changed within the city. Perhaps someday I will write a book about fieldwork at home, but for now I have tried to keep to the issue: the history of the East End Study Project and the contexts within which it was carried out. With some lapses, I have kept my own feelings and experiences out of the chapter.

Chapter 6, "The Cultural Economy of the East End," treats power and resistance as these play themselves out in the process of securing a living in the East End. The chapter is divided into three parts. The first describes the dominant economic pattern in the East End, and probably the central pattern in most working-class communities worldwide. Borrowing a concept from economic historian Karl Polanyi, I refer to this pattern as "householding," a noncapitalist pattern—often a resistance strategy—that gives highest priority to the provisioning of the group. In this case, we are talking primarily about extended family kin groups, but also about the East End community itself. Part 2 of Chapter 6 is about equivalencies in the East End, that is, about the nature and complexity of exchange relationships among East Enders: who exchanges what, with whom, and in what spatial and temporal contexts. Part 3 deals specifically with issues of gender and the informal economy.

Chapter 7 is about East Enders' participation in a city-initiated economic development plan. Initially, an out-of-town consulting firm was hired to create the plan as an architectural and engineering document. The initial position of the City Planning Department was extremely patronizing. From the outset, the plan emphasized the physical and geographical features of the East End to the exclusion of its human and social dimensions. The plan left out the people. Subsequently, after some local elites realized the need for a more humanistic approach, and after some city planners realized the importance of community input, the planning process came to include community leaders who sat on civic boards and attended planning meetings—the power relations were such that East Enders' physical presence, at least initially, did not translate into having East End voices heard in the planning process. At City Hall, when East Enders raised their hands to speak, they were often ignored. Trust was nonexistent between East Enders and the city. Minutes of the meetings left out the comments of East Enders.

Chapter 7 highlights the voices of East Enders in poetry, narrative, and dialogue; it does not attempt to cover the entire planning process, but it does show how East Enders fight back with words to counter the stereotypes of illiteracy and incompetency in planning. The plan implementation phase, which will take much longer than the planning itself, has brought new challenges, new struggles. The dynamics of these struggles over health, housing, heritage, and the maintenance of the community itself are subtle and complex, disjointed and, at the same time, relentless.

I have intentionally chosen a varied and somewhat fragmented style of presentation. East Enders are indeed living in a fragmented postmodern era. Life in the East End is, in many respects, unpredictable, uncertain, and, for many, without regular rhythms. Crises are common—accidents, hospitalizations, deaths, fights, layoffs, police harassment. Large community and kin networks provide wonderful safety nets; at the same time, being a part of these networks can take a substantial emotional toll, especially as the elders become ill and die. Funerals are frequent, and virtually everyone in the community is touched by each loss. When a young person dies of AIDS or leukemia, life in the East End temporarily comes to a halt. East End textures are rich, but they can also be very rough.

Processes of local colonialism permeate every aspect of East End life, sometimes overtly, usually covertly, but always when least expected. By local colonialism I mean the imposition of control from outsiders who are expatriates from other local communities. Developers are the prime local colonialists. For individuals, especially for community leaders, colonialism manifests itself in health problems, housing struggles, and the fight for the heritage center. It is a pervasive force with which the practice of community must constantly contend. Part of practicing community is thus dealing with the manifestations and remnants of colonialism.

The versions of colonialism described in Chapter 11 are very much a part of the local context, so local that they will undoubtedly be recognized, but not so local as to be idiosyncratic. Controlling the bylaws of the community council, described in Chapter 11 in a blow-by-blow fashion, is only one very typical example of how control by local outsiders can be attempted and, to some degree, accomplished in the community.

The presence of colonialism makes it difficult for East Enders to practice community in traditional ways—that is, by means of traditional institutions such as churches and local voluntary associations. By the same token, resisting colonialism becomes a primary way of practicing community in new and transformed ways that involve the hard work of creating and building new institutions. The creative strategies East Enders devise to preserve and revitalize the community are all part of resisting colonialism. These strategies include working with researchers, advocates, and citizen elites.

Colonial processes create their own pathologies, physical, social, and cultural (Chapter 8, "Health, Culture, and Practicing Community"). Health, culture, and the practice of community must be understood in the larger context of regional colonialism and the context of economic development that propelled rural people to migrate to midwestern cities like Cincinnati, Detroit, and Chicago in the first place.[5] Uprootedness, cash dependency, low skill levels, and powerlessness all create contexts within which it is very difficult for people to adapt successfully to urban environments. The more recent migrants are also the poorest.[6] These conditions, at least in part, provide the contexts within which the people and their health problems, described in Chapter 8, must be understood.

All successes, personal, familial, and political, seem to be only temporary triumphs. Many East Enders have told me that they worry when things are going well. Victories are both sweet and costly in a community in which the personal and the political are virtually inseparable. The chapters on health, culture and practicing community (Chapter 8), contested territory (Chapter 9), and a heritage center (Chapter 10) well illustrate these points. The highs are very high, so the lows are wrenching and nightmarish. The formal nonprofit corporations (see Figure 2) that have been established in the East End to deal with health, housing, and heritage—the East End Community Health Center, the East End Riverfront Community Urban Redevelopment Corporation, the East End Housing Preservation Fund, and the Pendleton Heritage Center—are deceiving in their formality. Chapters 9 and 10 particularly are also

Figure 2. East End Nonprofit Organizations

meant to illustrate the struggles involved in implementing the development plan.

The tone of the chapters in this book is as variable as the textures in the East End. The chapter on East End political economy (Chapter 6), for example, uses a completely different tone (much more analytical and academic) than the four that immediately precede it. Before the conclusion, one chapter discusses colonialism and power dynamics within the community and the city, another, the flood of 1997. The conclusion lends some comparative perspectives on marginality. The Postscript deals with some of the relationships between theory and practice that are implicit throughout the book. The order in which the chapters are presented is not necessarily chronological either, so to aid the reader, I have provided a timeline with major events defined.

Timeline

1969	City manager's plan for relocation of Columbia Parkway
1970	Plan "C" alternative presented by EEAC
1970	Outline Master Plan prepared by EEAC
1970	Establishment of Riverfront Advisory Council (RAC)
1971	EEAC requests planning assistance from the city.

	City Council, by resolution, gives priority to East End and Evanston in assigning planning teams to work with neighborhoods
1973	Existing Conditions study published
1974	East End Task Force established
1975	East End Area Plan published by City Planning Commission/East End Task Force
1977	East End Urban Design Plan published by the East End Task Force and the Department of Urban Development
1987	A Cincinnati councilman sparks renewed city interest in the East End
	Riverfront Advisory Council (RAC) assigned to develop a plan for the renewal of the East End
1989	LDR Consultants publishes Eastern Riverfront Redevelopment Strategy
Summer 1990	Neighborhood Information Committee formed
1990	Neighborhood opposition to LDR plan
	Matthew Marks, community organizer and advocate, approached by RAC members for assistance
	First study team formed, sponsored by Legal Aid Society, Urban Appalachian Council (UAC), and Applied Information Resources
October 1990	EERCURC (East End Riverfront Community Urban Redevelopment Corporation) enters into partnership with IDHF (Interneighborhood Designers of Homes for Friends)
January 1991	East End Community Report published by Legal Aid Society and UAC
	University of Cincinnati team, East End Study Project (EESP), organized to continue research
March 1991	City Buildings and Inspections and Health Departments shut down Betz Flats
April 1991	East End Neighborhood Recipe for Success formulated and approved by EEAC under Pete Evans's leadership

October 17, 1991	Pete Evans resigns as EEAC president
December 1991	Robbie Kale elected president of EEAC
January 1992	East End Riverfront Community Development Plan and Guidelines initial draft
April 27, 1992	Passage of "Recipe for Successful Implementation" by EEAC
May 1992	East End Riverfront Community Development Plan and Guidelines passed by City Council
July 1992	First meeting of Plan Implementation Team
September 1992	Resignation and impeachment of Robbie Kale
October 1992	First meeting of group interested in rehabilitation of Pendleton Building
December 1992	Urban pioneer Susan Pond elected president of EEAC
March 1993	Susan Pond resigns as president of EEAC
December 1993	Developers take over EEAC
June 1994	Gas station closes
November 1994	Opening of newly rehabilitated Betz Flats
May 1995	Opening of Lewiston Townhomes affordable rental units
May 1995	Market-rate housing comes on-line
December 1995	Unknowns run for president and treasurer of EEAC
January 1996	Unknown resigns and developer Elizabeth Jones becomes president of EEAC
December 1996	Developer Elizabeth Jones is elected president of EEAC and developer Anita Homestead is elected vice-president

2 | COMMUNITY IN PRACTICE

Overview: Inside the East End

Old houses and boarded-up buildings catch the eyes of commuters who ignore the 35-miles-per-hour speed limit on Eastern Avenue, the east-west artery that bisects the East End and parallels the river on the way to downtown Cincinnati. Nobody sees the tomato plants or the rows of beans carefully placed in backyards or the succulents and flowers that line Mr. S's walkway and garden. Nobody sees the sparkling floors and windows or the shiny table in Mrs. S's living room. Nobody knows exactly how hard she worked all her life in a home on the hillside, how she raised her son successfully alone in the face of racial prejudice and an alcoholic first husband. When she graduated from high school in the 1930s, local businesses were not hiring black secretaries. That is why she became a domestic worker who raised white children at the same time that she brought up her own. One year, she saved and saved and gave the money to her granddaughter instead of buying herself a winter coat. There are many Mrs. S's in the East End, black and white.

The interior spaces of East End homes are a mystery to outsiders, who, nonetheless proceed to make assumptions about what happens inside them. Stereotypes about child abuse, incest, alcoholism, laziness, illiteracy, disorder of all sorts abound and are perpetuated by people in power. One of my neighbors, who years ago was part of a Junior League project to build a multicultural preschool and kindergarten, asked me whether cockroaches still crawled in East End homes. I told her I had been in many homes where you could eat off the floor. The "raggedyness" of the exteriors belies the many tender realities of life inside, however. Indeed, there are boarded-up buildings, deteriorated houses, vacant lots, but if I were a toddler or a senior citizen, I'd rather live in the East End than anywhere else. There has almost always been someone there to care, to look in without intruding. But the community is changing.

Children ride Big Wheels and bikes treacherously close to the curb of Eastern Avenue. Worse, they ride in the street itself. Teens congregate in front of the recreation center waiting to enter at their appointed time—but not before. The center allocates certain blocks of time to children of different age groups. Younger children's programs function before 4:00 P.M. At 4:00, teens are allowed in. On one very miserable rainy day in 1994, two fourteen-year-olds I'd known since they were nine enlisted my help to get them into the recreation center early. They just wanted to play basketball in the gym and out of the rain and they were willing to take responsibility for themselves. I tried to convince a young employee of the city's Department of Recreation that the kids' word was good. The young worker, not more than twenty-five herself, refused. No amount of gentle persuasion would change her mind. The kids were silent when I told them; they nodded knowingly as if to store away the incident for future reference. Vandalism at the center is getting worse.

Grandmas and grandpas sit on rickety porches piled with odds and ends; interior space is at a premium in the East End. When weather permits, East Enders spend as much time outside as inside.

The community itself is spacious and the parks and riverbanks are enjoyed by everyone in Cincinnati. The river is very special—something not merely to look at, but to interact with, to use, to touch and feel and hear. One longtime resident, who has since passed away, used to take his boat to work downtown. When the river froze, people used to walk across to Kentucky. The river has spiritual meanings in the East End; power, force, presence, danger. It is the source of community and personal identity. East End culture centers around the river. When the river floods, which it does regularly, but to varying degrees, East Enders rally to do what needs to be done. The old-timers teach those younger how to handle the flood and its aftermath (see Chapter 13). Everyone helps. The river and its floods are part of East End life. The river is the symbol of home and its rebuilding after floods.

The steeple of Saint Rose Catholic Church can be seen from almost anywhere along the river. The red brick structure is a community monument, a thing of beauty and importance even to non-Catholic East

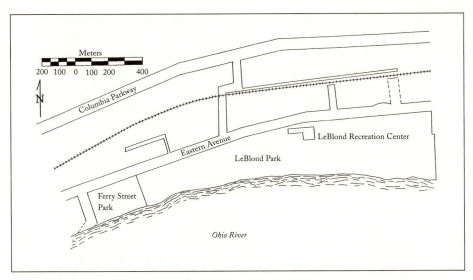

Map 5. East End Area: LeBlond Area

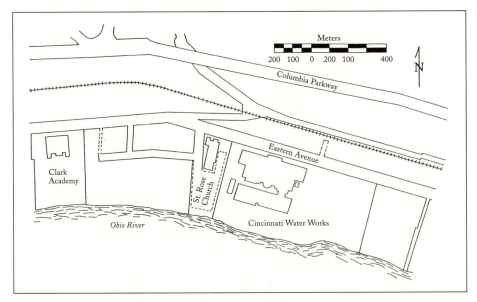

Map 6. East End Area: Saint Rose, Water Works

Enders. A large ruler painted on the back wall marks the flood levels of the river. Tourists who take the riverboats ask about the ruler and admire it. Inside the church, especially in the morning, the sun streams through the stained glass windows. On Sundays, the cars come from everywhere, Mount Lookout, Mount Washington; old Cincinnati families find special solace at Saint Rose.

Churches are important in the East End: they sustain hope; they symbolize stability. Priests and ministers command respect; they also receive criticism from real East Enders if they are standoffish, or if they refuse to become involved in preserving the community for East Enders. Some engagement with practicing community is essential.

At one time, there were many viable churches and ministries. Fritz remembers that First Evangelical Church had an active ministry in the 1970s. Now there are two main churches: Mount Carmel Baptist Church, which serves the black community in the East End and many black families from other communities, and Saint Rose Catholic Church, a large congregation that serves the entire city. How active and how involved these churches are in the community depends greatly on the leanings and personalities of individual clergy. In 1993, when the community was raising funds for the East End Heritage Exhibit, the church made a substantial donation. The pastor at Mount Carmel told me how difficult it was in the past to fight the city and raise the funds to build the addition on the church. He understood the sense of struggle.

Community history is told by elders to children. The children used to visit old Mr. Thompson, who would talk to them from his rocking chair. When he passed away, it was a loss to the whole neighborhood, but especially to the children. Old Betsy is gone now, too. Even with her Alzheimer's, she would laugh at a teenager's animal imitations as she held a great-grandbaby on her lap. Her many "adopted" grandchildren—really great-grandchildren—avoided her house for more than a month after she died; they didn't quite know how to deal with the gap her absence created in their lives, even though her daughter, herself a grandmother, tried to take Betsy's place. Grandmothers like Betsy can be found in most East End blocks; children adopt them.

The East End is only a stone's throw from downtown Cincinnati. In fact, the community's western border used to be a downtown street. The Ohio River is to the south. Across the river is Kentucky. The hillside, where the rich people live, imposes itself from the north so as to take advantage of the river views. On a sunny day, the river glistens. The boats appear to be gliding on diamonds. Social classes in Cincinnati correlate with the landscape.

The East End is not entirely urban—although it is within the boundaries of the city of Cincinnati. It is not rural, either, although people maintain their connections to the country by traveling back and forth between the East End and Kentucky or rural Ohio, by sending children to their grandparents in the country, or by simply knowing that the country is across the river, "out East" or "upriver." Six-year-old Adam keeps his calf at his grandmother's in Corbin, Kentucky. Old-time East End families have houseboats on the river, or, even better, they have land with large trailers for summer use. You'd be amazed how many people can sleep in one trailer.

A sense of smallness and familiarity permeates the community, especially if you know it well. Until June 1994—in fact, for twenty-five years—people honked and waved to Fritz, who managed the gas station on Eastern Avenue. Many stopped to chat and catch up on the latest news or to consult him about how to fix or acquire a car part. The gas station provided everything from parts to gossip to psychotherapy: what happened at last night's meeting, what a community leader would like to see happen at the next meeting, who was and was not talking to whom. Informal credit was issued to those in need of gas but in short supply of cash. Fritz would run a tab. When he got off work, he checked on Elaine's stove in a small house across from the station. His elder sister took the next shift; another took the third. His niece worked on weekends. Once home, he checked on old Mrs. Schiffer next door. (She was ninety-seven years old in 1995 and wanted to rent out part of her house, but couldn't. Fixing all of its code violations was simply too expensive.) A big chunk of Fritz's family is out of regular work because a community institution and a community-building institution has bitten the dust. After the station closed, Fritz spent a great deal of time doing odd jobs to make ends meet, almost double the time he worked before. He worked on cars, put in new motors, and did a variety of mechanic's jobs. Still, he was struggling financially. Finally, he went to work as a wage laborer for a car-detailing company. But this job took a heavy physical and psychological toll and meant many missed Health Center board meetings and time away from community work. His father worried that they were killing Fritz with his job. One night, they kept him working until 4:00 A.M.; he came home and slept for a few hours and then returned to work that morning.

A few doors down from the gas station, a seventy-four-year-old daughter took her mother (in her nineties) to the store; when the snow was heavy, they were both house-bound until the daughter's son or a neighborhood teenager shoveled them out.

A teenager skips school to take care of a younger brother or sister—maybe several. You can find any adult by asking the kids; the kids always know where the adults are, but the reverse is not always the case.

There is a sense of heritage here. The East End is not a temporary stopping-off point; neither is it a transitional stop on the way to somewhere else. It is home to renters and owners alike. Families who have rented houses and apartments have lived in the East End just as long, if not longer, than people who own. East Enders want to stay in the East End near family members and friends. While it is true that many people have been displaced and have moved to nearby communities, the tough strands of the neighborhood and kinship networks have not been broken. Rather, they have been stretched and extended to include all people who remain connected to the East End and involved in East End life, even though they no longer live in the community. The population figures do not reveal this sense of connectedness or the nature of long-term involvements in the community;[1] toddlers and school-age children are seventh-generation East Enders; teens and young adults are fourth and fifth.

Trolleys used to run up and down Eastern Avenue and stop for cleanings at the old Pendleton carbarn, which is planned for rehab as a community heritage center. At one time, grocery stores, bakeries, small apartment buildings, and churches lined the street. Ferry Street had comfortable houses on it and was only one of many such blocks. Now East Enders wait to see what is going to happen. The developers have bought up the land and the buildings in the name of progress. They have closed the grocery stores and the churches; they want to buy more land and more houses. Young lawyers, real estate people, working women are starting to move in. Already Volvos and minivans surround the ball fields when the weather is good and yuppies take the places of East End children on volleyball courts and in Jazzercise classes in the community recreation center. The Department of Recreation generates income by renting out community space to outside groups.

Plans and Planning

In May 1992, the City Council of Cincinnati passed an economic development plan (the East End Community Development Plan and Guidelines) designed to revitalize the community and at the same time preserve the East End for its residents. This was the most recent of many plans that had been devised by the city for the Eastern Riverfront. Plans from the 1970s have names on them that I recognize as current East End elders.

The planning process was long and arduous and required much energy, stamina, creativity, strategizing, and sheer stick-to-itiveness on the part of East Enders. In almost every discussion, community itself was being defined and redefined; boundary issues surfaced repeatedly. Exactly where did the East End begin and end? Who was a real East Ender? Who had the right to speak for the community—to tamper with its patterns of life, to silence community voices, or to threaten the autonomy and control of East End residents? In addition to the meetings at City Hall, hours and hours of community meetings were held in the heat of summer and the dead of winter.

If there was no place to meet, which was often the case, East Enders met in someone's house, in the park, or in a parking lot with papers spread on the hoods of cars. What were the issues? Affordable housing, housing for senior citizens, a community meeting place, market-rate housing, heights of buildings, densities, zoning, traffic, safety, eminent domain, green space, parks, railroad rights-of-way, bike trails, privacy, existing uses for businesses . . . on and on. Critical issues tangentially related to the plan but very important to East Enders emerged repeatedly: young people—how to keep them off the streets and occupied, "so they are too worn out to get in trouble," one leader said over and over again; how to keep children from swimming in the treacherous Ohio River when the pool at the recreation center was closed for lack of city funds; how to keep the young people from exercising their creativity through vandalism; how to determine the place of bureaucracy and its representatives in the community.

Recreation workers, social workers, teachers, children's services providers, and providers of psychiatric services, with a few exceptions, are all located outside the community. The Department of Recreation provides staff for the community's neighborhood recreation centers. LeBlond Recreation Center or LeBlond Park, as it is called by East Enders, has a shallow pool that is open in summer, a gym, a weight room, and several activity rooms. For many years, a cheerful and caring woman from an Appalachian community on the west side of town was at the center of all activities at LeBlond. Children of all ages, especially teens, spoke freely to her, told her their stories, their problems, and their dreams. A young man who also worked at LeBlond and who loved kids was promoted to a higher position in the Recreation Department. Most staffers last for less than a year.

The county agency that handles children's services has various locations, all outside of the East End. In practical terms, this means that there is no stable, familiar, and trusted social worker on which to rely in times of crisis. The closest substitutes for social workers are the nurses at the health center. They do their best, and East Enders do rely on them, but they are already overworked.

Within the East End, there is an adult education center and a Montessori school, but these are both underutilized by East Enders. In fact, in the 1990s, East End children have been a distinct minority in the Montessori preschool and kindergarten. The Junior League created the school in the 1970s to be a multicultural school, but over the years, East End children have been replaced by outsiders.

Psychiatric services, as such, are all located outside the community; those that are financially accessible to East Enders are centralized and impersonal; even these require traveling to "pill hill," the local name for the area where hospitals and clinics are concentrated. Such clinics are resisted strongly by East Enders. (See Chapter 8.)

At first, I heard talk of opposition over the plan between the community and "the city," whose representatives were elected officials who sat on City Council or staff members who had to answer to bureaucrats higher up. But who was "the city" really? Was it the City Planning Department, City Council, the Riverfront Advisory Council, the city manager's office, the Department of Neighborhood Housing and Conservation (which, in 1995, merged with the Department of Social Services to become the Department of Neighborhood Services)? As individuals from these initially intimidating institutions became known to East End leaders, "the city" became much less of a monolith to the community. Adversaries became allies almost overnight. But the reverse was also true. People who sounded like allies changed their minds or abandoned the community when pressure to carry out the interests of the powerful became too great.

Real East Enders struggle against the takeover of the community by outsiders—developers especially—but also rich people who can afford the expensive, market-rate condominiums that are now being built. Landlords refuse to fix up apartments; fires start mysteriously; more and more structures are bulldozed against the will of the community.

Ever-present factionalism plays itself out in many ways. Expatriates and local colonialists are powerful. They are the property owners. I call certain powerful outsiders "expatriates" because they come from and are seen by East Enders as belonging in other communities with other cultures, but they persist in claiming to be East Enders with the community's best interests at heart.

Will the Pendleton carbarn turn into a restaurant or a heritage center? The property owners on the street above the Pendleton do not want to see their investments diminished. Who controls the community council or the Plan Implementation Team? City officials insist that the community council represents the community, but does it?

How does a university-based research and advocacy team fit into this picture? Delicately and gingerly. It must walk on eggshells between factions and among personalities. Politics is very personal here. Strengthening the community's voice in the planning process became our first priority in the initial stages of our research. Strengthening the community's voice in the implementation of the plan has been an ongoing and very difficult task; research in the service of advocacy requires a long-term commitment to the community. But in a community that is being constantly defined and redefined, research and advocacy are risky business. Taking sides on even the most mundane issues can have serious consequences; at the very least, some people may refuse to communicate.

A Community Meeting: Neighborhood Boundaries and Local Knowledge

At the time, I didn't realize what an important rite of passage a Saturday morning East End special meeting about "the plan" would be for me. It marked my entrance—really, our team's invitation—into the community. Not only were most of the key people present, but the issues raised in this initial meeting continue to be key points of the plan itself and of the themes central to practicing community: neighborhood boundaries, education, underground wiring, safety, small businesses, taxes, and, of course, family and longevity in the East End. Over and over again, they have been argued and discussed at City Hall and in community board meetings throughout the implementation phases of the plan.

Doris Sells, an African American woman in her early seventies, kindly showed me the maps of "the plan" on the far wall upstairs in LeBlond Recreation Center. She apologized for the maps, saying: "There are lots of mistakes in it and I don't know how we are going to present to us [meaning real East Enders], but that's Jennie's problem." Jennie turned out to be a young African American woman, the project planner who was a staff member of the City Planning Department. As people gathered around the maps, flyers announcing a neighborhood cleanup the following Saturday were being passed around. There was talk of people without electricity. A large white woman wearing a sweatshirt with the words "East Enders, united we stand" seemed to know many of the people. She turned out to be a forty-five-year-old fifth-generation East Ender.

As chairperson of a committee established to keep residents apprised of meetings and all issues related to the plan and to coordinate community input, Doris called the meeting to order. She defined it as a workshop, saying: "We had a questionnaire to put ideas into the plan. The East End needs cooperation to get our job done." In a very soft voice, Jennie said: "We will go over a condensed version of the draft plan. We want your comments. We want to encourage group discussion around the plan."

The plan's first page addressed the linear character of the neighborhood and its different sections. The East Coast–based consulting firm had given names to the sections. "The neighborhood has to decide whether these names are appropriate," said Jennie, as she proceeded to describe the tentative plans for each section. At the time, I didn't realize how subtle and difficult to pin down the sections of the neighborhood were. Depending on whom you ask, you will get a different description of the segments of the neighborhood and a different delineation of the boundary lines for the East End as a whole. Some people will talk about Upper East End, meaning the segment of the neighborhood that is east of Delta Avenue. Others will call this eastern section Columbia Tusculum or Linwood. Everything west of Delta is then Lower East End. Others will agree on the definition of Upper East End, but will want to define Lower East End differently, as beginning at Saint Rose Church or the waterworks. Still others will not recognize the term Lower East End at all. Since the plan area includes only the area west of Delta, the divisions, Upper and Lower, are not very helpful. From the waterworks east (the Sunoco area) is the historically African American section of the East End. One old-timer (white) embarrassedly told me it used to be called "Niggertown."

An East Ender's knowledge is highly localized. From East Enders' perspectives, each block is distinctive, with key families, elders, leaders, and ne'er-do-wells. People who have grown up and lived in one part of the neighborhood will know that part intimately, but may have no knowledge of other parts of the neighborhood. It was no wonder, then, that none of the residents at this first meeting wanted to touch the issue of neighborhood sections.

One resident changed the topic completely and inquired: "Nothin' been said on education programs for children." Jennie responded that it was possible to project the number of families and children and work with the school board. Provisions for education could be implemented. There was a great deal of discussion about the heights of buildings, especially those affecting people's views from the north side. Someone said: "This is a neighborhood, not a pass through."

Placing utility wires underground evoked considerable discussion and continues to be a contentious issue in the community. The developers favor putting wires underground in order to improve the aesthetic quality of the community. The longtime residents fear the extraordinary costs that will have to be absorbed. "Don't put something like this on people that can't afford to have it done. That is a useless expense," said one resident who was soon to become the president of the East End River-front Community Urban Redevelopment Corporation (EERCURC). She is a deeply religious woman, black Appalachian by heritage. Her childhood was spent in the East End as the daughter of a railroad worker.

Concern for businesses along the river and safety measures at night were expressed as reactions to the bike trail allowed for in the plan. Privacy for people living near the trails also received attention. Caution lights and crosswalks where kids cross Eastern Avenue were mentioned by several residents. Safety continues to be an issue in the neighborhood.

Neighborhood grocery stores have disappeared from the East End almost entirely. At the meeting, one man reported: "We used to have five well-stocked grocery stores, now none. When I was a kid, they had tabs for the neighborhood people. We need to plan for small businesses." Another resident pointed out that when a local grade school in the East End was eliminated, a lot of small businesses disappeared: "Without a neighborhood school, we are not going to get the kind of development we need."

There was talk of families' longevity in the East End. A lot of people, renters and owners alike, had been in the community a long time. The area was changing. The same man, white and in his late forties, who talked about the grocery stores asked: "Why should people that live here have to pay raised taxes because people come here and build condos? Isn't there a way to prevent people from being taxed out of existence?

A person shouldn't be taxed out of their own house. We [our family] bought the house in 1936."

An Informal Community Center

Shortly after this community meeting, I met Robbie, a neighborhood leader, at the local bar. The River Inn is a small place with bar stools running along a counter in front and tables in the back. Pictures of customers, local celebrities—ballplayers especially—line the walls. Like most bars, it's dark inside. I had been there several times before.

The barmaids were all very friendly, and while I waited for Robbie, I watched children getting snacks and soda pop as they checked in with their mothers and grandmothers, some of whom were barmaids. "Put a pizza in for me," requested one hungry child, and the door of the micro-wave popped open. As the place filled with smoke and noise, the atmo-sphere grew livelier. The phone was ringing; people were talking and joking. Everyone knew everyone.

Robbie marched in with a large briefcase and proceeded to hand out section 8 housing forms. I then realized she was the woman wearing the "East Enders united we stand" shirt at the meeting I'd attended. Her elderly mother sat quietly at the rear of the bar, content to observe the neighborhood activities. More than a year later, Robbie admitted to me that when I first came into that bar she was having trouble figuring out what this "university broad" wanted in the East End.

I had never before seen a barmaid with a briefcase. That summer, I spent a lot of time in the River Inn, in spite of teasing from my stu-dents and colleagues. It was a very active community center—darts on weekends, cards, and a great deal of camaraderie. I felt comfortable there. I even suggested to a city employee that it might be useful to spend some time in there. She told me it would be perceived as "unprofes-sional" for a city employee to be seen going in and out of a bar. People in the East End do spend a great deal of money at the River Inn on booze; they do get drunk and into fights. The barmaids break up the fights and take people's car keys when they think it's not safe for them to drive home.

The following November (1991), after our team spent a summer in-terviewing East End families, I was sitting with Robbie at the River Inn. Robbie knows the community like the back of her hand. She also has her opinions about people, usually positive ones. She was giving me a rundown of people in the neighborhood who would be important to talk to—a kind of who's who of the East End but also an indication of her own racially integrated, intergenerational, community-based network.

Like most East Enders, though, she knows certain parts of the community better than others. She told me about a founding member of EERCURC, a board member of the East End Community Heath Center. She told me about a black woman who had been living in the predominantly white Lower East End as long as she could remember. The gas station area is considerably to the east of the River Inn and is, in many respects, a different neighborhood segment. It also lies to the east of Saint Rose Catholic Church and is the neighborhood section that claims ownership of the Pendleton carbarn. She described a talk she had with a talented black leader from a longtime East End family: "I hung out with his sister in grade school. He wants me to run [for president of the East End Area Council] because I have a mind of my own and I'm not gonna let anyone snow me."

She mentioned several other women, black and white, who were born and raised in the East End, including another barmaid who worked full time, took care of elderly relatives, and still played on a darts team at the age of seventy-three. She talked about how she knew three East End women who should be nominated for sainthood, two of the women (white) had passed away. One (black) still lived in the East End. She talked about her kin ties—ties between sisters, aunts, and nieces. She told me about an African American woman who owned a junkyard in an area of the East End that she knew less well. She also mentioned a man who was raised in the Lower East End but who had gravitated to the Upper East End.

Robbie talked about some other issues, especially those concerning East End kids: "We need a forum. Kids don't know whether they will be here from one minute to the next. Whatever it takes to make them feel like they are part of keeping this neighborhood together. We need to get Upper East End kids and Lower East End kids together."

On the subject of an upcoming election, she objected to the requirement that a person must have attended three East End Area Council meetings in order to be eligible to vote in an annual election: "If there could be a motion to have it be a community election without three previous meetings, we have a better chance of having the kind of council this area needs. Older people can't come to meetings. Don't discriminate against people because they can't make it to meetings. The criteria should be that you be a resident."

Practicing Community: Class and Power

The power elite of Cincinnati see the East End community as poor and Appalachian, that is, poor white, and mostly marginal hillbillies—authentic hillbillies. The term "subaltern," the newest social science jargon for people without power, is an understatement in this context. According to the power structure's definition, "Appalachian" means poor white to the exclusion of black Appalachians. In reality, the East End is a diverse community with a substantial (15 percent) African American and black Appalachian population.

East Enders see the neighborhood as home to powerless people—for the most part, without reference to race. The East End is a working-class community with the emphasis on a place called East End and a heritage shared by generations. East Enders' terms for the working class include "the people," "the common people," or simply East Enders. Local knowledge and local practice of community are crucial to the very survival of the East End.

As I have indicated, I use the term "shallow urban" to refer to a community that simultaneously exists in, is defined by, and is resistant to the city and its power structure while remaining connected (primarily through movements of people back and forth between rural and urban places) to the country. Shallow urban also indicates ambivalence about the city—resistance to committing to its ways and its rules. Bringing in law enforcement agencies or city officials to solve a local problem is just not done. If someone does call the police against another East Ender, that person risks severe criticism, at best. Ostracism and a forced move out of the community are often the next steps.

The practice of community reveals the dynamics of working-class culture at the local level at the same time that it requires rethinking some conventional (hegemonic) understandings of class and class culture. For example, ideas about patterns of interaction (sharing, exchange, trading) within the working class, ideas about the desirability of upward mobility, ideas about rugged individualism, about work, family, and community itself must be reevaluated. Some of the interactions described at the beginning of this chapter are examples of the practice of class and community among "real" East Enders. Chapter 3 elaborates, through actual family histories, the subtleties and nuances of working-class culture and social organization.

Interclass as well as intraclass conflicts are part of the definition and practice of community in the East End. The subtle, and not-so-subtle, manifestations of class conflicts—again as locally manifested—include power struggles around planning issues, control issues concerning bylaws for the Community Council, time allocation in meetings, and interpersonal dynamics between and among members of the same and different social strata. Developers and the city have clever ways of pitting East Enders against one another. Divide and conquer has always been a standard control tactic.

The community itself is vulnerable. Children feel a sense of uncertainty because they do not know how long their community in general, their house or apartment in particular, will last. At any given time, people can be co-opted: they can sell their homes; they can sell out their families. The question of where people will go once they leave the East End is a difficult one.

The ways class plays itself out at the community level and in the chambers and halls of city government are central to this analysis. The dynamic interrelationships and tensions between people with conflicting interests is a fact of life in the East End. The rhetoric of the powerful and the strategies used by the various class-based factions to control community building and community destruction come through strongly in meetings, especially Community Council meetings.

The Language of Class

"Ever'body says words different," said Ivy. "Arkansas folks says 'em different, and Oklahomy folks says 'em different. And we seen a lady from Massachusetts, an' she said 'em differentest of all. Couldn' hardly make out what she was sayin'." (Steinbeck 1976: 173)

I use the language written or spoken in the community to showcase East End voices in specifically defined contexts. East Enders speak and write a dialect of English that is somewhat different from the standard. This dialect, with some variation, is spoken by all real East Enders. Middle-class people are quick to criticize East End speech and modes of expression.

In certain contexts, the dialect itself, as is true of most nonstandard dialects, conveys a sense of powerlessness. I once heard an African American city official tell an African American East Ender that she needed to correct certain grammatical forms in her poetry. This caused me great distress, since, among other things, he didn't realize how important the dialect was for her form of expression. Being a real East Ender is very closely related to how well a person speaks this dialect, however, and I have tried to convey East Enders' words with as much accuracy as possible. In many instances, the voices that are speaking in nonstandard dialect are taking part in conversations, often very heated conversations, in public meetings where outsiders, especially developers and city staff, are speaking a nearly standard English. The dynamics of the language of class are very important, for they specify power relations that are not nearly as clearly manifested in private settings.

In the East End, dialect switching is very common; that is, depending on who is present, a more or less standard form of English may be used. An adult who is "watching" children will speak to her charges in one dialect and to me in another, which is closer to standard. Depending on what the issue is, a working-class dialect will be more or less true to East End English. Anger, for example, will eliminate a great deal of standardization, as will grief. Too much standard English will bring on accusations of snobbishness and uppityness, however. For schoolchildren, there are obvious conflicts. They are expected to speak and write standard English, but this is not the English they hear or are expected to speak at home.

Class Redefined

Using class and community as the focus of this analysis does not imply that there is unity or homogeneity within the community, or even within the coterie of grassroots leaders in the East End. Internal tensions are always present; when these tensions escalate to conflict or to the creation of an impasse in community-building institutions, meetings come to a grinding halt. Gender and race can also undermine class interests. And class interests clearly undermine community interests, even when all other things are equal.

My thinking about class has been influenced by the work of E. P. Thompson and others who have dealt sociologically with the concept of class in a postmodern context.[2] The model of class that (with some modifications) is most suitable as a model for the East End does not assume a system in equilibrium. Neither does it assume any holism or organic interrelationships either within or between classes.[3] Within the East End working class, there is not only conflict and the potential for conflict, there is also great variability and stratification. Some working-class families are indeed wealthier than others. The "wealthy" working-class families own land and houses and maintain large kin networks. Other families own some property, but do not base their standing on wealth alone. In fact, wealth alone is never the sole measure of a person's worth in the East End. Participation in church affairs, honesty, integrity, intelligence, generosity, and willingness to work are more important than wealth when East Enders evaluate one another. (The next chapter elaborates these points.)

On the surface, class solidarity manifests itself primarily as attachment to the East End as a community, that is, as people who share a common place of residence. But when one examines what it means to be a real East Ender, it becomes clear that there are various categories of residents, only some of whom are working-class people, that is, real East Enders. There is a history of union activity within the community as well as a history of identification with people of limited means, "low-income" people. One neighborhood leader refers constantly to what "the people" want in contrast to what the developers or outsiders want for the East End.

Anthropology has a long history of community studies in both rural and urban areas and traditionally has focused on groups that are marginal to state power structures. This book follows some traditions and breaks with others. In one sense, it follows the tradition of fieldwork in complex societies established at Columbia University and at the University of Chicago. The use of narratives, life histories, and diaries has been effective for keeping the reader close to the day-to-day life of communities.[4] This traditional approach has been continued by writers such as Jane Jacobs (1961), Herbert Gans (1962), Carol Stack (1974), and Ida Susser (1986) who have emphasized the strengths of working-class people in urban communities and continued the traditions of community studies.[5] They are all studies in which ethnicity has played a major part and in which local support systems based on kinship, friendship, and community are seen as bounded.[6]

This book has also been influenced greatly by ethnographic work in Europe, for example, Herzfeld (1987) on marginality in Greece and Cohen (1982, 1985) on identity and community in the British Isles. Cohen's work on the symbolic construction of community, especially his concept of "belonging," rings true in the East End. Even though his notions of community emphasize symbolic aspects, they dovetail nicely with E. P. Thompson's (1963) ideas about class as something that is in process, in motion in everyday, practical life in particular historical contexts "both in the raw material of experience and in consciousness" (pp. 9–10). Thompson's is a synthetic, practical, and fluid notion of class that embodies both the material and the symbolic aspects of everyday life and resists seeing class as a structure or category. Class culture is also central to his discussion, although he does not use the phrase. The most important point, however, is that Thompson's and Cohen's concepts of class and community are consistent with the ways real East Enders understand and experience the East End as a community. As one East End advocate put it, "It's not about being black or white, it's about being poor."

Class Culture and Power

The question of how East Enders see themselves and what sources of identity are available to working-class people in an era of deindustrialization points to work itself as a declining source of identity on the margins of the postindustrial state.[7] The place of community, of class culture and class identity, however fragmented, becomes important in this postmodern context.[8]

The ways in which members of our university-based research team dealt with the power relations we created and inevitably became a part of are also part of this ethnography. Our taking a strong position on the side of the grassroots leadership led to our team members' being treated politely, but coldly, by developers. At times, we had questions addressed to us publically that smacked of what one advocate called "outsider baiting." These incidents usually occurred in Community Council meetings when the developer-controlled council was losing ground. I discuss this issue in more detail in Chapter 5.

As community leaders were successful in achieving certain goals, or frustrated and exhausted by the endless meetings, rhetoric, and catch-22's created by the city bureaucracy, conflicts arose between East Enders and outsiders and among East Enders. Often, it was just when the greatest progress was being made that grassroots leadership fell apart. Power relationships and issues of control operate in the context of different community boards and in project-specific contexts. Who controls and receives credit for community projects is one issue. Social scientists used to frame these issues in terms of, for example, individualism versus the good of the whole or cooperation versus competition. But the processes in the East End are more complicated, or we now perceive them to be so. Race and gender come into play in ways that require untangling.

Which is the strongest source of identity: race, class, or community? When does working for the good of the community get carried too far, or wear too thin? How does the struggle for everyday livelihood influence grassroots efforts to maintain community? Do women experience these issues differently from men? Relationships between community identity, class, and power will be explored in this book. Is community a code name for class, or vice versa? What is the role of community heritage and history in maintaining a leader's credibility and trust? How is community itself redefined through revitalization? The term "working class" must itself be redefined to include not only wage labor, but all of the other multiple livelihood strategies that deindustrialization has fomented and that, indeed, have, historically, always been part of family-based provisioning strategies in some form.[9]

From a cross-cultural perspective, these approaches to understanding class culture and power are extremely important because they emphasize the variety of cultural forms within which a sense of belonging to class or community in a local social context can occur. These concepts are, thus, meant to be used to understand many communities, classes, and cultures at different times and places.

Summary

This is a book, then, about efforts to sustain community, about class culture and power—the power to control and maintain the community's identity and autonomy as a working-class community in the face of and in tandem with the forces of economic development. The East End community is constantly being defined and redefined in various contexts and in relationship to the city, the hillside dwellers, and the developers. East Enders must work almost constantly just to maintain the status quo, that is, to prevent the community from slipping away. Houses are torn down regularly. Well-meaning and caring parents move out of the neighborhood when they would really like to stay. The mother of a sixteen-year-old girl told me that she had to leave to protect her daughter because one of her daughter's friends put mattresses in boarded-up buildings so the kids could smoke, drink, and have unprotected sex.

There are subtle and not-so-subtle manifestations of class and powerlessness. In meetings at City Hall, there is community representation, but the voices of residents are somehow left out of the minutes; in hearings a clerk or a council member can silence a resident's voice by controlling the time allowed for speaking by cutting a community leader off prematurely.

Community meetings are also contexts for exerting power over working-class people. Developers dominate, both physically and verbally, by monopolizing meeting time and thereby controlling the agenda. The patronizing do-gooders who project their images of community in powerful ways but with supposed good intentions can upset consensus in a meeting just when it is beginning to be formed.

But there are also counters to powerlessness. Becoming known as an articulate speaker at City Hall—respected as an energetic and knowledgeable person and neighborhood leader—is one counter. Getting to know the city staff, forming relationships of trust with the insiders of city government is another. Learning how to use advocates and researchers effectively is still another. Learning how to marshall grassroots support and to plan for future projects while maintaining ties to outsiders who can help move projects along or avert crises is an ideal many community leaders strive for.

I have tried to tell the East End Story in the voices of the people. Context is important, however, and to some degree, it is reflected in people's voices. It may also be reflected in actions, which merit recording. My challenge has been how to maintain the anthropological voice, which I see as empathic, logical, and passionate, while keeping that voice autonomous and separate from other voices. The anthropological voice, while it need not be authoritative, must maintain its own sense of self, be its own "person." This means that it certainly can and, indeed, must speak on issues and take a stand and a position; to attempt neutrality is naïve at best.

Most important, my task has been not only to provide context but also to bring together the often dissonant community voices by presenting the many facets of an issue. The issues are not always rational; the stuff of ethnography is not always clear-cut. There are textures and nuances, subtleties and contradictions, as well as constant change. There is power in writing it down:

Cultures do not hold still for their portraits. (Clifford 1986: 10)

Cultures not only do not hold still for their portraits, they speed along before one can blink an eye. What seems to be a known fact or a *fait accompli* one day can be contradicted or reversed on the next. One interpretation or even description of an event or the meaning of a person's utterance after six months or a year can change completely. Time frames shape our understanding.

3 | BEING A REAL EAST ENDER: FAMILIES AND THEIR HISTORIES

We moved here when I was about three months old. And I was raised in what they call the bottoms. Now it's First and Fourth Street between Broadway and Bigelow—right behind Lytle Park. Between that street and Maple. I was just raised right in that area. We lived along First Street and Fourth Street. It was 1943 we moved to Newport and we lived over there a couple of years and we moved back after the '45 flood. And, ever since then we've been on Eastern Avenue.

Karl sees his mother every day; even if he doesn't talk to her she might yell a hello down from her house, which is practically across the street. She owns her house and "it's all up to par . . . Mom stays on top of it . . . it's a real old place, but it's all right, it's up to par, she stays on top of it. My sister's right across the street, wave and honk up and down and talk."

I begin this chapter with what is perhaps the most powerful, succinct, and vivid statement of what it means to be a real East Ender. It is a rendering (narrative) written by a fifth-generation East Ender as part of fighting back developers and stereotypes—practicing community with words. Ironically enough, and in true East End fashion, it is generous in its welcoming of outsiders.

Who are East Enders? Not the new kids on the block that have moved in to be on the ground floor of the revitalization of the East End, nor am I speaking of the speculators or the developers that have moved in like the fog that creeps in while you sleep. I am talking about the people that have stayed in this neighborhood through the closing of our schools, the closing of our businesses, neglect from the city and of course the floods that are a part of our lives. These are the East Enders that are on the brink of extinction. Make no mistake—true East Enders are on an endangered species list and in the East End poachers abound.

East Enders have earned that title, this has come from generations of the same families calling this home no matter what the cost to them. We have rebuilt after floods and fires. We have prevailed on our own with almost nonexistent help from the city, and we have fought back with words when we have been labeled illiterate, unwashed hillbillies. Most of this just happened because we are who we are, East Enders. But now we have a handful of outsiders and developers that wish to turn this in to their idea of the perfect upscale neighborhood with a great riverview and all the green space one would want for their children. And in most cases when money talks the poor walk.

There is a way to preserve the heritage that some have here, it is called the East End Community Plan and Guidelines. Not the Eastern Riverfront Plan that some of the new kids and developers wanted. In this plan there is a place for all classes and that is what has the developers and the new kids worried, you see they don't believe that true East Enders have any class. There is nothing that will stop some of the people from getting what they want, they will do or say anything to abolish the East End as we know it.

Where houses once stood are empty lots owned by developers waiting to build their condos and townhouses. That isn't enough for them, they also want to tear down the rest of the low income and stop any new affordable housing from being built, then and only then will they have the kind of neighborhood that they so desperately want.

This is why the East Enders that have called this home for generations must now stand together and say we will move no more. We must stand our ground for this has been the same ground that our grandparents and great grandparents have walked. I for one am not afraid to see development come, I yearn to see the first shovel of dirt turned that will mark a new beginning, and I am not afraid to live alongside of people that "have more than me" for no amount of their money can override the richness of this neighborhood and its heritage. With this in mind I am urging the true citizens of the East End to once again make their presence known, let's show that we know this neighborhood is truly one of class with room for everyone. (A fifth-generation East Ender)

Authenticity, Family, and Community

The question of who is an East Ender and the meaning of the expression "real" East Ender are not easily understood by outsiders. Being a real East Ender is an identity that is shared and admired by the elderly and children alike. Community membership cannot be taken for granted; being a real East Ender is an honored status that can often be achieved only after a family lives in the community for many generations. Once real East Ender status is achieved, however, a person does not sever East End ties easily. People with a family history in the neighborhood who have only a single relative left in the East End or people of Appalachian working-class heritage, which also confers membership in the community, are more authentic East Enders than a newcomer who owns property or runs a business.

Being a real East Ender is an identity that is also fragile, however, because the community is struggling for survival. The East End is vulnerable to market forces and to local and state bureaucracies—displacement and relocation, escalating property values and taxes. These are more intimidating to East Enders than the worst floods. Being a real East Ender is a great source of comfort, strength, and solidarity, even though maintaining the East End, its people, its heritage, and its culture requires constant work on the part of residents and grassroots leaders to ensure respect for and maintenance of the rich and long-lived traditions of a working-class family and community.

The experience of neighborhood neglect and deterioration, the experience of class discrimination and the sense of powerlessness that comes with fear of displacement, is very real for East Enders. The frustration with city bureaucracies intensifies when overgrown lots become mosquito infested, junkyards become health hazards, and boarded-up buildings become fire traps. The practices of everyday survival, the everyday practices of survival—the knowledge of ideals and the gaps between ideals of family and community and the everyday realities—can be overwhelming.

One of the best ways to understand real East Enders is to get to know East End people and families. Many are strong and resilient, large extended-kin networks. Others hang by a thread in the absence of adequate resources and social supports. Life patterns and everyday practices, evidenced by the closeness of neighbors and the blurred distinctions between family and community are the essence of community. Many East Enders are related to one another, by proximity and practical necessity if not by ties of blood or marriage. If the kids don't have a meal or a place to go, or someone's electricity is shut off, neighbors pick up the slack. When Casey's electricity was shut off, for example, Amy ran an extension cord from her apartment through Casey's window.

At the very least, everyone knows everyone else's business, especially the whereabouts of children and the elderly. While some of the relationships between and among East End families will emerge in the course of this chapter, a thorough treatment of the social organization of the East End would merit a separate book, for not only are East Enders related to one another through ties of blood, marriage, and practical kinship, but there are ties throughout the rural-urban Appalachian community that should be documented. Regional Appalachian neighborhoods and communities such as Price Hill, California (Ohio), Norwood, Over the Rhine, Fairmount, Madisonville, New Richmond, Amelia, Loveland, Milford, Lebanon, and Mount Carmel all have links to the East End.

Family is the number one priority for East Enders. Members of extended families often live very close to one another—in the same house or, more often, on the same street, in the same apartment building or section of the neighborhood. Family is the most important model for the community itself and for community groups. For both men and women, family obligations—being there to help any and all family members—take priority over all other obligations, including serving on community boards and attending meetings regularly.

One day I was sent by an elderly East End board chair to check on whether another elderly member of the board needed a ride to a board meeting. When I arrived at his house, I found his wife caring for her three-year-old great-grandson who lives across the street. She told me her husband had gone with their son to see about recovering some money he had paid for some goods at an auction. Apparently, when the son came to collect the goods after paying for them in advance, they were not turned over to him. An elderly authority was clearly needed to straighten out this situation.

Within the East End and among the families of people considered to be real East Enders, there is a great deal of variation in family rela-

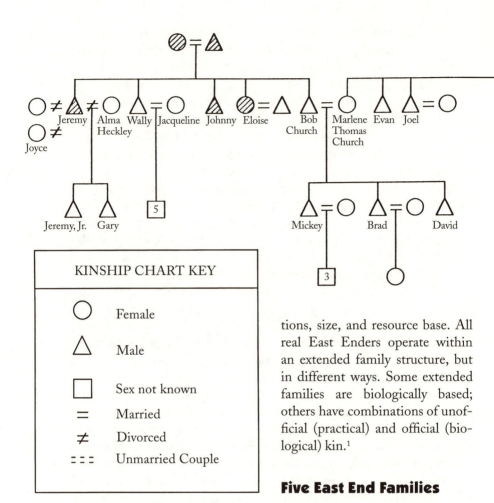

KINSHIP CHART KEY

◯	Female
△	Male
▢	Sex not known
=	Married
≠	Divorced
꞊꞊꞊	Unmarried Couple

Figure 3. The Church Family

tions, size, and resource base. All real East Enders operate within an extended family structure, but in different ways. Some extended families are biologically based; others have combinations of unofficial (practical) and official (biological) kin.[1]

Five East End Families

The families described in this chapter were chosen not only to indicate the range of families, resources, and configurations of relationships, but also to show the typical patterns of relationships among and between family members, friends, and neighbors. This chapter begins with two large, relatively well off, and stable East End families. The first family, the Churches, is typical of old, large, property-owning East End families. The Churches are a white family with roots in Kentucky, Ohio, and West Virginia. Their commitment to family, like that of many East Enders, can be seen daily as a set of regular interactions between and among people of different generations. The second family, the Simmses, is similar in structure to the first, although it is a

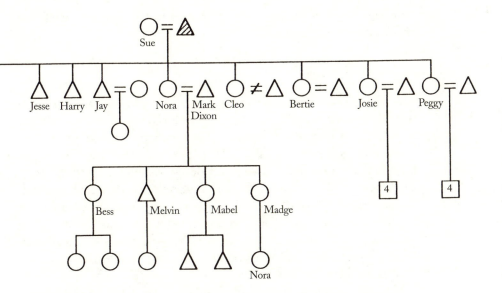

black family with roots in Kentucky. While each East End family is, in many respects, unique, there are many similarities between and among families.

The third and fourth families, both white, are less prosperous than the first two. While the McMillans own their own home, they combine government assistance (Aid to Families with Dependent Children, AFDC) with work in the informal economy—garbage picking, flea marketing, and garage sales. The Wrights are renters; so are the Hammonds. The fifth family described in this chapter consists of Karen Warren, a single black mother, and her children. All the families lived in the East End in 1991 and were still there in 1997.

The Churches

I love the river, I love livin' by it. (Marlene Thomas Church)

Bob and Marlene Church have spent their entire adult lives in the East End together with their extended family in a large house facing the river. Their sense of rootedness in the East End is strong and is based on longevity in the community and connections to family, friends, and neighbors. They also own several other properties and have been involved in both landscaping and used car businesses that employ East Enders. Bob Church is a large, burly man who loves to tease and tell jokes. Until recently, he was active in community affairs as one of the founding members of the East End Riverfront Community Urban Redevelopment Corporation.

Marlene's Family

Marlene Thomas Church was born in 1940. She lived in Over the Rhine until she was about ten, when the family moved to Hillsboro, a town in rural Ohio, "for a couple of years." The family then moved to the East End, where she met Bob. Bob Church, born in 1941, has lived in the East End all of his life. Marlene and Bob were married in March 1959. Marlene's mother, Sue, came from Kentucky. Sue's mother left Sue with her parents when she came to Cincinnati to get work; she brought Sue up after she got a job. Sue now lives in the first-floor apartment of Marlene and Bob's house. Marlene's father was raised in Charleston, West Virginia, and, before his death in late 1993, he lived with his wife downstairs from Bob and Marlene.

Marlene has five sisters and five brothers. Evan Thomas was born in Hillsboro, Ohio, and now lives in the East End. He installs auto glass. Joel Thomas lived with Marlene and Bob until he got married. He now lives in Amelia, Ohio, and works in heating and air conditioning. Jesse Thomas lives downstairs with his mother and is a roofer. Harry Thomas lives next door, in a building owned by Bob and Marlene. He is also a roofer. Jay Thomas lives in the East End with his wife and seven-year-old daughter. He is a tire changer.

Nora Thomas Dixon, who is the eldest sibling, had to quit school in the sixth grade to help with the family. She now works for a printing company. She is married with four children and lives in the East End. One of her daughters, Bess Dixon, lives in the East End and has two daughters of her own. Nora's son, Melvin, lives in the East End and has an infant daughter. Nora's daughter Mabel lives in the East End and has two sons; another daughter, Madge, has a daughter, Nora, and lived in the East End until 1990.

Marlene Church's other sisters include Cleo, who lives downstairs with her mother and brother. She is divorced and works in a plastics factory. Bertie, a cook at a local restaurant, lives across town and is married. Josie lives in South Lebanon, Ohio. She is married, has four children, and works at a nursing home. Peggy lives in the East End and works at Nutone. She is married and has four children, two of whom attend McKinley, the only grade school still operating in the East End.

Bob's Family

Bob's mother was originally from Kentucky but was raised in the East End. She died in 1951 from a "blood clot." His father came directly to the East End from Europe as an adult. After Bob's father died, Bob lived with his eldest sister, Eloise, and her husband until her death, after which he came to live with his brother Jeremy and now former sister-in-law: "I don't feel as though they cared anything about me you know, it was just takin' me in . . . I was 12, 13 years old, somewhere along in there, I practically raised myself. The old grocery store used to be across the street here and I went in there workin' . . . it was just a little rough." Bob was not the only one to experience difficulty. Johnny Church died in infancy. Wally Church, now retired from Hemmington Manufacturing, lives in Price Hill, a large Appalachian community on the west side of Cincinnati, with his wife, Jacqueline, who was raised in Price Hill. They have five children, four of whom live in Price Hill and the other in California, Ohio. Jeremy Church lived in the East End until he died of cancer. He was married three times; all three wives were from the East End. The most recent one, Joyce, now lives in Kentucky. Jeremy had two sons by his second wife, Alma (now Alma Heckley, an East Ender). Jeremy, Jr., lives in the East End.

Marlene and Bob have three sons, all of whom were born and raised in the East End. Mickey was born in 1960. He and his wife and three children now live in California, Ohio, where his wife was raised. Brad was born in 1962. On the recommendation of his teacher at Highland School, the local grade school attended by at least five generations of East Enders until it closed in the 1970s, Brad attended the School for Musical and Dramatic Arts, a magnet school that requires an audition for entrance. He graduated from this school and attended college for two years in Saint Louis and in northern Kentucky part-time for an additional year. He formerly managed an auto body shop and now owns his own garage, which employs only East Enders as full-time employees: Jay Thomas (Marlene Church's brother), Clay Kale, Larry Hammond and his son Ed, and Gary Church, Jeremy Church's son. Brad would like to find a building in the East End that he can use for storage of equipment and supplies as well as an office. His wife is a college graduate; they have a two-year-old daughter and live in Oakley.

David was born in 1968. He also graduated from the School for Musical and Dramatic Arts and now manages a tire shop in Fairfax, Ohio, a community very close to the East End. He lived with Bob and Marlene for a while, but he now lives in one of Bob's rehabbed houses.

Keeping the family close at hand and gainfully employed is a mark of being a real East Ender. It also means looking out for the employment needs of other East Enders. Whenever a young East Ender needs a job, Brad is considered as a job source. A lot of East Enders' work is seasonal; cold winters inevitably create layoffs for young male workers. When resources become short enough that rent payments are a problem, parts of families move in with relatives, either in Cincinnati, in a nearby neighborhood, or back in the country.

Livelihood and Nonmarket Economies

Marlene Church works as a bookbinder for a printing company across town. Bob Church has worked since he was a teenager. He dropped out of school in ninth grade and began working at a little grocery store across the street from where he lived. A few years later, he and the store owner set up a produce stand, also in the East End, and Bob ran the stand, splitting the profits with the owner. "I've done all kinds of things . . . went to work on the river." For most of his adult life, Bob has been a driver for Maple's Produce, a food distributor in downtown Cincinnati.

The Churches own their own home (a two-family building) and three other East End houses, some of which have more than one apartment. Bob bought all of his property with signature loans because no bank would grant a mortgage in the East End. They bought their own home, which they still occupy, from a friend's grandmother. They had been living in a rental house, but a tornado took off the roof. Bob got a signature loan, bought the house, and has fixed it up over the years.

The rents Bob charges are not always determined by his costs or by the market. He bought one house from an elderly woman, who continued to live there for a few years. Bob had some maintenance and improvement costs for the building and had to raise her rent. He continued to charge her much less than the going rate, however, because she could not afford to pay more and because he didn't want to displace her. He has rented the downstairs apartment in his building on several occasions, and once let a friend's sister live there rent free: "She was having some problems . . . and didn't have no one." Marlene's mother lives there now.

Bob has received numerous offers to buy his properties. One of his major contributions to practicing community is his resistance to selling his properties and his renting apartments to friends and relatives, often below market rates. He has even tolerated his places being "torn up." He says that all the offers to buy have come from outside the East End, either from speculators or "Hyde Park people who want a view of the river." He says he has bought some of his properties just to keep them out of the hands of "outside people" who only want to tear down the buildings and gentrify the neighborhood: "I bought my property when nobody else wanted it." Bob has fixed up his properties by doing most of the work himself. When a place is occupied, however, he usually sends someone else to do the maintenance because he doesn't want his tenants to think he's snooping. He is committed to keeping housing in the East End for East Enders.

Bob also fixes up boats. He and Marlene love the river and spend their free time on their houseboat, which they maintain themselves. Bob also bought a boat to refit, which he then sold. He proudly recalls how he salvaged a marine generator that had been submerged. He bought it for $150, rebuilt it, and still uses it on his own boat. The same generator would have sold new for $5,000.

In addition to boats, Bob works on cars. He buys them at auto auctions and resells them at a profit. His sons also work on cars in addition to their regular jobs. Bob says that he and Marlene have always been "able to get what nobody else wanted and make something out of it."

These labor-intensive efforts that add value to houses, apartments, boats, and cars are very important strategies for working-class people. They require the hard work, which has always been the keystone of working-class culture. The Churches can maintain a high standard of living and provide jobs and accommodations for family members and neighbors.

Practicing Community

Bob and Marlene see at least some of their relatives every day. Marlene's mother lives downstairs; David left home after he was an adult, and the other children drop by frequently. One day when we were talking to Bob, his brother-in-law came up the back steps, walked through the unlocked door, jovially slapped Bob on the shoulders, and walked out the front door. No one even looked up; it was a normal event in the East End. Doors are always open.

One of the reasons Bob and Marlene love their houseboat is that it is frequently filled with family and friends. Marlene says they don't see their friends as often as they used to, "only about once a week." Many of the

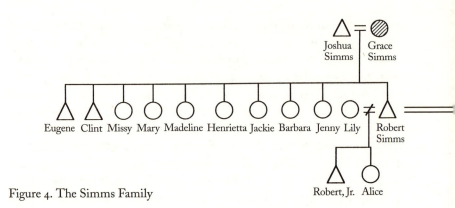

Figure 4. The Simms Family

people on their section of Eastern Avenue have lived there for years and are longtime friends: "People know each other, and help each other."

Bob Church is very close to James Strong, another East End family head who, with his wife and most of their nine grown children, lives just five blocks east of the Churches. James is much older than Bob. The Strong family is very much like the Churches, though, large, very solidly committed to family, longtime East Enders with most of the family living nearby in homes owned by the family. Says Bob: "What we've got is from the neighborhood, you know like James Strong up the street. He's a real good friend of mine . . . I talk to James . . . he's a lot older than I am but we're real good friends and we talk darn near every day on the phone and well we get together like in the summer time he's got a piece of ground up here on [Route] 52, and we go up and live on our boat up there for two to three weeks . . . and we try to take the grandkids . . . I go fishin' almost every day." Bob gives his fish to "a black guy that lives up the street . . . or I call Ed, he's a black guy around seventy something. I love to fish, but I can't stand catfish." Nothing is wasted or thrown away unnecessarily.

Bob and Marlene's block in the neighborhood has been very stable, although he acknowledges that new people disrupt the stability: "This block here has always been people that lived here from I'd say damn near from childhood." Bob is critical of outsiders and new people while acknowledging the longevity and stability of East Enders: "Well, you don't know the new people, there's a lot of people that moves in down here that all they think about is gettin' that check and gettin' drunk or gettin' high, which you're gonna find in any neighborhood. But you take like, okay, this house and like Lonny and Erma has been down here a long time, Tina, Joey, Miss Manley, Gladys, these are all people that's been here for years

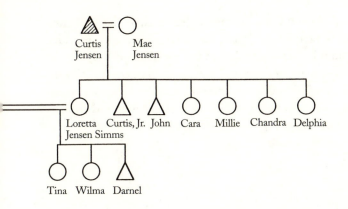

Curtis Jensen — Mae Jensen

Loretta Jensen Simms | Curtis, Jr. | John | Cara | Millie | Chandra | Delphia

Tina | Wilma | Darnel

and Miss Park over here on the corner and Chuck and them that live next door to them, all these people have lived here for years and raised their kids. Lonny's wife they moved here from Mount Adams, Manley's did . . . Ruby and them originally came from Mount Adams, that's the closest place to East End you know. . . . they got married, Joey and Ruby bought the house right here 2–3 doors down from her mom . . . Joey's sister lives up over top of him." Bob knows the neighborhood and its history intimately. The people and families he has mentioned are indeed the pillars of the East End community and are known to all real East Enders.

The Simmses

Loretta and Robert Simms are the heads of another very stable and long-lived East End family. Loretta is a small, unassuming woman whose appearance belies her inner strength. Robert is a large, strong man—a hard worker.

Loretta Jensen Simms was born in 1962. She lived in Madisonville, Ohio, a nearby predominantly African American working-class community, until she was eleven years old, moved to the East End for four years, and then, when she was fifteen, she and her family returned to Madisonville. In 1983, she moved with her husband to the East End. Robert, born in 1955 in Kentucky, has lived most of his life in the East End.

Loretta's Family

Loretta's father, Curtis Jensen, now deceased, was a meat packer in Kentucky. Her mother, Mae, was a cashier at a department store and now lives in Madisonville.

Loretta has four sisters and two brothers. Her brothers live in Madisonville. Curtis, Jr., is a landscaper, and John is a machine operator. Her sister Cara also resides in Madisonville and is a part-time office worker. Millie and Chandra live in Fairmount, an Appalachian community on the west side of Cincinnati. Millie is a factory worker; Chandra is unemployed. Loretta's sister Delphia is a hotel housekeeper and lives in downtown Cincinnati. All except Curtis are high school graduates; he left school in the eleventh grade.

Robert's Family

Robert's parents were also from Kentucky originally. His mother, Grace, is now deceased, but his father, Joshua, who is disabled, lives in Madisonville. Robert has seven sisters and two brothers. Jenny works at Providence Hospital and lives in Fairmount. Barbara is a factory worker and resides in Lower Price Hill, another Appalachian working-class community. Jackie and Henrietta both work at a dry cleaner and live in Fairmount, while Madeline, who lives in Kentucky, is involved in child care. Jenny, Barbara, Henrietta, and Madeline were all educated in Kentucky. Mary and Missy, who are East End residents, are both unemployed. They live near Robert and Loretta and visit them often. Clint is incarcerated, and Eugene is a junkyard partsman who lives in the East End in a house formerly owned by Robert and Loretta.

Robert has two children from a previous marriage, Robert, Jr., born in 1973, and Alice, born in 1975. These children live in the Simms household in the East End. Robert, Jr., dropped out of school after completing the eighth grade at Withrow High School and has been unemployed for a long time. Alice attends Withrow. Robert and Loretta have three children together, all of whom were born in the East End. Tina was born in 1979, Wilma in 1982, and Darnel in 1983. They attend Eastern Hills IGE (Individual Guided Education), a primary school outside of the neighborhood. Loretta notes that the kids do well in school. They have a lot of friends in the neighborhood and experience little if any racism in their predominantly white neighborhood.

Livelihood

Loretta Simms started working right out of high school. She has been a factory worker and a nurse's aid. She held a full-time job at Schneider's department stores for almost three years, where she worked in customer service and as an office manager. She then got a job at Cornwell Trust doing data entry while she held a part-time job at Schneider's. Loretta worked on data entry for fourteen months, but said it became too boring. She got transferred to a department where they return bad checks, which she indicates is more stressful but where she is happier.

Robert dropped out of school in eighth grade. He then got a job as a partsman at a junkyard until his back went out in 1984. Since then, he has not held a job and collects worker's compensation. Robert spends some of his time fixing cars for cash.

The first house the Simmses had in the East End was too small for their growing family. They lived there for only ten months. They bought their second house by signing a land contract because the bank would not grant another loan. Robert rented the first house to his brother Eugene, but found that being a landlord was too time consuming. He later sold it to Eugene.

The Simmses have done much to fix up the house, especially painting and remodeling their bathroom. They are not anxious to work too fast on their house, however, because the city might take it away through eminent domain. Loretta comments that "now it's like you don't know whether to invest in your house."

The Simmses own their house, five lots that adjoin their home, and one lot up the street. They also own a lodge at a resort in Batesville, Indiana, where they vacation. They have a tow truck in good condition, as well as three or four junked cars in the lots adjoining their house. They could not have purchased these things on Loretta's salary and Robert's worker's compensation alone. Loretta and her children frequently visit area flea markets and garage sales. They also shop at various large chain grocery stores and some all-purpose discount stores such as Schneider's.

Practicing Community

The Simmses see members of Robert's family daily, especially his sisters, nieces, and nephews. On Sundays, Loretta and the children go to church and visit Loretta's mother in Madisonville. Loretta talks to neighbors in the East End regularly, particularly concerning what she sees as impending development. She feels that the threats to the community have brought East Enders together. She has also been active in neighborhood activities. Several years ago, she took a seminar at a local university entitled "Community Awareness." She has since been a group leader for a citywide clean-up blitz.

Loretta has noticed dramatic changes in the East End. Displacement is ongoing. People are moving out because there is an acute shortage of places to rent. Businesses are also closing. Across from their house, there used to be a trucking company, but now the area is fenced in and overgrown with weeds. Loretta still maintains, however, that the rents in the East End are low and even a fairly large family can find a place to move into. She does understand though, that the city has approved four sections of expensive town houses. She fears that the city will claim the Simms house through eminent domain and give them only $15,000 for it. She believes that 90 percent of East End residents would rather deal with private developers, because they would get more money for their property. Loretta is not sure where her family would go if they lost their house: "There's drug dealing in Madisonville and Hyde Park is so expensive." Moreover, Loretta feels at home in the East End. She believes it is safe and states that in the area of the East End where she lives, there is virtually no racism.

The next three families are not as well off as the first two. They nonetheless come from similar backgrounds and live their lives in similar ways. Family members live nearby or in the region and interaction can be frequent. As resources become more and more scarce, however, stress within families like these mounts.

The McMillans

The McMillans, a white family, live in the segment of the East End that lies east of Delta Avenue, outside of the plan area (see Chapter 7). Their life and livelihood patterns are typical of many in the East End: hard work in several economic sectors, formal and informal.

Mandy McMillan was born in 1959 and has spent her life in the East End. At age sixteen, she became pregnant with her daughter Rebecca and was later married. The marriage lasted only a few years, because her husband wanted to stay at home and live from welfare benefits. She then married Jeremy, who was born in 1949 and also raised in the East End.

Rebecca lives with Mandy's mother, Betty Ann, to whom Mandy does not speak. Mandy's father is now deceased, but she recalls that he frequently drank. After a drinking episode, her mother would often have

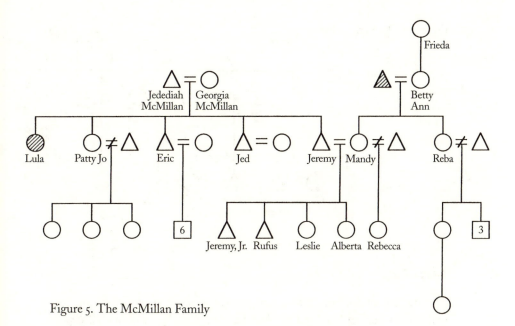

Figure 5. The McMillan Family

black eyes. Her grandparents were both born and raised in Kentucky. She is especially close to her maternal grandmother, Frieda, who lives in the East End, a block from the McMillans.

Jeremy's parents, Jedediah and Georgia, are from Arkansas and now live in New Richmond, Ohio, a rural area about thirty miles from Cincinnati. Jedediah was self-employed, doing odd jobs and tree trimming, while Georgia did kitchen work. They are now retired, which means that their livelihood comes from odd jobs and gifts from children, but not from wage labor.

Mandy has one sister, Reba, who lives in New Richmond and is divorced with four children. One of her girls has a child of her own. Jeremy McMillan has two brothers and a sister, all of whom live in the East End (one sister, Lula, is deceased). Jed is married and has graduated from nursing school at the University of Cincinnati. Eric is married with six children. Patty Jo is divorced with 3 daughters and is currently on welfare. Lula committed suicide a number of years ago.

Together, Mandy and Jeremy have four children. Their son Jeremy was born in 1978 and attended Eastern Hills IGE in Mount Washington. Rufus was born in 1977 and attended a local grade school. Leslie, who was born in 1984, failed first grade, and Alberta, who was born in 1989, has always been a sickly child.

Figure 6. The Wright Family

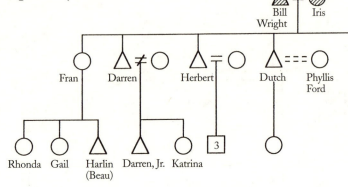

Livelihood

Mandy left school before she completed the seventh grade, and Jeremy will not let her get her GED: "He says I should stay home with the kids, can't find nobody you can trust to watch the kids." Now she collects AFDC. She also goes on her "routes" with the children. These routes involve "garbage picking," collecting of throwaway reusable items, and selling these items at flea markets: "I stay out to 1 or 2 o'clock. Routes are Sunday, Monday, sometimes on Tuesday and Wednesday and Thursday." She relates that most of her neighbors are on welfare, but says they also engage in garbage picking. On the eve of garbage collection day in a well-to-do neighborhood, pickup trucks and cars with small trailers drive through after dark to collect reusable goods that sit, discarded, on the curbs in front of large homes. This is a form of recycling that few people know about, and it often involves only a little cleaning and polishing of perfectly good appliances, rugs, couches, and other furniture. Mandy sells refurbished goods in the Pothandler's flea market—a market on the periphery of the East End.

Mandy traded some of her garbage pickings to get some body work done on her car. She then sold the car and bought the lot next to their house. She combines odd jobs with other informal economic activities. On one occasion, she painted a woman's porch in Mariemont, a nearby upper-middle-class community, for $25. She also can earn as much as $18 a day from collecting aluminum cans. She uses her earnings to buy toys for her children.

Jeremy has his GED. He is an alcoholic who combines taking advan-

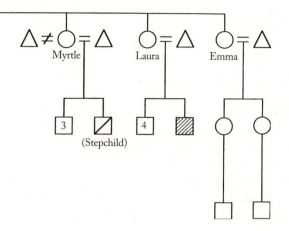

tage of Mandy's welfare with odd jobs, primarily in the neighborhood, cutting down trees, fixing old televisions, lawnmowers, microwaves, and mopeds, tasks typically performed by men. Since Mandy finds these throwaways in the garbage, there is cooperation between them in generating "extra" cash.

The McMillans' house was in Jeremy's mother and father's name, but now is jointly owned by Mandy and Jeremy. Jeremy is doing some remodeling on the house, such as replacing the ceiling. They are always short of cash and owe a substantial amount to the Cincinnati Gas and Electric Company.

The McMillans see members of Jeremy's family daily. Mandy says it is important to have family near. Her grandmother lives on the next corner. So does her adopted uncle, who lives with his girlfriend. She says she can depend on him anytime, especially if she needs money; however, she acknowledges that he "is all the time in trouble." He once stole several cars, but Mandy brought them back to prevent his arrest. Mandy is also close to some of her neighbors, including Lucy Ford and her husband: "I'll take her to bingo, to the store. She wants me to call her Mom and him Dad."

The Wrights

Fran Wright, a white Appalachian, was born and raised in the East End. She has lived her adult life in the East End and Fairmount. Her parents, Bill and Iris, now deceased, were born in Texas.

Fran has three brothers and three sisters. Darren left school in the ninth grade. He is currently divorced with two children, Darren, Jr., who was born in 1977 and attends high school, and Katrina, born in 1976 and living in Anderson Township. Herbert is a high school graduate. He and his wife and their three children reside in Loveland. Dutch lives in the apartment above Fran with his girlfriend, Phyllis Ford. He does odd jobs and is a house painter. He has a twenty-year-old daughter who left Withrow High School in the ninth grade. Myrtle currently lives with her second husband in Symmes Township with three children and one stepchild. Laura is married and had five children, one of whom died at age six. Neither she nor her husband completed the twelfth grade. Emma, who lives in the East End, left school after the ninth grade. She is married with two daughters. Both daughters have small children and are not married.

Fran has three children. Rhonda is in the fifth grade at Eastern Hills IGE. She suffers from kidney and bladder problems. Gail is a 1990 graduate of Peter Clark Academy, a special Cincinnati school for high school dropouts. Harlin (Beau) is a 1991 graduate of the same school. Gail and her mother both smoke heavily.

Livelihood

Fran did not complete the tenth grade at Withrow. She states that she has worked on and off but does not speak specifically of where her financial support comes from. All of her children live with her. Gail is a store clerk at the White Water Grocery in the East End. Beau does odd jobs for their landlord and wants to become a Cincinnati firefighter. Fran is also quite close to Phyllis Ford, who lives upstairs with Fran's brother, Dutch.

The Wrights pay rent on a two-family home. Fran pays $215 for three rooms and a basement; Phyllis pays $245 for six rooms and a bath. Their landlord, who lives in Hyde Park, seems to be the caretaker of the family, and, in fact, many of the appliances in Fran's kitchen belong to him.

Phyllis and Fran shop together and rely on each other for daily needs. Shopping expeditions usually include a large grocery store, an all-purpose discount store with a variety of large and small retail items from furniture to accessories, and stores downtown. Phyllis owns a car that both use often. If it breaks down, Beau is asked to fix it or to find someone in the neighborhood who can in exchange for food, cigarettes, and other necessities. Neither Fran nor Phyllis has a lot of contact with friends and family outside of the East End. Fran has an aunt and uncle who own their own home in the East End. She also has nieces who live nearby.

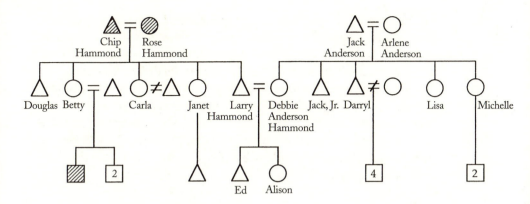

Figure 7. The Hammond Family

Fran is concerned that newcomers to the East End will come in and "run down" the neighborhood. Her son, Beau, comments that "you can't walk the streets without getting shot . . . drugs and alcohol is the reason for the problems. That's why I'm drug-free."

The Hammond Family

Debbie Anderson Hammond was born in 1954 and has lived all of her life in the Lower East End. Her parents, Jack and Arlene Anderson still live in the East End, and Debbie visits them often. Debbie became pregnant while she was in the eleventh grade. She was forced to drop out of school and soon after married the father of the baby, Larry Hammond.

Larry was born in 1951 and is a graduate of Withrow High School. He has lived in the East End for thirty-five years. Larry's parents, Chip and Rose Hammond, are now deceased. They lived in the East End a number of years before they moved to Kentucky.

Debbie has two brothers and two sisters. Jack, Jr., born in 1949, is a technical school graduate who lives in South Carolina. Darryl is divorced with four children and lives in the East End. His eldest son lives in Texas with his mother, while the other three children live in the East End. Lisa, born in 1952, is also a graduate of technical school and lives in Oakley, a nearby mixed-income neighborhood. Michelle was born in 1951 and is unmarried. She lives with her two children, both graduates of Withrow High School, in the East End.

Larry has three sisters and one brother. Janet dropped out of Withrow in the tenth grade. She lives in the East End and has one son who is in the Marines. Carla is a technical school graduate who is divorced and now lives in Fairfax. Betty lives in California, Ohio, with her husband. One of their children is deceased and the other two live in the East End. Douglas is a graduate of Withrow. He lives in Anderson Township.

Debbie and Larry have two children, Ed and Alison. Ed attended Withrow but was denied the right to graduate on time because a counselor said he was short a few credits. He and Debbie became angry with the school, so he transferred to Peter Clark Academy, where he graduated. He now does rehab work on buildings. Alison is in the fourth grade and is a very good student.

Livelihood

Debbie stays at home to be available to the kids, but works part-time as a bartender at the River Inn. Larry works for a distributing company in Sharonville loading trucks. Prior to that, he worked in the Bottoms, a harbor on the river.

Debbie and Larry rent an apartment above the River Inn for $250, which includes utilities. In the five years they have been there, they have had no rent increases. Debbie states that she would be interested in purchasing a house someday, although she does not want to leave the East End. She spends a lot of time at her parents'. Her parents have lived there for a number of years. Debbie and Larry have put money into the house in small repairs and general maintenance.

Debbie sees her family members and in-laws every day. Most of her friends are part of this extended family network. Each Saturday, she goes shopping and has lunch with her mother. She notes: "I take my mother anywhere she needs to go. I do my dad's chores, banking, post office, car tune-up." Debbie feels obligated to her parents, who have consistently provided Debbie and Larry with financial assistance. In addition, though Ed lives with Debbie and Larry, he often stays at his grandparents', a common residence pattern in the East End.

Debbie has always lived in the Lower East End and comments that she feels safe there. She says everyone knows everyone else and watches out for them.

The Warren Family

Karen Warren was born in 1960 and grew up in the East End. When she got married, she moved to Pleasant Ridge, where she and her hus-

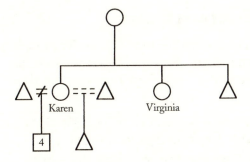

Figure 8. The Warren Family

band had four children. When her husband abandoned her for another woman, however, she moved back to the East End. She has recently had another baby with a different father. She supports her family with AFDC, but the family's yearly income remains under $6,000.

Karen's apartment is small. The air is close in the summer because her windows barely open. There are roaches crawling on the walls and furniture, so I sit gingerly on the edge of the couch. She seems to care deeply for her children, and her interactions with them are very caring. Her brothers come in and out of her apartment at will, without knocking.

She seems depressed and her personal appearance is sloppy. People say she is on drugs. Her sixteen-year-old daughter recently dropped out of high school and spends most of her time taking care of Karen's youngest child while Karen recovers from a complete hysterectomy. Karen had this operation after she was diagnosed with two ovarian cysts and cancer of the uterus.

Karen's sister, Virginia, lives close by and their mother, who works as a custodian in a local hospital, lives downstairs from Karen. Karen is the only one in her family with a car, and it has created great family problems for her. Her sister and her mother demand that she take them places. She does not have the time to do this, nor is she able to find child care while she is gone.

Karen is quite attached to the East End. Her neighbors know her children, which makes her feel safe. Moreover, many of her neighbors are people she went to school with and so she believes she can trust them.

Karen states that she takes her children to a pizza restaurant every week and allows them to order whatever they want. This is a tradition in her family: "I want to keep this at least."

East Enders' Perceptions of East Enders

East Enders do pass judgment on one another and on themselves. People fear unknown parts of the neighborhood. Says one homeowner from the Upper East End about people in the Lower East End who rent their homes:

> I used to feed their kids all the time—she knows nothin'. She didn't know how to read and write. She moved to the lower East End where she belongs—trashy people near Saint Rose and Collins. They have garbage . . . fat women with short shorts . . . kids running on the sidewalk. Here, a lot of 'em owns it. There, they don't care.

She continues:

> I know a lot of people, but I don't like how they live. They'll sit out and wait for their check. They'll clean up to go out and spend the check. They ain't got no self-respect.
>
> They was sellin' dope across the street. Before me and Jeremy got together, I was on it real bad, pot and speed. Me and Wally and them—we would forge prescriptions. His mom had a daughter and son that died from dope. Wally still on it. When I was eighteen, Jeremy used to drink real bad. We made a pact. He quit drinking, I quit dope. My first husband used to beat me.

The reverse is also true. Just as this speaker from the Upper East End criticizes people in the Lower East End, a woman from the Lower East End is aware that "outsiders perceive the East End as negative," but she believes they hear stories that aren't necessarily true. She does feel wary about the Upper East End, where she has heard of "older women being raped."

Common Sense in the East End

Clifford Geertz (1983: 10–11) has argued that common sense is "a loosely connected body of belief and judgment, rather than just what anybody properly put together cannot help but think . . . Common sense is not a fortunate faculty like perfect pitch . . . it both differs from one place to the next and takes, nevertheless, a characteristic form."

When East Enders talk about having a lot of common sense, they mean the opposite of "book learning." Actually, they mean a lot more. In the East End, common sense is really about culture in practice, how to live as an East Ender and member of, as one East Ender puts it, "the common people." Common sense refers to survival skills such as where to obtain food and housing when you really need it to local knowledge about the elderly and children. Cathy is an eighteen-year-old, extremely intelligent young woman who tells me in reference to her decisions about how much to charge for baby sitting that her charges are based on common sense. When the kids are asleep she charges a flat ten dollars for the whole day; when they are awake, she charges twenty dollars. These amounts represent a combination of what every East Ender knows about "helping out" a relative, friend, or neighbor and feeling adequately compensated for time spent.

Common sense is spoken about as inextricably related to being a real East Ender. On the one hand, it is what everyone knows; on the other, if we ask how it is that everyone knows something, we see that common sense comes from lived experience inside the East End over long periods of time. Outsiders do not have the lived experiences with the river, for example, that real East Enders take for granted. When outsiders do the appropriate things, as two city employees did during the flood cleanup in 1997 by staying extra hours to hand out cleaning supplies and organize relief efforts, they are thanked; East Enders are not thanked for doing what any real East Ender would do naturally. Thus, when East Enders work alongside city staff, East End leaders and residents see the staffers as needing to be thanked.

Given the tense relationships that have always existed between the city and the community, East Enders were surprised during the flood cleanup to see staffers voluntarily working overtime. East Enders expect one another to do whatever needs to be done, for however long, as part of common sense.

Being a Real East Ender in the Context of the City and the Vagaries of City Bureaucracies

East Enders have had a long and tempestuous relationship with City Hall and its various departments. In many ways, in fact, the city has had a major role to play in defining who East Enders are and how they view themselves in the context of the urban power structure.

The following conversation took place during a small meeting in the community a few weeks after the community leaders had learned that a trusted city employee, Seth Taxter, had been "yanked" from the neighborhood. The conversation is important because it indicates, among other things, a relatively rare and unusually positive relationship between community leaders and a city staffer. Seth was trusted for many reasons: he worked hard for the neighborhood, helping with the redevelopment corporation, with the drafting of the heritage center's bylaws, and with other neighborhood projects. He faithfully attended meetings, many of which he was not mandated to attend. Seth never "went by the book," as many social service providers were perceived by East End leaders as doing. He never stuck to a rigid nine-to-five schedule and had a low-key and friendly style; he talked very little but always when he thought he could contribute helpful information, especially about dealing with city bureaucracies. To the East End leadership, this "yanking" was just another of a long string of examples of the city's insensitivity to the needs of the East End community and to the ways in which East Enders work to improve the neighborhood, that is, by withholding trust until an outsider had proven himself. The reassigning of a trusted official caused disruption and a sense of personal loss and frustration. Once adopted into the East End family, it is a mark of disloyalty to leave it, even though he didn't choose to leave. To East Enders, leaving is abandonment, regardless of the circumstances:

Doris Sells:

It seems that every time we get our act together, the city pulls the props out from under us.

Elaine Winters:

We believe that it takes a lot to trust. We been tossed around so much.

In a very despondent tone, James Strong, an elderly longtime community leader and senior East Ender leans over and whispers that he wants to quit. Having heard this threat on numerous other occasions, I do not take what he has said literally, but, rather, as a sign of his repeated personal disappointment and frustration. He expresses his extreme distress by indicating to the group, and especially to Seth, that Seth was remaining in the adjacent neighborhoods of Columbia Tusculum and California but still was leaving the East End:

It seems awful personal to me when they let you up in Columbia Tusculum [the immediately adjacent now Yuppie-dominated neighborhood that East Enders consider historically to be part of the East End] and California [an adjacent river community that many regard also as part of the East End] . . . that's personal.

Seth invokes the authority of his boss, Wendell Jones:

I accept Wendell's wisdom.

Elaine Winters:

That's politics.

James Strong refers to another instance in which a city Recreation Department employee was yanked from the community:

They did it with recreation. They'd reassign him if they knew that we's gettin' along with him.

Shifts in city personnel are seen as undermining the neighborhood and as purposeful actions on the part of the city to inhibit neighborhood preservation, improvement, and revitalization. In these respects, the city is viewed by real East Enders to be in league with the developers and their profit-driven efforts to eliminate the East End as East Enders have known it.

4 | EAST END TEXTURES: HIDDEN DIMENSIONS OF BEING A REAL EAST ENDER

Introduction

The textures of the community—the sights, sounds, smells, emotions, humor, tones, feelings—are among the richest and most poignant aspects of life in the East End. The textures tell a different story from the kinship charts and narratives. They demand a different kind of attention. Yet they enhance all of the other elements of practicing community—family, local politics, and class culture. How does it feel to be in the East End, to interact with East Enders in East End spaces? Practicing community is not something abstract and philosophical; it happens day by day, hour by hour, often in intangible ways. A feeling of warmth and true spirituality is, to me, among the most dominant textures because it demonstrates the strong sense of belonging to people and place.

This chapter begins with prominent textures, ones that would immediately be apparent: noise and danger, the smells of factories where East Enders have worked for generations. Textures include community places, places out of sight, but important in the lives of East Enders, places known only to real East Enders: the soup kitchen, the Thanksgiving dinner for seniors at Mount Carmel Baptist Church, the alleys and the porches.

Social relationships also have rich textures: humor, joking, fighting, conflict. The chapter proceeds with a life-course framework to structure the many varied and unseen textures of life in the East End. Along the way, we see the high and low points: birth, pregnancies (wanted and unwanted), school experiences, jail experiences, the closing of a community institution, the elimination of community spaces, and the pluses and minuses of race relations.

The Senses

Space heaters roar in sitting rooms and punctuate conversations at odd moments. Voices rise to compete with these large boxlike presences that sit with chimney pipes rising out of them. They pump out heat—too much heat at times. Ann is constantly sweating; John complains that he is cold. Both are up in years, but they fight to turn the heater up or down. Blasts of cold air pass through leaky windows, and East Enders calculate how much heat they use. In winter, utilities can cost more than rent. Plastic over the windows helps some.

The din of the traffic on Eastern Avenue can be deafening. In summer, conversations on porches stop and start. Even in front rooms, East Enders have to shout over the noise. In winter, the cars splash slush on front windows with a startling splat. We can hear the traffic on the tapes of interviews; it drowns out the words and reminds everyone of the constant danger from the speeding cars, the insensitive proximity of outsiders who forget or don't think about or ignore the fact that they are speeding through a residential neighborhood, a place where people live and die, and where children stand in the dark waiting for school buses. TVs are always on in front rooms. The news, sports, videotapes of old movies, classics, cartoons provide background for daily life. An elderly man watches city cable and then reports the goings on at City Hall to his wife, a strong grassroots leader and chairperson of the Heritage Board of Trustees. Sirens. Fires are frequent in the East End, caused by faulty and old wiring, arson, smoking—sometimes in bed—space heaters again, kids playing with matches and cigarette lighters. The elderly worry constantly. In a community where everyone knows everyone else and where most people are related through ties of blood, marriage, heritage, neighborhood, and combinations thereof, sirens and ambulances bring instant concern. Word spreads—sometimes relief—sometimes sorrow. Children, especially teens, are the messengers. They know everything.

When the wind is blowing the right way, a sweet smell permeates the air for miles around. The large bakery (a factory) just to the east of the community, is baking cookies. The bakery used to employ a lot of East Enders; now only a few people work there. Elaine remembers when the bakery was generous and gave out boxes of cookies and crackers to all workers at the end of the week, just as the multinational but locally based produce company now gives out bananas.

When the wind is blowing the wrong way, the pungent, disturbing odor of solvent makes your eyes water and your head ache. A lithography company is the culprit—another East End employer. Several generations of East Enders have worked there.

In summer, roaches abound. Kids, especially small kids, treat them as moving targets. While not as big as the ones in the tropics, they seem more numerous and, somehow, more active. The same windows that leak so badly in winter refuse to open in summer.

Houses and apartments have mailboxes with locks on them, or no mailboxes at all; many people use post office boxes. Without locks on mailboxes, checks have been known to disappear, along with other mail.

People with cameras and clipboards are suspect. Will the city condemn my house?

In the basement of Saint Steven's Church is the East End soup kitchen. On regular days, it's a rather grim place, despite Dolores Young's careful strategies to keep the place cheery and the food plentiful. She cultivates the well-groomed Junior Leaguers and their male equivalents who volunteer there. She juggles work and family as well as race and class. She told me once how she had to show up at her son's school after he had been locked out of a classroom for arriving a split second late. "It's rough for black kids." She will drive across town for the best deals on hamburger, buns, vegetables—anything that she can use to stretch the very limited dollars in the soup kitchen's budget. At Thanksgiving, Dolores fixes a feast, turkey and all the trimmings. An elderly man is eating with his grandchildren. Even at Thanksgiving, the somber atmosphere prevails.

East End Area Council meetings are held in this same room in alternate months when they are not at the LeBlond Recreation Center in the Lower East End. The grimness hangs on as people peer around the evenly spaced columns. Perhaps the weight of the Seven Hills food pantry and clothing supply area upstairs makes itself felt. Seven Hills Neighborhood Houses is an institution in the East End. Without it, people would go without. But it is hard for East Enders to take charity. It is easier to ask for help for a friend in need.

The Thanksgiving dinner at Mount Carmel Baptist Church is very different from that at the soup kitchen. There are decorations. It's a celebration. The church is a sanctuary, a spiritual place. Thanksgiving is a dinner for senior citizens prepared by the younger women of the church, who crowd themselves and massive amounts of food into the lunch kitchen. There are trays and trays of turkey, heaping bowls of mashed potatoes, sweet potatoes, cranberry sauce, stuffing, and pumpkin and pecan pies. Reluctantly, the women of the church let me help, but I am not needed.

Alcohol exerts a strong presence in the East End. Kids talk about how some men get silly when they are drunk, while others get mad—angry, belligerent, violent. Accidents happen, people fall out of windows or speeding cars. Women battle alcohol, too, especially barmaids, some at very young ages. Some recover, saved by someone younger, often someone who needs them. Others grow old with alcohol—beer for breakfast, whisky for dinner—skin and bones but surrounded by loving grand-babies.

Drugs can be had, but they are hidden from outsiders; so is the bootleg booze. But many real East Enders are upset when they know a person is hooked.

Joking among adults is often couched in sexual idioms—with great affection, but with no intention of consummating a sexual relationship. Joking relationships, especially those between people of different sexes, sexual orientations, races, and generations, are about support, politics, and a semblance of grassroots solidarity.

Doris, a black woman in her seventies, calls Fritz, a forty-year-old white man, "love of my life."

Robbie "aggravates" Geoffrey, her son-in-law. The verb "to aggravate" has many meanings in the East End; it means both to give attention to and to bother or annoy. When an adult says to a child, "stop aggravatin'," this can be either a joke or a command to leave something or someone alone.

To someone who does not know the nature of and contexts for the close relationships between grandmothers and grandchildren, some of the exchanges of words may sound harsh or crude. A grandmother is just as apt to tell her grandbaby "I love you" as to say "Hit the road" or "I'll put a knot on your head" or "Get out of my face." An outsider hearing only the latter two without knowing the context or the nature of the relationships may read abuse, or at least some sort of roughness. In fact, it is often the case that the closer and the more affectionate the relationship, the more abusive-sounding the talk may be. When a grandmother says to a child, "I'm gonna whip your butt if you do such and such or if you say so and so," this is an expression of caring. "It's the people that don't talk that worry me," says one longtime East Ender. It is also the people who do not engage in joking or who are excluded from joking relationships who are the real abusers, although their abuse may be masked by polite forms of address.

Joking can be a way of practicing community by providing grassroots leaders with ways of coping with the hegemonic system, of dealing with everyday forms of powerlessness and resisting subordination and noblesse oblige through talk. A prominent woman who sits on an influential citizens' committee is very patronizing to East Enders, even though her dedication to preserving and revitalizing the community is very strong and her skills are excellent. At the end of a very long meeting in a City Hall conference room, a lifetime East Ender turned to me and in a very wry tone of voice asked: "Do you think she needs a hand down from her pedestal?"

East End Life Course

Birth

Four generations sit in a hospital room. Old Betsy sits quietly, as she always does, but this time she has a smile on her face. Robbie can barely contain her joy as she bustles around the room arranging things, chatting with another East End grandmother who came along for the occasion. That this other grandmother is black is insignificant. Black or white, grandbabies are grandbabies. A bundle of joy arrives to be greeted not only by her mother, father, and sister, but by two grandmothers and a great-grandmother. I feel privileged to be included in this wonderful event. I bring some Dr. Seuss books. Baby Emily, who was born that day, had her fifth birthday party in 1997. She is a great kid, loving, tough, feisty when she wants to get her way. She's surrounded by kin and, at age five, is old enough to help her grandmother care for a two-year-old.

Three infants live in one household, all named after flowers, each born to the daughters of a solid East End household. The grandfather is proud; he beams from ear to ear. He will support these kids even if their fathers don't.

Elaine brings her newest grandbaby to the health center board meeting just at the tail end. The baby is swaddled in beautiful pastel blankets against which her black curls frame her face. I have rarely seen Elaine so happy; her daughter is very pleased as all of us admire the newest addition to their large extended family.

Childhood

Bea, a longtime East End leader, organizes the children. Fritz, a pillar of the community, drives the pickup truck. The kids, equipped with gloves, rakes, shovels and garbage bags, ride in the back. They work hard. Fritz is very disappointed when the Community Council decides to budget $5,000 for a summer Blues Festival: "That's money out of the kids' pockets."

Accidents in cars or on motorcycles or bicycles are extremely common. Some accidents are serious; others just close calls. A child falls off a railing, falls out of a car. I don't know the accident rate, but it seems that one hears about narrow escapes and non-escapes regularly. People do get hit by cars on Eastern Avenue; some get killed. Cars also hit houses with some regularity, especially houses near the places where the road curves. But even on the straightaways, houses are vulnerable because they sit right on the street:

> She was with her younger sister. They were on their way to an older sister's house, in Norwood [a nearby small city that is predominantly Appalachian], to pick up a picnic table. It was Memorial Day and they were going to have a big picnic. A lady ran a red light at Linwood and Observatory [an intersection between the East End and Norwood], hit them broadside, spinning the car around in the middle of the street. Neither of the girls were hurt really bad. Scared. P. hit her knee on the dashboard. They took her to the hospital to sew up her knee.

Children sit quietly with crayons and homework at the East End Area Council meeting. A grandmother watches over them to make sure the work is done properly.

Robbie takes Ann, the granddaughter of a large East End family, in the car with the smaller children as she delivers cleaning supplies in the aftermath of the March 1997 flood. "Children keep you on an even keel," she says. The younger children adore Ann, who treats them as a little mother would.

Jamie takes care of Robbie while she is sick. Jamie is barely five. She also checks on the younger children in Robbie's charge.

Adolescence

I watch a dozen teenage girls practicing their cheerleading at LeBlond Recreation Center. The intricacies of their movements confuse me; it takes a lot of concentration just to watch them, much less to execute the drills. An older girl is helping them by showing them alternative ways to do things. "This is how they want to do it," says a mother proudly watching her daughter from the sidelines.

Pregnancy

Pregnant girls wait on the bench at the bus stop in front of the East End Community Health Center. They try to look older than their years and they do—heavy makeup, tight clothes, bleached hair that has taken much time to fix. They want a man. They want to look pretty; they have few sellable skills; neither do the young fathers. But what are their priorities, their hopes? The myths about pregnancy abound. "You can't get pregnant the first time." "When the moon is full, there is protection." "Condoms interfere with sexual pleasure."

> I don't know how they found out I was pregnant. I was three months along. They went off on me. My mom and dad went off on me. They were not at all happy. But I can't blame them. Looking back now I can't blame them.

A kindly aunt arranged for an abortion. They kept it a secret all these years. When Aunt Betsy died, all of the memories came back.

> I knew they wouldn't let me come back to school. I called them. They told me no. They couldn't be responsible for me over there. I'd a went.

> My two good friends. That I was talking about earlier. They had already quit school. They were out of school two, three school years when they got pregnant.

> Cindy didn't get pregnant right away. She was, like, nineteen or twenty before she got pregnant. Apparently . . . I always thought they were on some type of birth control. They never would confirm it for me, but I thought they were. Because I knew that they were playing around . . . long before that they were playing around.

I know more women than I would like to count who were raped and abused as young girls. They talk to me about it only when nobody else can hear. They still feel the pain. Some drank and still do to escape the memories. Others became depressed—deep depression hangs on—mood swings—sharp words—knifelike words that at times send close friends into states of total dysfunction.

SCHOOL

Bruce, a very pleasing, red-haired child, dropped out of school in the seventh grade. Before that, I used to pick him up once in a while in front of People's Middle School. Teachers were always giving him a hard time and calling him a slow learner. Maybe he didn't want to learn what they had to teach. He certainly knows the neighborhood like the back of his hand; he can name every member of every household on Gladstone and tell you how long each person has lived there:

> But I can't believe how the schools have changed. They were a lot stricter when I went to school. I mean, you got a paddlin' if you didn't mind. You do something wrong, and you went in the office, and you got a paddlin'.

> They let the corporal punishment go, and I think they let a lot of other stuff go down the drain too.

> They don't have no control over these kids that go to school now. They tell the teachers what to do.

> [The principal] has the kind of attitude that doesn't belong in this area. This area, 90 percent of the people that live here in the East End that have kids that go to this school are low-income people. They live on a fixed income one way or another. Those that do work, still get food stamps and medical cards and stuff like that.

> But this lady down here, uh, she's a [middle-class] black woman, and, uh, she just, I don't know, she doesn't, to me, doesn't have a lot of respect for the people in the neighborhood. I mean, it doesn't make no difference what kind of income you have, it's what kind of person you are that counts.

> He was placed in their special ed. classes, and they mainstreamed him as much as they possibly could . . . he was still acting out from the frustration and agitation and everything. He was still on the Ritalin.

> I think I was probably raised with morals; you know, I was raised from a down-to-earth attitude. I wasn't given any—you know, they didn't feed me things like, when you grow up maybe you'll be a millionaire—you know, stuff like that. It was common sense that got me through a whole lot. And the common sense that her and my dad taught me. I just . . . you know a person at Withrow told me, last school year. And it was sad to hear him say that. But, he told me last school year—and I don't think I'll ever forget that—he said "We are here to help the kids who want to learn . . . those that don't want to learn, we can't do much about" . . . if I was a teacher, or an

administrator, if I was one of those, I don't know, I would . . . knowing the kind of person that I am, I would probably say that, all right, those kids that are here to learn, okay. They're here to learn. They don't need a whole lot of help. But those kids that don't want to learn, are the ones that need our help. And that's not the way the system sees it.

We all grew up together, went to school together, skipped together.

LeBlond's recreation center was a big part of my life cause they had a lot of stuff for the kids, the teenagers and the younger kids. They had many things for you to do. There was baseball, there was football, there was basketball, there was pool. They had a pool table. And the swimming pool. And they had a dance every Friday night for teenagers. Which really gave them something to do. They don't have anything like that now. LeBlond's is still there and they have a lot of things going on, but they don't have the programs for the kids and the teenagers like they used to. And to me, that kept a lot of kids out of trouble. You know? It kept them off the streets. . . . they were there at the center and they were doing things. And it was a big part of my life and . . . I'm glad that we had it, and now I don't think, they're just not doing as much as they used to. Highlands School was the neighborhood school, I never went to Highlands because by the time I moved up there I was in junior high. But my kids went to Highlands, a neighborhood school, and I think that is also an important factor when you're young. Is to have a neighborhood school to go to rather than be bussed from one side of town to the other side of the town and go to school with complete strangers . . . neighborhood schools you basically know everyone, in my opinion, that worked. It worked for me and it worked for my kids, and I think that these kids now are like, they don't, they just don't have the same, I don't know how to say it. Goals or anything . . . they treat 'em like cattle. Herdin' em off here and herdin' em off there I mean. In the city to me it's so stupid, they're constantly complaining about the expense, and they create more expense for theirself by doing this, and there's nothing wrong with the neighborhood schools and that was proven with Highlands. Because, if there was something wrong with that building, the structure or something, then why is that building still there and in operation for the school that it's housing now? That to me is an important part of growing up, is being in your neighborhood with your neighbors, and your friends, and your family members and things. And going someplace like that. And East End had that. And I mean, I'm sure every other place had that, too, but, that was a big important part of my life and, I don't know, anymore it's not, it's just not the same anymore. With the kids now. My grandkids live here and go to school way the hell up there or over there. . . . there's a lot of the neighborhood things that we had when we were younger that I really believe that that's an important part of growing up. To have something like that. I just don't think the kids have it now . . . and I honestly believe if they had somewhere they could go and expend some of this energy on something good, all this that's going on wouldn't be. I just. I mean, I realize times change and things are different, but I still say go back to the basics cause it's gonna, I think it worked and I still think it would work. And I don't know what they plan on doing. I've heard so darn many stories about what they're gonna do with the East End. And if they're gonna put fancy high-rise condos and stuff down there, where the hell the people from the East End gonna go? They can't afford that. That's why they live down there. When I was younger and we lived down there, we was river rats. We, you know, lower than dirt and all that crap. Eastern Avenue! The river, that nasty river. Now all a sudden it's "the beautiful river!" same damn river. I mean, you know. Give me a break! We were always put down cause we lived down there. We didn't have the money to live in Hyde Park or Indian Hills, or, you know. So we were always looked down upon, at school, the other kids, you know. And that's one of the reasons I dropped out of school. Cause I didn't have the latest fashions. My dad said, "You've got clothes, wash 'em." You know, he didn't buy it . . . Eastern Avenue to me was home . . . you just have a certain place that you live when you're younger, and you consider it to be your home. Whether it's a house, it doesn't have to be a house, just the area. That's home. And I don't feel that way about it anymore because things have changed so much down there. And if they're gonna put condos up it's really gonna be changed. What'da they gonna do when the river rats come in!

Young Adulthood

Steve, a very bright sixteen-year-old, is "messing with a married woman."
Four new cases of tuberculosis are diagnosed the week of February 24,

1995, three new cases of HIV positive. I now know of three women, all in their twenties and all mothers of small children, who are HIV positive. What is to be done if these women die? Will the community adopt the children? Probably so.

Anthony, Robbie's nephew, has "come out of the closet." He was fired from his job, presumably for his sexual orientation. His sunny demeanor makes itself felt at the opening of the exhibit, *The Life and Times of East End Heritage*. Many of his relatives appear on the panels. He's a very friendly young man—warm with a quick wit and unassuming manner. For a while, he moved back to Kentucky—back home and away from the city. Now he is back.

City Council chambers, spring 1995: An African American council member and true friend of the East End has just reversed his position on the human rights ordinance. He no longer supports the inclusion of gays and lesbians. A public pronouncement from an East End leader follows, indicating her lesbian orientation by telling the story of a seven-year relationship with another woman.

Being in the Wrong Place at the Wrong Time

They're incarcerated right now. I know one of 'em is. And the other one's headed there. Because I know what he's doing. He's still going to school. And he's still at Withrow High School. But, he's selling drugs now.

Hank was sent away for auto theft . . . him and two other boys swiped an automobile. That's kind of . . . that's an odd thing to have go on around here now though. Most of the kids are going to jail for breaking and entering. Armed robbery. Or burglary.

Then Karl was gone to prison for six years. He was in and out for no serious shit, burglaries and stuff. When he was out he lived up on Delta.

Todd just got out of jail. He wants to turn his life around now, but it is very hard. He is twenty-four. Todd has been in and out of juvenile facilities since he was eight or nine. His mom took him away from his East End foster mother when he was six. His biological mother is the half-sister of Toni's real mother (Toni is Robbie's adopted daughter). Both women have been on drugs from an early age. His dad also used drugs. When Todd was fifteen, he went to adult prison for breaking and entering. By that time he was a habitual criminal. Todd's dad, Larry

Green, has a niece who is the mother of one of Clay Kale, Jr.'s children, Kelly, age ten (see Figure 18).

> [We have lived here] twenty years now . . . in the East End. We've . . . been here three years. We lived on Carl Street, right here for eleven years . . . and they sold that out from under us. So, we moved into a little house over there on Front by the flea market. We was only there for about—I don't think it was even a year—and the Board of Health put us out because it wasn't city sewage, and we didn't know it.
>
> They put us out over that and gave us three days to get out of there, so we moved down to what we call Lower East End, across from LeBlond Park.

A Rough Texture: The Closing of the Gas Station

Fritz says the station is going to close: "It's a done deal." Felix Leng wants it off his hands as soon as possible because the EPA is on his back to clean up the site. He has already been fined heavily for one other station he owns. Of course, Leng has no knowledge of or concern for what is really a very important community institution. The gas station is the most accessible and reliable meeting place, a place to exchange information: it, in effect, performs many of the functions that the grassroots leadership has in mind for the Pendleton Building.

All of the researchers and advocates rally for several weeks to see whether the gas station can be saved. Endless meetings take place at the gas station. Everyone—East End residents and leaders, researchers and advocates—hover around Fritz's big oak desk, which faces out the big window toward the gas pumps. Stacks of change, arranged neatly in rows, sit in the midst of years of scratches on the surface. Sometimes, Fritz lets the children play with pennies. We talk about turning the gas station into a small convenience store: we are trying to figure out some way for Fritz himself to purchase the property. We contact the best environmental attorney in the city for advice. He recommends that we follow certain steps.

But Fritz is reluctant. He can't take on the financial responsibility. Fritz is right; the closing of the station is inevitable. With the closing of the gas station in June 1994, a vacuum was created for the East End leadership and, consequently, for the community. "We couldn't get together," one leader told me. There was now no accessible place to meet informally and on the spur of the moment. Formal meetings are one thing, but informal, impromptu communication between leaders is more essential to practicing community. Keeping on top of things on a daily basis is what gives the grassroots a chance not only to discuss issues, but to involve other East End residents. If certain residents saw more than one car parked on the side of the gas station, they would stop to see what was going on and thus know the latest developments in the community.

RACE

In the evening he come out on the porch in his Sunday best. She be sitting there with me shelling peas or helping the children with they spelling. Helping me with spelling and everything else she think I need to know. No matter what happen, Nettie steady try to teach me what go on in the world. And she a good teacher too. It nearly kill me to think she might marry somebody like Mr. —— or wind up in some white lady kitchen. All day she read, she study, she practice her handwriting, and try to git us to think. Most days I feel too tired to think, but patient her middle name. (Walker 1982: 17)

To borrow Cornel West's (1993) title, race[1] matters to East Enders and in the East End. But race matters in some positive and negative, subtle and complicated ways that are not easily understandable until one spends a good deal of time in the community—talking to people, watching where people, especially teenagers, spend their time. The ways in which race matters have also changed over time, and people in different generations with different experiences both in and outside of the community have different thoughts and feelings about race.

Doris, a black woman over seventy, talks about walking to Withrow High School as a teenager growing up in the East End. In the late 1930s, when she graduated from high school, she wanted very much to have a job as a secretary; she was informed that she could not be hired because she was black. She and her mother both earned their livelihoods working as domestics in white people's homes on the hillside.[2]

Doris relates to me the story of her granddaughter, who, when she was four (in the mid-1970s) was taken to the LeBlond Recreation Center, where "they dirtied the pool so we could not swim in it." She talks about feeling uncomfortable at LeBlond, but also about how her son had black and white friends who came and ate and slept at their house. Her conclusion is that race relations are personal relations. She acknowledges "the people down there" (around LeBlond) as the Lower East End and as not being hostile, but not being overly friendly to blacks. She also mentions not spending any time "up where Donna West lives." Donna has been very active in community affairs. The midsection of the East End—the Pendleton carbarn, the gas station, Mount Carmel Baptist Church—is predominantly black. She talks about how she used to live in another house up near the ironworks—clearly also in the mid-section of the East End. Her son, now forty-seven, was born there and went to Highland School. Mostly blacks live in this area.

Elaine, a black woman in her fifties, told of a white couple requesting a hotel room next to hers at a conference because she was "a woman traveling alone." She also talks about white kids ignoring her greeting at the recreation center and of being called a "nigger" and a "black bitch" at the same place.

Marlene and Bob Church's eldest son, Mickey, got in a fight at Withrow High School. Some students had been throwing snowballs, and Mickey was first to walk inside the school after recess. Some black students "jumped him." Mickey was suspended. Bob and Marlene didn't want him to quit, but he dropped out during his last year, "tired of blacks ganging up on him." Marlene thinks that white teachers are afraid of black students and don't know how to handle them. Both Bob and Marlene say that the racial problems at Withrow come from blacks outside the East End. Bob says: "If anybody said I's prejudiced, I'd say he was crazy." The problem is not that East End people couldn't get along with blacks in the East End: "I was raised up with blacks from the East End . . . not much racial tension here." Bob says there has always been blacks in the East End and that neighborhood people get along fine for the most part. During the 1950s, blacks in the East End mostly lived on Eastern Avenue from the waterworks to Delta; that stretch is still predominantly black, but the neighborhood is more integrated now. Marlene returned to the high school then and said that it was hard being an East End student in a school where Hyde Park students went: "If you were from the East End and all that, you weren't considered to be 'in it.' Hyde Park kids could dress sharp . . . we couldn't . . . after a while, there was no reason to stay."

The assumption on the part of white leaders in the East End that race does not matter because whites and blacks have grown up together makes dealing with race and racism, both practically and conceptually, all the more difficult for East End leaders. This assumption also creates tensions among leaders. Black leaders will tell you that race does matter. On the surface and, in many respects, in day-to-day operations, the East End is a model of an integrated community with an integrated leadership structure. African Americans hold important leadership positions;

they sit on community boards. Churches, however, are not integrated. Mount Carmel Baptist Church is the black church; Saint Rose is the white church.

Some individuals are equally comfortable among blacks and whites. Fritz is one of them, Robbie is another. Both Fritz and Robbie are white. At the same time, a black person all of whose close friends are white is subject to criticism.

Race can and is manipulated in the East End to undermine class status, class identity, and the progress of grassroots efforts. When a black man, especially one who is young and handsome, filibusters to stall community projects, black women don't perceive him to be holding up progress; he is accepted and even praised, despite the fact that he tries to take over an older black woman's role as chair of a major nonprofit board. When a white woman criticizes the same young black man, she is accused of trying to take over things. But, once again, to read this accusation solely in racial terms is to oversimplify a very complex series of relationships among East End residents and leaders.

The Elderly

On Sundays we all go over Mom's, till everybody starts gettin' aggravated 'cause there's 50 – 60 of us all together with all the kids and grandkids.

The ability to learn, think, and reason is a gift from God and the most precious gift is the ability to store memories. What triggers a memory is as unpredictable as a spring rain. It could be a long-forgotten song or a picture unseen for years. It could even be something as unlikely as a green bean. Earlier today as I sat popping green beans for tonight's dinner (with a grandbaby in tow) memories of my grandmother came flooding back like a long-lost friend.

The kitchens I have been in are too many to count but none were as warm and comfortable as Grandma's. Her kitchen always had the smells of just-cooked food. For there was that ever-present kettle steaming on the stove. Three meals a day seven days a week plus all of the special treats ensured that the kitchen at Grandma's was the center of our family's life.

I remember popping green beans with my grandmother and listening to her tell what it used to be like in the East End. It was from her that I learned that I was a fifth-generation East Ender. I also found out from her how my mom and dad met in 1937 during the flood, they both fled the East End for Mount Adams and when they were introduced Mom called Dad a river rat. Mom and Dad never told us that story. It wasn't just the stories that kept me mesmerized, it was her strength and wisdom that I was drawn to. From her I learned tolerance for other people no matter their color or beliefs. . . . I often wonder why my dad did not get the same things from Grandma that I did. Maybe it was because she had to be away from her kids so much just to support them and by the time the grandkids came along we could have her attention as much as we wanted and believe me we wanted it a lot.

I wish Grandma could know Kelly [the speaker's granddaughter], there is so much that Kelly could have learned from her and there is so much that Kelly could have added to her life. I hope that I can pass on some of my pride in who I am and where I came from to Kelly as Grandma did to me.

When I sing to Kelly at night this brings back thoughts of my grandmother, the old hymns from church are the hardest for me. Grandma had a great faith and she passed this on. She was the reason that Clay [the speaker's brother] and I sang in the choir. Grandma's favorite hymn was "The Old Rugged Cross." She had a beautiful voice, and it has taken me years to be able to listen to this hymn . . . the green beans did much more than remind me of just how lucky I have been. I think I'll fix green beans more often.

Memories can be bittersweet at times but one thing they must never be is pushed so far inside that no one else can ever share them. Without the passing on of memories from generation to generation soon no one would remember where they came from or who they are, and that would be the beginning of the end for families.

Grandmothers, biological and adopted, are the keystones of East End social life. They pass on memories and traditions and they are there for their grandbabies. They are also the perfect role models, teachers, and sources of self-esteem for kids—calmer than mothers and older and wiser.[3]

One elderly East End resident states:

When I was in grade school, I had three brothers and my mom and dad, and my grandmother lived with us. She taught me how to make quilts. Yeah, embroidery an', and stuff like that. And . . . she was, you know, she was just a good friend. And, Grandma was very, oh, kind of outgoing person. She was, she made you feel like, you know, you were important. And, I don't know, I guess being around her most of my life . . . 'cause I can remember before she had to break up housekeepin' an' came to live with us. It, it was such a joy to go to her house, and she did all these good cookin' . . . she helped mother too—till she got sick. She had heart problems . . . but she was always a part of our house, you know, you never felt like she was a burden or anything like that.

Most East End children, at one time or another, have had intense contact with their grandmothers. Not all of these grandmothers are blood relatives; many are adopted in informal ways, not necessarily to the exclusion of biological grandmothers, but in addition to them. Grandmothers see themselves as playing a major role in the raising of their grandchildren. Other senior members of extended families may also take care of the children while the adult women work. "I've got another niece that's Carolyn. I raised her and her brother when they were little. I took care of them when their mother and father both worked. Johnny was in, I guess third grade when I quit watching them. Carrie was in the fifth, so I pretty much took care of them quite a long time."

The tradition of grandmothering tends to be passed on in families. That is, women with strong ties to their grandmothers tend to seek grandchildren, biological or adopted. Robbie herself now takes care of her two grandbabies full time while her "daughter," "the girl I raised," works. The grandbabies usually spend one weekend night with her as well: "I look at the babies sleeping and I know that whatever else happens in my life or whatever has happened in the past, somehow God has decided that I should have a double blessing."

Daughters and younger women take care of the elderly, as it is absolutely taboo to put a relative in a nursing home until every other alternative has been exhausted. Even when a person becomes almost impossible to care for, it is better to solicit help from neighbors and kin than to put an elderly relative "away," for this means that the person is being prepared for death.

BREAKFAST, JUNE 1, 1996

Doris is struggling with the decision to put her mother in a nursing home. She is at her wit's end and talks about having a nervous breakdown. The Pendleton is not her top priority right now. Fritz and Elaine listen; Elaine buried her mother about a year ago. They give her financial advice. "Take the money—at least 80 percent of it—out of your mother's account and move it to another account in another bank. Don't let the nursing home have it," says Elaine. The psychological elements mesh with the physically grueling tasks of taking care of an incontinent, combative, senile ninety-three-year-old. Elaine says: "That is one mean lady."

Doris talks about how much bitterness and resentment she feels against her mother, how her father wanted to die (of his heart condition) because his wife treated him so badly. Doris is struggling. She holds the belief that putting a family member in a nursing home is equivalent to a death sentence. She realizes that her mother's illness is killing her, though, up at all hours of the night, even in bed always keeping an ear out to see whether her mother is getting up and urinating on everything.

THURSDAY, JUNE 13, 1996

I hadn't been in Doris's cozy kitchen for a long time, ever since her mother came to live in the back room. The kitchen is warm—too warm on this June day. Beans cooking on the stove generate a lot of heat, also a kind of sweet smell that grows more intense as we sit at the red Formica kitchen table, now that her mother is in one of the finest nursing homes in Cincinnati. "The beans, Doris," calls her husband, C.A. "They're stickin'," she says, taking them off the burner. C.A.'s the cook in the family. He's in the adjacent bedroom watching the news—the bad news—about black churches burning in the South. "It's the Klan," he says. "You know what they're about—hangin' people, skinnin' them alive—black people." We watch the news together.

Just as I am about to leave, Doris sits down in a chair next to the bed. C.A. is impeccable in his suspenders and sparkling white shirt with the river sweep's logo. Every spring East Enders organize a cleanup effort along the community's river. C.A. and Doris are comfortable with one another. She spreads the "Extra" section of the *Cincinnati Enquirer* on the table. Her picture is there in color with Elaine's arm around her. They are standing in front of the Pendleton carbarn: "It was in my mother's papers," she says proudly, "from the summer of 1992. If you lose it, I'll kill you," she says. Her filing system is amazing, much better than mine, despite my office, my research assistants, and my four huge filing cabinets. Hers is in their bedroom, but mostly it is in her mind. "I sat down and thought about where it was," she says. "Then I looked in a pile of mother's papers, and there it was."

We talk about nursing homes. Doris fears destitution if her mother lives five to ten years. All of their property would be gone. The next day I return with color photocopies of the article. One for Doris, one for Claudia (a longtime advocate in the Appalachian community), one for the grant proposal Claudia is submitting for the Pendleton Heritage Center. I ring the bell downstairs. Doris and C.A. are upstairs. C.A. puts his head out of the window: "Doris will be right down." "Tell her to take her time," I yell up. I stand holding a brown bag of food for their supper—with corn chowder and roasted turkey. Doris does not like to cook and C.A. can get tired doing it.

After a few minutes, Doris opens the middle door between the laundry and the downstairs sitting room. She's wearing a red robe, slippers, and a bandanna on her head. I barely recognize her without her teeth and her beautiful gray wig; she's always so perfectly coifed. There are white tufts of hair peeking out from under her bandanna—"So white," I think. I've never seen her like this before. Her hair makes her look old. She settles into a low chair in the sitting room. I pull up a straight chair next to her as I count out her copies of the color photocopies, $20.79 for six copies. I absorb the cost, even though I know there is money in the Heritage Center account.

I've never seen Doris look so old. She shows me her swollen ankles and tells me how much she likes her young doctor (forty-four years old): "He used to be here at the clinic, Dr. Mendel was. Daddy, C.A., and I used to go to him. My daddy who died in '87 liked him so much. I wish you could have known my daddy." "I would have liked to know him," I say, thinking she is replaying her life now, her memories are haunting her and comforting her at the same time. She tells me of a social worker at Jewish Hospital who talked to her mother and said she was sweet. "She is sweet," repeats Doris. This is a very different view from the one Doris had a few weeks ago, and that I had been hearing about from the first time I met her. Doris had always complained about her mother, how self-centered, how selfish, how insensitive, how badly she treated her daddy. Now mother is sweet?! Perhaps she can be sweet only once she is gone—out of the house—on her way to the nursing home. Doris fears what her mother will do and say once she realizes she is not going home. She's going to the nursing home the next day.

Monday, June 17, 1996

Doris tells me she feels guilty about putting her mother in a nursing home. Yet she is happy they have her sitting up in a wheel chair. She is convinced her mother doesn't know where she is, but it is better all around that she is in a home. Doris sounds rested. She returns to Pendleton business. She talks about never revealing too much information to the city or the developers: "They always throw a monkey wrench in our business."

East End Ways of Death

JANUARY 10, 1994, MOUNT MORIAH CEMETERY

Life and death interfere with activism. Robbie's elderly aunt has died. I learn this on my answering machine. Robbie sounds very down. She gives her schedule, tells me she will be at Grey's funeral home and will call later. This is, to the day, a month after her mother's funeral. This aunt will be buried at Mount Moriah, the same cemetery where her mother's ashes were placed. Robbie suspects her aunt's burial will not be far from her mother's grave and decides she can't handle it. She is already a bit tired and labile because she has just spent the weekend with her daughter, son-in-law, and two granddaughters. Her furnace was out for a day and a half, and she had to stay there.

On Friday, she lost her wallet. Of course, this was upsetting. A man found it at the carwash and returned it to her door, money and all.

A rough month all in all for Robbie.

Her own mother's funeral was so close. Her ashes were placed in a family plot.

The day of her aunt's funeral is a very cold day. Betty Dawson, an East End woman in her twenties who often helped Robbie with child care, is there to help with the grandchildren. Matt Marksman, one of the advocates with training in theology, performs the ceremony. Robbie's uncle comes, as do a few advocates. The group attending the funeral is small but intimate.

A VIEWING AT A CHURCH IN KENNEDY HEIGHTS

I go to Elaine's mother's viewing with Doris. We take my car. The sanctuary is filled with people; the coffin is open at the front. The daughters are clinging to their mother for the last time. People mingle and speak to the sons and grandchildren sitting in the pews. Doris introduces me to everyone, since there are really two church congregations present: Mount Carmel Baptist Church, where Doris is a member, is well represented at this church in Kennedy Heights. The church is filled almost to capacity. The children are many—well dressed and extraordinarily well behaved. I feel comfortable and quickly forget that I am the only white person in the entire church.

James Strong, a burly white-haired man in his seventies, is flanked by his wife, Megan, and his daughter Kim as he (bent over) makes his way down the aisle of Saint Rose Catholic Church. His whole extended family is there to mourn the death of his twenty-six-year-old grandson from leukemia. I sit at the rear of the church between Elaine and Robbie and in back of Deborah Rows, one of the Strongs' many adopted daughters. East Enders are there in abundance—people I have seen many times at the LeBlond Recreation Center pool watching their kids in the summer or at the River Inn playing darts on Sundays.

The church itself is imposing: stained glass windows several stories high, sun streaming in from the window tops right onto the pulpit. As the Strongs get in their cars to go to the cemetery, they thank us for coming.

CHARLES BANK'S FUNERAL

Charles "Chuck" Bank, an East End institution, used to drive his boat to work downtown. He was a small, unassuming man who spoke with somewhat impaired speech. When he spoke at East End Area Council meetings, which was rare, the room always grew silent. He always had something important to say. He received respect from real East Enders on many counts. He refused to sell his house to the developers and he always stood up for what he believed. Many East Enders attend the funeral mass at Saint Rose. Kim, Megan and James's daughter, held the picture of Chuck and James Strong sitting on the bench by the river. This was the only recent picture of Chuck—one taken for the Heritage Exhibit. Two brothers-in-law. Chuck died of a heart attack down by the river he loved. He didn't suffer, Megan, his sister, said, the tears flowing. "Come and see us," she urged. I said I would. The local colonialists came. Kim was angry.

Political Textures

"They fight but they always come back," says one longtime community organizer. Consensus is fragile in the East End; so are friendships. But the stakes are high: community survival. Images of war abound. A few months after the East End Riverfront Community Development Plan was passed by City Council (in May 1992), a grassroots leader wrote the following about the tensions in the neighborhood:

AUGUST 26, 1992

Today at 1830 hours I went with plan in hand to meet the enemy at the LeBlond battlefield, but alas the generals were not there to command their troops and as in the case of most wars, where there are no officers the battlefront was quiet. Why did the officers not join their troops is a mystery, but fear not for they have not abandoned the fight—they will return again to fight another day.

This was not the battleground of their choosing nor were the liaisons from the city their allies. They were on the side of the opposing forces. This allows more time for them to try and muster more troops and plan their next confrontation. One must wonder if it will be a frontal attack or their usual sniping sneak attack.

In my judgement there will never be a cease fire, this war will only end with the complete defeat of one of the forces. In a battle between neighbors there is never a real winner. If we learned nothing from our country's civil war we learned that both sides lost and the healing is still not complete.

How do you stop the destruction of the neighborhood and the friends that you have always loved? There is no point for compromise, there is no middle ground. Is it right for so small a percentage of a community to decide the fate of the whole community? If both sides truly want what is best for the neighborhood why must there always be casualties? What is the reason for this war? Is it that some people would like to see not only the overthrow of the leadership but also the establishment of a dictatorship?

If there cannot be a common ground on which to meet, then there must be a quick end to the war. The plan of rebuilding that lies ahead for the East End cannot be a casualty of this insidious war. If this command cannot resolve the fighting then it is time for a new leader to come to the frontlines and put an end to this at once, so the healing can begin.

If the time has come for one side to strategically retreat and I choose to follow that course of action, I will do so with all sides knowing that I may have stepped back but I have not surrendered. Everyone will know that I will always be among the East End's troops and I will not hesitate to pick up the battle if the East End starts to lose this long, hard war. (Fifth-generation East Ender)

Tensions exist between community leaders; newcomers are perceived as trying to take over before paying their dues. Donna talks about how she was on the executive board of the East End Area Council for four years before she said a word at a meeting. She describes Robbie as wanting to take things over after only a few months. At the Friday, November 8, 1991, banquet at the VFW, Robbie makes a special point of showing me the table in front of us with Donna's whole family. The whole family has come to eat at the VFW, free of charge. The balance of self-interest and community interest is delicate.

Emotions Peppered with Politics and Politics Peppered with Feelings

MAY 1, 1993

There have been accusations of stealing, checks bouncing, some people not being paid for neighborhood cleanup. Tensions among the leaders in the community have been and still are high. Some leaders are so upset about the possibility of being subpoenaed to testify against another East Ender that they have become angry and silent. It is not a matter of being shy or embarrassed but, rather, a situation of escalating anxiety. Eva tells me she cannot sleep at night because she is so worked up about the possibility of testifying.

Settling disputes and conflicts within the community rather than taking them to outsiders, in this case, the courts, is the East End rule. The finances of the East End Area Council have been out of order. Community leaders realized that checks were bouncing. They have made every effort to set matters straight within the community, including phone calls, visits, meetings to urge reconciliation and the handing over of records. Their attempts have been met with resistance, primarily because the factionalism (between grassroots leaders and between these leaders and developers) has become so marked in the community that things have to be taken outside. This amounts to a rejection of the community safety net.

As it turns out, Eva does not have to testify, but the anxiety and anger remain. Tommy, a neighborhood leader, decides to try to work the tensions out by getting everyone around the same table.

I arrive late, as is my tendency. Red, Tommy, and Eva are already there. Quiet reserve hangs over the threesome. Eva is praying. She dips her tea bag up and down aimlessly. Tommy is looking distressed, and nobody is making eye contact. Eva rises and walks to the breakfast bar.

"This isn't gonna work," says Red.

Tommy looks at her: "No, but give it some time."

Eva returns, offers her prayers for the food prefaced by a tense "Excuse me."

Red, who has been accused of theft, finding the tension almost unbearable, takes her turn at the breakfast bar. While she is there, Eva, a close friend and fellow neighborhood leader, laments her own situation—her sleepless nights in anticipation of her testimony in court and her experiences with classism and racism:

> Everyone is worried about Red. How is Red? What about me? Do you think things have been easy? Rocks have been thrown through my windows.

Tommy orders a ham and cheese omelet. It arrives but he doesn't touch it. The waitresses are bustling around. Many of them are East Enders. We are surrounded by other tables. It's a good thing, too; the noise of the crowded restaurant dampens, even if it doesn't soothe the intense emotions.

Tommy says: "I just wanted to bring friends together, but I see now it was a mistake."

"No," says Red, and Eva concurs. Tommy excuses himself.

Pretty soon, all four of us have tears in our eyes as Red, regaining her composure momentarily, explains patiently and logically why no amount of money paid or admission of guilt on her part would have satisfied the opposing faction. She responds patiently to Eva's assertions that Red never admitted to any wrongdoing and resisted settling out of court. Red says again that nothing would have satisfied "them." Red is careful to tell Eva that one of "them" lied on the stand at her preliminary hearing.

The East End Area Council is clearly without leadership at this point. The grassroots leaders have been deposed, and there is no new leadership. After an inspiring inaugural speech in January 1993, Susan Pond, the urban pioneer who ran unopposed for president of the EEAC after the impeachment of Red, a strong grassroots leader, the previous September, handed in her resignation in March. She lasted barely two months.

In a more private setting, the quiet tears that were being kept under control at the table might have turned to anger, or at least to loud words. Eva is certainly angry and upset. As the former vice-president of the East End Area Council, she has been subpoenaed to testify at the preliminary hearing and has spent many sleepless nights trying to figure out how she can tell the truth and not harm her friend and fellow community leader. She is angry both at the developers and at Red. She resents the constant attempts by the developers to divide and conquer the community; she is also angry at her friend for putting herself in a vulnerable position by keeping bad records and writing checks that should not have been written.

Tommy, described by Red as "a bear of a man with the softest heart in the world" and who has a reputation for honesty and integrity, has set up the breakfast to try to get these two strong community leaders "back to talking." But while the emotions are somewhat tempered by the cheerful surroundings, our doting grandmotherly waitress stares down at the untouched food. Red explains that our talk is too heavy for us to eat. The waitress boxes up the eggs and home fries.

Throughout all of this, I am not sure what to say, so I say nothing. I feel honored to be there, but the emotions weigh on me; I work hard myself to fight back tears.

Tommy is very chagrined. He pays for the breakfast and the "therapy session" ends. But was it just therapy? He tells me the next day that his attempt to play mediator failed. He calls it a mistake; he will never do it again. I try, somewhat feebly, to say something about how talking is good, how it was a start, and how he should not feel that he has failed. But his emotions are obviously too tender for him to listen.

For a long time I wondered whether what I have just related is too personal, too intimate, too sensitive to be shared by writing about it. I came to realize, however, that these styles of conflict resolution between and among grassroots leaders, these ways of practicing politics and practicing therapy at the same time are patterns of practicing community. Knowing these practices is part of what it means to be a real East Ender. This was not the first time I had witnessed arguments and discussions that included tears.

Red's logical passion for the maintenance and revitalization of the community and Eva's passionate logic have continued to contest one another. Crimes against the community are not taken lightly, and one of those crimes is relying on outside adjudicators. Eva saw the possibility of resolution at the community level. She deeply resented even the idea of having to go to court, even the chance of testifying, this despite Red's statements that she never intended for Eva to have to testify against her.

It took some time to recover from our breakfast, which had evidenced so much emotion across the boundaries of race, gender, and, to some degree, generation. Tommy and Eva are almost twenty years apart in age. Eva is a self-proclaimed black Appalachian with roots in Kentucky. She is a fourth-generation East Ender. Red is a white Appalachian fifth-generation East Ender. Tommy moved to the East End as a teenager. He is a white man with roots in rural Ohio and Kentucky. Eventually Red and Eva made amends, although their friendship has never fully recovered from the court proceedings.

The legal system is good at pitting community people against one another. The local elites and stakeholders are even better at it. While these conflicts may sound trivial and personal, they are not trivial for the community, because it is essential that grassroots leaders work together in a variety of contexts, and on a variety of issues, all of which involve preserving and revitalizing the East End as a community. Whether or not they can succeed against the forces of the market system in achieving a neighborhood with a mixture of classes and races remains to be seen.

Meetings Formal and Informal

NOVEMBER 14, 1991

I arrive at LeBlond Recreation Center at 5:30 P.M., the usual time for executive board meetings of the East End Area Council. This is six months before the passage of the East End Riverfront Community Development Plan. I check out the cars to see who has gotten there—Elaine's brown one, Doris's tan one, old and rusted. Doris has said hitting it is fine as long as nobody touches her new one. Robbie's old blue boat of a car is there, too—this is the one she drives to work at the local bar: "When a drunk hits it at 2:00 a.m., I don't care."

When I reach the top of the long ramp that parallels Eastern Avenue, David, a Department of Recreation employee who grew up in the East End and works at LeBlond, smiles and says: "They're downstairs" and points the way to the basement ceramics room that doubles as meeting space for community groups. He knows I haven't come for Jazzercise or aerobics, as is the habit of Volvo-driving yuppies who pay the Department of Recreation to rent space that the community views as its own. I make my way through the large upstairs room of the LeBlond Recreation Center, one of the many centers owned by the Department of Recreation. The smell of Lysol and ammonia is strong from the bucket and mop standing where David left it. I quickly go down the back stairs to find Doris, Robbie, Elaine, Bunny Christy, and Pearl Clark, a recreation department employee who has worked at LeBlond for sixteen years. She is a real fixture in the community, even though she does not reside there.

Doris and Elaine are two black women who are lifelong East End residents. Robbie also grew up in the East End. Bunny does not live in the East End, but has many relatives here. The fact that there are two black women and three white women does not register with me until later, when I begin to think about some of the dynamics of this informal meeting—dynamics of gender, race, class, community.

The first thing I am told, apologetically, is that there is not, in fact, going to be an executive board meeting because the president of the EEAC, Pete Evans, has announced that there is no correspondence to deal with. (It does not surprise me that this man, one of the few yuppies in the community to hold office, does not want to face a group of very strong grassroots women.) I stand for awhile alongside the table waiting to see whether anyone is getting up to leave. Nobody budges, although two of the women are examining some molded ceramic figurines that are sitting on the shelves lining the back wall. I decide to sit down and join Doris, Bunny, and Robbie at the table.

Doris, who seems to be troubled about something, gives a short speech to the group: "I don't want to step in your business so you won't step in mine. When you step out of bounds you get your feelings hurt." At this point, Robbie, who always wants to include people and who knows the East End Area Council's history of helping people in distress, says that "he [the president of the East End Area Council] tried to help [on behalf of the Council] when Harriet Priest got hit." Bunny, trying also to mediate a potential conflict, says: "There comes a time when you got to put this stuff behind."

"The third floor is 'done for,'" Robbie continues, referring to a recent fire. "You pay more attention to these things around the holidays." Then, changing the subject or, rather, using this as the introduction to her next subject, Robbie asks: "Do you know anyone who will be by theirselves on Thanksgiving? Dinner at the River Inn, I've organized it. Some developers will donate pop. It's one thing if you have a family, but sitting there eating turkey by yourself . . . it's for people in the neighborhood who will be sitting by theirselves. I'm givin' them personal invitations. I don't want them to feel like it's a charity—just a get-together. Connie is there by hisself in the schoolhouse."

There is a brief informal discussion of the time conflict between a November 19 meeting at City Hall on the extension of the IDC (Interim Development Control) basically putting a halt to all development in the neighborhood and the Thanksgiving dinner to be held at Mount Carmel Church that same day at noon. Doris and many other women from

Mount Carmel will be at the church at 9:00 to set up the feast. Elaine announces that she is taking off from work to help with the dinner, even though she needs the money (she is paid by the hour as a secretary of a church). Robbie continues to encourage everyone to attend the IDC meeting if possible, even though there is general agreement that the IDC will be extended.

Doris, getting a bit agitated, says: "A few of us have let all of our personal priorities go to pot. Let someone else be interested. You can't be the pudding in every pot. Same old people."

Elaine, who is running for vice-president of the East End Area Council and will, if elected, have to give up her paid position as editor of the newsletter, reacts to Doris's outburst: "I'm gonna work twice as hard next year. There's nobody on this executive board that loves the East End more than I do." Elaine proceeds to display pictures of her grown children: "I need to stay editor because I need the money. Vice-president would be more helpful to the community than to be editor."

"Your voice can count on or off the executive board," adds Robbie.

Doris, in a somewhat resigned and upset tone, says: "I know I'm tired." (She is upset because the Information Committee no longer meets in her house and she has lost control of it.) She exits.

Elaine stands up and addresses the group: "I'm not tryin' to play religious, but I look up first and then I look at you. I don't put all my trust in man. I put all my trust in God. Pete Evans [former EEAC president, who resigned in October] and I have had more fights than anybody in this world. I am not mad at Pete. When I hugged Pete [at the November 8 banquet], I meant it. God is my leader. I don't worship men. This [involvement in the community] is something that I love to do. If it hadn't been for those two [brothers Bill and Mike Garner] I wouldn't been here."

The fact that Elaine was recruited into community work by Bill and Mike, two very powerful black leaders, and that she mentions them in the same breath as God, says something about the relationship between religion and power for black people in the East End. The combination of metaphors, religious and combative, is very important here, since it is often religion that calms people down and provides some sense of solace and hope for the future.

In the next breath, however, Elaine proceeds to talk about helping patterns in the neighborhood, especially the fact that Robbie and Fritz would take Elaine anywhere she needed to go. She proceeds to elaborate on a trip, mentioned earlier, to Dayton with the Christys, a white couple.

This, for Elaine, is the example that causes her to "look over Bunny's color." Bunny purposely asked Elaine to drive with them so Elaine would not have to go alone. Bunny made a special point about asking her husband whether another woman could drive with them, but did not think to let him know that the other woman was black. Elaine emphasizes her comfort with Bunny and her husband, Dublin.

Elaine then lashes out at Robbie, a white woman, but, in this instance, race is not the issue: "What goes on in the East End Area Council executive board stays right here. Dolores Young [from Seven Hills Neighborhood Houses] knows more about the East End than we know about Seven Hills. You don't tell everyone your business."

Robbie says: "How many times did I ask people to go to Seven Hills. I haven't told 'them' everything."

Everyone agrees that Seven Hills is a social service agency. Elaine says in reference to Seven Hills: "There has been times that I have been on my feet; I went to get things from Seven Hills and gave it to people."

This is a typical pattern; people feel comfortable going to a social service agency for the purpose of helping others, but not to help themselves.

Robbie, who is getting more and more upset at Elaine's accusations, at one point starts to cry: "Whatever it takes to get everybody workin' together. I understand that there is more than one way to do things. People say the executive board does things secretively." Elaine wants to know who these people are.

On the surface, Elaine's criticism of Robbie may seem curious in light of her praise of Robbie's and Fritz's generosity toward her. It is also curious because Elaine says she wants EEAC, Columbia Tusculum, and Seven Hills to get together. If, however, one reads the criticism in the context of Elaine's desire to protect Robbie as a member of the East End family and to strengthen grassroots efforts, the criticism begins to make sense and seems less of a contradiction in personal and political styles.

This last discussion does raise some boundary issues. Dolores Young is a black woman who runs the soup kitchen in the East End. Is Dolores an East Ender or not? Many people in the East End would answer in the affirmative; others would say that she distributes food and clothing in a preferential manner, that is, always giving to the same people or always giving the most desirable items to the same people.

Accusations of self-interest are common.

Pete Evans is known to be politically ambitious. Robbie notes that she sees Evans's car down at City Hall and that this is a continuation of his pattern of "going to meetings that we know nothing about." She says that in the last few months Pete, even though he has resigned as president, "has done a disservice to this community. Bush has his cabinet. The president of the East End area council has the executive board."

NOVEMBER 18, 1991

I go to LeBlond for an NSP (Neighborhood Support Program) meeting. This is a citywide program that gives $10,000 seed money to each community council to develop community projects. The projects are set by each community, and each year applications must be made to the NSP program.

No meeting.

House Burning

I call Doris, who tells me "a piece of bad news—Robbie Kale's house has burned."

I am shocked, especially because on the previous Thursday, Robbie had asked whether I would like to drive by the house on Congress Street that had burned. We saw a large frame house on the corner that was home to three families with five children altogether. The roof burned almost completely, damaging the second and third floors. One of the five children was seen walking barefoot a few days later. The Junior League is gathering clothing.

Now it is Robbie's house.

Toni, Robbie's adopted daughter, tells me that Robbie is at the River Inn. On the phone, Robbie sounds very down. She talks about how easy it is to go to the Red Cross for other people, but "hard as hell to go for yourself." My phone conversation with Toni revealed that Robbie had obtained coupons from the Red Cross to a large discount grocery store and to an all-purpose discount merchandise store for clothing and food. Robbie is most worried about two things: whether she will obtain permission to rebuild, and how her mom will handle the loss of a house with so many memories of her husband and son in it.

The next day, I talk to some of Robbie's close friends. Rita, a barmaid at the River Inn, tells me that Robbie "is much better today." Rita is the twenty-six-year-old mother of two children, Sandy, thirteen, and Jason, six. Her mother, Wilma, forty-seven and a known alcoholic, has worked as a barmaid at the River Inn for over twenty years. Wilma is "bored stiff" because all she does is play cards and watch TV. She says the daytime shifts are boring, but she quit doing nights a long time ago, except for Thursday nights, her "dart night." Her garlic pills keep her going. She does not seem interested in eating the microwave pizza she serves to bar customers. Her husband, Taylor, works for a book binding company.

Robbie is close to Rita, who helps her with her mom.

A conversation with Robbie a few days later reveals that she has been given unofficial permission to rebuild. She is relieved. For the moment, she has acquired twelve sheets of 4×8, $\frac{3}{4}$-inch plywood to prevent neighborhood kids from further stripping copper. She can use some of the wood to board up the house and the rest of it to rebuild. The beams and the wiring are still intact. "Mom will not be going back there tomorrow, but at least she knows she can go back."

5 | FIELDWORK AT HOME: THE EAST END STUDY PROJECT

Ethnography is actually situated between powerful systems of meaning. It poses its questions at the boundaries of civilizations, cultures, classes, races and genders. Ethnography decodes and recodes, tilling the grounds of collective order and diversity, inclusion and exclusion. It describes processes of innovation and structuration, and is itself part of these processes. (Clifford 1986: 2)

This chapter talks about the delicate relationships between research and advocacy in a shallow urban community that is a ten-minute drive from the university. How does a research team work in a community for six years? What are the issues and dynamics involved in conducting research and advocacy and how do these change? How is it possible to use research data to build upon and elaborate the strongest elements of the community? What are the logistics? Is it possible to communicate and use documented community strengths to negotiate with the city and with other power and funding sources for resources?[1] The timing of research and advocacy is very important. Timing principally involves the relationships between the research schedule and the daily, weekly, and seasonal rhythms of the community. Fridays are not good days to talk and visit. Grocery shopping, weekend child care arrangements, card games, all happen on Friday. Summer is not a good time to begin a project; East Enders are trying to relax, to have a break from power struggles, to have picnics and family reunions, to go upriver or simply to stay cool on porches. Air conditioning is rare in the East End and the humid, hot Cincinnati summers make people tired.

Most anthropologists spend no more than a year conducting research. Six continuous years in the field is virtually unheard of. Such a long time in the field has caused me to question many of the canons of contemporary anthropological research.[2]

The East End Study Project began officially in the spring of 1991, although some of the professionals and advocates on the team had spent a great deal of time in the community before this. Our aim during the first summer was to establish a level of comfort for both East Enders and researchers/advocates—to get to know East Enders as people. We collected detailed qualitative data along with what I have come to call "some good numbers"—longevity in the community, frequency and intensity of intergenerational ties, numbers of owners versus renters, caring patterns in and among households, and links between the East End and other working-class communities. These data are meant to counterbalance the "bad" numbers and deficits that are used so often to characterize the working poor—low socioeconomic status indicators, rates of illiteracy, rates of disease, and rates of school dropout.

Quantitative data are important, but they must be collected carefully. When a Head Start Program was being considered, our team worked with lifelong East Enders to calculate the number of children under the age of one year; in this instance, our three-year-old data were too old. We discovered an amazing number of infants within a radius of three or four blocks, seventy-five all told.

Training for research and advocacy is extremely important. In 1991, our multicultural team comprised a diverse group of people, including students from African American, Hispanic, and white Appalachian communities. Some graduate and some undergraduate students have been involved from the outset, and undergraduates have played very important roles in interviewing and in analysis. The original team consisted of ten students, who conducted intensive (three- to four-hour) interviews with seventy families. This team participated in an extensive weekly training program during the summer. Two years later, the team was joined by two other students, one a male graduate student who had been adopted as an infant into a well-to-do Cincinnati family and who had a very special sympathy for working-class families, the other a University of Cincinnati professor's daughter who was eventually to pursue a graduate degree in urban planning. Staff members from the Urban Appalachian Council joined social scientists and advocates on the team to talk about a range of issues, from the nature of interviewing, taping, and recording of field notes to how to write summaries to the logistics of fieldwork.

We processed feelings along with data in the weekly training sessions. Some members of our research team became so involved emotionally in the community that our sessions often turned into group therapy. The power and intensity of the fieldwork was overwhelming to all of us at times. Some team members were puzzled by the strength and friendliness of East Enders, given the everyday difficulties of functioning in small, confined spaces with very limited resources. Others were upset by the contradictions and anomalies; in some instances, the absolutely appalling physical conditions coupled with extraordinarily rich and warm human interactions. It would have been easy to overromanticize the charm and pathos most East Enders take for granted.

The weekly training sessions all took place in living rooms or around tables, both indoors and outdoors. Our team meetings were designed to guide the research and to allow for research directions and emphases to change. We tried to create a relaxed atmosphere in which members of the team felt comfortable sharing their intense emotions, frustrations, and triumphs. The African American students on the team had different feelings from the Hispanic student. Students with southern or Appalachian backgrounds also had different experiences. Some students decided to spend more time in the community than others, but virtually all were welcomed and felt positive about their fieldwork.

Our interview guide developed over several months. It was drafted, tested, and redrafted to produce a structured set of questions that still allowed—indeed encouraged—East Enders to tell their stories. We devised an elaborate interview guide that focused on collecting family genealogies, but that was also open-ended enough to allow us to learn about the East End from the East Enders' viewpoint. The guide was meant to be just that, a guide for talking to people.

Early on we rejected a rigid interview schedule because we wanted to encourage creativity among both fieldworkers and East Enders. We used artist's tablets to draw the kinship charts of the large extended East End families. We encouraged the sharing of life experiences, work experiences, and family memories. The students went in pairs to talk to East Enders at many different times. Many interviews were done on weekends and in the evenings. In the summer of 1991 we spent time in and around the neighborhood—at the recreation center, at the neighborhood bar, at the YMCA, and at community meetings.

The following is an excerpt from an undergraduate student's fieldnotes from the summer of 1991. I quote these notes extensively for several reasons. They capture the field experience as well as many of the essentials of the East End community. The descriptions dispel some strong stereotypes about bars and about the people who spend time in them:

> The bar was practically full with patrons; a black man (30s) at the end next to the door, a large white man with a pony tail and receding hair line, two white men (30s) talking with each other, a young white woman (30s) sitting, listening to them, plus an older white man and a woman at the end near the T.V. The only person seated at a table (near the T.V.) was Robbie's mother.
>
> Robbie introduced me to the woman next to me. The woman's name was May. She is a Christy and told me that she used to live in the East End. Next to her was her husband—a quiet man—and next to him was a woman and two men who turned out also to be Christys. Next to that group of three was Roy, a big man with a pony tail whose family has had property in the East End since 1936. May had lots to talk to me about. She said that she used to live in the East End, but when they closed [the schools at] St. Stevens and St. Rose she chose to move to Mt. Washington for the kids to go to school [at another Catholic grade school]. She told me all about her grandson who is 11 going on 20. Apparently he had been doing poorly in school . . . there were all kinds of conflicts with him and the teacher . . . the teacher says that he is bored and slow. His mother brought him to get tested at [a private grade school] and according to the tests he is capable of doing advanced work and should not really be having any academic problems. His grandmother May says that the teacher has problems accepting and dealing with his behavior and that her ego gets bruised because she is unable to handle him. He was then accepted into two elite private schools.
>
> May told me that her husband was the oldest policeman to ever retire and that she used to own two small businesses. She talked to me about this in the context of talking about the people in the East End. She says that many of them are not educated but it doesn't matter because they have a heart and are good people. She said, in reference to the city that "they" don't care one bit about these people down here and they want to keep them on welfare and they don't care to give them an education. May seemed to value education, which brought her to talk about her own life. With pride she told me the names of the schools she and her husband went to down in the East End . . . Highlands, Washington, and McKinley.
>
> We continued to talk about the East End and the River Inn. May told me that she comes to the River Inn about four times a week.

She told me that I should come around such. I asked Robbie if she thought that many people would come to Saturday's meeting where the neighborhood residents would draw up their own Eastern Riverfront plan to be recommended to the city. She said she hoped so, and that they're having an announcement printed and sending kids around to each house to distribute the notice. She wondered if a group [of developers] would get wind of the news. Robbie said that they've showed up at meetings before and have been vocal, but that they are primarily the people who live up on the hill above the parkway who work to preserve the green space as well as the view from the Parkway. She did not seem to take them in high regard, rather that they were out for their own best interests.

May agreed and had her own comments to add about the surrounding areas of the East End. When she mentioned Linwood I probed with specific questions—was Linwood considered a neighborhood? Yes, she said, and explained to me the parameters. We also talked about Columbia Tusculum. It used to be East End, but they started upgrading it and have tried calling it something else, but everyone knows it is the East End. May did say that there are some low income people living up there, but "it's all black."

SUMMARY:

I am at the point where I feel no apprehension in entering the establishment. I have been received warmly, and in two cases have been bought a drink. One might think that in a bar one is encouraged to drink an alcoholic beverage, especially after the hour of 8, however, this was not the case. I drank my diet 7-up, and several of those around me also drank soft drinks. Almost everyone else drank beer.

Not only did I feel perfectly safe, but I also felt entertained to a degree. Whether it was Wilma's bantering or Taylor's haircut, or little Jason sneaking up behind the bar to grab a beef jerky, these were all simple, but amusing events for any patron to enjoy. In the case of Robbie as barmaid, the patrons got a taste for the local news of political nature. [The community was in the throes of planning for economic development, preservation, and revitalization.]

Several of the patrons are not from the East End, but grew up there. One I talked to was living in Mt. Lookout . . . another lived in Anderson. They all indicated that they are regulars. Indeed the River Inn had a slew of regulars . . . I learned this fact by glancing through the photo album that Wilma had behind the bar.

The patrons are also of great diversity. I would say the average age is around mid forty, but in addition I have observed senior citizens, young mothers and children. Although the patrons are predominantly white, black people seem to frequent the bar as well.

There is dart night on Thursdays, and other events include card and bowling night, yet perhaps one of the most significant activities is a very informal one: food distribution. On both of the two afternoons I have been at the bar whatever was a surplus at the soup kitchen at St. Simons was offered to the patrons. Even I, who could have been considered an outsider was offered food on both occasions.

The main aim of the initial phase of research was to get to know people in the neighborhood and to begin to understand who was who in the interconnected families. East Enders tend to marry other East Enders; remarriage after divorce occurs more often than not to someone from the East End, or from another working-class community. When people move out of the neighborhood, they always return for long visits; many would like to return permanently. The large and quite elaborate kinship charts we constructed also showed us where residents came from in the region and how long East End residents and members of their extended kinship and friendship networks had lived in the East End. The Appalachian origin of East Enders was demonstrated over and over again. Grandparents and great-grandparents came from Kentucky, West Virginia, Tennessee, and rural Ohio. Many people also came from other parts of the rural South—Alabama and Georgia, for example—or directly from Europe—Germany, England, and Ireland.

Our research team met regularly throughout the summer and fall of 1991, and several of the team's original members still stay in touch with the East End Study Project. Several new team members have been added along the way.

Following this summer of intensive interviewing, the professionals on the team—I and two others who were also connected to the University of Cincinnati through Appalachian studies and urban planning—began more focused fieldwork. We started to attend board meetings, to spend time talking to East End leaders after the meetings had formally broken up, and to meet at the gas station to learn the informal patterns and practices of East End life. With time, East End residents and leaders became part of our team, and we became part of various community projects; research and advocacy became more and more intertwined.[3]

From the very first day in the East End, it has been impossible for me to read anything—ethnography, theory, fiction, journalism—without thinking about practicing community. Being "in the field" all the time took some getting used to, but anthropology "at home" began to feel very comfortable. Adopting the views of East Enders has become very natural to me, especially when I have found myself in professional and elite-dominated situations.[4] The more the "experts" claim to know about local politics, government, and so on, the more I realize how little concrete understanding they have of people and communities like the East End.

My hunches about the essential elitism of the experts have been confirmed at every conference or symposium I've attended that is devoted to topics concerning neighborhoods. I am amazed and chagrined at how much the professionals—the lawyers, the business people—talk and how little they say, and how little the community people are allowed to say in these contexts. Academic and civic conferences, with the accompanying credentialism and formality—keynote speakers, rigid and sometimes grueling scheduling—are by definition replications of the power structure.

Postmodern thinkers have already raised many questions about the nature of the anthropological endeavor, especially the traditional ways of dealing with so-called other cultures. The authority of the anthropologist's voice is being called into question along with the tools anthropologists have used for interpreting the meaning of culture. The ongoing field experience—in effect, living in the field as well as living at the university—provide the ideal context for reading, interpreting, and questioning the "canons" of contemporary anthropological theory, if there is such a thing, especially as it has developed in the last decade. I use the word "canon" intentionally, for it amazes me how quickly so-called criticism and cultural critique of anthropology itself can become entrenched in the elite world of the university.

Before I deal with some of the specific issues, let me say a bit more about the fieldwork itself and the larger context in which it was and is being carried out.

The East End Report

The East End Report, officially titled "The East End Community Report: A Community Survey and Report with Observations and Recommendations Regarding the Riverfront Redevelopment Strategy," provided the backdrop—indeed, the foil—against which the fieldwork began. I had heard nothing but negatives about this report from my very first day in the community. " 'They' are calling 'us' a bunch of screaming illiterates," Robbie told me over and over again. "We never knew we were illiterate until we read it in the East End Report." " 'They' think 'we' are stupid," said another leader, a black woman in her fifties. "Why?" I asked myself. These are the good guys, Legal Aid and UAC (Urban Appalachian Council), who conducted a joint study survey. What was going on?

In January 1991, "The East End Community Report" was published. It summarized the results of a survey sponsored by two leading advocacy agencies in Cincinnati: the Legal Aid Society and the Urban Appalachian Council. The report was based on a door-to-door survey of 180 community residents and key informant interviews. The survey and interviews were conducted from June through October 1990. As the subtitle of the report indicates, the impetus for the survey was provided by the Riverfront Advisory Council (RAC) Plan Group, which, in 1988 and 1989 worked with the City of Cincinnati staff and a private consulting firm to develop a riverfront redevelopment strategy and the related Riverfront Concept Plan.

The East End Riverfront Community Development Plan (hereafter the plan) (passed in May 1992) was highly controversial. As of the writing of "The East End Community Report," the ambivalence about the plan revolved principally around whether it would aid or harm the existing community, that is, whether it would displace residents and businesses or whether it would stimulate revitalization of the East End in ways consistent with East Enders' sense of community and class culture.

"The East End Community Report"
Study Design and Methodology

The area for which the development plan was designed and the study area for the survey overlap. A three-mile strip along the river from downtown Cincinnati to the main north-south entrance to the community—that is, three miles east of downtown—is the plan area. This is not the entire East End, for it leaves out the business district as well as a highly populated area to the east of Delta Avenue. The interviewers are described in the report as knocking on virtually every door in the neighborhood and interviewing household adults. Information was received from "perhaps one-third of the households in the plan area" (p. 2). The key informant interviews were with nine East End residents who were neighborhood leaders as well as other individuals who had special knowledge of the neighborhood and of the planning process. The purpose of the survey "was to gather information on the needs and concerns of current residents and to generate recommendations and strategies for protecting the interests of the existing community" (p. 9).

"The East End Community Report" has several theoretical and methodological problems. First, it focuses on households, a problematical unit for several reasons. The main units of social organization in the East End are intricate extended family networks, which always reach beyond the household and usually beyond the neighborhood. Households are fluid in composition and organization. Depending on the needs of the kinship network for housing, child care, food, and transportation, households expand and contract almost unnoticed. Nieces or nephews, for example, may move in with aunts or uncles. Often, the addition of a nephew means the addition not only of his nuclear family, but the addition of parts of his wife's extended family as well—a sister, a brother, with or without their nuclear families. Household composition may also vary within a given twenty-four-hour period: grandbabies stay at their grandmother's house during the day and occasionally at night, for example. The rest of the time, these children are with their own nuclear families.

Another problem is that the survey approaches the community from a "social problems" perspective and comes up with numbers that, while real in one sense, do not tell the full East End story. The following is a quote from the report (p. 7):

> The unemployment rate was 15%. Twenty four percent of the families had incomes below the poverty level. The "jobless rate" (calculated by adding able-bodied adults under the age of 65 classified as "not in the labor force" to those the census bureau classified as unemployed) was 50%, one of the city's highest. Almost half of the adult population had less than an eighth grade education and the dropout rate was 37%. The neighborhood ranked fourth in the city in functional illiteracy. . . . Almost one in four households was headed by a female and half of these families had incomes below the poverty level, but there are many blue collar and service workers and many two parent and extended family households. Thirty percent of the households received some form of public assistance. The median family income was $12,000.

The report does acknowledge the many strengths and positive features of the community, including "socioeconomic and racial diversity, a relative lack of racial tensions, strong kinship, multigenerational roots, and neighborhood networks in which there is much happiness, order, and mutual assistance" (p. 8). It does not elaborate these points, however, as it would be very difficult to do so using a survey methodology. Yet, the authors of "The East End Community Report" argue that "the positive aspects of life in the neighborhood are much more important than the list of social problems and that these features must be used as the basis for constructive planning" (p. 8).

The key findings of the survey consist of the following (p. 10):

(1) The East End constitutes a diverse stable neighborhood. The large majority of homeowners and most renters are long-term residents.

(2) The people of the East End comprise a mix of working class low to moderate income families, lower income families with unemployed or underemployed heads of household, and elderly retired persons. About half the households are headed by married couples.

(3) The East End is racially integrated and has been so for many years.

(4) The majority of East End residents are urban Appalachian.

(5) A large majority of East End residents like living in the East End.

(6) With regard to plans for redevelopment of the East End, almost all residents are opposed to any displacement of current residents, and both homeowners and renters fear that redevelopment will cause displacement.[5]

Responses to "The East End Community Report"

The community leadership did not hear the positive findings of "The East End Community Report" and immediately pounced on it as portraying the community "as a bunch of screaming illiterates." As of this writing, there is still criticism of the report, including the fact that surveys were conducted only between the hours of nine and five on weekdays, and thereby excluded many working people, for example, those who worked at night and slept during the day. The survey was also conducted in an impersonal manner without much thought to laying the groundwork in the community. The presentation of the report (both written and spoken) took the form of a fact-oriented, informational, and, again, impersonal statement.

In a real sense, however, "The East End Community Report" was a catalyst for creativity and empowerment. Two East End leaders began writing prolifically—poetry about the East End Riverfront Community Development Plan in one instance and prose about a range of topics, for example, family, politics, community, and individuals, in another. The writings are personal and political commentaries that tell the stories of the East End with an authenticity that cannot be replicated by outsiders.

But the writings are only one form of expression, one way of voicing and practicing community in the most positive sense. The energy in these writings influenced other community leaders and encouraged the formation of several new nonprofit corporations in the community: the Pendleton Heritage Center Board and the Housing Preservation Fund Board, to name two. In the interim, the plan, which consumed community meetings and caused grassroots leaders to eat, sleep, and breathe it, was passed with strong community input.

Research and Advocacy

From the outset, the guiding principles of our research have been anthropological in the most classic sense. East Enders must be understood as working-class people with roots in Appalachia, Europe, and the rural South. While East Enders are very special, they are not unique; they share characteristics with many other groups of working people in this country and elsewhere in the world—rural-urban migrants, immigrants, urban villagers, to name a few. This comparative, cross-cultural perspective is essential for the breakdown of stereotypes.

From the perspective of an advocate, if our aim is to understand the lives of East End people, then we must listen to multiple voices at the times and in the contexts within which East Enders wish to speak. Listening requires hearing many often very dissonant discourses and trying at the same time to keep the channels of communication open. This is not easy in a community that is becoming more and more factionalized along clear class and cultural lines and that exists in a larger urban context in which powerful outsiders control more and more of the daily life of the East End.

Adopting the position of a community-preserving advocate in the most proactive sense of the term is essential for working as a researcher in the East End. Playing the role of advocate is very tricky, however, when being a researcher is also one's task. At the very least, advocacy is very time consuming and requires taking positions, often very strong positions, that not only may alienate the opposing faction—in this case, developers—but also may run the risk of alienating the most well intentioned local elites—from women's political groups to the corporate executives and their wives who sit on city and, in some cases, community boards. The same words can be uttered by an East Ender and a university professor. From the former, though, the words are "community input" to be accepted, ignored, or acted upon, but the interaction is one between the powerless and the powerful; when a university professor says those same words, the statement is regarded very differently. Yet, in order to keep the voices of the community before those in positions of power, it is often necessary to repeat the words of a community resident, or to take a position that is not what those in power necessarily want to hear. As will become clear, there are many subtle and not-so-subtle issues here, from the control of time in meetings to the actual content of the positions taken by researchers and advocates.

Certain hard questions must be asked if we are to conduct high-quality research and if this research is to respect and enhance the diversity, energy, and richness of life in the East End. Using professorial status to the best advantage of the community, fighting the ethnocentrism of even the most well intentioned citizens and city officials, being a diplomat without selling out to the dominant institutions, all must be done in cooperation with community leaders. I must confess that there have been times when I have felt like putting on my "hillbilly redneck" sweatshirt, as East Enders would say; there have been times when I have come very close—and the longer I spend in the East End, the more tempting it is—to expressing publicly my frustration with the excessive verbiage and filibustering imposed by people of means on community residents who respond with polite, but seething, silence.

Sometimes East Enders tease me about my East End sentiments. On one occasion, after I had confronted a developer on his opposition to the heritage center, an East End leader admitted that she had never heard me speak in quite that strong a tone of voice ever before. Of course, the developer would not admit to opposing the center; he was simply using meeting time to criticize the plan's details. At such moments, all research agendas become irrelevant, and it can sometimes take days to regain any perspective at all. I had to observe myself for awhile as an anthropologist participating as an advocate. This was often very difficult, but it aided the return of a research perspective. I do not mean that objectivity returned, for I do not think there is such a thing; rather, I returned to the essential research questions, to the issues of practicing community. The return was difficult and painful because it involved playing leapfrog between positions inside and outside the community. I began to feel a kind of schizophrenia as my car, often several times a day, drove itself between the East End and the university.

The questions researchers formulate, the manner in which information (data) is collected, as well as the manner in which so-called results are presented to the community must be rethought with utmost sensitivity to community strengths, needs, and reactions. What kinds of data, quantitative and qualitative, should be collected and in what order? What circumstances—local (community and city), regional, and national—set the agendas for research and advocacy? EPA regulations, for example, as federally mandated, take precedence over state and city concerns. Where issues of environmental cleanup are involved, local residents and authorities must comply, even though compliance involves the closing of the gas station, the unofficial office of the unofficial mayor of the East End. The degree to which nonresident owners of property in the East End know or care about the consequences of their decisions and transactions remains a critical question for research and advocacy. What are the roles of community leaders and community institutions in setting research agendas and in organizing and disseminating information about the community? How can leaders work with advocates to connect research and advocacy? The relationships between researchers and urban institutions ranging across universities, advocacy organizations, local government, and social service agencies raise further questions about who is to use the data and for what purposes. All of these relationships engage researchers and advocates in practicing community.

The Need for New Measures

As an anthropologist, my own predisposition for in-depth ethnography (a people-centered, personal approach that is empathic and also analytical in its awareness of the larger forces impinging daily on people's lives) far outweighs the important, but nonetheless more impersonal, "number-crunching" approaches to social science research. This does not mean that ethnographers are averse to counting. It does mean that the contexts within which the numbers are collected are extremely important. For example, early in our research, in fact, during that first summer of 1991, one of the community leaders asked one of the student researchers whether I would be willing to give testimony supporting our preliminary report about the length of time apartment dwellers had been living in the East End. We had learned, after analyzing one set of interviews, that there was no difference between owners and renters concerning longevity of residence in the East End. We had given the preliminary results to the president of the East End Area Council, and we had made it known in the community that we were simply reinforcing and reconfirming "local knowledge"; that is, East Enders know exactly how long their neighbors have been there. Some renters, in fact, have been there for so long that they are perceived as home owners.

For Appalachians in cities, many of whom must struggle daily to maintain close family and neighborhood relationships in the face of impersonal urban institutions, a research methodology that supports and reinforces positive, personal, face-to-face relationships and knowledge is essential. Good ethnography, however, is highly labor intensive and, thus, expensive. Ethnographers should collect quantitative data, but these data must be collected and analyzed in specific social, cultural, and historical contexts that must be understood qualitatively in order to make sense of the data.

Numbers, while true and real, in a sense can be very deceiving. Population figures, for example, show drastic demographic decline in the East End over the last twenty-five years. But these figures do not reflect the large numbers of people who remain connected to their kin in the community and who would, given the availability of housing, move back to the East End.

Some new measures need to be developed, such as numbers of people connected to the East End by kinship even though they do not reside there on a full-time basis. Such measures will yield a much larger "demographic" picture than will census data alone. These measures will also present a much more positive picture of the community, because many former East Enders are just waiting to bring their skills and their families back into the community. Such measures are based on unconventional units of analysis, not households, not even the community itself, but the network of concerned kin and friends as working-class culture defines them. Without these new measures, we cannot understand the kinds of supports that East Enders have and that they in turn provide for people living outside of the community.

Cross-cultural Perspectives

An anthropological approach is based on a comparative, cross-cultural perspective that sees Appalachian people in cities, East Enders in particular, as sharing many of the same experiences as rural-to-urban migrants in cities around the world. For example, East End children may have at least as much in common with those children whose voices Oscar Lewis recorded from a barrio in Mexico City as with rural Appalachian children in the hills of Kentucky. The reasons for these commonalities are complex, but they can be understood, at least in part, by the fact that Appalachian people in cities and barrio dwellers in urban Mexico both originate in rural (that is, subsistence-oriented) communities and, to this day, continue to interact with people in rural areas by moving among rural and city residences. In such communities, rural and urban, extended families are the keystone of social organization, and intergenerational ties (especially between children and their grandparents, but also between mothers and daughters and fathers and sons) are the most important social relationships. These ties outweigh occupational status; responsibilities to members of extended families outweigh school or job obligations.

This cross-cultural perspective guides the process of understanding the heritage of East Enders and strategies for surviving in the city. If you ask a fifth-generation East Ender whether he or she is Appalachian, the answer, in all likelihood, will be negative. If, however, you ask that same person, "Where are your people from?" more likely than not, you will sit down for a series of stories, one more interesting and complicated than the next, about the origins of a person's family. Discussions of ancestry will reveal not only geographic origins, but also key features of family and community organization.[6]

I suggest a three-pronged approach to understanding the origins of East Enders' community. The prongs, so to speak, derive from a cross-cultural perspective and consist of geographical, cultural, and social structural features. Geography refers to place of origin (whether in the United States, Europe, or elsewhere), culture refers to adaptations primarily to rural environments (again, both in and outside of the United States), and social structural features refer to the importance of extended kin relations, especially intergenerational ties. Together, these three features allow us to create the threads not only of Appalachian ethnicity and identity in the East End but also of other ethnicities and identities. In the East End, especially among the black residents but also among whites, a person's identity as an East Ender overrides any association with Appalachian ethnicity. There are, of course, many places in the world where attachment to place overrides any sort of ethnic identity. The issue concerns the circumstances that create such strong place identities and that maintain them over time, even when a person no longer resides in the original homeplace.

Urbanism, Appalachians, and East Enders

To virtually all East Enders, the term "urban Appalachian" is a problematic, if not a contradictory, term. Many people reject the term "Appalachian" because they equate it with "hillbilly" or "ridgerunner" or some other stereotype. Even so, East Enders will go along with many of the projects sponsored by the Urban Appalachian Council (UAC), for example, because they see the programs as doing something positive for their children or because they are very fond of the woman who runs them in the East End.

More problematical for East Enders, however, is the term "urban," because East Enders consider themselves ignored and dominated by the city, on the one hand, and fighting and resisting city ways, on the other. Appalachian people in cities, especially East Enders, are, first and foremost, people who feel most comfortable in the country or in small-scale, face-to-face social settings and who invent and re-create such settings in cities. As I have already mentioned, East Enders give priority to family, kin, and neighborhood obligations, even when these conflict with obligations to jobs, schooling, and other tasks defined by the urban power structure as important, including opportunities for upward mobility. Priorities for sharing one's resources, however meager, and priorities that place responsibilities for kin and neighbors above personal needs and wants, create resistance to upward mobility. Personal relationships take precedence over bureaucratic dealings and skills. In some instances, mere contact with a bureaucracy such as city government—even going to City Hall and feeling comfortable there—might be interpreted in the community as "working for the city," that is, selling out the community for one's personal interests, financial or political.

Insensitivity to the strengths of local working-class culture comes in many forms. Powerful outsiders can impose judgments that damage individual, family, and community identity, even if their intentions are good (sometimes, especially if their intentions are good). Part of any research methodology must, then, work toward neutralizing the kind of ethnocentrism, for example, that uses such terms such as "adjustment," "upward mobility," and "success" in ways that imply deficiencies. If we look for patterns of success that fit urban, capitalist standards, we will almost certainly overlook the great strengths of working-class neighborhoods, especially the strong intergenerational ties and the informal educational processes that are preserved and maintained by older relatives and neighbors for the benefit of children and adolescents, often at the expense of monetary gain. Intricate patterns of exchange and gift giving (what I call "householding" in Chapter 6) ensure that no one goes hungry or without shelter and that children and the dependent elderly, especially, are cared for. When these kin and neighborhood support systems break down, the urban power structure tends to blame the victims or the informal health and child care providers. It often fails to comprehend that important community support systems have broken down when there is no one to ask for a ride or to provide temporary housing for people faced with eviction notices. Statistics such as employment rates, median incomes, school dropout rates, and proportions of renters to owners of homes and apartments do not reflect kin- and community-based exchange patterns, informal economies, and informal schooling processes, nor do they reflect the longevity of families or the tenacity of their ties in the community. Many East Enders could have purchased their homes several times over with the amount of rent they have paid over the years. They never had the credit lines or the cash down payments, however, because they shared their incomes with members of extended family and community networks.

It is the responsibility of researchers not merely to uncover these facts of social structure, but to help the urban power structure use these facts effectively, that is, for the benefit of people living in working-class communities. These are not easy tasks because the urban power structure will use every possible excuse to neglect working-class communities.

The Nature of Collaborative Research

Collaboration between and among East End community residents, advocates, researchers, and a few trusted city officials contributed to the different parts of this book. "Turn on the tape recorder," a community elder demanded when he wanted to be sure that the words of the developers could be checked and rechecked for the record. Or, a week or two after a particularly tense meeting, a community leader would ask: "Did you tape that development corporation meeting last week?"

The path between the East End and the university became more and more beaten with frequent sessions in labs and conference rooms to spread out old photographs for the heritage exhibit. The gap between the academic world and the world of working-class East Enders, while still immense, became a bit smaller. East Enders frequently came to the university, usually to the Anthropology Department, on occasion, to other events, such as conferences or seminars on the nature of community and the political process.

On several occasions, it became my task to provide diversity in civic gatherings. One such session I remember especially well, an evening event called "Politics for the People," sponsored by a local foundation. East Enders were the only "real" people there, that is, nonacademic and non-elite. Some of the women who had worked so hard to put the program together thanked me for bringing East Enders to the session. I watched jaws drop as wealthy men and women listened to the voices of people who had actually experienced hardship: unemployment, substandard housing, poor health, worries about basic necessities, noise, dangerous traffic, and drugs.

Research of this sort is not a pure, exact, or simple process. It is certainly not a science in the old positivist sense. The longer the research goes on, the more complex it becomes. Change is a fact of daily life and often takes on crisis proportions: someone's house burned to the ground; a relative or close friend died; a community institution closed. Living through these events with the community residents and leaders yielded real and practical knowledge about East Enders. But the experiences were often very intense, difficult both to experience and to process. Much of what I first wrote and thought was ethnography is now history.

The Evolution of a Research Project: Research, Planning, and Advocacy

Initially—beginning in 1991 and up to the spring of 1992, when the development plan was passed by City Council—the main point of our research and advocacy was to work with the residents of the community to secure a stronger voice in the planning process. The City of Cincinnati had hired LDR, a Massachusetts-based consulting firm, to design a development plan for the East End. As an architectural and engineering plan, it ignored the people. Even the planning process had focused primarily on the physical, geographical, and architectural aspects of the plan to the exclusion of social and cultural considerations.

Our collection of ethnographic data was designed to feed social planning considerations into the planning process. How? Often by injecting the planning process with social and cultural considerations in subtle ways. Accompanying an East End leader on visits to City Council members just before the passage of the plan turned out to be one such way. These meetings were often tense, but council members slowly became convinced that East Enders were indeed serious about the community and that they had a great deal to contribute to the planning process.

In fact, the community did succeed, to a large degree, in putting the people back into the plan, but not without the Herculean efforts of the East End leadership and residents described in Chapter 7. A provision was included in the plan whereby a percentage of the sale price of market-rate housing would be placed in the Housing Trust Fund. Guidelines for restricting heights and densities of buildings as well as a system of guidelines for environmental quality control (EQ), the first in the city, it should be noted, went into the plan.

As we will see, as the plan entered the implementation phase, these guidelines were used both for and against community interests. Witness the fights over the Lewiston affordable housing project (described in Chapter 9), when the developers attempted to use the EQ guidelines to eliminate affordable housing by increasing its costs, again under the guise of "concern" for the community.

For now, suffice it to say that the context for our research changed markedly after the East End Riverfront Community Development Plan was passed in May 1992. The community's leadership began to focus not on the passage of the plan by the City Council, but on implementing it. It was by no means a given that the plan would fly through City Council. Several on council regarded it as an antidevelopment, not a development, plan.

There had been many plans for the East End in the past (see the timeline), and the community was acutely aware of the fact that virtually all previous city-generated development plans were sitting on shelves or in filing cabinets. Prior to the passage of the plan by City Council, the president of the East End Area Council called researchers and advocates to a series of "brainstorming meetings" to create the "Recipe for Successful Implementation." This recipe, passed by the EEAC on April 27, 1992, the day before the plan was to be voted on by City Council, not only was a way of marshalling support for the plan in the East End, it also sent a strong signal of community solidarity to the city, thus building a strong base for implementation into the plan itself before it was passed. City Council passed the plan on May 28, 1992, a month later than originally scheduled.

Our research has been ongoing—always focused on the practice of community and always connected in some way to one or another provision of the East End Riverfront Community Development Plan. The research itself has lasted much longer than any of us ever anticipated.

While we changed the research methodology substantially as well as the direction and focus of the research, its overall aims have remained constant: (1) to gather data that would strengthen the voices of the community in maintaining its identity and integrity; and (2) to work with East End leaders to place the community in a stronger position to secure needed services and resources, including health, housing, and a community heritage center.

Researchers and advocates sit on community boards and committees. The presence of researchers and advocates on these boards serves to facilitate communication between and among the many people who have a stake in the preservation of the East End. Researchers and advocates can position themselves to serve the community in a manner that is comfortable for and useful to residents. Because all board members have equal votes on all issues, class and power differentials are softened when everyone is sitting around the same table in the community. Differential skills can also be combined more easily on community boards. East End leaders run meetings in a much livelier, friendlier, and more efficient manner than do university professors or administrators. More gets accomplished in one hour in many East End meetings than I have ever seen in weeks by meetings of university people. Time is indeed at a premium when market forces are at your door and work schedules, family obligations, and meetings must be dovetailed. When East Enders control meetings, posturing and pontificating are not tolerated; people are cut off, told their time is up, that they are straying from the issue.

It quickly became clear that there was little, if any, documentation of real life in the East End. The abundance of stereotypes, power maneuvers, colonization attempts blinded even the well intentioned to the day-to-day struggles and triumphs. Chapter 4 is one attempt to capture and portray those aspects of life that rarely appear in the social science record.

The East End Study Project was not without its stresses and strains. Sometimes the research became too intense for the students; sometimes it was simply too time consuming. The people who did the best fieldwork often had the most difficulty processing their field experiences. That first summer, the field team spent endless hours, often long into the night, working through the issues connected with doing fieldwork "at home." Scheduling problems at times seemed insurmountable. Students measure time in finite increments; they control time; they plan it. Dovetailing student time frames with life in the East End requires skill and patience. There are so many constraints and unpredictables involved in people's lives—sick children, doctors' appointments for the elderly, visits from home health nurses, and friends in need of help. Students were also worried about their own gut reactions. They did not want to be judgmental; at the same time, they found themselves having difficulty adjusting to the noises, smells, and what they perceived to be the sensory overload of the East End. The trucks on Eastern Avenue do make it difficult to hear yourself think sometimes. East End humor and the unconditional care that East Enders give one another, but especially children and the elderly, were noticed especially by the students; so were storytelling, oratorical, and writing skills. For a community that had been labeled underdeveloped, "illiterate," and uneducated, there was certainly a great deal being articulated. Later, when students better understood East End politics, they were amazed at the sophistication of East Enders' strategies and their sheer talent and sense of commitment.

East End residents welcomed the students warmly, but when a community resident would ask: "How come we have not seen so and so in such a long time?" I would have to explain, rather lamely, that so and so was off doing her student teaching or was cloistered in the library writing her dissertation or working on her master's thesis. In a community in which universities with a capital "U" are perceived as imposing symbols of wealth and power, my explanations were feeble, at best. I personally felt that it would benefit the students' academic work to maintain some manageable level of involvement in the community; many of them did. At the very least, I felt it would provide them some hold on the real world.

The research process in communities like the East End is not at all clear-cut or simple. Research requires advocacy, but advocacy is complicated, time consuming, and frustrating. Much of what one learns as an advocate is probably unpublishable or is a serious breach of confidentiality. At the same time, the confidence revealed in the heat of a power struggle indicates strength, resiliency, analytical powers, and a host of other compelling aspects of practicing community.

6 THE CULTURAL ECONOMY OF THE EAST END

Householding among Kin and Community

The cultural economy of the East End must be understood as a local economy that is embedded in community practices without being confined to the community. This means that East End economy simultaneously looks inward and outward. The community practice of householding maintains East Enders by using resources found both inside and outside the community and from both the formal and the informal economies.

In 1990, when I published a book about livelihood in rural Kentucky entitled *The Livelihood of Kin: Making Ends Meet "the Kentucky Way,"* I didn't understand the implications of the Kentucky way (as a pattern of householding)—neither its widespread applicability nor its potential for variations on common themes. One of the central concepts in that book was multiple livelihood strategies that are connected by householding, that is, the idea that making ends meet involves members of large extended kin networks working in several economic spheres throughout the life course in both simultaneous and sequential patterns. Wage labor in factories combines with other livelihood strategies—off-farm employment, subsistence farming, cash cropping, and flea marketing—in an informal cash-generating strategy. Cooperation among kin is essential to the success of multiple livelihood strategies, as these strategies creatively use and vigorously resist dependency on capitalism.

Cooperation among kin is essential to the success of multiple livelihood strategies. The concept of householding was created by economic historian Karl Polanyi (1944) to describe material provisioning processes at the margins of state systems. In Kentucky, the pattern of householding consists of a series of complicated and interconnected strategies for making a living in different economic sectors, formal and informal, rural and urban (Halperin 1994a). Cash cropping, for example, is one of several strategies that operate alongside wage labor in factories and unpriced labor: family members working on their own or relatives' farms produce both subsistence and cash crops. Family members also generate cash by selling goods in flea markets (marketplaces); they may trade goods with other vendors in the flea markets, in which case, there is no cash exchanged and no official record of the transaction. The crux of the matter is that families combine their resources (cash, labor, land, and capital) and allocate these resources in intricate ways that distribute resources among members of extended kin networks. Thus, there is circularity to the pattern of householding. The goal of the familial economy is not to move up the social ladder, but, rather, to make ends meet by keeping the kin network intact through everyday, ongoing livelihood strategies in a variety of sectors.

In 1996, as I was rereading *The Livelihood of Kin,* a strange feeling of familiarity came over me. I felt as though I were reading about the East End. Why? I asked myself. Are we talking about communities and parallel patterns in rural and urban economies? To some degree the answer is yes. Are we talking about common Appalachian patterns or common working-class practices at the margins of nation-states? How do provisioning strategies work in the East End? How useful is the concept of householding?

Many complicated economic processes and combinations of economic processes operate in relation to the livelihoods of East Enders; these cannot be fully understood by examining rates of employment or unemployment. Neither can these livelihood strategies be understood strictly in terms of conventional jobs. In fact, livelihood itself is so embedded in the social and cultural fabric of community life—in practicing community—that it is difficult to determine where to begin speaking of livelihood per se.

Livelihood in the East End is not just about earning a living and making ends meet, although it is that; it is about maintaining the family and the community, about preserving family and community resources and ensuring the ongoing life of working-class culture. For many East Enders, community work (all of which is voluntary) is just as important, if not more important, than work for pay.

This chapter begins with a discussion of the dominant economic pattern in the East End and, I dare say, in most working-class communities in the United States and in other urban parts of the world. This pattern is one I refer to, after Polanyi, as "householding"—very simply a mixed, predominantly noncapitalistic pattern that focuses on the provisioning of the group, in this case, the East End, and the maintenance of kin and neighborhood groups, loosely defined. Provisioning is carried out as a series of circular flows of goods and resources.

I then elaborate on the nature of exchange patterns in the East End by talking about equivalencies, that is, who exchanges what with whom and in what spatial and temporal contexts. I conclude with a discussion of the informal economy.

In order to understand the complexities of livelihood in the East End, I borrow the concept of householding from Polanyi, both because householding seems to describe what is going on in the East End and because it can be used even more broadly to understand the strategies of low-income working-class people who have been facing the deindustrialization of the nation-state. Whether deindustrialization comes in the form of chronic, seasonal layoffs, or whether entire factories are closed, as was the case for a large manufacturing plant in Norwood, Ohio, just outside of Cincinnati and about three miles from the East End, householding persists. It has remained a steadfast pattern that has gotten people through hard times. Householding is particularly useful for understanding how East Enders simultaneously adapt and resist postindustrial capitalism in the 1990s. It takes certain forms in rural contexts;[1] its basic pattern becomes transformed and intensified in the city, especially in times of severe economic stress.

Householding is one of Polanyi's most important and potentially most widely applicable, concepts.[2] For Polanyi (1944: 53), "householding has nothing in common either with the motive of gain or with the institutions of markets." It is a nonmarket, noncapitalistic principle that can operate in the midst of a market economy, however (p. 53): "Its pattern is the closed group, whether the very different entities of the family or the settlement . . . formed the self-sufficient unit, the principle was invariably the same, namely, that of producing and storing for the satisfaction of the wants of the members of the group."

In the East End, informal economic activities, the subject of the third section of this chapter, must be understood as one component in the pattern of householding. By informal economy, I mean all economic processes outside of the mainstream economy (see Halperin 1994a, 1996). Householding also provides the overarching framework within which exchange relations and processes of forming equivalencies must be understood.

Householding should be thought of as a model or analogy that we use to think with. It helps us understand patterns of pooling and sharing of resources among people living in different households or segments of households that are linked to a common place, in this case, the East End. All of the actual people or households involved need not be located in the East End. That is, participants in householding can be linked by a variety of means: former residence in the East End or kin ties in the East End, to name the two most important.

As a concept, householding has the capacity to deal with complex economic processes and combinations of economic processes. Also, it is designed to handle strategies of resistance to domination by political and economic elites in systems where there are constant tensions between the demands of local and regional elites and the material and cultural requirements of people who stand on the lower rungs of state stratification systems. Further, the concept of householding allows us to link market and nonmarket processes: from resistance to colonialism and domination by the market economy to participation in the informal economy and the priorities placed on maintaining kin networks and a sense of community in the East End.

Without being restricted to actual households, the concept of householding sheds light on the reasons metaphors of family and community are used constantly as codes for class and powerlessness in this Appalachian community. The concept of householding also allows us to understand the limits of both households and nuclear families as provisioning units. To my knowledge, this is the first use of the concept of householding in an urban setting.

As a concept, householding also accommodates fluidity and change. Part of its definition includes the fact that its component parts (both actual households and actual people) are constantly changing and vary according to economic circumstances, life-course position, state of health, and a variety of other features, including rural or urban location. We will see this in the following examples.

Householding in the East End

Karl doesn't want to take advantage of any low interest loans because he'd have to pay professionals to do the job when he can do it himself for much cheaper. "They give you a list of contractors and you have to pick from the list." Karl does all the work on his house; occasionally, when he has something to lift, he has John or a friend help him. Other than that, he does it all.

The goal of the whole process of householding is to provision the group, in this case, the kin networks that are linked to the East End community. Patterns of provisioning are rarely confined to a single household. When an extension cord is run from one household to another when the latter's electricity has been cut off, the link between households is very tangible. The favor will be returned at some time without clear expectations of the form the return will take. It may, in fact, be returned to a relative of the person who provided the electricity. The provisioning process, as I have said, is accomplished by means of circular flows of goods, services, and resources—food, cash, housing, child care, rides, automobiles, to name just a few of the essentials. Rarely is account taken of how much a person contributes to the householding process. Only in instances in which a person never contributes is that person labeled a "taker" or a "user." So-called users become too demanding and people avoid contact so as not to be "trapped" into doing something such as providing a trip to the store or a ride to or from work. In fact, any East Ender will tell you that everyone in the East End has someone they have to avoid so as not to be taken advantage of. Unfortunately, as one East Ender told me, "sometimes it's your own children that you have to avoid. Sometimes it's parents." Judy, for example, receives social security disability that comes to her because she has lead poisoning. It took some time for the family to receive Judy's disability. Judy's back paycheck was over $10,000. Her mother takes it and uses it to pay their rent. Other East Enders consider Judy's mother to be a "taker."

Normally, however, householding operates within several different kinds of units or groups: the extended kin network; the immediate neighborhood of unrelated East Enders, blacks and whites; the neighborhood at large. This last is rarer and usually applies to community work. The important point is that the worth of a person in the East End is judged primarily according to whether he or she is someone "you can count on" or "who would do anything for you."

The coordination, timing, and scheduling of the various elements of the householding process are critical for the process to work. Yet they can be intricate and risky at the same time. In the East End, coordination involves many different systems, including having East Enders work downtown or across the river in Kentucky in multinational corporations or their representatives (these firms have very rigid schedules with strict rules and requirements for time off from work); flea markets, AFDC, social security disability, part-time wage work, seasonally variable day work, and construction work. Bad weather prevents many people from working at almost any outdoor job. In the East End, outdoor jobs include, among others, bricklaying, construction, and landscaping. One young woman who works for a large produce wholesaler as an accountant risks her job every time she takes a day off from work, as she does fairly often to take a child to the doctor, to tend to a sick relative, or to attend a child's school function. One mother who works in maintenance was "written up" because she missed work to attend her child's end-of-the-year school program. Still another mother, who works for one of the largest uniform manufacturing companies in the country, relies on an East End grandmother to take her child to the doctor. Since she periodically is placed on "mandatory overtime," during which she works a twelve-hour day, her own mother, who is quite elderly and who already helps her with many daily chores, must have additional help. There are many such working mothers in the East End, including relatives who work in the same factories so that they can share rides to work.

Householding and Appalachian Communities

Householding is not new to Appalachian culture. Historically, rural Appalachian economies have consisted of sets of family-based subsistence farms designed to provision the family group with the material means necessary for survival. In 1880, Appalachia contained a greater concentration of noncommercial family farms than any other area in the United States.[3] The primary purpose of these family farms was to meet the direct consumption needs of the extended family, not to generate a profit. While householding operated in rural Appalachia within both large and small units that had various residence and settlement patterns in different environments, mountainous and nonmountainous, the aim of householding remained the maintenance of the family.[4] In the deep rural parts of Kentucky,[5] householding takes the following form: people marshall their family resources—primarily land and labor, but also tools, information, transportation, goods, and services—to construct livelihood strategies that serve to maintain the members of the family network. In rural Appalachia, small, family-run subsistence farms, operating relatively self-sufficiently, historically have been the primary units of livelihood. Often these farms were located on family land occupied by households of related family members. As children married, they established separate households on family land.

In the East End, the pattern of householding persists, but with many variations and transformations of the original rural pattern. Householding operates at political and material levels, that is, to provision the group as well as to maintain the life and well-being of the community. Maintaining the community through neighborhood politics is just as important as livelihood. In reality, community and livelihood are linked in complex ways. I will deal with the political aspects of householding at the end of this chapter, but suffice it to say here that householding at the political level also provisions the groups because it includes managing the preservation of the community against market forces. This management includes administering a housing preservation fund, seeing to the health of East Enders both within and outside the community health center, running the community urban redevelopment corporation, and creating the heritage center.

Householding operates within East End boundaries, but it is not confined to the East End. It branches out to include households in the nearby Ohio communities of Mount Washington, Milford, New Richmond, to name a few, as well as to parts of rural Kentucky just across the river. Also, householding involves sharing of work tasks, including childrearing. People have their primary work tasks, but they also create flexibility and variety for one another by passing tasks around from one family member to another, depending on the task and according to the age and life-course position of individuals. Men as well as women take care of children. Children sleep in the homes of their parents, often with co-sleeping arrangements, but they also stay with grandparents and other relatives on a regular basis. Here, too, grandchildren will share beds with their grandparents.

Nuclear families often maintain separate households, but there are almost always temporary additions—for several days, months, or even years. These additional household residents may be kin or neighbors, or some combination. When children become more or less permanent residents in neighborhood households, the adults of that household take on the roles of parents, even though a formal adoption never actually takes place and the child maintains contact with his or her "real" (biological or official) mom and dad.

Support provided by relatives of East Enders is essential for the maintenance of households whether or not the relatives actually reside in the household. Such support maintains a segment of the kinship network that may, over time, live in a variety of households, in or outside of the East End. Kin and, in many instances, neighbors (who may also be kin) are expected to help one another as needed. Taking a night job, taking on a part-time job, selling or trading an appliance or a car are just some of the ways East Enders obtain additional cash, or render cash unnecessary. We can see, then, in householding a pattern that consists of multiple and interconnected livelihood strategies associated with both capitalist and noncapitalist economic institutions (including bingo, the lottery, and card playing). Families combine their resources and allocate them in intricate ways. In times of emergency, when the river floods, for example, householding requires the whole community as its unit. Any available space, public or private, is available and shared as storage space for belongings that must be moved to higher ground. Such spaces range from several rooms on someone's second floor to the large unused space that is waiting to be rehabbed in the Pendleton Heritage Center (see Chapter 13).

The stories of householding are all different, but the basic patterning is the same. The patterns of householding that are based in but not confined to the East End come in many forms. Large or small numbers of kin may be involved at any given time; some kin may live close by; others may live in the region. The size of the kin group and the particular individuals involved in householding at any given time are variable. All East Enders have, in some way or another, been involved in householding; this participation is part of what it means to be a real East Ender and is a very important part of practicing community. Outsiders may participate in hierarchically ordered patterns of patron-client relationships, but they are not linked to the patterns of householding. Householding consists of sets of relationships among equals.

The following are three very different examples of householding. The first is a pattern that operates within a large extended family of official and unofficial kin. The second involves the whole community—or at least significant segments of it in a pattern of householding that occurs once a year at a community reunion. The third involves a large extended family of official kin. This family is so large that it is almost a community unto itself.

Carla Robertson's Householding Network

I was in the River Inn the first time, and . . . Penny's grandmother, Eileen Sands used to come in there every day. One day Mabel came down with her, with the kids, and um, I met Mabel. And, I didn't know her, you know, I didn't really know her, but I got to be pretty good friends . . . with Eileen's daughter Lisa who was like two, four, five, six years younger than I was, but she was pregnant, and when she was eight months pregnant her mom and dad threw her out of the house. And . . . she had to come live with my family because I was at, I was living in an apartment across the street from my parents' house. . . . I just took her home. I mean, she come into the River Inn . . . and she was all upset and I said "What's wrong?" and she said, "My mom locked me out." And I said "Well, we'll get you back in." She said "No, she told me not to come back." I didn't believe this, you know, and went down the street and Eileen just opened the upstairs winda, and being the kind, gentle lady she was, dumped hot water out the top of the winda, so. Needless to say, she [Lisa] went home with my family, and she stayed there until after Tim was born, and I had Tim till he was almost six years old. Cause Lisa wasn't ready to be a mother yet. And she came back when he was almost six years old and she took him away from me. And I, in those almost seven years, I got pretty close to Mabel and her family . . . she took Tim back when he was six years old. And now Tim is living in Florida with his stepfather since he was 15½ years old.

Penny McDonald takes out life insurance on her informally adopted mother (Carla Robertson), a forty-six-year-old white Appalachian life-long resident of the community and a fifth-generation East Ender, and on her adoptive grandmother, Betsy Robertson. Penny works as an administrative secretary in a major corporation in Cincinnati. Her husband, Geoffrey, is a construction worker. While Penny was in grade school and high school, and even through her early stages of marriage and motherhood, her adoptive mother, Carla, held a variety of wage-earning jobs (factory worker, convenience-store manager, barmaid). When Penny was in the primary and secondary grades, Carla relocated temporarily to a suburban area with an excellent school system to avoid sending Penny to the Cincinnati public schools. Carla is very proud of the fact that Penny graduated at the top of her class. Penny attended two years at the local technical college.

Carla is now back in the East End and spends her days taking care of her grandbabies and her great-nieces and great-nephew. These are Penny's children and the children of Carla's nephew, Al, Jr. (her brother Al's son). These five children are all under the age of five. Carla uses

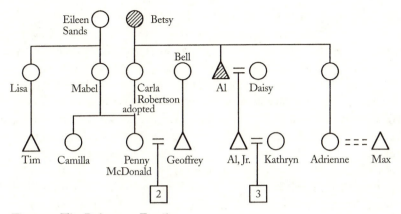

Figure 9. The Robertson Family

both Penny's apartment and her own to watch the children. In summer, she favors Penny's apartment because it is air-conditioned and has an outdoor pool. Carla often spends the night there as well. Periodically, Penny's sister, Camilla, Geoffrey's mother, Bell, or Penny's biological mother, Mabel, watch the children. Bell works at the bakery and Camilla is viewed as only marginally competent to take care of children. If Carla is ill, however, or if she has an appointment with her doctor, Mabel, Bell, or Camilla will be called upon.

Shortly after Carla's mother passed away, two of her kin (her niece Adrienne and her nephew Al, Jr.) and their families moved into Carla's apartment building in the East End. This was Carla's second apartment, which she moved into after a house her mother owned was destroyed. Al, Jr., moved from Norwood with his wife, Kathryn, and their three children, and Adrienne moved from Fairfax. Before this, Carol Conrad, a lifelong East Ender who had been abused by men, beginning with her father and continuing with numerous boyfriends, and abandoned by her mother, had temporarily resided in Carla's apartment. Carol helped Carla with her sick mother in exchange for Carla's protection from her abusive boyfriend and help watching her children while she worked at the local convenience store. Carol moved out when she chose her boyfriend's affections over Carla's protection.

Kathryn and Al, Jr., both work full time, she as a cafeteria worker and he as a car mechanic, a job he obtained from Carla's long-term relationship with Bob Church, neighbor and landlord in the 1900 block of Eastern Avenue. Bob Church's son Mickey runs a landscaping business, where Al has now obtained a job. Carla watches Al's three children during the day, unless it rains, in which case Al can be called upon to watch the children. From time to time, especially in summer, the children spend time with Kathryn's mother, who lives near Memphis. Daisy, Al, Jr.'s mother, and Carla's sister-in-law and wife of her brother Al, Sr., thanks Carla for relieving her of the large grocery bills she was paying when Al, Jr., and his family were living in her house in Batavia. Daisy gives Carla a hundred dollars or so every few weeks. At the same time, Al's and Kathryn's wages contribute to Carla's rent and other expenses. They pay half the rent and cover gas, electricity, telephone, and groceries. Carla's other expenses are covered by Penny and by the small amounts of cash Carla is able to generate by typing invoices for a local business. When her mother was alive, she received life insurance and a pension arranged by Carla's father.

Carla's niece Adrienne (Carla's sister's daughter) moved upstairs from Carla just after Carla's mother died. Adrienne helps Carla with the children when she is not working at the nearby convenience store. It is not uncommon to see Adrienne playing with Al and Kathryn's children on Carla's porch. Adrienne has a boyfriend, but no children; her boyfriend, Max, plays on a neighborhood softball team coached by Carla. From time to time, Adrienne and Carla "have words," usually over some matter pertaining to the children. Other services are traded as well. If Kathryn needs her car worked on, her cousin Don will fix her car and she will clean his house. Don will also fix cars for neighbors.

When the landlord decided to tear down the house, Carla moved temporarily to her adopted daughter and son-in-law's place. After a few months, when tensions between Carla and her son-in-law became too great, Carla moved in with a friend, Julie, and her sick father. Carla and Julie exchanged elder care for rent until Julie was fired from her job. Since Carla's services were no longer needed, she moved into her own place, a one-bedroom apartment in Newport near Penny. On the very first night in her new place, both of her granddaughters spent the night with her.

Elaine Winters

Elaine is a black Appalachian in her early fifties. She has spent her entire life in the East End, where her father worked on the railroad. Her mother, who passed away in 1995, was one of the oldest members of the Mount Carmel Baptist Church. Elaine owns a home in Avondale, an

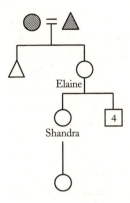

Figure 10. The Winters Family

African American neighborhood in northeastern Cincinnati. Her eldest daughter, Shandra, holds the title to her house in the East End. Shandra works two jobs, often lends Elaine her car, and provides her with cash when she needs it to supplement her earnings from her part-time job as a librarian in Kennedy Heights. Periodically, Elaine borrows her brother's car. Before her mother passed away, Elaine spent time sitting with her, a job she shared with her brothers. She brings her granddaughter to meetings in the community; the child always has a supply of books, crayons, and toys and never says a word.

Elaine is in charge of East End Day, the yearly black family reunion in the East End. Relatives come from as far away as Texas and Florida to attend the reunion. Elaine knows everyone and acts as the hostess for the party. She is Miss Elaine to children and young adults. Younger people in the East End call older women Miss So and So, a term of endearment and respect used by kin and non-kin alike. Kin terms abound at the reunion, and Elaine refers to Miss Billie as Grandma Ada and explains that it is "what everybody calls her." Elaine cooks an enormous amount of chicken and ribs on a huge grill on her front porch, and there are tubs of potato salad, baked beans, and soft drinks available. Her kitchen is an oven on this June day, and it makes the already sweltering afternoon seem air conditioned as one exits her kitchen. She proudly and generously distributes the delicious food to her family and her friends (black and white) from in and outside of the neighborhood.

East End Day is clearly about being a real East Ender and about practicing community. Deep yellow, almost gold, T-shirts with East End Reunion written on them are dated '93 and '94 so they will be good for two years. Royal blue shirts announce East End Day in white letters. The children play along the banks with the river as their backdrop. Fathers hold the very small ones, and Elaine comments that a little boy looks exactly like his father did when he was a child. She also tells a sixteen-year-old: "You are gettin' too grown." The elderly people walk slowly from place to place, one ninety-year-old woman on her daughter's arm. As I was sitting with Miss Vivienne and her nieces playing cards, a man came over, looked directly at me, and asked in a very kindly voice: "Are you an East Ender?" When I told him I was first generation, he nodded.

Elaine has many helping relationships with people in the East End. She ensures that her neighbor Ernest has food on a daily basis. He is an elderly African American who has serious physical disabilities and is alcohol dependent. She is very close to Fritz, a white man almost twenty years her junior, who helps her out with general handyman tasks. Elaine and Fritz engage in a great deal of sexual joking, something that everyone finds amusing, given the difference in their ages. Elaine is also close to Carla Robertson, who is one of the people she can count on for help. The relationships between Elaine, Fritz, and Carla are founded on their long-term residence and the longevity of their families in the East End. The fact that Elaine is black and Fritz and Carla are white is discussed frequently and is always regarded positively.

The Strongs

"They all know that they can go to James and Megan." James and Megan Strong, now in their seventies, sit at their dining room table showing us their family albums. Their memories document the history of the community from the arrival of Megan's father from Germany in 1925 right up to the present. As the afternoon wears on, the grandchildren trickle in from school. Around five o'clock, Kim, Megan and James's daughter, appears carrying a large covered pot and takes it into the kitchen. Megan starts to apologize for all the confusion, but there doesn't seem to be any. The children get their snacks. Every once in a while, other kin check in by phone.

The Strong family has been in the East End for several generations. James has been an activist in the neighborhood for more than thirty years. His name can be found on East End planning documents from the seventies. He was instrumental in getting the addition built at the LeBlond Recreation Center and has been part of the leadership structure of the East End Area Council. He is also a founding member of the Development Corporation and, most recently, has been an active mem-

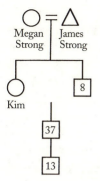

Figure 11. The Strong Family

ber of the Pendleton Heritage Center Board and the Plan Implementation Team. He gives generously of his time and wisdom.

Family is the Strongs' top priority. While a few of their nine children live in other Cincinnati neighborhoods, one child lives in their house, and two others occupy separate dwellings directly across the street. A son and his family live next door and a niece lives within shouting distance. You can find James Strong on any weekend gazing at the river. Usually, he's sitting with a family member, a brother-in-law or a grandchild. He spent most of his life running a boat-hauling business that took boats in and out of the Ohio. In the 1950s, his "boat dock" included a seaplane base. On holidays, the whole extended family comes for a huge dinner. One cannot help but wonder where nine children, their spouses, thirty-seven grandchildren, and thirteen great-grandchildren will fit in this house. Few houses are designed to accommodate that many people. Yet, somehow there is a sense of almost infinite space and spaciousness in James and Megan's house. Maybe it is their unlimited energy and warmth that creates such feelings of expansiveness in their small and cozy house.

Summary

We can see that the three examples of householding are very different. The groups themselves are differently constituted and differently sized; nonetheless, the patterns of provisioning the group (householding) are equally viable.

In the first example, Carla Robertson's householding network, the structure of the group is very large and complex. As members of the group move through the lifecourse, their needs and resources (educational, medical, social) change. Different segments of the group will relocate in order to accommodate a given situation. Education, for example, is very important. A parent will move out of the city, temporarily, in order to find a better school system. Small houses and apartments miraculously expand to accommodate additional family members. When cash in the city is short, the resources in the country can be called upon. Children can move in easily with grandparents. The proximity of relatives is important not just for social support, but for combinations of livelihood strategies that can be shared. Proximity of kin may be only temporary, however, as people move to gain better access to educational and job resources. Yearly family reunions pull the group together in one place, but only very briefly.

In the second example, Elaine Winters, we see householding writ large, that is, the group is really the whole black community, which itself consists of many self-contained, but interrelated householding networks that function very much like Carla Robertson's, and, indeed, like most of the families described in Chapter 3.

The last example of householding, the Strongs, also involves a very large group, but one of official kin. In many ways, the Strongs provide the mode of householding for East End families. The structure of the group is multigenerational and regionally based. The extended family is primary. It is not surprising that the Strongs and the Churches are in daily contact as families, for they are almost replicas of one another.

In all three examples, there are individuals who can be identified as key players. These individuals coordinate the provisioning strategies, but they do so in concert with other members of the group in complementary ways. No single person is in charge on a permanent basis. Rather, different individuals take on different responsibilities, depending on the situation. The division of labor is very complex—gender, intergenerational relationships, friendships, and neighborliness figure importantly at different times and in different contexts in provisioning these groups.

Householding is a provisioning strategy historically known to maintain groups—households, families, communities at the margins (lower echelons) of state stratification systems. In the Third World, householding operates in rural villages that must subsist while paying taxes to the state; householding also works in urban barrios to maintain families who are struggling in a cash-dependent economy. In the East End, householding is a provisioning strategy that is also a strategy to resist dependency on both the market economy and the state, for to rely on them would sacrifice family, community, and working-class identity itself. Welfare is only a very last resort.

Cultural Economies and Equivalencies: Resistance, Local Autonomy, and Appalachian Culture

Any practice is simultaneously economic and symbolic, in reality economy and culture march along intertwined with one another. (García Canclini 1993: 11)

This section elaborates on a concept from economic history, the concept of equivalencies, to understand several facets of working-class culture and community in the East End in particular and in Appalachian culture in general. These facets include exchanges of material goods and needed services, on the one hand, and donations of large amounts of time devoted to maintaining and enhancing community, on the other. Time spent doing community work is not easily measured; neither is it recognized or even acknowledged by the power structure as a legitimate form of work. In the East End, the amount of time spent maintaining the community as East Enders know it (that is, hard-line East Enders, as one city staffer put it) is enormous and includes time spent in meetings as well as time spent in informal groupings and on the phone. Often, the distinction between an informal grouping and a meeting is a fuzzy one. Sometimes what appears to be a meeting is actually a therapy or support session or a forum for the exchange of material and symbolic resources.

We can use the concept of equivalencies to understand on many levels how exchanges operate. Equivalencies describe how much and what kind of a particular good or service (broadly defined) is appropriate (that is, expected) in a given context. The concept of equivalencies is important for understanding the East End because, like many community practices, it is very flexible. For example, equivalencies do not require that transactions involve equal amounts or values; nor do they require that transactions or exchanges occur at the same time, or even at points close in time. Equivalencies operate both within and between different groups, albeit differently; that is, they can be thought of as operating among members, real East Enders, for example, or between East Enders and outsiders.

The most important, and the most powerful, point about equivalencies is that they are generic, that is, a culturally and institutionally neutral way of thinking about some key elements of exchange. Karl Polanyi first identified equivalencies as a generic alternative to price, which he saw as only one form of equivalency, a form set by forces of supply and demand in a capitalistic price-making market system. Polanyi recognized that prices set in such a market system were different, that is, subject to different equivalency formation processes from the prices set in localized marketplaces or in other contexts, such as communities, for that matter. He also saw, of course, that many goods, services, and resources were not subject to prices in any form, yet they were parts of organized formal and informal systems of exchange. One can begin to see that the implications of the concept of equivalencies are wide-ranging, particularly in contexts such as the East End, where the resurgence and elaboration of informal economies and other informal ways of doing things—institutions, if you will—can be seen as modes of resistance to capitalism in postindustrial states.

I should emphasize that conceptualizing equivalencies as a generic concept is different from saying that the problem of equivalencies is universal and can be understood identically in all cultures. Equivalency-formation processes (the processes that form or set equivalencies) exist in all cultures, but the processes by which equivalencies are formed will vary in different cultures and in different institutional contexts.

East End Equivalencies

I'll now turn to equivalency-formation processes—who exchanges what, with whom, how often, and with what constraints and restrictions in the East End. I should note that what I shall describe here is related to, but not the same as, householding. There are overlapping principles and processes involved, but the levels of interaction transcend the material domain of culture; in many respects, the transactions cannot be understood solely in material terms.

In the East End, equivalency-formation processes are very complicated. They involve highly personal relationships and subtleties, but they are not idiosyncratic. They are rule governed, but the rules take a very long time to learn; they change, and they are subject to nuances that are very difficult to detect, in part because of the strength of the informal economy and also because equivalencies are embedded in structures that are in the process of being built. That is, in a community that has been subject to so much neglect, physical deterioration, and displacement, one of the main tasks of community work is to maintain community through institution building and the resurrection of democratic principles and procedures in local government.

On one level, equivalencies are about the exchange of goods and services that are part of the complex provisioning strategy that I have called householding. But equivalency-formation processes also occur outside of householding. Exchange between unrelated individuals requires equivalencies that are different from those between and among kin. But keep in mind that unofficial (practical) kinship is just as important, if not more important, than official biological kinship. Provisioning of family and community with the material means of livelihood is essential, but, at least ideally, livelihood is not to be accomplished or sought at the expense of working-class identity and autonomy. By the same token, householding is not a strategy of upward mobility, but, rather, a strategy of maintenance—maintenance of culture and class through community. East Enders will take on additional responsibilities for children or for members of the community who are ill, for example, to the detriment of their jobs and their earnings capacity. Skipping days of work or reducing work hours is very common. When two young children were in need of care, their aunt and great-aunt cut back on work hours and on community board participation. When an East End young woman and potential community leader became severely depressed, an older leader cut her work hours and missed some critical board meetings to look after her. If anything, householding prevents individuals from garnering resources. In this sense, it is a classic leveling mechanism.

How do equivalency-formation processes work in the East End? A few general features of exchange are followed by an example of layers of equivalency formation processes:

(1) Exchanges within families and within the community are informal but, at the same time, highly structured along the lines of householding.
(2) Exchanges are ongoing and constant and operate in a circular fashion with gifts and chains of reciprocity, within the same generation, and among members of different generations.
(3) The largest unit within which exchanges occur is the community, sometimes broadly, sometimes narrowly conceived as neighborhood and kin networks or combinations of these.
(4) Exchanges operate on several levels. They are often not what

they seem in that credit obtained in one sphere of community life, say, the material sphere, can be paid back in another
sphere, but in a nonmaterial form.

In other words there are material and symbolic exchanges that are not
primarily about livelihood, survival, or subsistence, but about family
and political (community and class) loyalty and working-class identity.
These exchanges and their equivalency-formation processes cross lines
of race, gender, and age.

A Model of Equivalencies in Working-Class Culture

The following example provides a model for equivalency-formation
processes in the East End and, perhaps with some modifications, for
equivalency-formation processes in intact working-class communities.
This is a model because it indicates, after analysis, the ways in which
equivalency-formation processes operate at several levels (the individual
material level, the community political level, and the larger class level,
which overrides differences of race and gender). Equivalencies are embedded in working-class culture in multiple ways.

In 1994, Fritz told me that Elaine was depressed because she could not
afford to give gifts at Christmas. He explained that he was going to buy
her a gift, but that "it is not about that." Rather, he explained that she
was "always there," that he could call her anytime. "That is what it is
about. I can count on her."

Fritz, a thirty-eight-year-old white Appalachian, and Elaine, a fifty-
four-year-old black Appalachian/African American woman, have indeed exchanged many material goods and services. He has fixed her car
and arranged for her to purchase a car, moved appliances and fixed them.
He kept her house key and let her in whenever she forgot her own, which
was quite often. She, in turn, visited him, brought food, and invited him
to the annual East End Day. Formally, he managed a local business and
she earned $75 per week as a part-time secretary in a predominantly
African American community some distance from the East End, but
within the city limits of Cincinnati. She owns property there.

Another African American woman and her husband, Doris and C.A.,
also keep in regular contact with Fritz, and, although their exchanges of
material goods are limited, they visit regularly. C.A. walks past Fritz's
workplace at least once a day, stops in, chats, and checks on Fritz when
he is low. At any given time of the day or night, it was not uncommon

to see blacks and whites, old and young, mingling in and around Fritz's workplace, obtaining goods and services, information, gossip. When Pearl Clark's son was severely injured, she came first to Fritz. Pearl describes herself as old enough to be Fritz's mother.

THE POLITICS OF EQUIVALENCIES

Fritz and Elaine both chair important community boards, as does Doris. Fritz and Elaine sit on one another's boards, as do Doris and Elaine. All three sit on the East End Riverfront Community Urban Redevelopment Corporation (EERCURC), for example. Their commitment to affordable housing, including that for seniors, is unconditional. They are ecstatic when the board's staff person gives such an impressive report to the Plan Implementation Team that even the developers cannot oppose the latest efforts to build affordable housing. In fact, at the April 1997 meeting of the Implementation Team, all attempts by developers to block affordable housing failed miserably, and the staffer was complimented by the chair, who is a retired corporate executive.

Fritz, Elaine, and Doris are part of a very talented and energetic coterie of grassroots leaders who share strong community ties. All were born and raised in the East End and spend countless hours on community work, including sitting on city boards and committees and spending time testifying before City Council and meeting with various members of city government. In addition, all three, from 1990 to 1997, played important leadership roles in the East End Area Council, the community council that is the major contact point with the city. By sitting on one another's boards, they are giving and sharing time for community work. The material and social costs of this work are high, because they include time spent away from cash-generating work and from family. Community work is political labor and there are also political costs. The elite faction goes after strong grassroots leaders in multiple ways—legally, politically, emotionally—and tries to silence their voices at City Hall.

I now want to return to Fritz's statement about his exchanges with Elaine. Initially, he seems to be talking about altruism and selflessness, and, indeed, on one level, his behavior and Elaine's are extremely generous. He expects no return; neither does she. Similarly, C.A. and Doris give their support to Fritz unconditionally. On another level, however, equivalency-formation processes are driven by ties to community and class; community, although very important as a homeplace, is also a code word for class, as in the expression: "We are members of the East End family." Here "family" substitutes for "class." Grassroots leaders exchange and share time on community projects and on the sheer maintenance of community, endless hours in meetings in the East End and at City Hall. In part, these community-based and class-driven equivalency-formation processes are a response to powerlessness; in part, they are also a strategy of resistance to price-making equivalencies under capitalism and to the people who hold the market system dear. Community labor is noncommoditized. It is political work with economic ramifications.

When the developers in the community tried to rewrite the bylaws of the Community Council to "turn the East End Community Council into the East End country club" by instituting selectivity and exclusion in membership, Fritz chaired the grassroots group that worked to return the bylaws to their original democratic form. Among the issues that received the most attention were membership in the EEAC and community board composition boundaries. As of this writing, the issue of bylaws for the EEAC still has not been resolved. To orchestrate a response to the elite faction's bylaws, breakfast meetings, requiring food, child care, and meeting space were provided by grassroots leaders. The meetings of the grassroots bylaws committee often lasted three to four hours as strategies were created to maintain the East End community as East Enders know it.

The Urban Informal Economy in Cincinnati's East End

The urban informal economy, although not called that, is extremely important in the East End, as it increasingly is for all working-class communities at the margins of postindustrial states. East Enders—young and old, black and white, male and female—work and get paid "under the table." Virtually every extended-family network has members involved in the informal economy. How much of the East End GDP is generated in the informal economy is difficult to calculate, but it is substantial. In many cases, it comprises more than half of the household's income.

There are, in fact, many kinds of informal work arrangements and combinations of formal and informal work arrangements of some longevity in the East End. Jobs are passed on from generation to generation. It is difficult to imagine how life in the East End could perpetuate itself without the informal economy, for work in the informal sector is what provides East Enders with the autonomy and control necessary to maintain working-class culture and community.

Unfortunately, the term "informal economy" often carries a negative valence of black marketing, bootlegging, or illegal drug trading. While these activities certainly go on in the East End and will probably increase as the national and regional economies worsen for working-class people, the illegal elements of the informal economy are not at present the most prevalent or widespread. Here, I want to focus on the traditional, paid-under-the-table informal economy. By that I mean the unofficial, long-standing, but unrecorded income and resource-generating strategies that have existed for East Enders and for other working-class people for many decades—often alongside and in addition to officially recognized sources of income.[6]

Fritz, Chris, and Brenda worked for an absentee owner running a retailing business until it closed in spring 1994. They sold candy and soda that they purchased on their own at large discount supermarkets and were paid by the hour. They kept careful accounts of the goods sold and did their best to cultivate steady customers. People went out of their way to shop there just to have a conversation with Fritz, who also managed the store. Fritz, Chris, and Brenda also owned and managed some rental property within the community. They often bought goods, especially clothes, at the various marketplaces. These goods included work gloves from Little Miami Flea Market and Christmas items from East End Flea Market on Kellog Avenue, just on the edge of the community.

These two marketplaces, Little Miami Flea Market and East End Flea Market, are part of the region's rotating system of periodic marketplaces. They are utilized by East Enders for both buying and selling goods, although more goods are bought than sold there. While these market-places allow East Enders to generate some cash outside of the formal economy, they primarily provide the opportunity to purchase essential items, including food and work clothes, at rates that are lower than almost anywhere else. Little Miami Flea Market and East End Flea Market are among the marketplaces that are closest, geographically and culturally, to the East End. East End Flea Market is on the periphery of the East End itself, and Little Miami Flea Market is in Kentucky just off a major interstate. Little Miami Flea Market is much larger than East End Flea Market and is a major node in the regional system. It houses permanent, indoor stalls as well as temporary, outdoor ones. This means that East Enders can rely on certain vendors to supply work clothes, gloves, and other essentials. East End Flea Market is an intermediate marketplace in the regional system. Intermediate markets not only are smaller, but their pool of vendors is much less stable. Some vendors sell every week; others are less regular. When East Enders cannot find something at East End Flea Market or if the price is too high there, they go to Little Miami Flea Market.

Combining Formal and Informal Sector Jobs

Paul Brooks, a railroad worker for some thirty years, has a stand at the East End Flea Market. He specializes in making shoes, boots, and other leather items, such as belts and wallets. He makes these items in his house or in the back of his van while he is selling. In addition to his leather goods, he collects old railroad memorabilia, such as lanterns, by going to closeouts at other marketplaces. While he does not offer the lanterns and other memorabilia for sale, they represent a considerable investment and they could, of course, be sold if cash were needed. Paul's wife, Pauletta, helps at his stand at East End Flea Market. She deals mainly in ceramics—Santa figurines at Christmas, cookie jars at other times of year. They also sell at the Little Miami Flea Market.

The goods sold at East End Flea Market are quite varied. Mrs. March has "a little bit of everything": clothes, name plates, and little bells. She also cuts keys. Allen and Annie sell at East End Flea Market as an adjunct to their antique business in central Cincinnati. Stained glass is their specialty. One East End resident said: "A lot of people go up there [East End Flea Market]. A lot of stands will let you lay away. There are two stands that lay away toys. People get clothes for kids." Thus, with reference to consumables, the local marketplace is extremely important. Trading among vendors themselves is also very common.

Once a person has an official (taxed) income, the way is clear for additional (untaxed) income to be earned. The reported income shelters the unreported earnings, leaving individuals free to generate substantial amounts of unreported cash without arousing suspicion. For instance, people with regular jobs deliver advertisements door to door. The preparation for delivery often involves groups of people who bag the advertisements and then deliver them on Saturday or late Sunday night. Payment is made according to the number of advertisements in each bag. One former seller revealed the following:

I had two routes . . . all the bags you could hang on the mailboxes. I could make as much as $700 per week. You had to take out your own taxes. Pink pages [a large booklet of ads] are 11 cents per book. One time, we delivered [soda] pop samples. They gave you one can of pop for each house. There's a lot of people who do not want things delivered. We got a lot of pop that way.

One East End woman, who is white with racially mixed children and who has, over the years, experienced employment discrimination that resulted in very low-paying jobs, worked delivering advertisements for sixteen or seventeen years. She'd have many of the neighbors' children out with her; she not only kept the children occupied, she paid them. Within the East End itself, delivery of advertisements starts at one end of the community and goes out to the other, an area that exceeds ten square miles.

Combining Informal Sector Work and Government Assistance

Many women on AFDC also work and do not report their earnings. Cathy spends a good part of her week collecting clothing, kitchen utensils, and odds and ends to sell at East End Flea Market on Saturdays. If items need fixing or cleaning, she must spend time getting them ready to sell. She tucks the earnings away for a variety of purposes: emergencies, toys for her children, food in a pinch. She also earns cash as an unofficial child care provider. Child care can safely be performed by women on various forms of government assistance because payments in cash or in kind can easily be made under the table. Often the reciprocal system is very complex, with the same person providing services to several families. The children come from a combination of kin, neighbors, and friends. In exchange, one family may reciprocate with housing, another with the loan of a car when needed.

Social Security Disability Insurance (SSDI) provides a baseline "official" income on top of which cash can be earned in the informal economy. In fact, all sorts of informal work arrangements are possible, from yard work and landscaping to child care. A person may not be able to perform a repetitive, physically demanding job in a factory, for example, but may be quite capable of mowing lawns, painting houses, taking care of children, or performing clerical work—all unreported.

Informal Food Distribution

Soup kitchens and food pantries have their formal and informal aspects. At the end of each lunch at the soup kitchen, located in the basement of a former church, Jim Cane drives a truck through the East End with meals for people in the neighborhood, many of whom have members employed in both the formal and the informal economies. He gives special attention to the elderly, but he also delivers to large families who are struggling to make ends meet. There is always an abundance of bread and rolls from the Pebble Hill Bakery, which specializes in whole wheat, no-fat products, which Jim distributes freely. He often leaves a pile of leftovers at the River Inn, where people can help themselves without the stigma of having the truck parked in front of their house.

Jim drives his truck back to "the Pit," a combination bar and gambling parlor, a place where many legal and illegal informal economic transactions occur. "There's people in every block who do things people don't know about." The Pit also functions as an informal food distribution center. Food is prepared on outdoor grills and given out for the asking. Outsiders are not welcome here. East Enders, however, especially lifelong residents, use the Pit as a gathering place, informal soup kitchen, and source of goods, both legal and illegal.

Odd jobs are numerous and are usually obtained through neighborhood or kin connections. Income from them is not reported officially. For instance, Rose drives Casey to work on Monday. She cleans houses in a nearby wealthy neighborhood. When Casey is not working, she helps Rose watch children, some of whom are their common grandchildren; she also cleans furiously while she babysits. Gary, Casey's son and Rose's son-in-law, cleans the bank in the evening after his job as a construction worker is over. Rose fills in for him when he is unable to clean. Rose also cleans and types invoices for Wagner's Windows, a company with offices in the East End.

When East Enders speak about odd jobs, they do so tentatively and reluctantly. It is, of course, in a person's best interest to treat these odd jobs as occasional (sporadic) and inconsequential. Such light treatment conceals the real economic importance of these informal work tasks, including selling in marketplaces. The autonomy and control possible in the informal sector cannot even be approached in low-wage, often dangerous, and grueling formal sector manual jobs. The additional cash generated in the informal economy, whether in marketplaces, odd jobs, or other informal means, is not insignificant. Without this cash, families would not survive.

Maintaining a baseline income and health benefits is, more often than not, the main point of regular employment and government assistance, whether AFDC or SSDI. For women with children, "the welfare" is more useful for the medical card it provides than for the meager income it yields. The medical card provides both free health care and free or nearly free medicines.

Gender and the Informal Economy

One of the chief characteristics of the informal sector is that it is flexible. Odd jobs, for example, can be performed at odd times (evenings, weekends)—at times outside of the regular work schedule and in combination with a variety of other tasks.

Flexibility of work tasks, hours, and division of labor is an essential part of working-class adaptations to industrial capitalism—now post-industrial capitalism—in all of its various forms. In the East End, however, where the gendered division of labor is essentially complementary—with men and women sharing the essential tasks of production and social reproduction—the flexibility of the informal sector is just as critical, if not more so, for men as it is for women. Many jobs held by males are seasonal or subject to the vagaries of the weather. In many families, a husband works the night shift and his wife works in the daytime, or vice versa. They share child care. Informal sector work can be fit into the interstices of formal work schedules. For example, work on cars, a predominantly although not exclusively male activity, can be done at many different times and places. Payment for car work is not declared for tax purposes.

Flexibility in scheduling does not mean that this informal work is idiosyncratic or random. In fact, a rather organized and complex division of labor operates within many informal work groups, including community-based male work groups. For example, automobile repair work is shared among groups of East End men. Brothers will help one another. Individuals will specialize in different aspects of car repair. Stevie Watts is the best transmission mechanic. David Soames is the best motor mechanic. Jack Franz is an expert on brakes. If Fritz can't do something, he will send people to David. Many men are generalists. Robert Simms and Jake Dawson can take any car apart and put it back together.[7]

If we recognize that the basic livelihood strategy in the East End (and communities like it) is one of participating in a variety of economic sectors, formal and informal, then we can see that the flexibility of both work and family is very important for everybody. This is one of the reasons that extended families are so important; if one person is not available to do a job, another will, in all likelihood, fill in.

Conclusion

How do we understand the local cultural economy of householding and the place of the formal and informal sectors in the context of culture, class, and power in the East End? Is the informal sector a marginal, stopgap sector? Is it a free enterprise sector? Is it the sector that allows for autonomy and control of working-class life and livelihood that works best in combination with a formal sector job or government income? Is it the route to a formal sector job? For example, working on cars and being paid under the table while one is working for a taxable income elsewhere can develop into a full-time formal and taxable job, given certain conditions. If, for example, the appropriate garage can be found for a reasonable price, then an informal work group might become the joint proprietors of a small business. But most East Enders work or have worked for significant periods of time, either alone or in combination with informal work, in the formal sector. Factory work is still very common, as are other forms of wage labor, including domestic work.

Informal economies are complicated and varied at the margins of nation-states. To explain exactly why the patterns of participation in the informal economy are the way they are requires an understanding of some of the deeper layers of working-class culture as these can be viewed in relation to the basic components of the informal economy.

In the present case study, the rotating periodic marketplace system is a key institutional component of the informal economy in both rural and urban contexts. In fact, marketplaces are not only key institutions, they are key places—meeting places, landmarks, nodes in the communication system. In many respects, this marketplace system links the rural and the urban economies and cultures. Marketplaces are themselves very complex places. Both rural and urban people buy and sell in the marketplaces, albeit to different degrees and with different kinds of goods.

If we examine the use of the marketplace system in the rural and the urban context, however, we see some very different patterns. In the country, especially in the shallow rural, the marketplace system might be said to constitute the keystone of the informal economy; it is the largest single contributor to cash income earned outside of the formal sector. In the rural context, selling in marketplaces can be viewed as a form of "off-farm" employment that provides much more autonomy and control than a factory-based or other wage labor job, precisely because vendors can determine their own level and schedule of involvement in the system. In the city, the marketplace system plays a much smaller part in the informal economy and thus in the overall local economy. It is one of many informal cash-generating and goods and services–generating strategies. One rarely finds full-time (extensive) sellers in the marketplace system residing in the city, for example.

There are several reasons why urban dwellers use the marketplaces to a much lesser extent than do people in the country. Given the pressing necessity of cash in the city for daily maintenance, it is difficult to make a living entirely from the informal economy. Thus, only an East Ender who already has a steady source of income that does not consume all his or her waking hours can hope to earn significant supplemental cash through marketplace selling. Odd jobs, for example, do not combine well with marketplace vending; both are too irregular, and neither pays benefits. In urban settings, it is much easier (requiring much less investment, preparation, and time) to work at odd jobs, but a person must do so extensively in order to make ends meet. There are also more odd jobs to be had because of the close proximity of higher-class people with whom East Enders can establish patron-client relationships. Painting and yard work can be performed easily and flexibly by East Enders in wealthy communities without declaring income.

Once a person has a formal sector job, all other work need not be declared. Formal sector jobs are also much more accessible in the city than they are in either the deep rural or the shallow rural areas. There is usually someone in the urban kin network (often several people) who holds a formal sector job. From the vantage point of most urban households in the East End, the higher prevalence of formal sector jobs makes the system of rotating periodic marketplaces much less central in overall livelihood strategies. While some East Enders do sell goods in marketplaces, none are extensive or regular vendors. Most people are peripheral sellers in that they sell sporadically in only one or two marketplaces, usually the ones closest to the East End; that is, they do not travel the market circuit. They use a few other marketplaces, but as buyers only. Most people use the marketplaces as sources of inexpensive consumables. Odd jobs play a much more central role in the urban informal economy than does cash generated from selling in marketplaces.

The relationships between kin networks, informal economic processes, and overall livelihood strategies are intricate and changing constantly. In the rural context, kin are extra labor to help out wherever needed: in marketplace booths or on farms, especially at harvest time. The returns for helping are substantial. Virtually all rural people involved in marketplace vending have access to the products of the agrarian system through trading relationships. This access to agrarian products is especially easy for vendors who sell in the major markets in the shallow rural part of the region.

In the urban context, especially if all or most members of the kin network reside in urban places, family members will have great need for cash. Work can be unsteady or scarce because layoffs and bad weather prevent men from working outdoors. Women have easier access than men do to low-paying domestic work, but the incomes of both men and women must be spread over a substantial part of the kin network. When male incomes are sporadic or nonexistent, the incomes of women must be spread even more thinly. The number of people who have secure jobs with benefits are very few.

There are many ways to conserve resources, especially cash. One common adaptation is shared living space. It is not uncommon to see six members of an extended family residing in a one-bedroom apartment. The six family members often represent four generations. The intergenerational division of labor, a very common pattern of resource conservation in the East End, can, and often does, work in the following manner: elderly family members take care of the children while the parents are working in the formal and informal sectors. When additional family members broach the idea of moving into this already-crowded space, the line must be drawn, usually by the person who holds the lease. Under conditions of scarce living space and scarce cash, tensions that can break up the extended family unit can be created in a variety of ways, not the least of which is a high phone bill run up by a nephew or niece who constantly calls home to the country.

Layoffs often result in return migration. Going back to the family homeplace in the country eliminates rent payments and provides easier access to food. After being laid off, Rose's nephew decided to return to the country so as not to become a drain on the kin network's resources. After his girlfriend found a job in the city, he returned to Cincinnati. In fact, there is often a seesawing residence pattern in which people go back and forth from country to city as often as once per month.[8]

From a regional perspective, these multiresidential patterns, in which people move in and out of urban, deep rural, and shallow rural areas, are important because they mean, among other things, that people are moving in and out of different economic sectors. They also mean that people are moving around a region and are not permanently rooted in a single place. In this Appalachian region, there are cultural consistencies, such as the various rural and urban versions of the Kentucky way, that, combined with a widely consistent pattern of social organization, render the utilization of a regional economic unit possible. In many parts of the world, if such consistencies ever existed, they are now gone.

Informal economic processes are difficult to study, much less measure in terms of amounts of cash earned and goods traded. Many of the data included here, especially the sections on the urban informal economy, were revealed in confidence. The inferences are my own. The patterns I have described have been observed over a six-year period. While these data are in some respects the proverbial tip of the iceberg, there are many, many icebergs, and I suspect that, as the U.S. economy continues to deindustrialize, the informal components of the urban economy, and their overall importance in the local cultural economy, will only grow deeper and larger.

COMMUNITY PLANNING: EAST ENDERS' PERSPECTIVES

The People's Version

Putting the people in the plan—that is, The East End Riverfront Community Development Plan and Guidelines—especially in a community as long-lived and as factionalized as the East End, has been difficult, to say the least. The planning process, a very complicated, arduous, and contentious process, took place in the years immediately preceding May 1992, when the plan was passed by City Council. In 1987, the Riverfront Advisory Council, a citizens' advisory group to the city, was assigned to develop a plan for the renewal of the East End. Neighborhood leaders had seats on the RAC, but it was not until 1991 that any significant level of trust was achieved between the RAC and the neighborhood.

The plan itself is a bland and faceless document. Not a single photo has a person in it. The writing is dry and sterile. The document reads as though it were describing a laboratory or a superhighway, not a community. The human elements of the plan are there if one looks long and hard, but, essentially, it is about spaces, buildings, roads, and infrastructure. Most plans are. Such is the nature of plans.

Understanding the plan and the planning process is very difficult and complicated; depending on who is speaking and who is listening, a different understanding of how the plan came about will emerge. Different readings and interpretations of the priorities and the power dynamics occurred every day. Even the official document that emerged at the end is itself only one interpretation of the planning process. It reflects the power structure of the city and, indeed, of the country as a whole.

The community, its leaders, and its residents interpret the plan very differently, and these interpretations greatly influence everyone's perceptions of the plan and its implementation process. One way to understand the plan and the planning process from East Enders' perspectives is through the writing that poured forth from community leaders and residents: poetry, narratives, speeches. These texts are as important—indeed, perhaps, more important—as the planning document itself. The poetry is written by a community leader who was, from the outset ("from jump street"), intensely involved in meetings, hearings, and the entire planning process. The themes in her poetry are powerful, heartwrenching, and religious. The poems are about resistance to the commodification of the community, about East Enders as people just like anyone else, just like the powerful people who are fighting to maintain their views of the river and their upscale lifestyles. The narratives are also written by a community leader, a person with a very different, but no less committed, dedication to the preservation of the community. Both the poetry and the narratives were written in the year preceding the passage of the plan by City Council in May 1992.

Rather than attempt a blow-by-blow description of the planning process, I try in this chapter to present the major planning issues in the East End from East Enders' perspective. I emphasize East Enders' perspectives rather than those of the planners and city officials because these "official" views are well represented in the planning literature and because an emphasis on people is consistent with our research team's original mission in the East End, namely, to strengthen the voice of the community in the planning process.

The people's view of planning has yet to be presented systematically and coherently. In order to do this, I look at two things. First, I have selected excerpts from community planning meetings. Most of those documented here were held in the East End, but some took place at City Hall. Second, although by no means secondary in importance, are the texts written by East Enders in part as responses to being labeled "illiterate" and in part as highly articulate expressions of heartfelt feelings and political savvy. I see these activities—meeting and writing—as critically important ways of practicing community.

This chapter begins with the only titled poem, "The East End Rap," written by the East End poet laureate, as I call her. It first appeared in the monthly newsletter, *The East Ender*, published by the East End Area Council. Many people, including some grassroots leaders, thought the poem was too harsh, "too angry," even an embarrassment to the community. Others liked it, thought it was powerful, "articulate," strong.

"She can write," said one East Ender at a community meeting held just after the newsletter came out.

To me, the poem is an ode to the neighborhood, to its people. It is one way—a very articulate way—for its author to engage in practicing community. It is an expression of commonality, a chronicling of important community events and institutions: private property and the facts of home ownership; the Riverfront Advisory Council and its Plan Group; the citizens' group set up to advise the city in the planning process; the closing of Betz Flats, a thirteen-unit apartment building in the middle of the East End plan area.

The poem has its high points and low ones. It is optimistic—a wish list—about the need for neighborhood meeting places (the Pendleton and the firehouse) and about preserving East End land for East Enders. It is logical, but its logic is local and community-based; "we have more to lose than the city has to gain." It also expresses vulnerability, the results of displacement itself, and the consequences of powerlessness. More than anything, though, the poem claims ownership of the community, not just because the East End is and has been home to seven generations of East Enders, but because, symbolically, the East End is more than a place, it is an identity that confers a sense of belonging regardless of whether a person currently lives in the East End. The poem ends with a plea to the city, "Don't take our home by 'urban renewal,'" and a statement about our common end as humans:

September 1991

The East Ender
Published by the East End Area Council
Seven Hills Neighborhood House
East End Branch

THE EAST END RAP[1]

East End residents' needs are in vain
We have more to lose, than the city has to gain
We love our neighborhood and we want to remain
That's why we're asking for "no! Eminent domain"

Doris, Bonnie, James and Bob have nice homes
And would love for the city to leave them alone
The yelling and screaming has come to a groan
All we can do is weep and moan

Hey! City hall I'm sure you already know
Sometimes we're high and sometimes we're low
If we had the Pendleton and the firehouse Eileen's heart would glow
But recreation is saying that picture will never show

Being on the R.A.C. we've tried to put up a good fight
But I'm getting so I can't sleep at night
People are saying white is black and black is white
It can make you feel you are losing your sight

Since the Betz Flats has been made to close its door
Most landlords are kicking out the poor
Being thrown aside like an apple core
So the rich can accumulate more

The grabbing and snatching of our land by the rich
Makes us feel we have a bad case of the poison ivy itch
The cemetery is full of the poor and the rich
When we all die, we'll go in the same type of ditch

We know we live on priceless land
And it can be taken with the shake of a hand
Michaels [the city manager], city council and mayor
We the East End residents are going to take a stand

City planning we know you're not going by the "golden rule"
We the East End residents are not stupid and we're no fool
So please city council we're begging you don't be cruel
Please! Don't take our homes by "urban renewal."

Will all the evictions and condemnations ever cease?
Our neighbors are being kicked out like they are sliding on grease
It would be nice if we had the grandfather clause lease
So when you come to take our land the preacher will shake
His head and say, "Let them rest in peace."

Planning began in a tense environment in which there was virtually no trust between the community and the city. Communication between the community and the city was tense. Gradually, however, the grassroots leaders and advocates worked to bridge the gaps.[2] For a while, at least, people turned around—both East Enders and city people. While the structure of city bureaucracy did not change, at least the faces of the bureaucrats grew familiar and, in a few instances, working relationships gradually reduced the tensions as people came to trust one another. East

Enders grew much less hostile. The city also started listening. The chair of the Riverfront Advisory Council planning group acknowledged repeatedly how important strong grassroots leadership was to the whole planning process.[3]

The East End Riverfront Community Development Plan and Guidelines is the product of hours and hours of work on the part of East End residents and leaders alike, on the part of the city staff in many departments, especially Planning and Neighborhood Housing and Conservation, on the part of City Council members, and on the part of many dedicated advocates who gave their time generously to be involved in a very long and contentious process. Even the name of the plan was controversial. East Enders had to fight hard just to have the words "East End Community" on it.

The Official Version

The planning process began for the East End in 1987, when the Riverfront Advisory Council and the Cincinnati City Planning Department, at the request of a city councilmember, set out to redevelop the East End Riverfront neighborhood. The initiative for the planning process came, then, from City Council, not from the East End community. The RAC, defined in the plan document as "an officially designated citizen advisory group to the City Manager," had community representation.

The planning process went through numerous stages. The RAC adopted the Eastern Riverfront Revised Concept Plan in December 1988, the Eastern Riverfront Redevelopment Strategy in June 1989, and the Eastern Riverfront Implementation Analysis in December 1989. As the plan describes it, the planning proceeded as follows:

> In the summer of 1990 the Department of City Planning, in association with the RAC, requested proposals from qualified planning and design firms to prepare an Urban Design Plan and Guidelines for the East End Riverfront. The team selected was headed by EDAW, Inc., of Alexandria, Virginia, and included the local firms of Jones and Speer (architects), the H. C. Nutting Company (geotechnical and environmental engineers) and Vivian Llambi Associates (landscape architects and planners).

The result was a document: *The Community Development Plan and Guidelines.* It was produced by EDAW, Inc., under the direction of the RAC, the City Planning Department, Department of Neighborhood

Housing and Conservation, representatives of the East End Area Council, the Columbia Tusculum Community Council and residents of the East End Riverfront Neighborhood. Such is the official introduction to the plan.

Meetings, Plans, and Politics

The following is a description of an East End Area Council meeting that took place in 1991, before the East End Community Development Plan was passed in May 1992. It was, in many respects, typical of the meetings that dealt with the plan, as it covered zoning, housing, tax abatements, and eminent domain. Neglect and powerlessness were also evident. In many ways, this meeting foreshadowed the key themes of subsequent meetings, especially with respect to relationships between the city and the community. When the president declared that "telling the city to go to hell won't work," he really put his finger on city-community relations. He also acknowledged the frustrations with the city that have only escalated and intensified with time.

East End Area Council (EEAC), August 5, 1991

Pete Evans, president of the EEAC, chairs the meeting. Pete first became involved in the community in 1982, when he needed to get a zoning change. He grew up in a home located at the edge of Mount Lookout, East End and Hyde Park, and still lives there. He is a large man, impressive not only because of his size but also because he is an articulate public speaker. He has been elected president of the East End Area Council five times; however, what took two to three days a month when he started now takes twenty-five days.

After the minutes are approved, someone from the group of approximately fifty people moves that the regular meeting agenda be postponed and the Eastern Riverfront Urban Redevelopment Plan, as the plan was originally called, be addressed. The motion is solidly supported by the residents, but first several announcements have to be delivered:

- A public conference on zoning will be held at City Hall on August 14, 1991, and another on August 15.
- The upcoming Wednesday City Council meeting will consider the proposal for "points of sale inspection." This provision would require an inspection for code violations before any house or building was sold.

- A Regional Neighborhood Network Conference will be held on September 16–18 in Fort Wayne, Indiana. The group agrees that the East End Area Council will send no more than six participants.
- Rent applications for single parents who would like to live in the Lewiston Townhomes [affordable rental housing; see Chapter 9] can be obtained from any member of the redevelopment corporation.

Since March 1991, 120 East End residents have been evicted and 120 more are "slated for eviction in the next month." Pete Evans notes that 940 people live in the area of the recent evictions. The 120 residents who have been displaced represent a 13 percent loss in six months.

There is a brief discussion about the building known as Riverview Apartments. Several tenants had asked the housing director for help in bringing in the health and building inspectors. After the health inspection, building inspectors were called in and issued eviction notices to thirty-three people, stating that they had thirty days to relocate. Family relocation services was called in to assist the residents.

THE PLAN

As a preface to the discussion of the city's recently unveiled plans, Pete comments that nothing in the plan addresses the needs of a "community." Such needs include low-income housing and senior housing and other more technical issues related to tax abatements.

When the floor is opened for comments and motions, one of the urban pioneers, Susan Pond, speaks her mind for some time. She believes there has been a conscious effort by private owners who buy up property to neglect the neighborhood and its buildings. She uses the term "urban blight" to describe the neighborhood and insists that neighborhood residents reject the plan as it is written. She believes that the neighborhood should cry "bloody murder" for what is about to happen, namely, the selling of the neighborhood.

Next begins a discussion about zoning. An employee from the City Planning Department attempts to explain the different zoning districts. There will be new zones created to meet the needs of the city. One resident accuses the city of using the East End as a guinea pig to try out its ideas. The man from the planning office tries to assure everyone that city planning is an evolutionary process and that no one should expect codes in any neighborhood to stay the same forever. He points out that the last zoning change occurred in 1963.

A husband and wife who raised eight kids in the East End were forced to move when their house was taken by eminent domain. Many East End residents are afraid of eminent domain, even though the city representative assures everyone that City Council resolved in April that there would be no eminent domain involved in the East End plan. In spite of the city's continued assurances, however, the residents still feel uneasy about the issue and believe eminent domain could be exercised in the future.

One resident points out that City Council has resolved not to exercise eminent domain on any occupied buildings in the East End. The residents express their fears of eminent domain's being applied to unoccupied buildings, however. The same urban pioneer who spoke previously speaks up again and declares that eminent domain will inevitably come in a different form—through property taxes. Taxes will skyrocket and people on low and middle incomes will not be able to afford the rates.[4]

One man says that a politician stated sixteen years ago that there wasn't enough voting power in the East End for politicians to pay attention to the needs of the community. The speaker feels this is especially true today. Other statements at this community council meeting include the following from East End residents:

The city wants the East End to be middle- and upper-income people.

We won't be able to afford to live here.

The only changes they made [from a previous draft proposal] was the green space—none of the changes we recommended occurred.

Several of the residents cite Adams Landing, a very large, upscale high-rise at the western edge of the community near downtown, as something to watch. They say that the same family that owns Adams Landing owns most of the property in the East End. Another resident insists that everyone should pay attention to what is going on all over the city. The example cited is the development in Over the Rhine, low-income housing covering a half-block and cramming 130 families (300 kids) into one of the worst "crack and prostitute areas. In ten years, these developers will be able to do anything they want with the property."

After hearing all of the comments, Pete Evans declares that telling the city "to go to hell won't work." He asks for recommendations on what the residents feel should be done with the plan.

A motion is made to take a vote to reject the plan. After discussion, another person moves to table the first motion so that alternatives to the plan as presented on July 27, 1991, may be discussed and recommended. After much discussion, the EEAC votes to reject the urban design plan as drawn up by the city.

The residents agree to meet to draw up their own plan. The meeting is scheduled for Saturday, August 10, 1991, at 9:00 a.m. at LeBlond. The residents agree that the city should not be invited. One longtime East End resident and community leader points out that the residents made a seven-point proposal three years ago, and *none* of the points had been incorporated into the plan they were now discussing. The seven points included the need for the following: • one- and two-family residences; • a grandfather clause for taxpayers who lived in the East End before development to exempt them from property tax increases; • housing for seniors; and • low-income housing.

The final motion of the night is a move to have the neighborhood recommend a plan and have City Council vote by November 1, 1991. This date is significant, given the upcoming City Council election. The idea is to make incumbents accountable.

The final comment is made by the representative from Associated Neighborhood Practice, Inc. (ANP) of Hamilton County,[5] who feels there are still many residents who have no idea what is going on. She points out also that there are residents who cannot attend meetings because of their work schedules (many people work on night shifts). She recommends setting up an office in the community to make the latest information about the plan available for study. She also notes that very similar kinds of development issues are surfacing in other neighborhoods in Cincinnati and that a coalition of neighborhood councils should be formed in order to gain strength.

Information Committee Meeting

The Information Committee was set up to convey to the community information about the plan. Meetings were held at the home of the chairperson. Some people sat on the couch and on soft chairs, others perched on straight-backed chairs. Grassroots people as well as developers attended. These meetings always exhibited some tensions—tensions it took years for me to understand. In a nutshell, there were tensions among grassroots leaders; there were also tensions between grassroots leaders and developers.

The Information Committee meetings focused on information obtained by East End leaders when they attended RAC Plan Group meetings at City Hall. From the outset, there were three community representatives sitting on the RAC, two from the East End and one from Columbia Tusculum, the wedge of yuppies who live in what historically has always been called East End.

East End developers did not attend RAC plan group meetings because they were not invited; therefore, they did not have easy access to information about the planning process. The developers on the Information Committee thus used these meetings to "pick our brains" (as one East End leader put it) about what had gone on in Plan Group meetings at City Hall. While the Information Committee was still meeting, there were efforts being made on the community level to include all East End players in the planning process. At this point, real East Enders still controlled the EEAC. It was after the developers took over the EEAC that Information Committee meetings were perceived by East End leaders as "brain picking."

I should note here that there were problems with the Information Committee from the outset. Several grassroots leaders, some of whom had been excluded from the meetings when they were convened at the chairperson's home, succeeded in moving the meetings to the recreation center. Clearly, this move represented a loss of power and control for the chairperson, and it did not contribute to grassroots solidarity, either. In fact, the move to LeBlond created divisions among grassroots leaders that still exist. Nonetheless, the community residents and leaders continued to interact with city elected officials and with city staff. These interactions occurred both in the community at meetings and at City Hall—in City Council chambers and in various offices and departments. In early 1992, the Information Committee disbanded.

The City and the Community: Practicing Community by Resisting Commodification

March 12, 1991

The following excerpt is taken from a letter to the East End Area Council from a city councilmember.

Dear East End Area Councilmembers:

I might take issue with your comment on the elected officials spending neither time or money in your neighborhood. The "Eastern Riverfront Plan" alone has brought me and other Councilmembers to the East End many times in the past year, and as you are very aware, we are still attending meetings on this issue. An enormous amount of City staff time which certainly translates to "dollars" has gone into "that Plan."

Very truly yours,

———,

Councilmember

At this time, there was great distrust of the plan because it drew attention to the East End as a place with property too valuable for East Enders to own. An East End leader responds:

That comment let us know it is "the plan" that is the concern of the East End community. We are a piece of valuable land, not people. You and so many other city officials feel you are doing us a favor, by popping up every now and then. No! This does not excite us at all. All you are doing when you do show up is, to show us we did not "exist" in your minds until the "plan." You have not been out here for the concern of the people that live out here. But for the concern of the people you feel should be living out here. We are only being considered (conned is a better word) because of the plan. If we complain about some of the things you all want to do out here, we are told well we can go to another neighborhood and help them. We may be labeled to be illiterate and dumb poor fools, you are in for a rude awakening. We have sense enough to fight for what is ours.

We are a rare community, some poor and some moderate, but we are rare. There is no community in the city of Cincinnati, where people live under the conditions we live under and have no racial or economical problems. We have lived side by side through the hard times and through the good times. We know we are somebody. We are proud to live in the "East End."

We have weathered the floods and we are going to stand steadfast and unmovable. We've been a forgotten community, but we've earned the right to keep what is rightfully ours. When we were coming up as children, people would ask where do you live? We would say the East End, their reply was oh! You're a "river rat." That comment never bothered us, because we knew who we were and have always been proud of it.

I must commend you all for waiting as patiently as you have, to watch our neighborhood "deteriorate" so you could come in and move us out. It took 25 years for you to realize how run down the neighborhood is. But we know you knew all along what you had in mind . . .

This is a personal stand, I do not want to be transplanted somewhere else. I am in the East End because I chose to be. East End is in my blood and in my heart. Do not start coming down on us with your building codes unless it is life threatening. Clean up your own back yards before you start with us. It took 25 years of neglect. Give us some good faith funding.

Yours very truly, I'm sure.

At its base, commodification is dehumanizing. To receive attention all of a sudden because the community sits on valuable land wanted by wealthy people is repugnant to real East Enders. The emotions in this letter are impressive. While there is certainly anger, there is also a strong sense of the practical realities—the need for safe housing and the need for resources to revitalize a deteriorating neighborhood.

This letter preceded the East End Area Council's "Recipe for Success" by about two weeks. In some ways, the recipe was a response to the author's concerns. In other ways, it was simply another, less passionate, way of expressing the same concerns.

April 1991: The Recipe for Success

Under Pete Evans's leadership, the East End Area Council formulated and approved the "Recipe for Success" in April 1991, almost exactly one year before the actual passage of the East End Riverfront Community Development Plan by City Council. The "Recipe" consisted of a series of recommendations for the revitalization and preservation of the community. *The East End Neighborhood Recipe for Success* reads as follows:

1. Maintain the East End as a neighborhood without turning it into a housing project.
    A. Majority of new construction should be of single and two-family homes.

B. Scale back total number of proposed units.
2. A commitment of no eminent domain against existing residential structures by the City of Cincinnati.
3. Provide that Municipal Code 740-9B include the East End Riverfront plan in order to provide for relocation fees to residents due to owner initiated displacement. This should be made retroactive to March 1, 1991.
4. The creation of a housing trust fund.
    A. For rental rehab loans or grants.
    B. For construction of senior citizen housing and low-income rentals.
5. Tax abatement for existing residential units for a period of 15 years.
6. Provide that the plan not be required to pay for itself at the expense of the community.

This last point was a purposely oblique reference to the issue of underground wiring for utilities—electricity and telephone in particular. There is still concern on the part of residents that the costs of underground wiring will be passed on to them.

The RAC's response to the "Recipe for Success" was generally supportive of the neighborhood's wishes. The RAC did not, however, support the housing trust fund directly. The language in the RAC response to the East End Neighborhood Recipe for Success is simultaneously formal and vague. Witness its statement about the creation of a housing trust fund:

A number of loan programs currently exist for which many of the East End area residents would qualify. Federal regulations and guidelines limit the eligibility of structures located in the floodplain and floodway. The RAC agreed that language should be included in the plan that acknowledges the need to stabilize the existing neighborhood population and the need to investigate innovative ways of addressing this issue.

THE RIVERFRONT ADVISORY COUNCIL'S POSITION ON THE EAST END NEIGHBORHOOD'S RECIPE FOR SUCCESS (REVISED 9/5/91)

Anger, Hope, and Fight: The Poetry of Planning

The plan aroused very strong feelings in the community: residents should come first; the city should demonstrate more respect for East

End residents and leaders; discrimination against the poor, black and white people alike, is not acceptable by East End standards. Some of the strongest feelings are expressed in the poetry of planning. These poems are about practices that preserve the community and address specific questions, such as whether parkland should be preserved as green space or used for much-needed housing. They also bring up general issues, such as the relationships between the rich and powerful and the poor and powerless. The relationships between the hillside people, what the East End poet laureate calls "the view people," will be seen in poems that focus on the nature of social stratification in Cincinnati.

As the planning process intensified, the poems became more focused. Traffic on Eastern Avenue is the subject of an entire poem, for example. In their own way, the poems comment on the history of the planning process from the perspective of one real East Ender. Her voice is not unique, however; it represents a synthesis of community feelings that derives from her life experiences as an East Ender and from her close relationships to fellow community leaders. When I was rereading these poems just after the March 1997 flood (see Chapter 12) caused houses to be torn down quickly and indiscriminately, the themes rang truer to me than ever—especially those about power, negative stereotypes, and insensitivity to practicing community. To hear East Enders talk about the river is one thing. To actually see East Enders deal with the river is another.

The following three poems are addressed to the city and to the positioning of East End residents and leaders in the planning process. Positioning must be regarded holistically, that is, in the context of the city of Cincinnati as a whole and its social class and power configurations. The first poem acknowledges class and power relations both as they have affected the East End's history and as they will determine its future. The poem complains about the disproportionate power held by the wealthy in the planning process and worries about the possible extinction of the community. It also argues for the dignity of the poor and the strength and resilience of a community of poor people.

One of the most significant passages in the poem is in the last part of the fifth stanza:

We keep telling you our community, "is like no other"
so quit trying to judge us from our cover.[6]

The uniqueness of the community from East Enders' perspectives is an underlying premise of the practice of community. It is based on a series of multistranded relationships and beliefs: the close relationships to the river, as both a source of beauty and a powerful spiritual force, but not as a salable commodity, and the fundamental belief that what is in the heart is more important than what is in the wallet. It represents a commitment to the quality of cultural life (especially family and community relationships). Family responsibilities take precedence over all other concerns. Income sharing is the rule, and fixing a house takes much lower priority than helping a family member, friend, or neighbor in need. The passage is really about resistance to the profit motive, about bucking the mainstream values of greed and market-driven economic development. Superficial inspection of the community "from our cover," is not, in this East Ender's view, appropriate because it does not begin to capture the quality of human relationships in the community. This first poem acknowledges the realities of class structure and power in the city by emphasizing the fact that the people on the hillside that overlooks the East End (Columbia Parkway Trust) and the yuppies who have taken over a part of the East End have power over East End residents.

> East End residents have become the minority
> Columbia Parkway Trust, Columbia Tusculum, and developers is
>   the majority
> If you have our interest at heart why should they have so much
>   authority?
> We've been criticized, victimized and itemized
> To those who feel they are superior I hope you get cut down to size
> If some people had their way we would be pesticide
> Hoping to make us petrified
>
> Being poor is not a crime
> Just hope you never lose your last dime
> We've been through some floods, storms and rain
> But we made it
> Some things have caused a lot of pain
> But we made it
>
> For the past 25 years we've been stumbling in the dark
> Instead of caring about us, you're concerned about the parks
> You say we shouldn't take an attitude
> Have you done something, where we should have some gratitude?
>
> We can say you are gratuitous
> Because some of your tactics have been very vicious

We keep telling you our community, "is like no other"
So quit trying to judge us from our cover

When you start talking about what we deserve
Just be fair and honest and don't get on my last nerve

Everyone is trying to protect their views
You can't know the pain it causes, until you've walked in my shoes

How would you feel if we said "small-fry politicians" should be
    roasted?
And the whole East End community should be toasted?

What the city has done for the East End is 2%
But they want us to trust them 100%
I keep telling you we are not dumb and we are not stupid
And you can't win our hearts because you're not cupid

I've always been told if you dig one ditch you'd better dig two
Because the first one you dig may be for you

With your money, you can live and live well
But I thank god, you can't pay your way out of hell

In the final analysis, this poem is about trust, really, the absence of trusting relationships between the city and the East End community and the questioning by the poet of the city's assumption that East Enders will blindly trust authority. The poet makes a plea for empathy by appealing to the reader's sense of fairness. The suggestion that those in power consider reversing roles with East Enders is a not-so-subtle reminder, on several levels, that we are all human. The religious imagery here works to counter the realities of power.

The anger and pessimism in this poem is countered by the next one, which, while it treats many of the same themes, is much more upbeat, hopeful—even optimistic. I have placed these two poems next to one another in order to illustrate the many mood swings experienced by leaders in the community. The poet takes the upper hand in this poem, as a parent would with a child, especially where a lot of energy is required when one is tired after attending meeting after meeting. There is a real sense of energy in this poem.

I hope that we are finally on the right track
We don't need any outsiders and trouble makers holding us back
Instead of your hat, put your head on the rack
It is truly late when I hit the sack

There are times when I've felt we have been set up
If you have our interest at heart you will back-up
But 25 years of neglect by the city why not help us get up?
So we can get to work and fix up

I pray that the building inspectors will not be out there in force
Riding our backs like they're riding a horse
We're hoping they'll clean up their mess first of course
And treat us fair so there will be no remorse

Why can't you all be legit?
Your lack of concern for us just won't quit
Close your mouth and go in a corner and sit
At times you almost make me have a fit

The air that Hillside Trust, Columbia Parkway Trust and Columbia
    Tusculum
Breathe is very cool
And they picture the East End residents being underdogs and fools
"God said: he would make my enemies my footstool"
We realize we are at the river and not a pool

Keep the East End residents in the plan
You know what we want and you know where we stand
I'm tired of outsiders deciding for us about the plan
Because if the city wanted to get rid of us they would give them
    a hand

We were left alone for 25 years as if the city had forgotten
And just as they wanted the neighborhood became rotten
We've got the you know who's breathing down our necks
As if to say why should we care about the East End who gives
    a heck?

We are poor and small in number
There hasn't been much rest and very little slumber
Outsiders don't see our homes or the people it's the landscape
I wish there was a way East End residents could escape

The developers and the people concerned about their view
If you don't have our interest at heart what good are you?

"God said it" and I believe it, that we are all equal
But I know it's hard for you to believe we are really people

I know I've put the East End resident's first
If the faithful were not out there fighting things could be worst

There are two meanings of the word "faithful" here: faithful as in faith in the community, and faithful as in believing in God and the essential humanity of all people, rich and poor.

The last poem in this set was written less than a month before the passage of the plan. The dominant metaphor in the poem is combative and militaristic. It sets East Enders against "the enemy," in this case, the "view people," that is, the wealthier people who live on the hillside above the East End. The view people have, of course, a great deal of power with the city. The Hillside Trust and the Columbia Parkway Trust are two groups that represent the view people. There were, in fact, alliances made between the view people and the East End residents in opposing the tall buildings proposed by developers and land bankers. The poem also manifests a sense of entitlement to the East End as well as a sense of the importance of home and place: "Our homes are all we got." The depression[7] triggered by anxiety and uncertainty over both the loss of particular homes and the loss of community can be found in the eighth stanza.

April 6, 1992
My name is Eileen Waters and I love where I live
You've been taking from us now it's time to give
This is our neighborhood and this is where we want to live
We are human beings and we can't go in a sieve

There are still many things that needs to be done
We've just about won the fight, but the battle is yet to be won
The needs of the East End residents must be priority number one
Working hard and fighting for us all has not been fun

I've upset the enemy
Because so many times they've upset me
Asking us to protect their views and not drive on their street
I could let them alone if they would just let us be

View people our homes are all we got
Have you thought about this of course not
We know our land is real hot
Outsiders quit acting like you hit the jack-pot

View people and developers you've got to stop all this fuss
It's not what we can do for you but what you can do for us

You get on our nerves so much some people want to cuss
We've greased ourselves up so we won't rust

There are times when I get very upset
There is a point I have to get
My name is Eileen and don't you forget
Because if you do you'll be sorry we ever met

Why can't we complain for goodness sake
You'd be upset if your homes were at stake
How much ruckus do you think, you would make?
I've had more to lose than I can take

Unless you have something to lose
You would know I don't get mad because I choose
These many months I've been given the blues
Believe me I've been paying my dues

To our neighborhood they all came
Developers, Hillside Trust, Columbia Parkway Trust, Columbia
    Tusculum
They are all playing some kind of game
When the lot of you would be put to shame
If anything goes wrong the East End residents will be blamed

I don't take having our homes on the line lightly
And I will fight for us all rightly
With the community interest at heart nightly
When things start happening it will be sightly

Meetings

April 6, 1992

"Only God" can give us the sunshine and the rain
Man to worship man would surely be insane
In order for us to appreciate the joy he has to give us some pain
My love for him I will not abstain

No I haven't dotted every i and crossed every t
And I'm not in bed with the enemy
You try volunteering it is not easy as you will see
So tired at times you'll be

My mornings, afternoons and evenings too
Going to meetings after meetings to help me and you
East End residents there is still so much work to do
The "implementation" Eileen Waters plan to see it through.

There were dozens of meetings between April 1991 and April 1992. All community residents and leaders worked on a voluntary basis. Doris and Elaine went by bus to City Hall, in the rain, in the snow, in the heat of summer. When Robbie's car was working, she drove everyone downtown. Sometimes I drove.

The burdens and costs did not come only from time spent in meetings. Meetings required preparation as well as debriefing. Time away from family, from rest, often from food, debilitated health and stamina, which, for some leaders, was already marginal: high blood pressure, diabetes, arthritis, ulcers, "nerves" were already daily facts of life.

In December 1991, the grassroots gained control of the East End Area Council and grassroots leaders made every effort to convince City Hall, especially members of City Council, that, indeed, the residents of the East End should have first priority in planning. To East Enders, plans are for and about people.

The meetings were long and arduous—often three hours or longer. The process was painstaking. A very forceful minority leader stood up and read the plan, line by line. Every zoning regulation, every height and density restriction was scrutinized carefully. His strong presence, in combination with the commitment of the EEAC board, kept the meetings on track. It took Herculean strength on the part of grassroots leaders to prevent speeches, posturing, and filibustering from those who had other priorities than maintaining the East End for its lifelong residents and their families. It also gave the community, for the first time, a sense of strong participation in the planning process. In the year preceding the passage of the plan, the grassroots leaders were committed to working with developers in a cooperative manner without selling out the community.

On April 15, 1992, the East End Area Council met and it became clear that the leadership in the community, both formal and informal, was committed to revitalization of the neighborhood through development of a range of housing types. At that point, the leadership viewed high-income development as being honor-bound to contributing to a housing trust dedicated to the rehab, building, and purchase of low-income housing. Part of the sale price of every market-rate unit would, presumably, be put aside as a contribution to the East End Housing Preservation Fund, a community-based group with its own board of trustees.

Working with the city and with developers proved to be a very rocky process, however. All sorts of interests came to the forefront. For example, the sale of Ferry Street Park to a housing developer created a great deal of controversy. There were hours of hearings and meetings in the community as well as at the Park Board headquarters.

East End residents were divided on several issues. Some wanted to preserve the green space. Others agreed that the parkland should be used for housing, but did not want it sold to developers. At one meeting of the Park Board, a representative of an environmental group, with no idea of the needs of the East End, came to the meeting uninvited to advocate for green space. The grassroots leaders argued for housing. Some urban pioneers argued against the sale of the parkland.

Park Board hearings became very heated at certain points, as did East End Area Council meetings. Had it not been for the determination of a coalition of black and white grassroots leaders, who argued that housing was more important than green space, the Park Board would not have agreed to sell Ferry Street Park and the adjacent Vance Street property to developers. At this point, leaders' thinking was that some cooperation with developers was necessary for community revitalization. The leaders expected some reciprocity from the developers.

Traffic

Traffic on Eastern Avenue has always been an issue. While the speed limit is officially 35 MPH, I have been passed many times while I was going 45 or 50. Since the East End neighborhood is bisected by Eastern Avenue, which runs parallel to the river, and since Eastern Avenue functions as a commuter corridor running east and west between the wealthy suburbs to the east and downtown Cincinnati to the west, the very character of the neighborhood, for both longtime residents and newcomers, depends on traffic safety.

The Riverfront Advisory Council spent hours and hours talking to traffic engineers, safety engineers, and other professionals, who told the neighborhood only what residents already knew. The traffic on Eastern Avenue must be controlled—more traffic lights, more police presence. Residents pointed out that there were other, wealthier neighborhoods on the same commuter corridor that had police cars on many corners during rush hours. People dared not speed, as they did on Eastern Avenue.

The "Traffic" poem portrays a residential community invaded and violated by speeders who simply do not realize, or refuse to acknowledge, the human elements of the East End neighborhood, or even to see that it is, in fact, a neighborhood and not just a pass-through between the suburbs to the East and downtown. The seriousness of outsiders' disregard for East Enders is emphasized in the poem. The poem appeals to all East End parents to speak up and commands all outsiders (commuters and metro drivers alike) to respect the community as a residential neighborhood. The poem is long, almost relentless and droning, much like the traffic on Eastern Avenue.

April 14, 1992
My temperature rose and I wanted to yell
Traffic speeding down Eastern Avenue like a bat out of hell
Come on traffic engineers, come out of your shell
If you do your job, Eastern Avenue will become a show and tell

All this speeding, we don't and won't condone
Eastern Avenue is not an expressway nor a speed zone
We can talk all we want to, but the speeders need to be shown
There is so much worry and concern about our own

What kind of price do we have to pay?
Our children are on Eastern Avenue each and everyday
Please don't let it be the wrong kind of "pay day"
All East End parents speak up you should have the last say

The way people are speeding, we know it's illegal
It seems their mission is to run down all East End people
This is not the way we want to be under St. Rose's steeple
"God said it," I didn't, "we are all created equal."

The cars cannot keep speeding as they've done in the past
Something must be done, and done real fast
Will some have to die? Or end up in a cast?
Is stopping the speeders that big of a task?

I'm going to fight with both tooth and nails
You can't bring someone back to life by putting someone else in jail
The price to pay is too great for us to fail
As you know we've already been told; "we're a ship without a sail."

Education is taught common sense you're born with (there are
   some exceptions)
Let's not wait too late, where we'll end up with a bunch of stiffs
Then all of city hall, will be ready to take the "fifth"
And when someone gets hurt, the blame they will want to shift

To all the commuters in your cars and the drivers of metro
35 miles per hour on Eastern Avenue you're supposed to go
Concern and respect for our community you will and must show
This is a residential neighborhood, the speed limit is not too slow

Our children and elderly are special to us as yours are to you
If this was your neighborhood, you would be concerned too
You know the speeding must stop, so why not take your cue
Take care of our safety so we don't have to hear the words "code
   blue"

Please take the time, and do something about what's being said
Are any of you leaders? Or do you all have to be led?
Do the words: "ashes to ashes, dust to dust" have to be read?
Please don't wait till one of our children end up dead.

Looking toward Implementation

The next two poems, written in the last weeks before the passage of the
East End Riverfront Community Development Plan, are poems of cooperation, of looking forward to the implementation of the plan. They
are hopeful poems that represent some sense of empowerment, but they
also show clear recognition of where the real power lies. The bottom line
is "Let's get to work."[8]

The tone of the next poem is one of cooperation—with the city and
with developers. The tone is also friendly and humble, not angry, and
it shows a sense of accomplishment from the hard work of the planning
process.

April 20, 1992
Now hear this; those of us who own, we don't want to rent
Hoping that working on the plan is time well spent
Don't weigh us down with property taxes where we have to walk
   around all bent
Remember: you said this plan would work without costing us a cent

We the East End residents have felt the kick of the shoe
But, at city hall the only ones that came were the faithful few
Some volunteers got tired and said they were through
Little does some people realize there is still work to do

I feel good about the work we've done
Our fight (plan) has just about been won
But the battle (implementation) has just begun
Come to city council meeting on April 28th and be counted one
 by one

As you know our community is an experiment
And it's not supposed to cost us for improvements
There is a need for us all to make a commitment
And the city should make a long overdue investment

We're being put under a magnifying glass
Being told over and over and over we have no class
You've got to do more for us, than you have in the past
Then you won't have to tell us not to sass

All city departments you are 25 years late
Our community city hall you need to accommodate
Whatever your plans I hope you formulate
The neglect of our community we will no longer take

Such a heavy burden on us have been laid
So many tough decisions have to be made
We can't work in the sun, we'll do our best in the shade
Our community we do not want you to raid

Our community existence is on the line
To know we've been heard would be oh so divine
Residents and the city need to combine
If you want to rate us from 1 through 10 we would rank number nine

I don't feel that I am always wrong nor am I always right
And for the good of our community I will always fight
For 25 years we've been in the dark, now it's time for us to see the
 light
When the builders start building it will be a beautiful sight

It is the feelings of some that we rank third
The way we've been treated is absurd

Please city councilmembers please let us be heard
We are fully aware you have the last word.

Three important themes related to practicing community emerge in this poem. The first concerns the concept of the East End community as "an experiment." It is an experiment in diversity, in both race and class, and it is an experiment in planning. The poet is not opposed to revitalization, however. She very much favors building. A subsidiary theme here is the request that the city accommodate the community: "Our community city hall you need to accommodate." The second theme might seem to contradict the third, but the two taken together indicate a delicate relationship with the city. These themes are indicated in the lines "The neglect of our community we will no longer take," implying that there is a great need for resources to come into the East End, and in the line, "Our community we do not want you to raid." This last line requests community autonomy and control over resources, land, and homes. These last two themes require a delicate balance in order to revitalize the community while preserving diversity of community to include real East Enders.

How to strike a balance between preventing neglect and raiding? The plan itself is ambivalent. For example, it supports the preservation of historic buildings, but it does not specify who is to preserve the buildings and for what the buildings should be preserved. Thus, while the community sees the Pendleton Building as coming back to the community as a community meeting place and heritage center, the city is quite ready to consider selling the building for use as a profit-generating business or some other purpose that completely relinquishes community control over it. There is a fragility here: "Our community existence is on the line." The poem ends with the recognition that power is in the city's hands: "We are fully aware you have the last word."

The following poem continues in a cooperative spirit, but, unlike the last one, it conveys a certain sense of empowerment and strength while recognizing the realities of the power structure and the position of East Enders in the class stratification system. It even contains some humor. The poem ends with a real call to action, for people to, in essence, practice what they preach.

April 27, 1992
No matter how far, you've gone in school
Remember the world is full of "educated fools"
So be nice, be kind and be cool
Let us all try to go by the "golden rule"

To anyone who can be so becloud (to confuse; as an issue)
Making sure of what you say, and say it out loud
We're not dead yet! So we don't need a shroud
If something goes wrong, I pray that it's in a big crowd

When we talk about our homes some people balk
Oh! But they want us to listen when they talk
They keep us on our knees, so we can't walk
And leave us so upset to where we have to sulk

I've been asked by some: what about the city I can't believe?
For 25 years our community has been deceived
No money for infrastructure have been received
If they had shown some concern for the residents, I would be
    relieved

So many times they've made me want to belch
Telling us they were going to give us some help
Treating us like a bet they've made, and now they want to welch
Believe me I can do without all this nonsense myself

I've been trying to give the city a hand
Because I'm still somewhat skeptical about the "plan"
We the residents want to live at "peace" on our piece of land
But if we are treated fairly, I'll be the city's biggest fan

In every battle there are some casualties (renters of the East End)
And of course some liabilities
We're working hard to keep our properties
We are going to die fighting and that's a reality

We are between the devil and the deep blue sea
This is not a place we want to be
And you've heard what we are considered to be
Not A B C or D but, the end of the totem pole X, Y, Z

I want our community to grow
But dealing with the greenway, can we stand the flow
The outsiders want to help us and show
But will they be around when it comes time to sow?

People want the East End to be the playground for the whole city
Those who feel we need parks more than we need homes that's
    a pity

I hope they don't think that we feel they're witty
Let's quit playing and get down to the real nitty gritty.

April 28, 1992, was the scheduled date for City Council to vote on the plan. It was by no means a sure thing that City Council would pass it. In the months prior to this, leaders of the East End Area Council visited each member of City Council to talk about the plan's merits.

On April 27, a special meeting was held of the East End Area Council to discuss, vote on, and pass "The Recipe for Successful Implementation." This "Recipe," which was modeled on the earlier *East End Neighborhood Recipe for Success,* treated all of the key issues in the planning process from the community perspective; these issues should now be very familiar from the poetry, a poetry I have come to think of as the poetry of class.

The affirmative vote passed by the East End Area Council on "The Recipe for Successful Implementation" constituted an affirmative vote on the plan itself. The "Recipe," in fact, became a part of the plan document and was one of the strongest indications that, indeed, the voices of East End residents had been heard.

The first provision of "The Recipe for Successful Implementation" set up the Implementation Team (East End Riverfront Implementation Advisory Committee) to oversee the revitalization efforts as specified in the plan. Other provisions included capital improvements, traffic, social services, housing, and the Pendleton Building, referred to as "The Pendleton Club."

Following is the text of "The Recipe for Successful Implementation":

APRIL 27, 1992
THE RECIPE FOR SUCCESSFUL IMPLEMENTATION

1. East End Riverfront Implementation Advisory Committee.
   There is a need for a community based committee to oversee the implementation of the plan. This committee would insure that this plan moves forward in a way that makes the project manager/team and all involved City departments accountable to the community.

2. Capital Improvements
   MSD [Metropolitan Sewer District] needs to start a clean-up of the banks and river to stop the direct dumping of raw sewage into the Ohio River. This is a violation of federal law and MSD needs to be held accountable.

3. Traffic Flow
   Traffic engineering, public works and the Safety Department

should be directed to work toward making Eastern Avenue a pedestrian-friendly street. Seven A.M. to nine A.M. and four P.M. to six P.M. [parking] restrictions need to be lifted, thus, making Eastern Avenue two 8 ft. parking lanes and two 12 ft. travel lanes at all times.

4. Social Services

The health and educational services in the East End need to be improved, expanded, and tailored to community needs. A mechanism needs to be created to bring about the return of a neighborhood school.

5. Housing

- Senior housing must become a reality with housing available for both independent and assisted care living.
- Rehab housing and new city-assisted/low income housing has to come on line with all avenues explored for the development of the floodplain. The need for rehab assistance in the floodways must be addressed.
- A Housing Trust is essential for the survival of the current population of the East End. A housing trust exclusively for the East End has to be privately funded and organized with a board of trustees composed largely of East End residents.
- NHC must develop a blueprint for housing in the East End with a projected amount of new, city-assisted/low income housing and rehabbed housing to come on line yearly. The director of NHC would be directly responsible and accountable to the city and to the community.
- Building inspection processes should be revised to separate safety issues from aesthetic concerns.

6. The Pendleton Club: The commitment of private monies with help from the city to restore the Pendleton Club to its historical form immediately to be a vital part of the East End Community. An official meeting place would cement the relationships between East End Residents, Developers and the City to make this a plan of cooperation.

As this book goes to press, there is a Housing Preservation Fund Board in place with a majority of its members East End residents. The board has met only once, however. The Pendleton Heritage Center Project has come a long way, but is still not a reality (see Chapter 10 on the Pendleton Heritage Center). The first new affordable rental units were opened in May 1995 as the Lewiston Townhomes (eleven units). Betz Flats has been rehabbed and reopened (thirteen rental units).

The Implementation Team did indeed come into being, headed initially by two co-chairs, an East End leader and a retired executive with links to strong religious institutions. The pair of co-chairs was later replaced by the chair of the RAC Plan Group.

The strength of the grassroots did not please some people, however. One very vocal black grassroots leader on April 17, 1992, Good Friday, received a phone call telling her to "watch your back," repeated three times. She was very scared. Another strong leader, white, was told by a developer that if she really cared about her elderly mother, she would give up her responsibilities in the community. She also received threatening phone calls of a different sort, one of which informed her while she was at work on April 11, 1992, that there was an ambulance in front of her house. This was clearly trumped up to upset her, for she knew that her elderly mother was visiting her sister. She also received a call saying: "If Ferry Street goes, so do you, watch your back." This was a reference to the controversial Park Board property.

The Passage of the Plan

Despite the threatening phone calls, the extraordinary efforts on the part of grassroots leaders to inject a strong community voice into the East End Riverfront Community Development Plan paid off. A summary of these efforts was presented to City Council by a grassroots leader, complete with images of war and struggle but with a community at least temporarily united:

April 28, 1992
To most people, Tuesday April 28, 1992 is just another day. But to the East End community it is the first day of the rest of our lives. Our dream is to be able to spend that time in the East End if we choose. This sounds dramatic, but it is a fact of life if this plan you have before you today does not include the things we have brought before you in the past, there could very well be no place for us in a revitalized East End's future. To this committee tonight, we have brought our follow-up to the recipe for success. It is the recipe for successful implementation. In this document you will see what we feel must be done to insure this plan not only creates an improved East End, but that it creates improvements for the people that have been there through the deterioration of our neighborhood.

The EEAC last night had a special meeting so that we could come here tonight and present to you what we hope will be a solution to some of the things from the past few years that have put a stop to this plan. Please know that we are here as a community united, as one that has been through some battles with the city and come out the stronger for it. No, I do not think this plan is ideal, but I do not feel that it leaves us out as it did in the past. The war has not ended, but a cease fire is at hand. And for this I am proud—proud that this neighborhood has fought as long and as hard as it has for what we believe. It has not been a war without casualties—for we have lost many of our friends through displacement. But I would hope, that like any other war, once the fighting is over, the rebuilding begins. And with this rebuilding some of our friends can come back home to enjoy what we have won through determination.

For the first 45 years of my life, the most I ever did to improve my neighborhood was to put my garbage out Monday nights and try to have the cans back in by the weekend. It took the flood in January of 1991 to get me to my first area council meeting. I needed help in clearing away the drift left behind after my river view went back into its banks. My next meeting was after the Betz Flats was vacated. It became evident to me that everyone in the East End lost something with the loss of The Flats and it was going to take everyone working together to regain what we had lost. So here I am today. We still haven't gotten the families back that we lost, but we also have not forgotten them. Nor have we erased the memory of how The Flats went down. It is easy to blame the owners and the city for what happened that day, but the East End needs to assume some of the blame too. You see we let this plan take over our lives and let things go on that should have been stopped long ago. If we truly believed that the East End was being ignored by the city and that there was a deliberate attempt to let our neighborhood get into the shape it's in today, why, in God's name, didn't we stand together before the city brought a plan out here and demand to be treated as part of the city that now wants so desperately to be part of the East End? Why did we wait for all of the displacement to occur before we took a stand? For my part it was not facing the changes that occurred in the East End over the last 25 years. It was seeing the old East End when I drove down the street, not the neighborhood that other people from the outside see. And why did we let petty arguments get in the way of standing together working toward a positive solution.

To all my friends and neighbors, I apologize for all the years I've stood back and let the other guy handle things. To Pete Evans, the Wests, Lora Robin, Nick Brown, the Ezzards, the Simms, Bunny Christy, and to all the others that were involved before it became fashionable to do so, the East End is very grateful. To the 1992 team, that I am proud to be part of: James Strong, Bob Church, Doris Sells, Jonathan Wiley, Madeline and Mark Jones, David Park, Sara McQueen, the Seelys and Josh Isaacs, all I can say is thank you for helping me learn. This position I hold as president, I do not hold alone, and to the other presidents of the EEAC, Fritz Franz, Mike Garner, and especially Elaine Winters, thank you for making a difficult job fun most of the time. I could not thank the people from outside the community enough for what they have done, but I cannot leave it unsaid: Jessica Allen, Keith Baker, Ned Benson, Matthew Marks. To Gary Michaels, thank you for Arthur Blair.

Special thanks to Jim Cane, Pearl Clark, Claudia Pauly, Jim Spencer, Len McFarland, Davis Farley, Nathan Trapp, Donald Compton, Lisa Knoll, and all the members of the RAC. To Janet Munson. When I started in March of last year, I was told you were one of the enemies. Well that couldn't be more wrong. Not only are you not the enemy, you have become an ally to the East End. Everything you have done to bring me up to speed on this plan went well beyond the call of duty. My deepest thanks to you.

I would be remiss if I did not acknowledge the following three names. The reason will be obvious when I say:

Your majesty, please . . . I don't like to complain,
But down here below, we are feeling great pain.
I know, up on top you are seeing great sights,
but down at the bottom we too, should have rights.
We turtles can't stand it, our shells will all crack!
Besides, we need food. We are starving! Groaned Mack.

So to Yertle the Turtle and my hero Mack thank you for making your view on the subject of views very clear to me. To Dr. Seuss thank you for the child's view on a very sensitive issue surrounding this plan.

To my mother, Toni and Jamie, thank you for all the understanding and support, even when I should have been at home with you. You are the reason I do the things I do. To Kelly, you've been through the battles with me, and at three years old, you are a shining example of what 7th generation East Enders can be. And now maybe things can get back to normal.

All the acknowledgements just given makes it seem like this plan is over, and I am now back to the East End and City Hall can get back to normal. Well it just ain't so. Until this plan is done, until everyone is home again in the East End, until all the things that the East End so desperately needs are in place—until then, I'll be seeing you in all these old familiar places, for you see, once you get involved, it's hard to go back.

Epilogue

After the plan was passed, the city planner in charge of it received a series of presents from the community. One was a T-shirt with the words "First Generation East Ender." She remains a trusted friend of the community.

8 | HEALTH, CULTURE, AND PRACTICING COMMUNITY

*T*his chapter is about health and illness—but not in the conventional sense. It is about health and illness in a broad, holistic, community context in which health is the responsibility not only, or even primarily, of parents, relatives, and professional health care providers but of the community itself, of neighbors and friends and community institutions. These institutions certainly include the East End Community Health Center, but they also include churches and gas stations, kitchens and porches. Caring for other East Enders in a myriad of ways—sometimes even in ways that do not appear immediately to be related directly to health—is part of practicing community.

The perspectives used in this chapter build on the work of Benjamin Paul (1955) and others who have taken cultural issues seriously in thinking about health care delivery. These orientations are still unconventional in several respects. They focus not on patients as autonomous individuals but on patients as parts of families and as members of a community that constitutes a social and economic class of the working poor. Patients, then, must be understood as part of a community and class dynamic that has to be understood over time.

Generational issues are very important. Some health problems occur generation after generation. Some of them have a genetic base; others are related to environment. Daily conditions have major consequences for health and disease. Faulty wiring can, and often does, lead to fires and residential displacement. Frequent moves place additional stresses on health. Chronic poverty contributes to neglect and creates fear of hunger and cold. Overwhelming responsibility for dependents, especially small children and the elderly, may cause chronic anxiety and tension.

As people move through the life course, and as the various life-course points become defined in the context of working-class culture and community, health issues arise and are managed in ways that are specific to culture and class contexts. Teenage pregnancy and depression, for example, must be understood in the context of poverty.

The culture-bound syndrome that East Enders refer to as "nerves" is common,[1] but is not idiosyncratic to the East End. The syndrome manifests itself as depression and anxiety and is found worldwide under conditions of rural-urban migration, rapid culture change, and increased dependence on and shortage of cash. Health, culture, and community—the health repercussions of culture contact, migration, urbanization, and the like—have been long-standing topics in social science and medicine. Migration at any time and from any place is stressful; so, too, are displacement, unemployment, and all of the other processes that lead to poverty, inequality, and oppression. Alcohol further complicates and impedes adaptation to any new environment, especially urban environments, which require relatively large amounts of cash (compared with rural areas) for family survival. In rural areas, people certainly need cash to purchase necessities, but cash is not the sole source of food, for example, which can be grown in gardens on homesteads. Livestock—a few chickens, pigs, or cows—contributes greatly to the protein supply in rural areas. Food processing and food storage for future use are still very much a part of livelihood in rural Appalachia. Any visit home to the country will yield some food, fresh, frozen, or canned.

Rural-to-urban migration patterns, changing gender roles, and transformations in family structure are factors that place urban Appalachians at risk for serious health disorders. A number of transitions, rooted in economic, life-course, and institutional processes, affect the health of rural Appalachian migrants in cities. These include change in physical environment, adaptation to an urban versus a rural way of life, change from dependence on subsistence production to reliance on wage labor, and change in social networks.

In these contexts, Social Security Disability Insurance (SSDI) must be understood as part of a complex series of cash-generating coping strategies that provide a secure source of income for people struggling at the margins of the state. The time demands of informal economic activities (see Chapter 6), another coping strategy, are not to be underestimated, however. The resultant stress often takes a heavy toll on health.

Not all situations are problematic. To assume that all adolescent pregnancies are automatic disasters is as inappropriate as it is to assume that all are handled with ease. One of the benefits of the extended family and of strong community ties is that there are safety nets, both temporary and long term, for people in need of support. The example of teen pregnancy in this chapter is important because it illustrates how an event that the power structure views as a tragedy can, in fact, be a positive event for an entire extended family, including a very supportive seventeen-year-old father. From a health policy perspective, if teen pregnancy is a fact of life in the community, then, the most culturally sensitive approach may be for health care providers to facilitate the most viable family and community-based support system. This may mean identifying supportive grandparents or other adults and ensuring that these adults have enduring relationships with teen parents and their children.

In this vein, the roles of strong women in working-class families must be understood. In some instances, when these strong women become ill, the whole family falls apart. In other instances, one strong woman can provide the glue that holds the family together.

This chapter focuses on a set of model patient cases that are based on real patients seen in the East End and at the health center. For reasons of confidentiality, however, they do not describe any person or family exactly. To represent not only a range of health problems, but also a range of life-course issues that relate to health and illness has not been an easy task. These health problems are certainly not unique to the East End; they are associated strongly with rural-to-urban migration, poverty, and stress. They are serious, and they tend to be reproduced and passed down in families.

One case involves a young teenager who, at age thirteen, made several suicide attempts but refused conventional care. Another describes an elderly woman, now deceased, who had Alzheimer's disease; she was incontinent, combative, and disoriented, yet her daughter refused to put her in a nursing home because to do so would have been the equivalent of handing her a death sentence. Another patient, who has never really defined himself as such, is a man who has experienced severe depression but who has never, to my knowledge, sought therapy from anyone formally connected to a health care institution. Instead, his "therapists" are East Enders who provide therapy in their own ways—but also in true East End style—by being there for him. Summaries of the critical issues in each patient case are presented before the patients and their histories are described in detail.

To read about people and families who are ill to the point of experiencing serious loss of function may be grim, even jarring. For those unfamiliar with the range of biopsychosocial issues in communities like the East End or for those who simply do not want to confront the serious illness problems that poverty and displacement can create, this chapter will be difficult to read. The realities of day-to-day existence can be very difficult for East End families. Food requires cash, which is often scarce. Dwellings are in disrepair; air conditioning is virtually nonexistent and, when window fans break, the humid air hangs in small, difficult-to-ventilate apartments. In winter, leaky windows and poor insulation create the opposite problem. Transportation to and from the grocery store, the health center, the drugstore, the hospital often requires efforts that are beyond the capabilities of mothers with small children. Phones are a luxury and are disconnected and reconnected regularly.

Many East Enders cope with illness on a daily basis, but it is considered inappropriate to discuss personal concerns about illness at a board meeting or even at an informal gathering. In fact, any mention of illness is considered to be an excuse—and not a very good excuse. "We all have personal problems," is a phrase heard often in the East End. Yet illness in families plays a significant part in the functioning of community boards—whether or not people attend, how well they are functioning when they do attend. At times, as we have seen, meetings can turn into "therapy management groups" in the sense that they become support groups for people in distress.[2] My focus in this chapter, though, is on individuals and families who are experiencing illness problems.

The East End Community Health Center

This chapter begins by placing the health center in the context of the community and the city. The East End Community Health Center is part of a network of federally funded community health centers. It is a very busy place, small and understaffed; it turns away patients, much to the chagrin of its excellent staff, who understand first and foremost that East Enders will seek health care outside of the East End only with great reluctance. The East End Community Health Center has a full-time attending physician, three full-time nurses (one RN, two LPN's), a pharmacist (part time), and a part-time pediatrician (Tuesdays all day and Wednesday and Thursday mornings).

If you are an East Ender, it is acceptable to use the term "clinic" to refer to the health center; if you are an outsider or a developer, you must say "health center." "Clinic" carries negative connotations as a place where only poor people go to get health care.

The East End Community Health Center is a model of culturally sensitive, community-based primary care, one that certainly could and should be replicated in other community settings. The director of nursing, Elizabeth, is an especially impressive person. Her communication skills alone could be the subject of an entire chapter. Not only can she convince a pregnant teenager to receive prenatal care, she can talk to the Junior League women, the neighborhood business leaders, and the architects of the new health center (which opened in June 1997) with ease, grace, and sincerity. Elizabeth is a strong patient advocate; "The patient is always right" is her motto. She tells me that there were some issues with an older doctor, who expected the nurses to take care of him, an old familiar pattern, she explains. "Our first priority is always to take care of the patients first."

Elizabeth has earned the title of "boss," a true term of endearment. It is to her that all of the regulars turn; at times, they refuse to talk to other nurses. When Elizabeth is not there, the patients may transfer their loyalties temporarily, but they always go back to Elizabeth. She mothers patients and staff; she scolds them; she supports them; she trains them. When she sees staff with an "attitude," she helps them change to become more cooperative, supportive health care providers.

One person does four jobs in the East End Community Health Center: reception, phone answering, billing, appointments. Nurses not only take care of patients, they pay bills, answer phones, and train new doctors. At other health centers, a single person does each of these jobs. In the East End, three nurses and one physician see as many patients in one month as twenty health care providers see in other, larger health centers. "We are turning away patients," Elizabeth laments. "How many?" I ask. "We are too busy to keep track," she replies. It is clear that more space is needed desperately. But more space occupied by more patients demands more staff. The transition from the old to the new health center will take time and skill.

The board of trustees is a community-based board with a majority of its members East Enders from various walks of life. One board member is an elderly black woman who has lived in the community her entire life. Another is a white woman who is a retired courier. Another is an East End property owner, a white woman, who describes herself as property poor. A white male real estate investor who was born and bred in the East End also sits on the board. The board president is a dedicated white Appalachian man whose family migrated to Cincinnati when he was a young boy.

In 1993, when I was asked to join the board, I was very hesitant. I said no at first, not wanting to influence decisions directly (by contributing to discussions, voting, etc.). The issues under discussion at board meetings were, after all, the issues I was trying to study—where and how to build the new health center, whether to close the pharmacy, what kind of equipment to buy. The board president urged me to reconsider; so did several other members. I agreed and have learned an enormous amount about what it takes to run a community health center, everything from accounting to auditing to record keeping to, of course, patient care. The teamwork required of the staff is almost superhuman.

The front door of the East End Community Health Center abuts Eastern Avenue in Upper East End. "It's a wonder there are not more wrecks out here," says one of the nurses as she peers out to the street from a second-story window. People drive fast and their brakes screech as they stop in front of the Queen Cafe, the health center's nearest neighbor to the west. Eighty-year-old Opal Whitmore, a lifelong East Ender and senior board member lives next door, on the eastern side. She's a very spry woman.

One day as I was driving down Eastern Avenue, I pulled over to say hello to her and she talked to me for an hour, all the while leaning on the broom she was using to sweep her sidewalk. "We don't rent out the downstairs anymore, honey," she told me. "It's just too much trouble." I hadn't asked about her apartment beneath her living quarters, but it was obviously on her mind. Her husband is something of a recluse, so she enjoys the company provided by her proximity to the health center, especially when she is called on to be a cosigner on checks for Health Center projects. She has established close relationships with the nurses, one of whom retrieved Opal's false teeth after they fell out during a bad spell. Opal was so grateful, she repaid the nurse with a large and quite costly box of perfumes. Her knowledge of East End history is vast and she has a wealth of old photos and newspaper clippings to embellish her detailed narratives. When she gave me several of her albums to look at, I was afraid to touch some of the pictures, they were so brittle from age. She even had a picture of the health center when the building was a savings and loan. She became a board member emeritus in 1996, just after the board agreed that she was having trouble following the basics of managed care.

New board members, especially East Enders, are always being sought.

The president welcomes people who want to get involved. In 1996, a barmaid from the Queen Cafe became a board member by virtue of her lifelong residence in the East End.

On days when the health center opens at nine and closes at five, patients sit quietly in the rows of chairs that face the receptionist in the small but cozy area that is the main waiting room on the first floor. Men and women hold small children; women monitor their toddlers. Occasionally, people come in cussing, upset, and on the verge of losing control. Mostly, though, the patients wait quietly, talking in low tones, comforting children with fevers, earaches, and colds. Posters on the walls warn against shaking a baby, encourage the use of free smoke detectors, and advise regular checkups. There is a WIC (Women, Infants, and Children) poster on the wall. Pamphlets explaining the availability of Lamaze childbirth classes are neatly piled on the reception desk.

The health center's smallness, intimacy, and warmth have both pluses and minuses. Upstairs in the bathroom next to the medical records and between the record office and a small conference room where the staff retreat to eat lunch is a bathtub with feet. The atmosphere is warm, homey, small; the nurses call people "honey." The small examining rooms and a small office are behind the reception area. Patients have to be careful what they say to the doctor or the nurse because everyone is within earshot. The opening of the old bank vault that used to function as a pharmacy takes up one side of the waiting room just under the stairs that lead to the medical records room. The pharmacy had to close in 1996 because it was running a $1,500 monthly deficit. Since the new health center's groundbreaking in June 1996, every dollar is needed to be sure that it can function. A large deficit can no longer be absorbed.

Everyone agrees that the East End needs a new health center. The present one is indeed tiny; privacy is impossible. There literally is nowhere to go to have a confidential conversation. Patients withhold information. The board agrees that patient privacy is a real problem and considers privacy to be a high priority in the design of the new health center. When the president of the health center's board of trustees speaks of the new building, his eyes light up.

Doctors, young and old, pass in and out of the East End Community Health Center. A young one who had a gentle manner with patients left for an immunology residency. For a short time, he was replaced by an older doctor who, before joining the University of Cincinnati Family Medicine Department, had spent twenty-five years as a solo practitioner in a solidly Appalachian county in rural Ohio. Elizabeth was afraid they were wearing him out. The pace at the health center can be very hectic. She decided to take only existing patients—no new ones who needed lengthy intake physicals. Now there is a new young doctor, just out of his residency at a high-powered teaching hospital in Cleveland. He was born and educated in Nepal and has a special interest in Appalachian people. His gentle manner and caring attention to sensitive aspects of patient care have gained him immediate acceptance in the East End community.

A Monthly Meeting of the Health Center Board of Trustees

THE NEW HEALTH CENTER

The president of the board calls the meeting to order. It is clear he will take no nonsense as he sits at the head of a long table (two folding tables placed end to end and covered with paper) fashioned each month just for the board meeting. The first topic is the new health center. A few people want to control the whole process—from the design of the facility itself to the control of the choice of the architects and construction company.

The executive director of both the East End and the Mount Auburn Health Centers sits opposite the board president. He handles any filibustering and manipulative behavior with a gentle, soft-spoken manner, but with an iron hand. He explains that the board will hear presentations from several architectural and engineering firms that will be chosen from a larger set of firms. The executive committee, composed of the board president and the executive director, will narrow down the choices.

The board hears four presentations, each an hour long. The president hands out a checklist for the board members to fill out on each firm; there is some resistance—"Why can't we just vote?" someone protests. He responds by saying, "We are using federal dollars, we must have evidence of our selection process. We must document."

The board's selection of architects and engineers is made only after much discussion at other meetings and vigorous grant writing on the part of the executive director. The health center currently has $300,000 in federal funds and $75,000 in city funds for the new health center. A local bank has provided the mortgage to cover the remaining costs.

THE HERITAGE EXHIBIT

The motives of the American radical engaged in organizational work will be viewed by many people and organizations with suspicion, cynicism and hostility. They will measure him with the only measuring stick that a materialistic society has taught them, one that is marked in units of selfishness, exploitation, money, power, and prestige. They will wonder and ask, "What's in it for him?" "What's his angle?" "What's his cut?" "There must be a catch in it some place—what is it?" "People don't do things for nothing—what's he doing it for?" (Alinsky 1989: 89)

The next topic of the board meeting is the heritage exhibit, a collection of photographs and narratives officially entitled *The Life and Times of East End Heritage*. This project was designed by community leaders to operate as a tool of empowerment. The health center is acting as the fiscal agent for the project, although the project itself does not belong to it, but, rather, to the Pendleton Heritage Center (see Chapter 10). At the time the heritage exhibit project team was writing grants to support the exhibit, the strongest East End nonprofit organization with tax-exempt status (501[C][3]) was the health center.[3]

At a meeting on February 23, 1995, the same few who want to control the design of the new health center at this meeting wanted a list of the checks written for the creation of the exhibit from the more than $20,000 obtained through grants. The health center's accountant presented a summary of the project's funds ending December 31, 1994. The summary was brilliant—specific enough to indicate where the money was spent, but vague enough so as not to reveal specific details.

Questions about who benefits from grant monies have come up before. When we first started collecting photographs for the exhibit, one of the first questions asked was who was getting paid by the grant? At that time, I took great pains to explain that the monies were necessary to make slides of the old family photos and to construct the exhibit itself. All of my own professional services were being donated to the project, as were the countless hours spent by East Enders and consultants. Several members of the East End Community Health Center Board, who are also members of the Pendleton Heritage Center Board, went to great lengths to underline the voluntary nature of the project when the issue was raised again at the February 23 board meeting.

I am convinced that the questioning of the allocation of heritage exhibit funds is the work of a set of colonialists (see Chapter 11) in the East End whose divide-and-conquer techniques include accusing researchers and advocates of profiteering from grant funds and then co-opting grassroots people to turn East Enders against other East Enders and against researchers and advocates. The joint efforts of the executive director, the president of the board of trustees, and other strong grassroots leaders have not allowed these colonialists to gain control of the health center.

Patients as People

The following descriptions of patients are based on actual illness problems seen at the East End Community Health Center. To protect patient confidentiality, no individual patient is described exactly. Some ethnographic liberties have been taken to integrate the details of patients' lives into East End culture and community.

Linda

Linda Carter, in 1996, is a forty-five-year-old white Appalachian who suffers from chronic anxiety ("nerves") and substance abuse. She is part of a large family of rural to urban migrants. Like her father, she is a heavy drinker. Like her mother before her, she became pregnant as an adolescent and feels overwhelmed by her responsibilities to her nuclear and extended families. Her mother and her sister, Jeanine, in particular, are very demanding. She seems always to be caught in a web of emotional and financial obligations that she cannot fulfill. The third generation—Linda's children—seems to be following the pattern of adolescent pregnancy, high anxiety, depression ("nerves"), and early school dropout. Linda's case raises questions about the relationships between social stress and illness.

> "Never mind," Helen said sharply. "We're fixing to be late, that's all. I'm taking Vonda Louise in to Valleydale to the doctor." She cast this news back over her shoulder as she hurried down the walk. "She's just about out of nerve pills." (Lee Smith 1995: 213)

Linda spent her younger adult years working as a waitress in a small restaurant and bar on the outskirts of the East End. In her early childhood, she lived in a small town in rural Ohio, but moved to the East End at age three. She is a chronic sufferer of the not unfamiliar Appalachian culture-bound syndrome called "nerves," which is often very severe and incapacitating.[4]

Linda's presenting symptoms include a history of chronic headaches, chest pain, and a variety of other somatic complaints, which may be linked to her low self-esteem and high levels of anxiety. In the past, she has complained of tension headaches, migraines, chest pain, shoulder and back pain, and chronic diarrhea. In addition to these, she experiences bouts of depression and anxiety, which she describes as "nerves," and long periods of abuse of alcohol, street drugs, and prescription drugs. She has tried to kill herself several times.

Family History

Linda was born in 1951 and has eight siblings. Both of her parents were heavy drinkers and, at times, smoked marijuana; they frequently separated but never divorced. Because of his drinking, Linda's father had difficulty holding down a full-time job. He took odd jobs periodically, often working several different jobs in one week. He occasionally took a temporary factory job. In his later years, he lived with Linda but contributed no money to the household. He died in 1985 of liver disease. Just before he died, he was showing signs of dementia.

Linda's mother, Bea, was pregnant with her first child at sixteen. At age sixty-three, she is a heavy smoker and suffers from emphysema. In 1975, she was diagnosed with panic attacks and often complained of an intense anxiety when she left her house. She feared that she would do something inappropriate in public. In addition, she feels that Linda and her other daughter, Jeanine, impose on her and depend on her too much. At the same time, she becomes angry if they fail to visit her regularly, at least several times per week. She often laments that she has failed her daughters and her son Herman because all three have taken drug overdoses. Moreover, she has had considerable trouble dealing with her youngest son, Benny, who has been a problem since his adolescence if he does not get his way. Bea attributes this tendency to the fact that Benny's father died in Vietnam when Benny was an infant.

Linda dropped out of school after completing the seventh grade. At age thirteen, she was treated for pelvic inflammatory disease. Her early years with her husband, Eric, were marred by his alcoholism, his subsequent abuse of her, and his conviction for breaking and entering. He was released from prison in 1978, at which time he took a maintenance job at a school. Together, they have five daughters, though Linda has had several miscarriages and an abortion.

The children have been a consistent source of stress for Linda, who supports the family through Aid to Families with Dependent Children (AFDC). The eldest daughter began bearing children at age fourteen and now has three children. She lives in a neighboring community. Molly, Linda's second child, suffers from low self-esteem and anxiety,

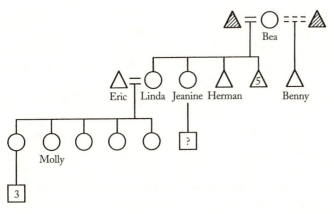

Figure 12. Linda Carter

which she calls "nerves." Her family describes her as "following in her mother's footsteps." She also smokes heavily and complains frequently of asthma and shortness of breath. Both the eldest daughter and Molly have left school.

The children have had a tendency to act out in response to Linda's substance abuse and suicide attempts. Children's Protective Services has consistently been involved in the affairs of the family, although the children have never been removed from the home.

Clinical Care

Linda has been a patient at the East End Community Health Center since 1975. She is malnourished and visits frequently for a variety of complaints. She often looks tense, with an agitated affect, and talks about suffering from "nerves." The nurses at the health center have provided her with regular, but informal, counseling. The sessions are not scheduled and these are not psychiatric nurses. She often requests refills for her prescriptions of Elavil and Vicodin, used to treat her recurrent headaches. She also requests more "nerves medication."

In 1988, she became very depressed and began to abuse Xanax, an antianxiety agent. She also began to disregard her appearance. She refused to bathe or wear her false teeth. She complained that she had many problems with her children and other family members. She had trouble controlling her children at home, and the children's teachers were concerned about possible attention-deficit disorder. These problems became overwhelming for Linda and precipitated several suicide attempts. She was referred for counseling to Central Psychiatric Clinic, but she refused to seek help outside of the East End. Her refusal to go to other referred doctors can be understood, in part, as her fear of unfamiliar health care settings that might discriminate against her for being poor. Her already demonstrated problems involving loss of control and sense of autonomy would be sharpened in these outside-the-community institutions. East Enders commonly refuse referrals.

Many of Linda's complaints appear to be linked to her overwhelming family responsibilities, both financial and emotional. Her mother and siblings insist that she buy them food, even though she has four girls of her own to feed. When her sister Jeanine had a number of health problems, she expected Linda to take care of her children. These added responsibilities came at the same time Linda felt overwhelmed with the care of her own children. Her husband's conviction and his alcoholism placed additional strain on their relationship.

Linda's physical problems can be understood as her way of coping with anxiety. She then requests medication to alleviate her symptoms. By turning her social stress into medical problems, she tries to validate and seek support for her family problems from the health center staff. She also avoids the stigma the community generally places on mental disorders. The staff members express great sympathy for her but, at the same time, they are frustrated by the sense of helplessness they feel when Linda returns to the health center repeatedly with little or no improvement. Even attempts on the part of the primary care physician to recommend a "counselor" rather than a psychiatrist, meet with repeated rejections.

Loni

Loni Kiser, born in 1941, is a white Appalachian who is part of a large East End family all of whom are seriously ill with several chronic diseases. The resources to deal with their health problems are scarce. In addition to many issues surrounding noncompliance with medical treatment, the Kisers' patterns of illness present issues for the treatment of chronic disease as it manifests itself in multiple and complex forms. When the mainstay of the family is incapacitated, the health of the entire family is threatened. Diets are broken and compliance with medical regimens breaks down.

Loni's medical problems include a history of diabetes, renal disease, and COPD (Chronic Obstructive Pulmonary Disease or emphysema).

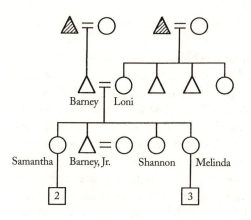

Figure 13. Loni Kiser

She also has high cholesterol and triglyceride levels, is a smoker, and at 5'6" and 250 pounds, is significantly overweight.

Family History

Loni is married to Barney Kiser and they have four children. She was formerly a cashier at a dry cleaners but had to quit because of her failing health. She had spells of nausea that she attributed to the chemical exposure.

Loni's family has a history of renal disease. Her father died of kidney failure at age forty-five. Her two brothers have been on dialysis since they reached ages thirty-two and thirty-six, respectively. Her sister has been ill for some time but has never been diagnosed with kidney disease.

Her husband, Barney, was born in 1938 and is currently receiving SSDI after having a heart attack in 1980. He also suffers from tuberculosis, diabetes, and hypertension. Before the onset of his multiple problems, he drove a truck for a large trucking company based in Lexington, Kentucky. Barney's father died of tuberculosis a number of years ago.

Shannon was born in 1960. She has had a series of short-term jobs: waitress, beautician, and cashier at a local convenience store. In 1993, she was assaulted and raped while at work alone at a 24-hour convenience store. Her injuries required twenty-five stitches. She was documented to be HIV negative before the rape and is now HIV positive. Before the rape, she was diagnosed with depression and was treated with antidepressants. She talked about being abused as a teenager by a boyfriend who was much older than she. She has a sixteen-year drinking history and occasionally smokes tobacco and marijuana. She currently lives in West Virginia.

The Kisers' daughter Samantha was born in 1966. She is a food service worker and has recently moved out of the East End because of the scarcity of affordable housing. Her new residence is in Spencer Hill, a large apartment complex that people call "little East End," in Mount Washington, a nearby Cincinnati neighborhood. Many East Enders have moved to Spencer Hill, because it is one of the closest sources of affordable housing. Samantha is currently without health insurance. She has suffered from kidney problems since 1981, has high LDL and triglyceride levels, and is obese. She also has diabetes and hypertension. She takes insulin in order to treat her diabetes, but has considerable difficulty following her diet. She has two children, one of whom is five years old, has asthma, and is on daily inhalers. The other is seven and has been diagnosed with attention deficit disorder.

Barney, Jr., was born in 1970, and, like Loni, is significantly overweight (5′8″, 228 pounds). He suffers from diabetes and hypertension. Since dropping out of high school, he has been working as a parking attendant at a local restaurant. He is married with no children. He also has trouble taking his medications and following diets and continues to drink and smoke heavily, despite the risk to his health.

Melinda was born in 1977. She has not yet developed any signs of renal disease or diabetes, but smokes and drinks frequently. She became pregnant at age fourteen, had a miscarriage, and subsequently gave birth to three children, all with different fathers.

Clinical Care

Loni has been a patient at the East End Community Health Center since 1986, when she first began to feel sick. She had her first episode of renal disease at age forty-two. In February 1995, she developed some paralysis on her left side, possibly due to a stroke.

Loni has been receiving treatment for kidney failure at the University of Cincinnati's Dialysis Center after referral by the East End Community Health Center. She stopped smoking for six months in 1972, but now smokes more heavily than ever, despite repeated attempts on the part of nurses and doctors at the health center to urge her to stop. Her lung problems have worsened as a result. In 1986, while she was in Bethesda Hospital, she was put on a special diet to control her weight as well as to manage her chronic medical problems.

The Kisers are a very close family; they attend church together, and in the summer they go on weekly camping trips. Loni suffers greatly, however, from the added stress created for her by her family's serious health problems. She is adamant that they follow their diets and keep regular appointments at the East End Community Health Center. Loni comes to the health center frequently to have her blood pressure and sugar levels checked. When her own health problems worsen, she is often unable to look after her children. On one occasion when Loni was hospitalized, Samantha refused to follow her diet. As a result, her diabetes got completely out of control. With close monitoring and careful dietary control, the Kiser family is able to keep health problems under control.

Chelsea

Chelsea Nelson, born in 1981, is a fifteen-year-old white Appalachian mother of a six-month-old baby. Chelsea's adolescent pregnancy was carried through with supportive family members, including her parents and the seventeen-year-old father of the baby. Her pregnancy is typical of many adolescent pregnancies in the East End because abortion and adoption are viewed very negatively. Any baby belongs to the family. Had the family been unable to provide support, it is very likely that someone else in the community would have adopted Chelsea's baby informally. This is part of practical kinship, that is, the creation of family ties when necessary.

While Chelsea's family is relatively well off, they have had to struggle to provide for her and her baby. Chelsea lives in the East End with her mother, Della, and her father, Wes. At age fourteen, she became pregnant and left school shortly thereafter. This was an unplanned, unwanted pregnancy, which was very difficult for her parents to accept. They eventually resigned themselves to helping Chelsea with the new baby, since neither abortion nor adoption was acceptable to them. They believe they are responsible for the child and comment that "it's ours." East Enders virtually always keep their children, so Chelsea and her parents have not behaved in any way outside of the cultural patterns of the community.

Family History

Chelsea is a very attractive young woman who is known in the East End as one of the "street people," teenagers who "hang out" on the street and are active in teen gangs. One of the favorite locations for teen street

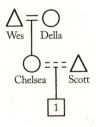

Figure 14. Chelsea Nelson

people is a bench marking a bus stop just west of the health center. Chelsea can be seen "hanging" on the bench with the father of her baby. In this environment, Chelsea is exposed to teen fighting, drugs, and sex.

In the East End, a young woman's self-esteem is connected to how sexual she appears to be. There is likely to be pressure from others—"you get you a man"—to take part in sexual activities at an early age. Chelsea must also appear to be "tougher than any of the boys" and occasionally takes part in "turf wars."

Chelsea applied for a medical card to pay for the expenses of her pregnancy. Even though her thirty-three-year-old mother will be the one to raise the baby, Chelsea felt that she wanted to handle her prenatal and delivery costs on her own.

Scott, the father of the baby, is a seventeen-year-old East Ender who, at the time of the baby's birth, was a full-time student at a vocational school. Before enrolling in this school, he was out of school for some time and unable to find work. He talks very positively about his woodworking projects at the vocational school and is planning to become an apprentice to a cabinetmaker when he graduates. He was supportive and very involved throughout Chelsea's pregnancy and has remained involved in the baby's life.

Clinical Care

When Chelsea first became pregnant, she went to the East End Community Health Center. During the pregnancy, Elizabeth, the head nurse, became very concerned about her because, at 5'6", she weighed only 115 pounds. In addition, she had been in a street fight, although she was unhurt. With the support of her family, she was able to attend childbirth classes.

The baby was born in June 1995 and was healthy except for some slight jaundice. After Chelsea had the baby, her family and Scott rallied around her to provide for the care and financial support of the baby. They were determined that neither she nor the baby would be forced to accept public assistance.

Chelsea has since gone on birth control and says she wants no more children. She and the baby visit the center regularly for checkups.

Lucy and Randy

Lucy Simpson Rosin represents an extreme case of difficult adaptation to the urban environment. Shortages of cash related to low-paying and insecure jobs, access to alcohol on the job, and the difficulties of juggling work and child care responsibilities all contribute to high levels of stress and morbidity for the entire family, particularly for Lucy.

In 1996, Lucy Rosin, a white Appalachian, was sixty-one years old. She was born blind in one eye. She has a history of chronic depression and "nerves." She has been hospitalized for depression and has attempted suicide eleven times. Lucy uses both the East End Community Health Center and University Hospital. She has a history of respiratory problems, arthritis, and asthma.

Lucy's husband, Randy Rosin, is a sixty-year-old white male. He suffers from cirrhosis of the liver. He was disabled after being shot four times in the abdomen and legs in February 1981. He is now on SSDI.

Family History

Lucy and Randy have lived in the East End most of their lives. Lucy was born in Mount Adams, a formerly Appalachian neighborhood in Cincinnati that is now completely gentrified. Her parents were from Madeira, a town with some farms to the east of Cincinnati. She remembers that her father's parents had an eighty-acre farm in Harrison, Ohio, where she would sometimes spend the summer. Randy's parents were originally from Tennessee and West Virginia. His father worked in the coal mines in West Virginia for many years until he developed black lung disease.

Randy quit school in fifth grade. He worked for the City Department of Public Works and then as a furniture mover before he was shot. Lucy wanted to be a seamstress when she was younger. She now tends bar and collects social security. Her access to alcohol is constant because of her job. She talks about changing jobs so that she will not be tempted to drink.

Randy and Lucy rent an apartment above an East End bakery. The apartment is in poor condition, and the Rosins are forced to turn on the gas stove for heat. Moreover, their roof has structural damage and leaks

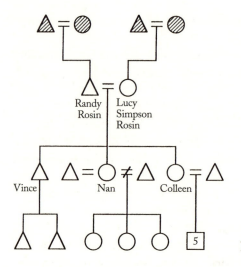

Figure 15. The Rosin Family

every time it rains. They have tried to patch it, but their landlord refuses to provide the materials.

Lucy and Randy have three children. All three dropped out of school in the tenth grade. Their son, Vince, is thirty years old and lives in Denver. He has been in and out of jail, mostly for minor offenses. He is unmarried and has two sons. Both of the Rosins' daughters, Nan and Colleen, live in the East End. Nan has three daughters from her first marriage and has since remarried. She also works as a barmaid in a local establishment. Colleen is married with five children. She has worked at various jobs, in nursing homes, restaurants, and the local convenience store. She has had to rely on neighbors and friends to "watch" her children, however, and she is constantly juggling her domestic responsibilities with her work obligations. She has lost several jobs after taking time off to care for her children when they were ill. In early 1996, she was hospitalized in Bethesda Hospital for a nervous breakdown. Her husband has worked at several temporary jobs, which often include working the night shift. When he can, he supplements these with odd jobs in landscaping, car repair, and house painting.

Clinical Care

Lucy has had problems with her vision since birth. She was born blind in one eye. She had five surgeries to correct the condition, which kept her out of school until she was seven. She now suffers from cataracts. Lucy also has asthma and regularly uses an inhaler. In 1981, she was hospitalized for pneumonia. Lucy has a history of chronic depression, which she refers to as "nerves." She states that this depression is related to stress concerning her children: "I let things build up." In her last suicide attempt, she drank vodka until she was unconscious.

In November 1990, she attempted self-mutilation by trying to "slice [her] guts up," for which she needed thirty stitches. She was hospitalized for a month after this suicide attempt. She comes to the health center regularly to talk to the nurses about her "nerves." Currently, she takes Valium for the condition. She has a history of drug abuse. The doctor at the health center has talked to her about smoking and sent her for pulmonary function testing at the University of Cincinnati Hospital. She was found to have the beginning signs of Chronic Obstructive Pulmonary Disease.

Randy uses the University of Cincinnati Liver Clinic. He suffers from cirrhosis of the liver. He is supposed to have plenty of fresh fruit and vegetables as well as a low-salt diet; however, he and Lucy are on food stamps and, since they share all resources with their children, do not have enough money to maintain such a diet. He also has had many health problems related to the shooting. Randy states that the shooting happened when he got into a fight with a neighbor. They were both drunk at the time.

Caroline and Gary

Rural-to-urban migration has hit the Reed family hard. In 1955, they came from rural Ohio to Cincinnati after they could no longer make ends meet on their small tobacco farm. A large family and a series of psychosocial stresses have created serious health problems. The Reed family represents another extreme case of difficulties initiated by rural-to-urban migration: domestic violence and substance abuse.

In 1996, Caroline Reed, a Caucasian, was sixty-eight. Her presenting symptoms include a history of chronic back pain, stomach disorders, headaches, and depression. Her husband, Gary, was born in 1925 and died in 1985. Before his death, he had numerous health problems, including high blood pressure, chronic back pain, and heart problems. He suffered from bouts of depression and had long periods of substance abuse (alcohol and prescription drugs).

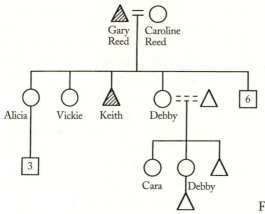

Figure 16. The Reed Family

Family History

Caroline was born in Hamersville, a rural town in Ohio. She is a first-generation rural-to-urban migrant, as was Gary. He was a bus driver for a number of years until poor health forced him to go on SSDI. Domestic abuse was a way of life for Gary and Caroline, who often "beat each other up" in "knock down fights."

The Reeds have ten children. One of their daughters, Alicia, is forty-five years old and has a serious alcohol and drug abuse problem. Because of this, Caroline and Gary were forced for several years to care for her three children, one of whom has several learning disorders, including dyslexia and attention deficit disorder. Another daughter, Vickie, was injured in 1985. She too, has a substance abuse problem. Keith, born in 1962, had a history of cardiac problems. He developed myocardial ischemia at age twelve and was treated for a seizure disorder. He passed away in 1988.

Debby, born in 1956, suffers from low self-esteem and has recovered from several overdoses of hard drugs. She is also known to abuse prescription drugs, which she buys and sells on the streets. She is the victim of domestic abuse by her common-law husband. They have been together for over twenty years. She also suffers from frequent, incapacitating headaches. Debby has three children, a son and two daughters. Her daughter Cara suffers from epilepsy. Cara and her boyfriend moved to Kentucky and, while there, robbed a Pizza Hut. Cara refuses any treatment for her epilepsy and refuses to use birth control.

Debby's other daughter, also named Debby, has a young son. In 1995, she had to take him to Children's Hospital after he fell out of a window while the adults were having a party and were not paying attention. Children's Protective Services was called and considered taking the child away from his mother to be raised by his grandmother; however, they were informed by the social worker that the baby would be better off with his mother.

Clinical Care

Caroline has complained of back pain for a number of years, but its etiology remains unknown. Her peptic ulcer has caused her considerable pain, and the health center nurses describe her as often coming to the East End Community Health Center "screaming and cussing." In 1983, she began to vomit blood and subsequently had surgery. She suffers from incapacitating headaches as well as depression and anxiety, which she refers to as suffering from nerves. She has not been treated for these conditions.

Like Caroline, Gary also suffered from depression. He had a serious substance abuse problem and drank heavily every day. He also abused prescription drugs and smoked for forty-three years, despite being constantly short of breath. Gary had dangerously high blood pressure and in 1979 was hospitalized for chest pain. Later that year he had a heart attack. In 1981, he began to receive SSDI due to a chronically dislocated knee and back pain. His problems with mobility worsened in 1982, when his back pain became so severe that he was unable to leave his bed. He died in 1985. Caroline collected a large sum for back SSDI.

Because of health problems, the Reeds became dependent on the welfare and disability system. There is evidence of widespread substance abuse, domestic abuse, and sexual abuse—Gary was accused by Caroline of having sex with one of their daughters. Given the very high levels of tension in the family, it was difficult for the children to feel any peace. They constantly fought over money and squandered substantial amounts on alcohol and entertainment. Caroline moved to Kentucky in 1996. Her children strongly disapprove of this and believe that "she's leaving us." This separation anxiety has caused further stress for the family.

As first-generation rural-to-urban migrants, the Reeds appear to suffer from a type of situational depression that results when people move to the city. Families from rural areas seek economic opportunities in cities. Once they arrive, however, they are forced to take low-paying jobs in which they have little control over their own resources, time, and labor. Thus, when they cannot attain economic success, they experi-

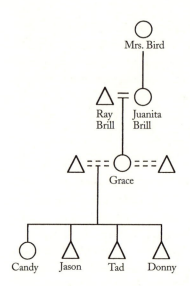

Figure 17. The Brill Family

ence relative deprivation, anger, and disappointment. East End Community Health Center professionals call this depression the "East End Syndrome." It is known more commonly in Appalachia as "nerves."

Candy

Low self-esteem is the central issue for thirteen-year-old Candy Brill, who is an attractive and intelligent white Appalachian.

Her presenting symptoms include a history of depression and anxiety. She often mentions that her nerves are bothering her. She has attempted suicide twice. Her family, however, has been reluctant to seek treatment for her.

Family History

Candy has three siblings: Jason, ten; Donny, six; and Tad, eight. Her mother, Grace, is a heavy drinker, as are her maternal grandparents, Juanita and Ray Brill. Ray works in a book bindery. Both Juanita and Grace are waitresses. The children spend a great deal of time around the restaurant, which is an important place in the community.

Grace was pregnant with Candy when she was twelve years old. At age twenty-four, Grace learned that she was HIV positive. She constantly teases Candy about the prospects of her becoming pregnant soon.

Candy is determined to avoid pregnancy, although she spends enormous amounts of time trying to attract boys by putting on dramatic makeup. She dyes her hair bright blond and constantly changes her hairstyle. She can be seen walking up and down Eastern Avenue or hanging out with other teens in front of the recreation center.

Clinical Care

In 1994, Candy was admitted to Children's Hospital after attempting suicide by drinking turpentine and taking pills. Her family swears they will never return to Children's Hospital. They claim she was treated very badly there—discriminated against for being poor. About six months after her hospitalization, she began talking again about killing herself. A close friend of the family suspected she was being abused by her mother's boyfriend and that she needed to talk to someone about it. The friend asked whether I would talk to Candy. I agreed on the condition that Candy and her mother keep an appointment with a child psychiatrist at Central Psychiatric Clinic who agreed to see Candy without charge.

Candy's emotions were labile; at several points in our conversation her eyes filled with tears. She talked about her family, about how important the East End is to her, about her worries that the East End is slipping away from East Enders because developers are building houses that the poor cannot afford. She was worried about her brothers and the kind of trouble they might get into hanging out on the street.

After repeated urging to get Candy and her mother to keep the appointment, it became clear that their resistance to Central Clinic was more than a matter of scheduling. Since I felt strongly that a psychiatrist was needed, I arranged for the family friend to contact Candy's great-grandmother, Mrs. Bird, who lives downtown. "If anyone can get Candy and Grace to do something, it's Mrs. Bird," the family friend in the East End told me. The attempts to contact Mrs. Bird were unsuccessful, however, and Candy never went to see the psychiatrist. The underlying issue here was Grace's fear that the social workers and psychiatrists at the clinic would decide that she was a "bad mother" and remove Candy from her household.

Ella

Ella Jenkins was a seventy-eight-year-old black Appalachian who, from the early 1960s to 1997, suffered from high blood pressure (hypertension).

Family History

Ella's parents migrated to Cincinnati from Georgia in 1923, when she was four years old. Her mother had no other children. She was a hard-working woman who worried constantly about Ella's well-being in a household with an alcoholic father. She feared that he might abuse their daughter while she was at work.

Ella was a very responsible child who did a great deal of work around the house. She was rather withdrawn and spent most of her time with her family. She completed high school and went immediately to work. She and her mother were domestic workers for some forty years each, and Ella took her mother's place when her mother decided to retire. They worked for a white family in Hyde Park. Ella has no children of her own, and she never married. Ella's father worked for the railroad.

Clinical Care

The health professionals at the East End Community Health Center had difficulty getting Ella to come in for appointments. They arranged for a visiting nurse to come to her home, but still, her blood pressure remained out of control. In 1995, her blood pressure became more difficult to control, and there was concern that she might not be taking her medications. She consistently had a blood pressure between 210 and 220; normal blood pressure is usually between 110 and 130. She seemed to have problems finding transportation to the health center.

Ella's blood pressure, while high, did not manifest any symptoms. There were no headaches, nosebleeds, or signs of dizziness.

When the health center's pharmacy closed in 1996, Ella had a great deal of trouble getting her medications. She was unable to afford them and, even if she could buy them, she would have had trouble getting to the nearest pharmacy, which, while close to the East End, is inaccessible by public transportation.

Ella was a proud and stubborn lady who was very set in her ways. During the flood of March 1997, she refused to evacuate without her cat, which was nowhere to be found. She was found dead in her home immediately after the flood. It is unclear whether she had a stroke or a heart attack.

Betsy

Extremely close relationships between the generations create often overwhelming responsibilities for adult caretakers of the elderly. In a culture

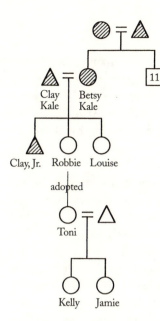

Figure 18. Betsy Kale

that regards the elderly as a regular and expected family responsibility, the elderly are kept out of hospitals and nursing homes until the last moment. While all members of the extended family help, so do neighbors and friends.

Betsy Kale was a seventy-five-year-old white Appalachian who suffered from Alzheimer's disease. The disease was advanced, and Betsy suffered from severe memory loss, combativeness, and incontinence. She has had a series of urinary tract infections and skin rashes caused by her refusal to bathe regularly. Her daughter adamantly opposed putting her in a nursing home.

Family History

Betsy was born in 1919, one of twelve siblings. She married Clay Kale, Jr., in 1940 and gave birth to three children: Clay, Robbie, and Louise. Clay III died in 1990 from complications caused by an injury during the Vietnam War.

Betsy had a variety of jobs throughout her life, including waitress and barmaid in the East End. Betsy's husband worked for a trucking company until he died in 1984. Betsy received $1,000 per month from his life insurance. She lived with her daughter, Robbie, until her death in 1992.

Clinical Care

Although Robbie was Betsy's primary caregiver, many other family members (including great-grandchildren) and neighbors contributed to her care. At one point, Robbie took in a young woman and her children because the young woman "is so good with Mom." At other points, young women and teens spent several hours daily caring for Betsy, including bathing her and giving her meals.

Betsy was first evaluated at the Alzheimer's Research Center after Robbie became convinced that her medications might need to be adjusted. Periodically, though, she would require acute care. At one point, she was brought to the emergency room by her daughter after she had fallen off a chair at home. She spent an inordinately long time in the emergency room on that occasion (on a gurney with no food or water for more than eight hours); Robbie, who is normally a calm person, grew increasingly agitated and finally succeeded in having her mother admitted to the geriatric psychiatry unit. She was thereupon placed in restraints and given medication for a urinary tract infection. The restraints upset Robbie even more, since it did not appear that Betsy required them and Robbie viewed them as a severe form of imprisonment.

While Betsy was in the hospital, a young resident tried to convince Robbie to place her mother in a nursing home. The resident was quite adamant, in fact, that Betsy was unmanageable at home and that, because of her combativeness, incontinence, and tendency to wander at all hours of the night, Robbie would be wise to give up trying to care for her mother at home. What the resident did not understand was that for a working-class Appalachian person to place any loved one outside of the home was the equivalent of a death sentence—"putting Mamaw away."

What is striking in this case is how important the great-grandchildren were to Betsy's well-being, and how important they were to reducing her level of disorientation. When Betsy refused to get in the car to go to the doctor or when she refused to take a bath or eat her meals, her great-granddaughter Kelly—a very mature four-year-old—became a miracle worker. Kelly took Mamaw by the hand and led her wherever she needed to go. No one else in the family could get Betsy to eat, to bathe, or to get in the car for doctor's appointments the way Kelly could.

Betsy's final hospital stay was a very difficult one for her family, who remained at her side around the clock. Four generations kept watch and helped Robbie make the very tough decision against another surgery. Her adopted daughter finally convinced her that Betsy was much better

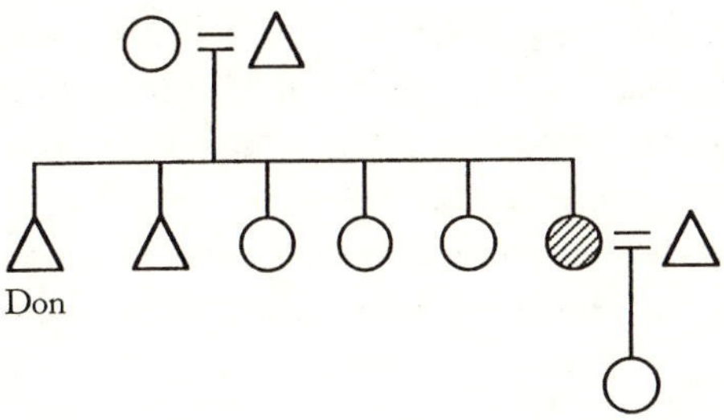

Don

Figure 19. Don Lands

off "in heaven" than she was suffering with Alzheimer's. On the anniversary of her death, her great-grandchildren fill balloons with helium and release them to Betsy in heaven. Every once in a while, Robbie talks about how much she misses "Mom."

I first met Betsy in the River Inn, sitting quietly in the back. Her quiet presence kept her daughter in balance. She came along to all the meetings, large and small, never said a word, but always listened. I remember her especially at the birth of her great-granddaughter Jamie—how happy she looked. Then she began to have symptoms of Alzheimer's. She grew frail, lost weight, refused to eat, became combative, wandered, and took off her clothes. She had become a different person.

Don

The following patient, Don Lands, received care from fellow East Enders and leaders outside of formal clinical contexts. The perceived seriousness of Don's condition and East Enders' realization that community issues had some part in his becoming depressed sparked a whole group of East Enders to monitor his condition, initially on a 24-hour basis, and subsequently on a daily basis.

Don is a thirty-eight-year-old white Appalachian who is very much involved in community affairs and who periodically is subject to bouts of severe depression, triggered by job loss or by criticism from close friends and other community leaders.

Family History

Don is part of a large family of rural-to-urban migrants. The family came to the East End in the late 1960s from Martinsville, Ohio, because there were no jobs in the small town. He is the pillar of his family; he oversees family finances and worries about the well-being of all of its members. The household consists of two adult brothers including Don, three sisters, and their parents. "We live pretty good. We're not cramped. We got enough space. Each person has their own room." Don had another sister who died in a car accident in 1985. The daughter of this sister now lives part of the time with her father and the rest of the time with Don, her uncle.

Clinical Care

In 1995, after a series of "words" with Meg, a close friend and also a community leader, during which she accused him of being lazy and an irresponsible person with respect to keeping a job, Don fell into a deep depression. He refused to talk to anyone, and he sent a letter of resignation to an important community organization.

His family and the group of guys with whom he plays darts on the weekend, were very protective of him. At one point, he seemed to disappear. Community leaders and advocates became very fearful for his well-being. Jerry, one of the community leaders, decided to call Bill Rower, with whom Don plays darts. Jerry told Bill that Don was walking the riverbanks. That night, Willy and Chuck, close friends, walked with Don for several hours and finally returned him safely to his house.

For the next week, a whole set of East Enders, including Cori and Al, who lived next to Don's place of work, checked in on him. The nonprofit board from which he had resigned had a special meeting to urge him to return. A letter was sent signed by every member of the board. He had either a phone call or a visit from someone every hour on the hour for the next several weeks.

He recovered, gradually. The hours and hours spent by East Enders who instantly formed a safety net to support him cannot be measured, but they certainly saved the health care system a great deal of money.

Summary and Conclusion

Health, culture, and community in the East End are intricately related. The patients described in this chapter are based on the kinds of illness problems most commonly seen in the community, both at the health center and in the community at large. What can we say about illnesses and illness patterns in the East End?

Diabetes and hypertension are among the most commonly seen health problems. Many people suffer from both, along with others such as ulcers, arthritis, obesity, and a variety of psychosocial problems. While "East End Syndrome" ("nerves") is not officially in the Diagnostic and Statistical Manual of Mental Disorders and while it has not been included in any epidemiological studies, it is prevalent in situations of poverty and stressful culture contact throughout the world, albeit under different labels—nerves, *susto, ataques de nervios.*[5] Depression, anxiety, headaches, suicide attempts are some of the most common symptoms.

Drinking, often heavy, is extremely common, in bars as well as homes. Any schoolchild can tell you how to deal with different kinds of drunk people; men and women, young and old battle against alcohol. Some do stop drinking; others continue to drink their meals and grow thinner and thinner. Alcohol poisoning occurs with some frequency; the last person who died from alcohol that I remember was twenty-seven years old.

Adolescent pregnancy is clearly a significant health issue. Birth control is often not used; neither is the practice of safe sex the norm. Myths about sex abound. "You can't get pregnant the first time." "You are less of a man (woman) if you use protection." Babies are raised by older women—mothers, aunts, grandmothers of the girls. I remember many conversations with health center staff about how to introduce birth control in effective ways. The reliability of different forms of birth control and the ways in which different forms work well or not so well for different age groups are issues.

Support groups and facilities for people caring for children, places outside of the home where children can be taken to play in a safe environment, and sharing of child care would all contribute to stress reduction for mothers and grandmothers. Attention-deficit disorder is a label easily pinned on East End children—but not only on East End children. One wonders what happened to the category "children with a lot of energy." Children who rarely experience any sense of safety, peace, and calm are bound to act out.

The policy and public health implications of these cases are far-reaching. Young women tend to seek help at the health center; young men do not. Some practical and creative ways of recruiting underserved groups of patients must be developed.

If we acknowledge that most adult women in the East End work outside of the home at some point in their lives and if we understand that, for the most part, the extended family is expected to pick up the slack, then we must ask about the supports—community supports, institutional supports—needed by the extended family. Adult children in extended families tend to bear heavy burdens, especially in caring for the elderly. Social service supports for a range of problems are needed, from day care centers for Alzheimer's patients to someone to check on the family. A community-based social worker would be a great asset.

The economic development of the community, regarded holistically, is critical for its health and well-being. By this, I mean jobs. The commercial and infrastructural features of development are important, but the human elements of development that enable individuals and families, especially children, not only to survive, but to thrive in healthy, creative ways are more important than any physical improvement for the future of this working-class community. While this may sound idealistic, the level of caring in the community (as we saw with the last two patients) shows that community human resources can be used very positively and that they ought to be supported, nurtured, and elaborated. High-quality, reliable, and culturally sensitive adult day care and child care supports would contribute greatly to stress reduction in the East End. Any day care center would ideally need to operate around the clock, since parents work many different shifts. Grandmothers in the neighborhood would need to be involved both as models and as advisers. Day care supports might include something as simple and as low cost as a safe place for child care providers to bring children to play.

In all cultures, when mothers cannot feed themselves and their children, they experience excruciating psychological pain, manifested as "nerves" in the East End, or what the health professionals in the East End call "East End Syndrome": anxiety and depression manifested in their mildest somatic forms as headaches, backaches, and other stress-related illnesses, and in their most serious form as depression leading to successful and unsuccessful suicide attempts. These are culture-bound syndromes in a broad sense. They are the products not just of rural-to-urban migration, but of deindustrialization, downsizing, and other structures that lead to job loss, cash shortages, in short, intensified economic and social stress.

9 | CONTESTED TERRITORY: THE STRUGGLE FOR AFFORDABLE HOUSING IN THE EAST END

Contested Territory

The East End is now contested territory. Land bankers, real estate speculators, and slum landlords (and these are not mutually exclusive categories) want to acquire and hold onto as much property as possible so that they can, in both the long and the short runs, glean as much profit as possible. To them, preserving the East End for East Enders might be a nice idea or something that they might pay lip service to in the hallowed chambers of City Hall, but when it comes right down to it— dollars and cents, that is—community preservation must not interfere with profiting from investments. Thus, for example, if the Pendleton Heritage Center will lower the value of developers' property on Hoff Avenue, it must not be built. Similarly, if affordable housing must be built, let it happen in a confined area so as not to interfere with the value of market-rate housing.

Contestation rarely happens directly. That is, developers will never come right out and say that they fear declines in their profits. Instead, they choose to pick away at the details of community projects. "The Pendleton is too expensive; it would be better to tear the old building down and build a new one for the high cost per square foot," they say. Or, they will say that the roof line is wrong or that another design detail is wrong on the plans for the Lewiston Townhomes. They will object to the placement of the driveways or even the placement of porches and windows. Many of these "well-meaning" suggestions are intended, of course, to increase the cost of affordable housing and thereby render it no longer affordable. It is easier to eliminate something by suggestions than by any kind of direct criticism.

Affordable housing must be just that—affordable. This means that rental units must be between $200 and $250 per month for two-bedroom units and $300 and $350 per month for three-bedroom units. Houses for sale must be between $60,000 and $90,000. They must be air-conditioned, and they must have hookups for washers and dryers and for cable TV. Affordable housing must be designed for humans in hot, humid Cincinnati summers; builders must not make assumptions about what is necessity and what is luxury. Affordable housing must also be well managed, so as not to insult the dignity of residents. Sounds simple, doesn't it? It isn't.

By just about anyone's definition, most housing in the East End is substandard. As in many low-income areas, abandoned and dangerous buildings in the East End create safety hazards for children and teens, who regularly "tear up" the plywood panels nailed over windows and doors. There is a high rate of arson.

When the Betz Flats closed, more than ninety people were displaced. An older man sat crying on the sidewalk; the East End had been his lifelong home. The social agencies tried to help, but there was nowhere in the East End for people to go. When the time came to talk about rehabbing "the Flats," the community spent hours and hours debating the details of the renovations—everything from financing to the actual design of the apartments. Community leaders stuck to their commitment to affordable housing and, through sheer persistence, forced a positive vote in the Area Council. Had the developers had their way, the Flats would have been torn down to make way for market-rate housing. Yet, when the Flats did open, the developer president of the Community Council had no trouble taking the credit.

While rents are generally low by overall Cincinnati standards, they are high considering that landlords spend next to nothing on repairs. I know of a bathtub that fell through from the second to the first floor. Rats can be heard and seen in the middle of the night. High ceilings make un-insulated and already difficult-to-heat apartments impossible to keep warm. Plumbing is always a problem, and residents use their ovens and stove tops for heat in winter.

I remember helping a family move into a small apartment. We piled their belongings into a corner so that we could paint the walls and the floors first. Lead-based paint peeled off in multiple layers as we were painting. It would have taken weeks to sand the floors down to bare wood. It was one of four units in a building, two upstairs and two down-stairs—a typical East End apartment building.

There are no high rises or housing projects. The one upscale high-rise visible from most parts of the East End, but actually located on the hillside, is criticized by East Enders as an eyesore. There are many single-family and two-family units. Most houses are quite old, having been built in the 1930s and the 1940s. Dwelling units stand next to and across the street from businesses, some small, some quite substantial. Many lots are vacant now and weeds are a constant problem.

The number one issue in the East End is affordable housing. For the past twenty-five years, the loss of housing units for East Enders has been dramatic. Between 1992 and 1994 alone, some eighty units were lost, including the closing of Betz Flats and the displacement of some thirteen families. The Flats reopened in 1994 as the first rehabbed affordable housing in the East End in over thirty years.

A Ribbon Cutting

Kelly's Landing, opened in May 1995, represents a real victory for the East End community: eleven three-bedroom units renting for $355 per month. This is the first affordable housing to be built in the East End in over thirty years. Officially, these are known as the Lewiston Town-homes; in the neighborhood, the project is referred to as Kelly's Landing. The traffic on Eastern Avenue both muffled and punctuated the speeches at the ribbon cutting. The mood was jubilant but tense. Board members of the East End Riverfront Community Urban Redevelopment Corporation, the Neighborhood Development Corporation, were there in force. The majority of EERCURC board members are East End residents. EERCURC's mission is to bring back both new and re-habbed housing to the East End.

People important to the community were also there in significant numbers. The director of nursing for the East End Community Health Center, a mainstay of the community, was there. Benjamin Tate, an elderly African American gentleman, veteran of the civil rights movement and longtime community organizer, represented Associated Neighborhood Practice, Inc. He had a big smile on his face. Keith Baxter, a devoted advocate and friend of the community, even though he worked for the city, attended proudly. Representatives of the lending institutions were there in force, along with housing advocates from all over the city. Members of the board of Interneighborhood Designers of Homes for Friends (IDHF), another nonprofit organization that was partners with EERCURC on the Kelly's Landing development, were well represented.

Their chairperson is a prominent Cincinnati attorney noted for her leadership and management of the Attorney's Services Association.

The onlookers were in the sun, and it was very hot, even though the river sent an occasional breeze. Megan and James Strong, two of the oldest and most respected pillars of the community, were a quiet presence. James had his seventy-eighth birthday in 1997. Megan stood behind James, as she always does. She is a tiny woman whose small frame is further diminished by her husband's bulk. When he is sitting, they are the same height. He has trouble walking now, but his involvement in EERCURC from its inception and his long history of community activism cause the younger community leaders still to see him as leading the charge to preserve and rebuild the East End community. His quiet commitment inspires all who know him and he remains active on the EERCURC board.

The Lewiston Townhomes are on prime riverfront property, and part of the tension derived from developers' disbelief that such prime property could indeed be used for affordable housing. The president of the EEAC, a developer and longtime opponent of affordable housing, sauntered in late and stood lurking behind everyone in one of the garages next to the food supplied by the management company.

The preparation for this event was long, arduous, and contentious. Many present were remembering the hours and hours of meetings in the community and hearings in front of City Council and the City Planning Commission—the long-winded and relentless picking at the details of the Lewiston development—roof lines, driveways, porches, and, at one point, a retaining wall to hold back the hillside on the north side of Eastern Avenue. Originally, there were two sites for the Lewiston Townhomes, one on the south (river) side of Eastern Avenue and the other on the north side across the street from LeBlond Park. The "LeBlond site," as it came to be called, was abandoned because of the cost of the retaining wall. No one ever came right out and said that East End developers were opposed to affordable housing because it would reduce the value of market-rate housing. A Legal Aid attorney and IDHF board member spent countless hours preparing testimony to defend affordable housing in general and the Lewiston Townhomes in particular.

Given this background, Reverend Hubbard's invocation carried meanings that he himself might not even have been aware of, although his sense of struggle is certainly clear and powerful. Everyone was solemn; Doris held my hand and others linked theirs.

Reverend Hubbard, pastor of Mount Carmel, prays:

Let us pray, God, our father, we give thanks to Thee for the occasion that brings us together this morning. We thank Thee our father for the combined efforts of all of those who have worked faithfully and diligently to bring this project to fruition. We are mindful, oh God, of the struggles and the trials but today we are able to look in smiling faces, rejoicing hearts, and wonderful spirits. We pray, oh God, that the spirit that brought this project into being will continue throughout our community, throughout our lives as your people on earth. Oh gracious God, we know that all things are possible with Thee and without Thee nothing can be done. Thank you for the faith of those who continue in the face of opposition and press forward, may their lives and their efforts be realized. We pray in His name and for His sake. Amen.

Robbie told those gathered that Reverend Hubbard had graciously "allowed us to meet in his building, provided meeting space for the development corporation board [EERCURC] when there was no other place to meet. I want to thank Reverend Hubbard and let you know that he is a big part of the East End and what is going on here." The attorney for the development corporation, Paul Silver, added: "Thank you for the use of your church for these many months. The EERCURC board has really needed your assistance and you've been wonderful." Before introducing the mayor, Paul referred to the perseverance it took to keep the project going.

The Mayor

The mayor's speech was a masterpiece of community practice and local knowledge. She acknowledged the hard work of consensus building on the part of grassroots leaders as well as the local opposition to the project; although she was vague on this point, anyone who participated in the many discussions understood the nature of the local opposition. She also injected a spiritual element into the discussion of community institution-building that is very rare, especially because her comments placed the Lewiston project in the context of the East End Riverfront Community Development Plan and all of the very difficult and long planning efforts on the part of community residents and leaders. In effect, she acknowledged factionalism at the local level and the importance of creating and implementing economic development plans that preserve communities for community residents—in this case, working-class Appalachians, black and white. Local leadership was the critical ingredient here and she knew it. She was a real neighborhood person complete with a sense of humor:

> When Robbie asked me if I would come and be part of the ribbon cutting, I was in a difficult position to refuse. We were both holding garbage bags cleaning up Eastern Avenue. I wouldn't have refused even if we weren't doing that.
>
> This project is the product of a long-term, tremendous commitment and effort on the part of everybody who's here, but also on the part of the East End community. I remember when I first got on City Council, the focus of the Community Development Committee was the East End Plan and Paul Silver was instrumental in working with others throughout the East End community to get the East End Plan approved. These homes, which are for low- and moderate-income families, were an important aspect of that plan and an important aspect of the community's commitment to making sure that people from the community would remain in the East End, regardless of all the other parts of the plan that involved re-development and development—that the commitment was a balanced commitment. The resolution of the East End Plan and the adoption by Council came about only because of the tremendous work of Robbie and Paul and others who are here and their commitment to neighborhoods, to low- and moderate-income housing, but also their willingness to work together and to come up with a consensus that not just everybody could live with, but that everybody knew was in the best interests of the community. [Some, even some of the most progressive members of City Council, regarded the plan as an antidevelopment plan that would reduce the city's taxes.]
>
> I personally felt that it was an experience which really gave me a sense of what planning and neighborhood development truly is all about. It only happens when you have real leadership. The other thing that I was very proud of when it came to this project was that when push came to shove and it really did come down to subsidizing these units for $90,000 a unit, there were questions raised and there were legitimate questions raised. But what Council understood was that if we were going to see these units done and we were going to see low- and-moderate income housing in our community, we were going to have to bite the bullet and that even in the face of then what was the local opposition, continue with our support. Daniel [Todd, a councilmember] is here and he remembers that and he knows that it took a lot of tough work to make sure that we still

ended up with the votes, but we did it—and so, on behalf of the City of Cincinnati and the Council of the City of Cincinnati, we are very proud to be partners with all of you in this project.

We really want to congratulate everybody: the builders, the developers, the financiers, the city departments, the community, everybody who has had a hand in making this a reality and made a reality for eleven families—decent, affordable, good-looking housing in the East End community. Congratulations to all of you.

The mayor's speech was impressive in its coherence and her memory of the history of the East End. It was also a spirited, inspired speech that originated in her own involvement while she was still a regular member of City Council who worked closely with the East End plan. As the person with the largest number of votes in the 1994 election for City Council, she then became mayor.

A former city councilmember and attorney for EERCURC, Paul Silver, thanked numerous people. He clearly knew the residents of the East End, especially the leaders, personally. He mentioned all of the founding members of the development corporation by name. He gave community leaders their just recognition, which is very different from most ceremonies of this sort in which community residents and leaders are hardly mentioned.

He adopted a style that was very close to reminiscing and storytelling—unusual for a prominent attorney and elected official.

I remember when we were finally getting the plan done. A lot of people really questioned whether we could actually fit in low- and moderate-income housing into a community as well as middle- and upper-income housing. There were a lot of naysayers, a lot of people that didn't think we could do that. I think this [project] is a testament to Robbie's faith in the plan and her roots in the East End. She's really made an extraordinary contribution and I know and she knows that nobody will let her stop now.

Paul introduced the president of IDHF. He was the person who had agonized the most over the delays and the details. He mentioned breaking ground to begin building across from LeBlond four years earlier to the day:

We ran into some obstacles, but we persevered and we remained true to our mission, which was to provide affordable rental housing for families. First of all, our partners, the East End Riverfront Community Urban Redevelopment Corporation, our lenders.

He makes a special point to thank the architect Tim Wexel and the attorney Jack Sinclair who really sweated out the critical moments. Before introducing Daniel Todd, Paul Silver made some incisive comments about the difficulties in accomplishing the Lewiston project. As he mentioned Daniel's perseverance, he said:

> It shouldn't be so difficult, but as Daniel and I know from years of trying to collaborate—We thought Over the Rhine was tough; this, conceivably, might even be tougher. The good news is that we have a plan; some wonderful things are happening in making that plan into a reality not just a dream. Let me let Daniel talk about this and what he sees for the future of the East End.

Daniel Todd:

> I know the sun is hot out there, because I was standing out there, so I'm going to be brief. This is a day of celebration. We owe a lot to Paul; when I came on Council, Paul was already leading the charge; we owe a lot to Paul and Robbie and Elaine and others. There are some great people in this community. As I travel around the city and I look at some of the worst conditions in our community and come here and see the possibilities, it only continues to inspire me to see that we can do a great deal for those who felt that they have been left behind. And so this is an important effort today. We want to continue to make affordable housing for everyone in our great city. We have great people who really care.

Paul then calls on Robbie:

> The most important people are the people who have stuck through this from the very beginning—the James Strongs, the Elaine Winterses, the Doris Sellses, the Bob Churches, who never, ever thought that this wouldn't happen. And Megan Strong, who stands behind James no matter what he does and has to hear all our complaints when we call to get a hold of James, said something a couple of weeks ago that brought all this home to me. Megan said: "We build houses where houses never stood before. We have affordable units that cost no East Enders their homes." We've given eleven East End families back some homes after we lost a lot of them. So, James's a great man, and you know what they say about great men . . . thank you, Megan.
>   Last night when I was trying to decide what I was gonna say— I never say what I'm goin' to—I decided that Paul Silver does have

a title—as far as the EERCURC board and the Pendleton committee, Paul Silver is the mayor of the East End. I can't tell you the amount of hours that Paul has put into the EERCURC board to make sure that we're legal, and up and running right. I guess we're all going to have to cash in pop bottles or something to pay him because he hasn't seen anything yet. I want to thank Paul for hanging in there with us. Keith Baker [a trusted city staffer] came in a little bit late. Keith, this would not be a ribbon cutting without you. He's been our adviser, our confidant; I still sneak a phone call to Keith. The only reason we had Jessica Allen [a trusted county agency employee] is because of Benjamin Tate [an activist and community organizer]—for all the training sessions he did—with different East End boards, that meant something to us; we still fight, but he tried. I think the one thing that's came from all of the fighting are eleven affordable units.

What got me moving last night was hearin' two three-year-old little girls in a bathtub laughing their heads off because they were having fun and they were back in the East End, where they belong. And that's what it's all about. These kids are back home. One of them is a seventh-generation East Ender and the other is a fourth, so that's what this is for.

The EERCURC board is here in mass: Cammy Pound, David Cafe, he is helping with the Pendleton, Doris Sells, who's chair of the Pendleton board, Anna Kim, who's also part of the East End health center board, Ester Tull who has been a part of the East End and her family for as long as any of us remember; and Elaine Winters who is now the vice president of EERCURC but during a couple of very hard years when we couldn't figure out who was running the show, Elaine was there as president. I wanted to acknowledge our EERCURC board. James Strong is still a part of the EERCURC board, but he decided not to climb up the steps. I'd like to thank them for everything they've done to help do this [project] . . . this is not a one person thing and I've gotten a lot of credit, but it's kind of like a jigsaw puzzle; they had it all laid out and all I did was kinda come in and put in the last few pieces.

That brings us to Matthew Marks. About five years ago, if Matthew Marks had walked in my house in the East End I'd a' probably throwed him out the back door. Matthew was part of a project in the East End of research and they did a report that a lot of us took exception to.[1] Matthew, being the person he is, figured if we were griping about it, that he couldn't be totally right and we couldn't be totally wrong, and vice versa. So he came back and Matthew has stayed; he helped get the EERCURC board solid again he got some other researchers involved, and out of that came the exhibit that is in the garage behind you—one panel of the exhibit. Matthew Marks has been a driving force for five years and I'll never put Matthew out a back door again.

Paul:

There is a lot more to do. People thought we couldn't have a community with different socioeconomic groups. We couldn't have a community that didn't care about each other. There are so many fourth-, fifth-, and sixth-generation East Enders that are here— give them the opportunity to stay here. Thanks for asking me to emcee this wonderful occasion, it's truly the sense of fulfillment of the dream, I think there's a lot more to do and I think everybody's aware that we're just getting started in the East End. I think that many people felt that there was a long period and not only did it take a long time to come together with the plan but I think the most important thing was that we didn't forget about it. I think there was a period where a lot of people felt that we couldn't have a community that didn't displace people or that had different socioeconomic groups living together or one that cared about each other and made sure that those who wanted to live here and live out their lives and generations as Robbie said, there's so many fourth-, fifth-, and sixth-, seventh-generation East Enders that are here, the important thing is not only to give them the opportunity to stay here but also to the work of those who have worked so hard in the past and also welcome those who live up the hill (as Robbie is so fond of saying), I think that that's exactly what this project is all about.

Matthew Marks:

Before the closing prayer I would like to ask Doris Sells to say just a few words about the Pendleton Heritage Center, which will be another phase in the East End redevelopment.

Doris Sells:

I want to say that this is indeed a great day for me because I only live a block from here and every time I walk down to the mailbox I'll be able to see these buildings and also when I walk up the other way one block at the light, that is the Pendleton Building which we, hopefully, will renovate, it will be a community building for the East End. I grew up with that building, I could give you the history of that building of seventy-three years, my years and it is a dream of mine that it be kept for the East End, for the people of the East End, and anyone else that would like to share it. We're grateful today I'm happy to say I have had a lot of support from all organizations from the EEAC up and down and we hope and pray that they will continually bless us and work with us. Thank you.

Matthew Marks:

Oh God of our mothers and fathers known by many names throughout the lands, you have guided our forebears through their ups and downs, triumphs and failures, in their efforts to keep their promises to you and to each other. You have guided us through this project and you have given it to us as a sign of hope for the people who live in the East End, for people who've been displaced and might return now, and for new people who might come to fill the empty places. This reminds us of your call to Nehemiah and his followers to rebuild the city of Jerusalem . . . it's that kind of work that our cities are in need of now, and it is we who you have called to help with that. Bless the families who will live in these homes, bless this community, and bless our city, amen.

Just one week after the ribbon cutting, in the early summer of 1995, it was discovered that, according to the tenant screening criteria established by the management company, Simms Hale, with the approval of the Lewiston Partnership (IDHF and EERCURC), anyone convicted of a felony within the last five years could not be a resident in the Lewiston Townhomes. Further, to have EERCURC board members living in the development represented, according to IDHF, a possible conflict of interest. A very tense meeting followed the informal discussions and phone calls about the conflicts of interest. The meeting was tense because approvals had been granted for the president of EERCURC to move in as a resident child care provider for a young mother of two young children. She had pleaded no contest to a felony charge several years before.

To challenge the right of an East End resident, especially a talented grassroots leader, to affordable housing was to challenge the very definition of community in the East End. But this was only the beginning of the next stage of trouble for the East End Riverfront Community Urban Redevelopment Corporation and for affordable housing in the

East End. After a summer of little activity (all boards take some time off in summer), it was time to talk about new projects for EERCURC. The Lewiston project had yielded a few thousand dollars in developers' fees to EERCURC as co-partner with IDHF, but the 501(C)(3) had still not been granted and EERCURC had not identified a new project. From the perspective of the IRS, this meant that, as a board, EERCURC was not active, and therefore not deserving of nonprofit status.

Was this another catch-22? Yes, in more ways than one. The community leaders at the Lewiston ribbon cutting ceremonies thought that one leader was receiving recognition and claiming credit for the project without proper acknowledgment being granted to the others. A few people thought that this leader not only had taken over EERCURC, she had formed alliances with those in power. The practice of community had been violated. EERCURC meetings were difficult to orchestrate and, when they did occur, they were tense. I remember one meeting in which two leaders almost came to blows.

Shortly thereafter, in the winter of 1995–1996, a new EERCURC president and executive board were elected. Meetings were calm and peaceful. Advocates worked with the board on goals and objectives, tasks of a staff member, board expansion, and future prospects. A year after the Lewiston ribbon cutting, a staff person was hired, and a new project is about to come on line. The project involves the construction of three new, owner-occupied affordable houses on Eastern Avenue. Lending institutions are in place and *pro bono* legal services have been procured from one of Cincinnati's premier law firms. The board has been strengthened and restructured to maintain community control while at the same time involving needed financial and other technical expertise.

10 THE HERITAGE CENTER COMES OF AGE: PERSISTENT LEADERSHIP, STRUGGLES, AND DREAMS

APRIL 21, 1992 [1]

We are getting closer to the Pendleton, we hope to regain
Our cries of the past three years have not been in vain
To everyone that would listen, I truly did complain
Recreation you had me worried now I feel now you are humane

The Pendleton would bring back so much good
Having access to the place where a lot of my loved ones once
    stood
It's been a long time coming, and I prayed that it would
Be given back to the East End community as it should

So many times I felt, how impossible it seemed
Wondering if it was a dream?
Hoping and praying they would see the glow and the beam
Now when we talk about the Pendleton you'll know what I mean

City Hall it is truly a must
You need to do what ever you can to build up our trust
We know the Pendleton is old and there is some rust

The Pendleton can serve the whole East End community
Having the Pendleton may bring us unity
And then there will surely be some harmony

Hoping that the help from everywhere the money will flow
So when we have our meetings everyone will know
That the Pendleton is the place to go

Thanks to everyone who is trying to make this dream be real
The Pendleton can be ours and we will have the seal
Everyone has been upfront and we have made no deal

The East End area council, we need a place of our own
And the Pendleton can be the East End area council's home
Where we can be reached on the telephone
With the Pendleton we won't have to feel we are alone

In getting the Pendleton, would be on recreation's part a good
    stand
At least we would know we are part of the plan
If we get the Pendleton, I will be your greatest fan
It will be time to "strike up the band"

Without the Pendleton we been from pillar to post
Sometimes we were cold, at times we felt we would roast
We need the Pendleton the most

At times we felt we were the lost, the last and the least
But on the opening day of the Pendleton, there will be a big feast
Hoping that then all the rumors will cease.

A Community Place

There is no place in the East End for the community, a place for community groups to meet, for community records and correspondence to
be kept, a place from which information about community events and
projects, upcoming hearings and meetings at City Hall can be dissemi-
nated. The community groups and boards are nomadic; they move their
meetings from place to place. In some cases, the movements follow a
more or less regular pattern. The East End Area Council, for example,
holds its meetings in Upper East End one month (at Saint Steven's
Church) and in Lower East End in alternate months, at the LeBlond
Recreation Center, a city-owned and -managed facility. I say more or
less regular because this alternating cycle is often broken, because there
is a competing event at the church or at LeBlond, sometimes referred to
as "the park." Meetings can also be relocated because the leadership of
the EEAC has simply decided to do so.

Other community groups do not have even this minimal pattern of
regular meeting places. That is, while the LeBlond Recreation Center
is always a possible meeting place, it is often double-booked, noisy, or

both. In summer, the favorite meeting room (because it is the only part of LeBlond that is air-conditioned) can be a difficult place to meet. Since the room is right next to the swimming pool, its restrooms function as locker-rooms. Other meeting places include the Mount Carmel Baptist Church and the health center. But these places belong to other groups. EERCURC has no home; neither does the Pendleton board—not even a temporary one.

In order to practice community under these conditions, community leaders must be flexible. But even the most flexible and skilled leaders have difficulty running a meeting in a noisy room or with mosquitoes biting in 90-degree temperatures, as happens in LeBlond Park. None of these places belong to the East End as a community; that is, none are under community control. All of them require reservations with city staff weeks in advance, thus preventing spontaneous gathering or impromptu meetings.

Meetings occur in homes, but there are both positive and negative aspects to meeting in private space. As cozy as most East End homes are, someone will feel uncomfortable or left out and, perhaps, not show up for the meeting. Someone—usually, but not always, the person whose home it is—will dominate the meeting, control the agenda. Public space is much more accessible and people do not have to guard their words as carefully for fear of offending a host or hostess. There is a city ordinance prohibiting private meetings of community groups for just these reasons. Thus, although meeting in a person's home is almost always more comfortable than meeting in a public place, the latter is almost always preferable. The question is where? This question is the backdrop to the Pendleton Heritage Center (PHC) project.

History

The Pendleton Building is a red brick structure that sits on the north side of Eastern Avenue in a predominantly African American section of the East End. Known in the community as the "Pendleton Club," the building used to be a carbarn where trolley cars were repaired and serviced. Before that, it was a railroad station. When the trolleys stopped running on Eastern Avenue in the 1940s, the Pendleton Club became a social hall and recreation center for the East End's black community.

The Pendleton carbarn holds many fond memories for East End residents. Doris remembers going to dances and socials in the Pendleton Club, just a long block east of her house. Others remember going there

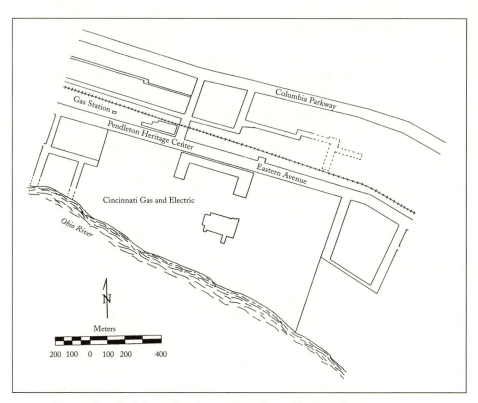

Map 7. East End Area: Gas Station, Pendleton Heritage Center

to play pool and Ping-Pong. To bring it back has been the dream of grassroots leaders. Renovated, it would provide a home for the East End community as old-time East Enders once knew it: a place for meetings to be held, information to be kept and transmitted, a place to provide a sense of permanence and continuity in a rapidly changing and revitalizing situation of economic development. Symbolically, it is a monument to East Enders' central role in shaping a new East End in a way that is consistent with past practices and patterns of class culture.

In the 1970s, the Pendleton Building was taken over by the Department of Recreation and used to store swimming pool supplies. The building was, from East Enders' perspective, defaced by the placement of a garage door in its southeast façade. The passage of the East End Riverfront Community Development Plan did bring with it the removal of the Recreation Department and its supplies. In September 1992, several months after the passage of the East End Riverfront Community

Development Plan in May and the motion to deed the Pendleton Building to the neighborhood as part of the "Recipe for Successful Implementation," a small group of residents, researchers, advocates, and city staff began meeting to plan the renovation.

Initially—that is, before it became a freestanding nonprofit corporation with the name Pendleton Heritage Center—the Pendleton Club Committee was a subcommittee of the East End Riverfront Community Development Plan Implementation Team, a diverse group of people brought together by the grassroots president of the East End Area Council to oversee the implementation of the development plan. The team was co-chaired by an East Ender and a retired corporate executive. The East End Plan Implementation Team included developers, grassroots leaders and residents, researchers, advocates, representatives from the Riverfront Advisory Council, and people with expertise in, for example, housing, real estate, and economic development to donate to the plan's implementation. A report dated May 12, 1992, from the assistant to the city manager for special projects, who also acted as staff liaison to the team, notes that "the Implementation Team, made up of East End Area Council (EEAC) members and other groups/organizations, was to serve in an advisory capacity both to the City and to the Area Council." The Pendleton subcommittee was appointed at the first meeting on September 10, 1992. From the outset of the plan implementation process, there were researchers and advocates from the East End Study Project involved in all groups, as advisers, board members, and observers.

The autonomy of the Implementation Team and its Pendleton subcommittee, and their positioning as an independent advisory group situated between the EEAC and the city, was an intentional strategy on the part of the grassroots leadership. Community leaders felt strongly that a separate implementation team that included developers but that also involved advocates who had the community's interest at heart stood a better chance of functioning to preserve the community. Community leaders also knew from firsthand experience that a community council controlled by real East Enders was extremely vulnerable and subject to the vagaries of local and city politics and power relations.

From the very beginning of the Implementation Team's existence, the developers wanted to place it under the East End Area Council, which they soon came to control. There was also some grassroots support for placing the Implementation Team under the East End Area Council. After all, the EEAC as the community council was the local entity that represented the community in the eyes of the city. For some two years, however, the Implementation Team remained an independent entity, albeit an increasingly weak one.

It is not merely coincidental that in the fall of 1992, just a few months after the plan was passed and the Implementation Team was in place, there were strong efforts made to impeach the grassroots president of the EEAC, and the city began to express concerns about the EEAC's ability to function. The events surrounding the impeachment and the instability of the EEAC are extremely complicated and I will not treat them in detail here. Suffice it to say that a combination of factors and forces both on the grassroots side and the developers' side worked to contribute to an unstable community council.

The important point here is that throughout all of the turmoil in the EEAC, the Pendleton Club Committee persevered. Its strong and organized leadership combined with social service agency staff support to create a well-oiled, although still fledgling, organization. It also had considerable support from one city staff member and from strong members of City Council. The committee continued to work toward the rehabilitation of the Pendleton Building.

In February 1993, the Pendleton Club Committee began seriously to explore its establishment as an autonomous nonprofit corporation that would develop (that is, rehabilitate and operate) the Pendleton Building. In the course of these discussions, the Pendleton project was named the Pendleton Heritage Center. The Pendleton Heritage Center Board of Trustees was created as part of the process of incorporating as a nonprofit entity with the help of one city staff person and a *pro bono* attorney. The board wrote bylaws that were approved by the state of Ohio. The Pendleton Heritage Center became an autonomous nonprofit corporation in December 1994, a little less than two years after discussion of nonprofit status began. There was still much work to be done.

In March 1994, the original city staff liaison to the East End, a man who had always been a true friend and advocate in the community, was replaced by another individual. As I look back on the first meeting without him (the details of which are related in Chapter 3), a real feeling of sadness washes over me. Gone now is one of the few city employees ever to receive the full trust of real East Enders.

The Pendleton has enormous symbolic significance in the East End, especially for those elderly African Americans who remember spending time there. It is a community space that carries a very positive valence—as one that "may bring us unity" because it would legitimize the rights of East Enders to have a community building and not be forced to move meetings to every nook and cranny of city-controlled space.

When the Pendleton poem that starts this chapter was written, the main divisions felt by real East Enders were those between themselves and the developers, who wanted to see the community used for commercial purposes, and between the community and the city, which wanted to increase its tax base by encouraging upscale commercial and residential development. City officials and staff were constantly asking questions about the East Enders' ability to operate the building. As this chapter will show, there have also been divisions among and between grassroots people.

Board Meeting

Pendleton Heritage Center board meeting—the ground floor of Le-Blond Recreation Center. Deep shelves line one wall. In the past, they held ceramic molds and figurines; now they exhibit books donated by the wives of the Cincinnati Reds; the title *Exodus* stands out in bold white letters. There must be over a thousand books. A stove on the far wall, a washing machine and refrigerator next to blue dishes and an electric frying pan, all donated by the Cincinnati Reds' wives for teen cooking classes. I bring a thermos of coffee and the blue cups come in handy.

The tables are arranged in a squared-off U. The latecomers sit at its corners. Doris, the chair of the board, sits in the middle so she can see everyone clearly; she always watches with a sharp eye as she moves through the agenda. I am amazed and impressed by her powers of concentration, since I know she has just put her ninety-six-year-old mother in the hospital for evaluation after several weeks of constant worry about her "downhill slide." Children play in one part of the room; a six-year-old twirls her not-yet-three-year-old sister in a padded desk chair. They take turns. Their sounds are noticeable, especially during the pauses in

Figure 20. The Pendleton Heritage Center

the conversation, but no one complains. Their grandmother apologizes to the group for the periodic interruptions from the children.

"It's okay," replies one of the professionals at the table in a calm and friendly tone. He's a kindly man in his late forties. The meeting goes on with no pause.

First Agenda Item: Parking for the Pendleton Heritage Center

The project manager of the East End Riverfront Community Development Plan reports on the gas station parking site—once an East End institution and now a torn-up lot with a small building diminished further by plywood boards and the word CLOSED painted in big red capital letters. The owner of the station shut it down when the EPA began asking questions about site pollution. He is in the process of using Superfund money to clean up the site. Fritz, the manager of the station for twenty-four years, sits on the Pendleton Heritage Center board. The gas station site is the ideal place for the Heritage Center's parking: it's right next to the Pendleton Building; it's flat; it's large enough for the Heritage Center to expand; and it could accommodate a range of projects to stimulate economic development and generate funds for the Heritage Center. A weekend flea market, a fruit and vegetable stand, a convenience store are only a few of the ideas East Enders have talked about for the gas station site. Fritz, a longtime resident and community leader, has agreed to manage the Heritage Center building.

The new project manager for the PHC received information about the gas station parking site on January 11, 1995, and sent it to the deputy city manager. The information about the number of spaces and the multiple uses of the parking lot, as well as about the "environmental cleanliness" of the site, is critical because, without proof of adequate parking, the city zoning board will not approve building permits and the city will not release the funds ($175,000) for the rehab.

The groundwater test came back with no problems. It appears, then, that any contamination is contained within the soil. Blacktopping might be sufficient to contain the contamination, but the board must await the report of the environmental engineer after cores are taken to get information on soil contamination. The environmental engineer expects to have this information back by the end of January and a report by mid- to late February. This report will be given to the owner of the gas station site.

Robbie asks whether anyone else has expressed interest in the gas station site. She knows how strongly the developers oppose the Pendleton Heritage Center. She also knows that those who own property on the street on a hill overlooking the Pendleton Building would like to turn it into a restaurant or use it for some other commercial purpose. She has experienced having things taken away before. Doris is a bit impatient with the prospect of waiting another month or more before proceeding: "Is it feasible for us to contact the architect? We don't want to just sit and do nothing."

"If it can be done for nothing," pipes in the project manager. Clearly, without the release of funds, an architect cannot be paid.

Second Agenda Item:
Leasing or Owning the Pendleton Building

"Do we want to lease or own the Pendleton?" Doris is very systematic in her efforts to ensure that everyone on the board has a chance to speak. She begins at one end of the U-shaped table with Robbie, who responds: "We should have title to the property. We would have access to historic tax credits if we have ownership. If it is our responsibility it should be our building." Doris moves right past a visitor (even though the visitor was quite prepared to contribute to the conversation) to Elaine, who says: "I would like the neighborhood to feel this is ours instead of renting it from the city. Paul Silver (who was then a member of City Council) was to ensure that it belongs to the neighborhood as a focal point."

James Strong points out that the previous discussion about owning versus leasing the building concerned issues of liability. He is in favor of owning the building as long as the liability issues are resolved. The only developer on the board who is one of two representatives from the developer-controlled EEAC, agrees that a nonprofit corporation could own the building and says: "Personally, I always prefer owning to renting, but I am not sure I understand the issues."

Robbie points out that, even if the community leases the building, "We will have to be covered and pay insurance, even on a 'lay away plan.' The city will not cover liability."

Third Agenda Item: The Fund-Raising Plan

The discussion turns to the fund-raising plan and to Jacqueline Piedmont. Jacqueline has just recently become involved in the Pendleton Heritage Center, that is, only since fall. Initially, she became involved with the fund-raising for the Heritage Exhibit, but it soon became clear that her interest was high and her involvement would strengthen the community's position vis-à-vis the city's cooperation. Jacqueline is a member of Cincinnati's elite, although her family originates in Kentucky. Her Appalachian roots connect her to the community. It also was becoming increasingly clear to the PHC board that the city probably would not be forthcoming with the next phase of the fund-raising plan and that city staffers were skeptical of the community's ability to operate the building, that is, pay bills, provide maintenance, and so on. Jacqueline's efforts and her connections add credibility to the board's ability to run the center.

Jacqueline's style is low-key but forceful; she is clearly a very experienced fund-raiser. She points out that before we put together the fund-raising plan, we need additional information. She explains that, right now, she and the co-chair of the fund-raising effort, who is also her brother-in-law, are thinking about two separate endowments: (1) a building fund endowment equal to the value of the building; this is the contingency fund to cover unforeseen costs; and (2) an operating endowment. Jacqueline points out that there are added costs to what is in the operating budget: "We need to tell donors what percentage of their donation will go for what. We are thinking of asking for $1,000 lots and planning a two-year concentration of fund-raising. Donors also like to know what the membership is doing."

At this point in the meeting, the city staff person says that after the original $175,000 is exhausted, the Pendleton Heritage Center Board can do what it wishes with private funds. The $175,000 is for rehab only: "The core of your decision is whether you want to assume all responsibility for habitation and maintenance of the building. The motion was made by [Councilmember] Todd to deed the property to the neighborhood, but this board said that it was not ready to own the building. Now the board is having second thoughts about leasing."

As the discussion proceeds, it appears that ownership requires as much responsibility as leasing. Montgomery, a board member who is in real estate and who is also an appointee of the EEAC, points out that "if it gives us greater flexibility in funding then let's go with owning."

Jacqueline says that "it would be wise for the board to look at owning issues seriously. You want this to be set up for success." She asks: "Who would be responsive to help deal with a crisis? Which way gives more autonomy? The conditions of ownership is an issue. We need an attorney to clarify the issues."

Doris asks for a vote: to own—7; abstentions—1; against owning—0.

The board agrees that it needs legal and accounting advice. Montgomery agrees to talk to real estate lawyers, but he adds the problematic idea that any lawyer worth his salt will have to be paid and that the board might get someone *pro bono* but that person might be less competent.

The city staff person, Pendle Erenrich, gives the board some sample leasing and owning written arrangements. He points out that board members are now developers and building managers.

Doris adds a contrasting spiritual element to Pendle's extreme practicality: "A home—I had no other dream." She quickly gets her feet on the ground and asks Robbie to get the plans from Samco's architect. Samco was the principal contractor for the rehab of Betz Flats. As the meeting ends, Doris assigns additional jobs to board members and fundraisers: Bob Snider will examine the building; Montgomery will follow through on obtaining legal advice; Jacqueline will talk with Montgomery about legal people. She points out that they will be flattered to be asked. Robbie will call Samco for plans. Doris ends the meeting by telling the lone developer on the board: "We need you." She thereby incorporates the opposition through personal persuasion.

The Fund-Raising Team

The following week sees a meeting of the fund-raising team itself, during which Dan Moyers is introduced to the group. Although Doris is very tired now that her mother is home from the hospital, she tells me that, as chair of the board, she could not very well miss meeting the new fund-raising co-chair.

He is clearly a person with a corporate style—pleasant and businesslike. The meeting proceeds with a larger, site-oriented perspective brought by architect/planner Mahir Duran. Clearly, the building is useless without parking, and the parking site can be used, if designed well, for multiple purposes. A weekend flea market, held when the center would be closed and not in need of parking, not only would generate funds for vendors to earn a living, but rental fees charged for selling space on the parking lot could go to the PHC's operating expenses. A fruit and vegetable stand or a convenience store owned and operated by an East End family would provide jobs in the community. These ideas are critical to the fund-raising plan, since money must be found for all aspects of the Heritage Center and its projects, including the traveling Heritage exhibit. This discussion is quite lengthy, but it is crucial because it brings the whole Pendleton project back to the general economic development issues in the East End. If community revitalization is to be accomplished, income must be generated for people as well as for projects. The linking of institution building to concrete aspects of people's lives and livelihoods must be kept constantly in the forefront.

The PHC's Operating Plan

In the fall of 1994, almost a year before fund-raising efforts began and just before nonprofit status was approved, the PHC board submitted an operating plan to the city manager. This plan was designed to demonstrate the community's ability to run the building. In order to generate rental income, but still maintain space for community groups to meet and store records in office space, the PHC board divided the square footage of the building roughly into three: (1) community space, (2) rental space, and (3) shared space. These decisions were made only after many meetings. Even after the board made its decisions about the basic division of space, there were many details to be ironed out in the process of producing a document with the title "Operating Plan for the PHC."

The spatial arrangement of the operating plan can be summarized as follows: (1) fully accessible facilities, meeting all Americans with Disabilities requirements; (2) a kitchenette; (3) adjacent parking; (4) an assembly hall (occupancy of ninety-six) suitable for meetings, presentations, programs, and community events; (5) a conference room (occupancy of twelve to twenty); (6) two very small or one small office to be shared by PHC, the Area Council, and the Redevelopment Corporation; (7) rental space (600 square feet) ready to be completed to suit the tenant's needs, with a separate entrance, access to building facilities (e.g., bathrooms, parking, and kitchenette), and shared access to conference and assembly hall negotiable.

The operating plan also delineated the functions of the PHC, although these were purposely left vague. The PHC would function, in the main, as a community center and home for East End community boards. Office space and meeting space (large assembly hall and smaller conference room) would accommodate this main function. Income would be generated from the rental space and from short-term rental of the assembly hall, conference room, and parking lot (for flea markets and event parking). The proximity of the East End to downtown puts it in an ideal location to run a shuttle service.

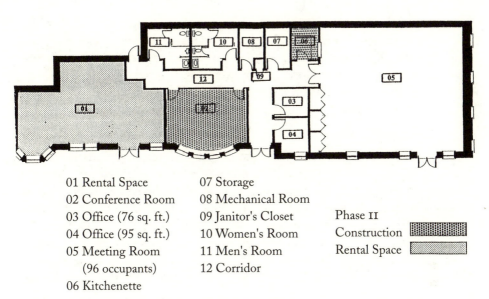

01 Rental Space
02 Conference Room
03 Office (76 sq. ft.)
04 Office (95 sq. ft.)
05 Meeting Room
   (96 occupants)
06 Kitchenette

07 Storage
08 Mechanical Room
09 Janitor's Closet
10 Women's Room
11 Men's Room
12 Corridor

Phase II
Construction
Rental Space

Figure 21. The Pendleton Heritage Center Floor Plan

Since there were no computers or printers in the East End that could be used by the PHC board, the board chair, Doris Sells, accompanied by two other board members and an advocate from the Implementation Team made regular trips to the west side of downtown Cincinnati in late August and early September 1994 to the offices of Associated Neighborhood Practice, Inc., of Hamilton County. There, the board members worked with the ANP staff person assigned to the East End to hammer out the details of the operating plan on his computer. The numerous trips to ANP were time consuming and tiring, especially for the elderly members of the board.

The City's Response to the Operating Plan

The PHC board's budget and operating plan was submitted to the city manager on September 15, 1994, two years after the group began meeting. It took the manager over two months to respond.

A Letter from the City Manager

We are driving to a meeting in Councilmember Daniel Todd's office. Doris is in the back seat reading the letter from the city manager responding to the operating plan and budget. The letter is dated November 23, 1994. Doris is clearly upset as she reads the letter aloud.

The letter begins in a complimentary fashion, but then turns to a series of "concerns" that Doris interprets as throwing yet another set of obstacles in the face of the community. It is addressed to Ms. Doris Sells, Chair, Pendleton Heritage Center Board, and begins as follows:

Dear Ms. Sells:

The Department of Neighborhood Housing and Conservation (NHC) and the Office of Research, Evaluation and Budget (REB) have completed a review and analysis of the budget and operating plan for the Pendleton Heritage Center. Your timely submission and the quality of the document enabled NHC and REB to address the issues relevant to the redevelopment of the Pendleton Heritage Center. The Pendleton Heritage Center Board should be commended for its work.

After reporting that the split sewer system "should be ready for hookup in January of 1995," and thereby taking care of what had been (so the community thought) the major stumbling block to the renovation of the Pendleton Building, the city manager turns to his "concerns" about parking and makes it clear that these concerns must be addressed before funds can be released for renovation and before the city will consider appropriating additional funds.

The first concern is the contamination of the most suitable parking site, the gas station site. The manager does not realize, or at least does not acknowledge at this point, that the owner of the gas station has paid into the Superfund, an insurance system that, with the payment of a substantial deductible, will ensure the cleanup of the site. The tone of his next comments is also very negative, especially concerning the cost of environmental cleanup in relation to the feasibility of the site:

• A preliminary evaluation of the gas station site by the Fire Division and the City's Office of Environmental Management during the removal of underground tanks showed significant contamination of the soil. Environmental remediation could make the development of this site for parking economically infeasible. The City expects to receive an official report from the Ohio Environmental Protection Agency in early January of 1995.

The manager's letter expresses additional concerns about the PHC's ability to generate income to cover annual expenses. He mentions two public event facilities already operating within the immediate vicinity. He returns to the operating budget and to possible shortfalls created by vacant rental space. He also expresses preference for a paid building manager, not a volunteer. He ends with the following:

> To summarize, after reviewing and analyzing the budget and operating plan for the Pendleton Heritage Center, the City's primary concerns are the provision of adequate parking for the facility and the tenant and rental income assumptions included in the operating budget.
>
> The City Administration remains supportive of your project. The $175,000 previously budgeted for the Pendleton Heritage Center remains in place. A member of my staff will be calling you in the next few days to schedule a meeting to discuss these issues.

The letter is signed, City Manager.

Doris responds in writing to the manager and addresses his "concerns" one by one. She writes on behalf of the Pendleton Heritage Center Board, first thanking the city manager for his letter then making it clear that she does not want the progress of the Heritage Center impeded in any way. She makes a few concessions, but basically she sets the facts straight:

> January 3, 1995
>
> Dear Mr. Cirrus:
>
> On behalf of the Pendleton Heritage Center Board, I would like to thank you for your letter of November 23, 1994 in response to our budget and operating plan for the Pendleton Heritage Center. We are very pleased to learn that the split sewer system should be ready for hook-up in January of 1995. We are, however, very concerned that the issues you raise not impede the progress of our heritage center.
>
> Here is our response to your concerns:
>
> 1. Parking: the cleanup of the gas station site is proceeding. It is our understanding that the owner of the gas station has initiated the cleanup of the site immediately to the west of the heritage center.
>
> Since he has paid into the superfund, he is in the best financial position to accomplish the cleanup. Once this is done, we plan to proceed on the purchase of this site. The Cincinnati Gas & Electric site is a very undesirable option because of its location across the street and the dangers presented by crossing Eastern Avenue.

2. Generating income to cover annual expenses and competition from Carnegie Library and Seven Hills center as public meeting and event facilities: the Pendleton Heritage center complements the existing facilities by performing different functions for a different population within the East End community. It does not present competition:

A. The rental space will be used to provide missing and much needed services heretofore absent from the community and indeed from the entire east side of Cincinnati. The Alzheimer's association and Head Start have made preliminary commitments. There are no Alzheimer's or Head Start facilities in the area at all.

B. The population from which the scheduled events will be drawn (weddings, reunions, parties) is completely different from that served by the Carnegie or the Seven Hills facility and these facilities are not used for family events. These buildings are not available for rentals. Currently, the American Legion and recreation center in Fairfax are rented by East Enders for weddings, parties, etc. which certainly illustrates one of the needs that the Pendleton Heritage Center will fill in our neighborhood.

C. The Heritage Center includes space for community exhibits, as well as for Head Start and Alzheimer's.

D. Multipurpose parking site: the gas station site can be multipurpose. It has great potential as an open air marketplace that the neighborhood can use in certain seasons to generate income for the heritage center.

E. A market analysis would be appropriate were the building larger than 3,000 square feet. As it is, there is little space that has not already been designated for rental.

Fund-raising team: the Pendleton Heritage Center has established an experienced fund-raising team. The fund-raising team has begun to establish a revolving endowed fund to cover any shortfalls in the operating expenses.

3. Maintenance: the board already has a list of volunteers who will donate up to 5 hours per month for maintenance and landscaping.

There are several examples of nonprofit civic organizations in this city that have operated with a great deal of volunteer labor, the Esquire Theater and the Arts Consortium to name two.

A building manager (paid) will oversee the maintenance. Due to size and limited foot traffic the building manager will be part-time and paid approximately $10,000 per year.

We hope that this letter answers your concerns and that you will find yourself in a position to release our $175,000.

We now have our 501 c(3). We also hope you do not forget about our recent budget request for phase two of the Pendleton project.

We look forward to meeting with you on Wednesday, January 4, 1995.

Sincerely,
Doris Sells
Chair, PHC Board

This letter was copied to the mayor and two councilmembers along with members of the Plan Implementation Team and members of the Riverfront Advisory Council.

After Doris's letter was sent to the city manager, the PHC board met with the assistant city manager and representatives from REB and NHC. The board was told that once the parking issue was resolved, the funds would be released. A promise was made at that time to the effect that the funds to purchase the parking lot would come out of a separate fund. This promise was later withdrawn.

The Long-Term Context

The themes in Eileen's poem "We Are Getting Closer to the Pendleton" dealing with the centrality of the Pendleton as a symbol of community past and present (April 1992) take on added meaning when they are seen from the vantage point of June 1995. More than three years after the passage of the East End Plan, the PHC was still not a reality. No funds had been released. While a great deal had been accomplished—Articles of Incorporation, a 501(C)(3) in hand, a strong board—parking still had not been acquired and renovations had not begun. Neither had a program been agreed upon for the building. Instead, there were voices calling for a redefining of the roles of board members—an attempt to tear the group apart, or at least to stall its efforts. There was even a swipe at the leadership of the PHC.

The following excerpts are from a meeting of the PHC board in the early summer of 1995. The PHC meeting followed a prior meeting requested by grassroots PHC leaders with the newly established city Department of Neighborhood Services (a merger of Neighborhood Housing and Conservation and Social Services). At the city meeting, the new director of Neighborhood Services placed a new demand on the PHC board. She required that tenants for the PHC's rental space be secured prior to the release of the $175,000. The PHC meeting convened to discuss this new demand in the context of the meeting with the new director. The meeting was dominated by a man who was a relative newcomer to the East End:

Montgomery:

It's paramount that everybody understands a role and the capacity of that role . . . I'm not an expert myself and I'm not a parliamentarian per se, but I've sat on enough boards and am currently on enough committees and witness how they operate to where I can definitely say that we're kind of missing a beat or so here and I think until we start operating as a Pendleton Heritage Board property everything else is going to flap in the wind. I think it's important that we have our roles defined. . . . I'm not certain that maybe Carlene Mauve's [the new director of the Department of Neighborhood Services] letter and the meeting is because there is mystification in her understanding over those various roles or the capacities, so we can wait and let those be resolved by Carlene Mauve and other influencing factors outside of PHC or we can take the initiative and resolve those within PHC . . . I take exception to it being something where Carlene Mauve has to call a meeting to figure out where PHC is in this.

Robbie:

Let me clarify that. Carlene did not call this meeting. We asked for it so we could orientate Carlene to what's going on out in the East End seeing as she's new. Carlene didn't ask for this meeting. We asked for it. She was grateful for it.

Montgomery:

I guess what I'm asking now with the current state of mayhem or confusion that we have, are we ready and prepared to go to Carlene Mauve with a host of variables and "we don't know yet" and "we're still working this out" or would we not do better as a PHC Board to tidy up our own board roles, our own understanding over what it is we intend to do. I think it's going to be important that when we go down there that we are represented very clearly as a PHC board that is in control and capable of this project or we potentially will stand to lose it.

Robbie:

I think Carlene realizes that the PHC board is capable of doing it because the one thing she made clear on Monday was that any contract done for the development of the PHC was between the city and the PHC board as the developer, and then the PHC board could have their choice of who they'd hire as an architect and who would do the work to complete the PHC.

Montgomery is defining the situation as one of "mayhem or confusion." He repeats: "The clarification of roles is still very much confusing."

Robbie:

We didn't really go down there to ask the city for anything. It was for Carlene to get to understand what PHC was and what EERCURC was and where we were at.

Montgomery:

Just as you say that I certainly don't have a problem with an informational meeting wherein you explain to her what PHC is about and who we are. Certainly, if in fact it can be accomplished within the same meeting what EERCURC is about and who they are. To necessarily presume or to place both of those organizations in the same basket and say here is our project I think may be a little bit premature.

Robbie:

It was not addressed that way, Montgomery; you're assuming things.

At this point, Elaine interjects:

Please, Montgomery, let me say something. I was not at the meeting but I was under the understanding that EERCURC and the PHC would go down there not to say: hey, we've come down here to be the developers [of the PHC]. It wasn't like that. It wasn't like that. You have to live in this community to know that you don't go down there by yourself and try to talk to those people down there because they'd never listen to us. We always have to go as a group. . . . we have been trying to find out how much the parking lot is going to cost. Pendle never would tell us, so we had to go to his boss to find out. I'm not underhanded as far as this project is concerned and I feel that my time is just as important as anybody else's that lives on top of a hill or whatever. . . . I am going to stay on PHC and I'm going to stay on EERCURC boards and I feel that I am going to consider Robbie's feelings and I'm going to consider yours, but don't make it look like we're down there trying to connive and sneak something up.

Internal discord is difficult to interpret, especially when the central figure in the discord is a relative newcomer to the East End and is one of the newest PHC board members. It is difficult to say whether the foregoing dialogue is a deliberate filibustering attempt to gain control of the PHC, whether it is simply a need to hear oneself talk, or some of both. Given the larger context, however, and given how upset grassroots leaders were at this meeting, one begins to wonder how many more years must go by before a tangible heritage center will come about.

The principal speaker, Montgomery, has recently become the real estate agent for one of the developers in the East End, Jo Island. The fact that he lives in the East End and sits on two community boards adds to the representation of developer interests on local governing groups.

Here we see the co-optation of a group's effort by a self-interested outsider who claims to be an insider. This is, as we will see in the discussion of local colonialism (Chapter 11), an increasingly familiar pattern. That the stalling and filibustering is done primarily by men, black and white, in groups led by women, black and white, is worth noting. But what separates the grassroots leaders from their opposition is not gender or race, primarily, but power and class position. Even relatively subtle differences in power and class can divide community residents and leaders.

A Need for Change

By the fall of 1995, it was clear that the way the PHC board was proceeding had to be changed. The elders on the board, in particular, were quite pessimistic that any real progress toward releasing the funds and "getting the building up and running" could be made. At several board meetings there were more advocates in attendance than there were East Enders. At the same time, many obstacles had been overcome. The sewer work that prevented the building permit from being issued had been completed. The parking issue was now resolved, but only after the city used $55,000 of the $175,000 set aside for renovation of the building itself to buy the lot.

There was still the problem of securing tenants for a building that had not yet been renovated. The amount of funding for renovations was a serious problem, especially in light of the fact that the fund-raising efforts had disintegrated after the elite co-chairs of the funding team began to witness the internal dissension in the community.

The PHC board began to explore other options that would, in effect,

URGENT MEETING

SAVE THE
PENDLETON!!!

TUESDAY, SEPTEMBER 24, 1996
4:30 P.M.
MT. CARMEL BAPTIST CHURCH

W E   N E E D   Y O U !

PENDLETON HERITAGE CENTER

*The Pendleton Heritage Center: Preserving the East End's history,
celebrating its diversity, and promoting its future.*

Figure 22. "Urgent Meeting" Flyer

save the Pendleton Building for the community. The board's thinking
went as follows. Given the difficulty, indeed the great struggles, to build
institutions, what sorts of institutions can be linked to the PHC that
would protect it from the attacks of people with colonialist interests and
from the general inertia of city bureaucracy. Of course, the board did not
state the issue in this way, but the question of protection from the local
power structures—and also help in dealing with these structures—was
essential.

In December 1995, the PHC approached the Urban Appalachian
Council, which had a long history of providing services in the East End
as well as in other Appalachian communities in Cincinnati. The central
question was whether the UAC would operate the PHC on behalf of the
PHC board. The PHC board would be responsible for the center and
therefore remain in control of major policy decisions, uses, and programs, but would contract its daily operations to UAC. Under this arrangement, community groups, including the PHC board, the East End
Area Council, and the Redevelopment Corporation would meet in the

PHC and use office space there. UAC, along with other social service organizations, would operate programs in the community. Rental of space, both long and short term, would be arranged through UAC.

At the same time, PHC approached ANP about increasing its involvement in the East End. ANP has been involved in housing efforts, education, and social services in the East End. Specific needs for PHC included possibly providing staff support as well as a role in operating the center. A partnership between UAC and ANP became a possibility. Between early 1996 and the early summer, UAC and ANP representatives had several meetings to discuss possibilities for collaboration.

Summary

In 1993, as a result of the city's budget process, the city allocated $175,000 for the rehabilitation of the Pendleton Building. By spring 1997, some of the money had been spent on preliminary architectural drawings and on the acquisition of the parking lot, but the $120,000 left in the allocation had not yet been released to the community.

The mission statement in the PHC Articles of Incorporation speaks of a home for the East End community that would help "preserve its history, celebrate its diversity, and promote its future." As of early summer 1997, a new fund-raiser is on board and a new contractor is ready to rehab the Pendleton Building. It still belongs to the city, but it stands completely untouched and empty. The city says that it will release the $120,000 when an additional $45,000, needed to complete the renovations of the building and the parking lot, is raised by the new fund-raiser. Is this requirement just another one of many hurdles? The process of institution building has been slow at best.

11 LOCAL COLONIALISM AND THE POLITICS OF FACTIONALISM

Colonialism needs to be analysed and theorized because its pervasive and enduring ramifications are all too evident, despite decolonization and the increasing frequency with which the term "postcolonial" is applied to the present. Like modernity or capitalism, colonialism would seem so fundamental to both the larger dynamics of global history and power relations, and to many more immediate aspects of our lives, that the desirability of analysing and reinterpreting "it" must be obvious. (Thomas 1994: ix)

Ethnographic work has indeed been enmeshed in a world of enduring and changing power inequalities, and it continues to be implicated. It enacts power relations. But its function within these relations is complex, often ambivalent, potentially counter-hegemonic. (Clifford 1986: 9)

Appalachia is a good example of colonial domination by outside interests. Its history also demonstrates the concerted efforts of the exploiters to label their work "progress" and to blame any of the obvious problems it causes on the ignorance or deficiencies of the Appalachian people. We believe that there are peoples all over the world who have experienced this sort of "development" and consequently live in conditions similar to those found in the mountains. (Helen Matthews Lewis)[1]

Local Colonialism

> Colonialism can be seen both as a historical moment—specified in relation to European political and economic projects in the modern era—and as a trope for domination and violation. Culture can be seen both as a historically constituted domain of significant concepts and practices and as a regime in which power achieves its ultimate apotheosis. Linked together, colonialism and culture can be seen to provide a new world in which to deploy a critical cartography of the history and effects of power. (Dirks 1992: 5)

Colonialism is about power—the fact that some people have it and some don't. It is about outsiders imposing themselves on insiders. Colonialism operates in many contexts in the East End and, indeed, in the city at large, in everyday interactions on the street, at City Hall, in community meetings, board meetings, even at funerals when the colonialists show up and make East End families angry with their smug and arrogant presence.

Colonialism must be understood holistically; it is simultaneously a political, economic, and cultural process. Colonialists operate on all three fronts. Politically, colonialism permeates the chambers of City Hall. People of influence receive resources from the city, respect from the city, guidance and technical support from the city. Powerless people experience roadblocks, hoops to jump through, and more obstacles. The case of the Pendleton Heritage Center is a primary example of local colonial processes operating in political and cultural arenas. Economically, people with property—landlords, business owners, even homeowners, to some degree—dominate the East End. The struggle for affordable housing is another case study in colonialism. Culturally, colonial processes are often, although not always, very subtle. Colonial discourse—that is, the words spoken by the colonizers (outsiders) to or about the colonized (real East Enders)—is pervasive. The discourse may be more or less constrained, depending on the context. Within the community, colonialists will talk at great length and with very little attention to politeness, much less to whether or not they are insulting or patronizing real East Enders. Outside of the community, especially at City Hall, colonialists are more restrained. In fact, publically, they say what they think city officials and real East Enders want to hear. It is in their interests to act as though the East End is a united community, because resources from the city will flow more easily that way. Colonialists conduct their private negotiations behind closed doors.

Local colonialism and colonial processes can operate between people who are of the same or different races, speak the same language (albeit different dialects), wear the same (or similar) clothing, went to the same school, and even grew up side by side. One can actually be on the periphery of power while being ostensibly in the center of it. That is, a person can live officially in Cincinnati, an urban power center, and, in fact, occupy a marginal power position, much like a person living on the margins of the Third World. "Local colonialism," then, is a phrase I use to refer to processes of domination and control that have a local city origin and that operate to adversely affect the East End community.

Colonialism and its offshoots, power for a few and powerlessness for most people (to borrow from John Gaventa), is a long-standing pattern in Appalachian culture both in the country and in the city.[2] If you ask an East Ender about power, the lack of it will be immediately apparent by statements such as: "Those people on the hillside are those with power and money" or "The world works by the golden rule. He who has the gold makes the rules" or simply, "We are a community of poor people. I live in a raggedy house, but I wouldn't live anywhere else." Humor and creative language may not confer power as such, but they do go a long way in making life bearable under often difficult circumstances.

Power relations are complex in the East End. In many respects, do-mains of power and influence—what power is for and about from the East End perspective—are difficult to pin down. So too are the various contexts within which people wield power. A community council meeting reveals different power dynamics from those of a smaller meeting or an informal meeting. Meetings within the community are different from those that take place outside of it, even if the same people are present. Power can be simultaneously formal and informal, subtle and blatant, appropriate and inappropriate, vulnerable and stable.[3]

Within the neighborhood, authentic, grassroots, working-class iden-tity is clearly linked to what it means to be a real East Ender. It is closely related to trust, to longevity in the community, to "being there" when someone needs help, and to devotion to family and community. Forms of outside control, whether from the city or from developers or both, continue to violate East Enders' sense of what it means to be a real East Ender, and what is most important for East End families and for the East End community. Community leaders who have fought long and hard to bring about positive changes in the community have their efforts constantly undermined at the local and the city levels by market forces and by representatives of those forces as well as by other institutionalized forms of power—schools, courts, hospitals, to name a few.

Within the community of real East Enders, seniority is a major source of social and political influence. Senior community leaders have authority because of their knowledge of the past and their life experience; they often have large extended kinship and friendship networks that, in effect, represent a potential constituency, political faction, force of resistance to outsiders, or all of the above.

Resistance to local colonialism can take many forms: a vote in the community council in favor of new or rehabbed affordable housing, a vote to support the Heritage Center. But even the most respected senior East Enders are constantly having their influence undermined by outsiders who want to claim authentic membership in the East End community by calling themselves East Enders. Most of these "wannabe insiders," as one East Ender calls them, are small-scale developers of one sort or another (landlords, small business owners, or property owners) who either do not live in the community or who live there only sporadically or part time.

The wannabe insiders do not understand real East Enders' sense of identity and belonging because they define power and control exclusively in material and economic terms, not in cultural, ethnic, and spiritual ones. The people whom East Enders, especially East End leaders, consider to be of greatest threat to grassroots power—"the greatest pain in the you know where"—are not city officials, but outsiders who try to "join" and control. They manipulate local community people by imposing a certain kind of rigid order and by asserting their superior class status, managerial skills, and generally greater ability (because of their time and money) to impose themselves on the community. To a large degree, these wannabe East Enders claim to know what is best for the community. They say that they care about the community and about East End people, but they are viewed by real East Enders as self-centered, materialistic, and controlling in the most manipulative sense of these words. Most important, no matter how hard they try to be real East Enders, they are viewed by the grassroots leaders and residents as outsiders.

There are East End residents who appreciate and value highly the sense of order and the absence of overt conflict that can temporarily be imposed by an outsider-controlled community council. That these appreciative residents have been the subject of subtle and blatant forms of colonial domination, however, is a subtext that the grassroots leaders well understand.

This chapter begins with a lamentation about upcoming community council elections volunteered to me by a longtime East End developer and businesswoman who has been active in community affairs since the seventies. She is lamenting the "outsider" status of developers. Her speech is followed by presentation of a new set of community council bylaws by a developer named Payne. It is based on an actual transcript of the presentation of the bylaws by a developer at an East End Area Council meeting, although certain details have been changed and the text has been shortened substantially. The nuances of language and presentation style are very important here because they indicate the subtle power plays that are accomplished by drawing speeches out and by taking up valuable time in the meeting with attention to every minute and often insignificant or irrelevant (to the task at hand) detail. Elaborating on the obvious and speaking in an overly wordy, deliberate fashion are only two of the techniques of colonial control. The last section of the chapter deals with some of the ways East Enders resist colonialism.

Outsider Status Lamentations

The following is an unsolicited monologue told to me on the eve of the 1994 Community Council election. Although the person speaking is not running for office, she is objecting to being labeled "an outsider" by "real East Enders" because, as a property owner, she feels her legitimacy as an East Ender should go unquestioned.

In this particular election, several races pit small-scale developers who claim to be East Enders against neighborhood people. The monologue begins with a confessional lamentation: "I put three doors in [that old building] and they would take cars and bust through. I didn't have to put all the money there." She continues in a voice full of emotion: "I felt that I was doing good for the neighborhood. I don't like it to be so slanted. I can't see the big put-down for outsiders who make it liveable. Nobody thinks of all the sacrifices!" There is a pause. Then returning to thoughts about personal sacrifices and investments, the speaker criticizes East Enders for placing food and luxuries before the needs of the neighborhood:

I could be living in Indian Hill [the wealthiest community in Cincinnati] with all the hundreds of thousands of dollars I put in the East End. Increased value is due to us. We get labels and put-downs. We make sacrifices that improve the neighborhood. We are property-poor. We eat baloney sandwiches. Food comes last. With East Enders food and luxuries come first. We're outsiders yet we contribute jobs. We contribute jobs for local people.

Referring again to the other developers and voicing a sense of real injustice the speaker says: "Every day we are down there working. That's not fair to say that a person is an outsider."

Returning again to the theme of making sacrifices: "I wasn't spending it on me, I was putting it all down there. I am not in their [the other developers'] category. I see Mr. Payne with buckets of paint. I don't go for this put-down."

Returning once again to the developers' running for office: "You [the developer] have to run for president because nobody else would run. She is a qualified professional woman who will give her time and make sacrifices."

Changing the subject back to East Enders: "I've had bad experiences with these freeloaders. I'm pro–doing something for yourself. I raised money. I've been involved since the seventies. I get upset when I see people call them outsiders."

Bylaws

Bylaws are extremely important to all nonprofit organizations in the East End. East Enders spend enormous amounts of time creating them, and bylaws are constantly consulted when any matter of protocol arises. *Robert's Rules of Order* is also consulted regularly. Such formality is unusual in the normal course of things in the East End and is used by both East End factions, real East Enders and developers alike. The parliamentarian, one of the offices of the East End Area Council is the keeper of the bylaws. Since 1979, this office has been repeatedly held by a senior, extremely well respected real East Ender.

The following is a presentation given by the developer chairperson of one bylaws committee of the East End Area Council. The setting is a large room in the community recreation center. People arrange themselves informally throughout the room. The East End Area Council is a nonprofit corporation with bylaws that must be sent to the Internal Revenue Service as part of the process of obtaining a tax exempt I.D. number.

I will quote from the existing (adopted in 1989) bylaws extensively with the note that the bylaws revisions have already stimulated a great deal of negative discussion about power and control in the community at large. To quote one East Ender: "This is an attempt to turn the East End area council into the East End country club." Occasionally, I note certain paralinguistic features (pace of speech, loudness, pitch, tone of voice) in brackets at the end of a passage because these features illustrate additional ways of exerting power and control.

The chairperson of the committee to revise the bylaws is a developer who begins his presentation as follows: "I am not really going to worry about—you are familiar with them [the old 1989 bylaws]—probably conversant enough with them that you don't need to carry them with you [chortling]. I have to make some assumption and that's a valid one, isn't it?"

He proceeds to define the nature of the changes and the differences between the old bylaws and the new ones he is proposing. He uses phrases such as "total revision" and in the next breath indicates that "total revision" does not mean "total change." Thus, he sets up a rather confusing framework at the outset. People who are not familiar with the old bylaws and who have not read the new ones really have no idea what kinds of changes have been made. Has he merely edited the old bylaws, as he tries to indicate by saying that "we've corrected grammatical structure" or have the bylaws indeed undergone "total revision," a phrase that implies more than mere editing?

> What I want to do is this: what we have done through this bylaw process is to arrive at a . . . essentially a total revision of bylaws. Okay? When I say a total revision I don't mean total change. We've corrected language. We've corrected grammatical structure. I will talk with you about some areas in which we've changed substance and then if you have questions we'll go into as much detail as you want, so that you're prepared a month hence to say we're gonna buy or we're not gonna buy or here's what we want to do.

It is not clear whom "we" refers to, but he is clearly using the pronoun in two ways: to refer to the Bylaws Committee and to refer to the body of the East End Area Council. He proceeds to distribute the copies of the proposed revision of the bylaws: "If you will let me start. Let me start . . . talk it through with you. That's what I'd like to do. If at any time you have questions, raise your hand and we'll try and deal with it."

He begins to go through the revisions and skips very quickly and lightly over an issue that has probably generated more discussion and debate than any other: community boundaries. This is one technique of control, that is, ignoring burning issues.

> Article one is unchanged. Article II. The Boundaries. We think there SHOULD be some changes perhaps, but there is no change. Exactly as it is today. Number 3: Purpose. Purpose is essentially the same as it was except we've cleaned up the grammar and ah, ah made a restatement if you will, but haven't changed the basic content.

The implication here is that the previous authors of the bylaws were deficient, since the grammar needed cleaning up—a clear criticism.

He speaks slowly and deliberately:

The first change comes in membership and it's more CLARIFICATION [he speaks with emphasis] than anything else. Ah . . . there were some ambiguities in the language as it exists today and what we tried to do is be very clear about it. Basically, we said, that there are resident members, the people who live in the East End and then there are non-resident members and non-resident members are people in two categories: people who have a legal tie to the East End because they own property or they work here. In other words, they're involved in the East End. And a second category of non-resident members are people who just have an abiding interest in the East End. In that regard, no change really from what we've got in the present bylaws but simply a better clarification as to the distinctions that we're making.

Again, speaking of ambiguities is another criticism.

He neglects to turn people's attention to the provisions in the membership section of the new bylaws that make it possible at any meeting for a nonresident member to have membership rescinded by a vote of the majority present at that particular meeting. Certainly, this change goes way beyond "clarification."

With regard to the provision for suspension of nonresident voting privileges, he invokes a higher authority, namely, a city ordinance: "In part this ties to the City ordinance that all communities were required to adopt, um, some three, four years ago now . . . and carries on to a petition . . . anyone can petition to have non-resident voting privileges withdrawn. If somebody DOES petition then the organization is required at least once a year to vote on that if somebody . . . if somebody in fact petitions us to do so. So provision is there for that." He skips over this matter rather hurriedly, however, with legalese. He makes rather light of the provision, in fact, but as we shall see, the significance of this change is not lost on real East Enders. They understand that all it would take to vote a former East Ender (a real East Ender who no longer lives in the East End) off the council would be a stacking of any given meeting with developers. Payne moves on quickly, however:

Article V. Officers and their duties: I think there's little change here except that we've . . . we've adopted a tabular form of what the responsibilities of each of the officers is. The officers are the president, the vice-president, recording secretary, corresponding secretary, financial secretary, we've dropped out account. We had financial account secretary. We dropped out the word account and simply made it financial secretary but haven't changed the responsibilities. Treasurer—and parliamentarian.

Here he is acting as though the membership of the council cannot read for themselves. He then proceeds to describe at great length a rather significant change in the bylaws:

> We are proposing to add 2 trustees to the board. And we're doing that for a couple of reasons: First of all, the board, you'll discover a little later, the board is going to be made up *only* of elected officers. The president is no longer going to be able to appoint members to the board to serve at the president's pleasure, that is not going to be the case anymore, if you adopt our proposal. Our thinking is as a council, we want to elect who's on the board, who our officers are, and so they are the people who make up the, who make up the board they and them alone.
>
> With regard to the trustees we said, well . . . if we made it only the elected officers, that's seven, let's in fact name two trustees at large without portfolio other than the council may assign, and let's do two things: we'll name two trustees, each December we'll name one for a one year term. That means that if everybody else on the board changes, we should have at least one person who sits there who says well now last year this is what we did. So we've got a trustee to provide continuity from one board to another and so we've added two trustees, one to be elected each December for a two-year term. The only ones who automatically would have two year terms, although officers can be renominated and reelected if we should chose to do so . . . and they should choose to do so. That's the thinking for that.

The idea of providing some continuity on the board is certainly a good one, but what the real East Enders are most worried about at this point is a community council dominated and controlled by developers to the point where the board will consist entirely of developers. If the board is to represent the community in the broadest sense, the Area Council's Executive Board should have on it a representative from each of the other boards in the community, that is, from the Heritage Center board, the Development Corporation, the health center, and the Housing Preservation Fund. From the developers' point of view, however, this would give real East Enders too much representation.

The chair proceeds with a series of images that refer to the changeover from old to new officers. His presentation implies accusations about disorganization and the murkiness bordering on dirtiness of the old system. He refers to the new system as "very clean." The new language is very, very critical of existing practices:

> We have cleaned up, however, when authority changes. What we've provided for is a transfer of records meeting. Immediately after the election,

the incoming president and the incumbent are going to set the date on which they're going to have a transfer of records meeting. And at that meeting, we change the guard. Okay? We'll still have the formal installation in January, but so far as this never never land that exists in the East End today, when we have an election and then it's never clear as to when do you go to the new officers—that meeting will be announced, the transfer of records meeting— it's very clean—up to that point it belongs to the one crew, from that point on it belongs to the next. [Notice the vocabulary of ownership here.]

Building on this theme of disorganization, he proceeds to discuss how much better the revisions are in formalizing procedures. The implication is that he has created order out of chaos:

Okay? We've provided this business—somehow in the East End, we've had more than our *share* of the opportunity to remove people from office. So we've, we've *formalized* that just a little bit using the guidance from Robert's and standard parliamentary procedure you'll find on page 5 that we've talked about the impeachment and removal from office—no real surprise except that to impeach an officer or trustee will require five votes of the board. In other words a nine-member board—five of them, a majority, and you see that's really closer to two-thirds. If that person is impeached, then that bill of particulars comes to the Council and we must by a two-thirds vote, decide to pitch that individual. So we've made the provision for it, but I think that we've made the stakes high enough that we aren't going to run in to doing it without thinking very critically about if that's an appropriate course of action for us. We have said too, that if you're impeached from office that involves membership revocation: "Any person who is impeached or either resigns prior to trial by the Council, or is convicted by Council shall be removed from membership in the Council shall not be eligible for membership for three years from the date of resignation or conviction."

Almost anticipating the opposition to this provision that will develop in a moment, he invokes Robert's Rules of Order to justify the provision that revokes membership in the council upon impeachment or, rather, "conviction," as he puts it. His use of words such as "trial" and "conviction" lends an authoritarian tone to the bylaws that is foreign to a community that prides itself on settling its disputes in a personal and sensitive manner, most often with the advice and help of elders.

Moving on to the next topic:

With regard to vacancies—on page 6, the vacancies of situations is essentially unchanged. It belongs to the board and we would—we've made one minor change. We've said when the board has to act, [he chuckles]—one of our problems has been the board hasn't bothered to act and we're goin' to help 'em a little bit because in the event they don't take care of it we're going to help them take care of it.

The condescending and insulting tone here is not lost on the audience. People look around at one another, since many of the people in the room have sat on previous boards of the East End Area Council.

He proceeds to committees, making it clear that the Plan Implementation Committee, a team of diverse people designed to be an independent body advising the city and the Area Council, is now under the control of the East End Area Council. This means, of course, that whoever controls the Area Council controls plan implementation. Now that developers control the Area Council, this provision is a self-interested one that also presents a conflict of interest. He also puts down the Implementation Committee by saying that they don't care whose auspices they are under. This is patently untrue, since the Implementation Committee has discussed this issue of control numerous times and East Enders have insisted that the team remain independent. Real East Enders have resisted the control of implementation by the Area Council because they want to keep implementation out of local politics.

Committees [he speaks very slowly and deliberately]: We have reduced the number of standing committees and named specifically a Membership Committee, a Finance Committee, Neighborhood Support Committee— those exist right now—an Implementation Committee. What we've said here is the Implementation Committee is a part of the East End Area Council rather than simply being something that floats in limbo. Now Donald Compton, who's been the fellow who's done the coordinating for the Implementation Committee is aware of this course of action. So it's not a surprise—I don't know that it's been discussed by the Committee per se and I don't know that they really care.

This last statement is completely unbelievable. Having participated as a member of the Implementation Committee from its inception, Payne knows that the numerous attempts by developers to place the Implementation Team under the Area Council have been rejected for several reasons. The Implementation Team was modeled on the Riverfront Advisory Council, which was established precisely to act in an advisory capacity to the city and the community on the East End Development Plan. One of the reasons the Implementation Team was not placed under the Area Council was to protect it from the vagaries of political factionalism and local-level politics.

He then jumps to a different topic, but maintains a lecturing tone: "One of the things we've said here is, the community wants to continue to reach out to draw resources from the broader community for the benefit of the East End. The Implementation Committee in our assessment is clearly one of the arenas that gives us the opportunity to do that. It would be our hope that this practice would continue." It is very clear that Payne's proposed bylaws exclude the chairs of standing committees in East End from sitting on the Executive Board of the East End Area Council. He continues: "Again, these committee persons would not be members of the board *unless* they happen to be committee chairmen in addition to being elected officers, okay? But by virtue of chairmanship of one of these committees they would not automatically be members of the board."

The explanation for this exclusion of committee chairs is complex. On the surface, it appears that the president of the Area Council, at this point in time, Payne's wife, would have decreased power to determine who sits on the board, since they would all be elected. At the same time, given that a developer virtually controls the council, perhaps there is a feeling that all elected officers in the future, or a majority of them, will have the developers' interests at heart. Since committee chairs are often community people, and since increased powers have been given to the board in this set of revised bylaws, the exclusion of committee chairs, in effect, excludes real East Enders.

He continues to emphasize the fact that few changes have been made in the proposed bylaws from those of 1989. In fact, as we will see presently, not only have there been substantial changes, but the changes fly in the face of what real East Enders consider to be the best interests of the community. Payne's technique, however, is a well-known one. He is attempting to appropriate the local culture by saying that his proposed bylaws are consistent with what has gone before, when in fact he has changed both the spirit and the letter of East End law.

Elections

Again, Payne invokes images of cleanliness and clarity in his discussion of the Election Committee:

> We have cleaned up the election committee situation a little bit in that we tried to make a little more clear so that there would not be the misunderstandings that have occurred in some past elections. For example, we had

the unfortunate situation where some, some candidates have been at a disadvantage because some other candidates have distributed literature. Most inappropriate [he uses a tone of castigation as though he were literally slapping wrists]. The by-laws said that was inappropriate but it was done and nobody challenged it. We *tried* to deal with that here, so that everybody plays on a level playing field and there is no misunderstanding.

There are two important issues here. The first is that candidates in the past have submitted biographical statements to the community newsletter and this publication, *The East Ender*, published the statements written by the candidates just before the election. Such statements were written and submitted to the Election Committee, also chaired by Mark Payne, but they were not published in the newsletter. Also, a full-page article appeared in the main local newspaper featuring a developer who was running for vice-president. His opponent felt compelled, in light of the Election Committee's failure to print any campaign information, to hand out some informational leaflets. Payne leaves out these facts and proceeds: "We added article X., really we haven't because you will recall that after Veronica Mullenbrock became treasurer, she prepared and the Council adopted a financial policy. We broadened that to be a financial policy and annual audit, but it's essentially the language which you have already reviewed and adopted for the operation of our financial operations and that has been incorporated."

There is an interesting shift from "you" to "our" in the last sentence. Payne does this consistently. When it suits his purposes he says "we" or "our." When he wants to distance himself or exert control, which he does throughout his presentation, he says "you" or, worse, "you people." This constant switching is a control technique in and of itself.

Article X. Precedents and Amendments—simply provide for how we go about amending the by-laws if we wish to do so. No change in your basic procedure from what we have today. Again, we've simply cleaned up the language and hopefully made it consistent throughout the document. Now I have gone through hastily because I thought you wanted to go through hastily but I'm prepared to take as much time as you'd like to discuss any issue or the rationale that's a part of any of it if you'd like to do so.

He does not include any other members of the Bylaws Committee in the discussion, nor does he acknowledge the participation of the other members of the committee. It becomes clear that there are no other members.

As the floor opens for questions, the tone of Payne's presentation changes from one of calm control to one of slight frustration. He pauses and then launches into a pedantic and patronizing tone and raises his voice: "Many hours have gone into the language here people, and I don't want us to end up adopting something that we haven't thought through the implications of. Okay?"

Discussion of the bylaws continues. Real East Enders are very restrained even though, throughout the discussion, Payne continues to hurl insults at the community. At one point, for example, on the question of election procedures, he says:

> The election committee gets to decide how they conduct the election. They're the people who conduct it. Now, we tried to tighten up a little bit so that the election committee can do that. What we've done . . . We've been disgraceful in our behavior as a community with regard to the way we have conducted elections. We have people who have just showed up . . . we tried to deal with that, in part . . . people who just showed up and made it a shouting contest."

At another point, he talks about sign-in sheets as evidence of attendance and voting privileges. Here he adopts a pompous tone: "There are people who maintain, 'Oh, I didn't sign in,' . . . That's tough. In the real world, you know that when you come to the Area Council there's not a calling of the roll. The sign in is the roll call. And if somebody hasn't done that, I don't care if they've been here *without fail*, they didn't do their job. They can't fault us, for that."

Nobody actually challenges Payne's presentation of his revised bylaws, even though there had been a considerable amount of criticism in the neighborhood. Fritz does suggest that the proposed changes be published in *The East Ender,* however. Fritz also suggests dropping some extra copies of the proposed bylaws at the gas station, which, at this point, was still open, so that he could pass out copies to those who were interested. Payne resists this idea: "Let me be clear about something. I don't feel that we have to be in the business of making distribution of these by-laws, per se. That's not our job. If someone is interested in this organization, and wants to ask what are your by-laws, you give 'em without hesitation."

In a somewhat hushed and subdued tone he proceeds to insult the community even further:

> There are literally, there *have* to be hundreds of copies of the existing by-laws distributed in this East End. Now most of them have long since been burned because people haven't bothered to keep 'em—they carry 'em out o' here, they don't read 'em, they don't use 'em, they just pitch 'em. And

if . . . my concern, Fritz, is this: because of the *cost*, you figure, we're doin' seven cents a page, that's why it's back to back . . . When we do the *final* [version of the bylaws], when we do the final, the [word] "proposed" will be off, it will be "as adopted" on a given date, and then we will do, instead of back to back, *I hope* we could do just one side. But even then, I think we ought to be very *jealous* . . . if you're not gonna use 'em, then don't take 'em. They are always available if you want, the parliamentarian has 'em, the officers will have them. Those people in the community who are interested in what they say, will have them. But just to pass them out for toilet tissue . . .

There is grumbling from the floor and at this point Madeline Payne cuts off her husband and suggests that "we can announce in the newsletter that we are going to be voting on the by-laws and we can use our voice mail number."

Payne then becomes frustrated and shouts: "People, I'm, I'm . . . some o' you, some o' you, are questioning me deliberately about this. *I'm not interested in making a distribution!* If somebody wants to subscribe to the paper, let 'em subscribe. But I'm not in the business of giving it away. And if somebody calls you for one, you can have it and pass it to them."

The tension in this dialogue is escalating as real East Enders exchange looks and their eyes continue to roll.

Fritz: "That's all I'm asking."

M. Payne: "But I don't feel. I would not feel you go through the business of saying wouldn't you like to have one. I think that's not the way to do it."

Fritz: "That was not what I was . . ."

Payne doesn't let Fritz finish, but finishes for him: "That was not what you were thinking."

Fritz: "I was thinking on the same order as if there's someone should call me."

M. Payne: "Right, I think that makes sense. Put your number so that you can be contacted."

Fritz: "Yes, ma'am."

Fritz is so restrained and calm that the people in control do not notice how angry he is.

Boundaries Once Again

The boundary issue surfaces, to which an elderly East Ender replies: "The East End Area Council . . . Columbia Tusculum overrun our boundaries. We didn't overrun them. We made that decision so many times. We didn't overrun them, they overrun us."

The very naming of Columbia Tusculum, originally East End, is itself a power move, an overrunning of East End territory. Taking control again, Payne says sternly:

> The situation is this: the City ordinance that provides that every council (you know, we didn't used to name the boundaries, we didn't used to). City Council adopted a City ordinance that requires each community to do this. They acknowledge that that will result in overlap, and overlap isn't bad. So we, we indeed can bring you the maps that we looked at . . . we finally decided that the boundary makes sense. Let me tell you what the boundary is, just for your amusement or amazement.

To make light of boundaries is inappropriate at best, since East Enders take their history and their boundaries very seriously. The city and the developers are constantly trying to shrink the East End, and boundaries are, for a variety of reasons, constantly contested. Payne's tone is very patronizing:

> It begins out at Kemper Lane and Columbia Parkway. It comes out Columbia Parkway to Delta. It gets to Delta, it goes north on Delta to Kroger Drive, and then, it does a miraculous thing, it goes from the intersection of Columbia Parkway and Kroger, through the bridge loop yonder, to Wooster Pike and Eastern and then it turns south to the Ohio River. I don't know what you may think south is, but if you're very critical as to its turn south, it just goes out toward California. Okay? Because that's south! Now, that's what the by-laws say and then along the Ohio River to Kemper Lane. I don't disagree with you that this would be something that somebody could look at some time in the future. We talked about just making it the plan area, and excluding all the rest of it. One of the very regular people who that would exclude is the lady sitting right back here.

His tone implies that his audience has no knowledge of the geography. He points to a white-haired woman, Veronia Cable, who is a resident of Columbia Tusculum and who has been attending East End Area Council meetings for at least forty years.

Voting

The liaison from Associated Neighborhood Practice expresses some concern about these bylaws being voted on at the next monthly meeting (May 2, 1992): "My concern is if folks didn't hear about this."

Payne responds in an angry tone:

I won't buy that. This was on the agenda for March. One of the things that happens in the East End . . . we take care of all those people who don't bother to take care of themselves. No dice. We've done it on a business-like basis, we've prepared it, we've come prepared to discuss it with people, we'll make provision in the Newsletter so they will get copies. This business about going out and delivering it to somebody because they are nice people—we're finished. That isn't the way a business runs.

James Strong, another old-timer who has been involved in a leadership capacity for thirty or more years, makes a strong argument for decisions to be made by consensus, not by a single person. He also views the community broadly. This is an implicit rejection of the "business mentality" put forth by developers. Actually, the "business rhetoric" is simply another control device. The fewer people who actually look at Payne's proposed bylaws, the less the criticism of them.

The developer interests then begin to coalesce for quick adoption of the proposed bylaws. Again, the "business" images prevail.

Montgomery:

Before we get out of hand, I think as there has been extensive discussion on that. A comment was made here that it is this group and this meeting where we conduct our business. And it's unfortunate that this meeting's not well attended or more attended by citizens of our community. I think those of us that have taken a couple of hours out of our week or our day to be here. We should respect the fact that we're here to make decisions and those that are not—well we're sorry for them. For anyone that does have a concern that wants to call in, recognize that they've been absent, ask for minutes of the meeting or get caught up on any of the issues discussed, we'll be happy to share that with them. But for those of us that are here, let's make decisions and move ahead.

Madeline Payne pushes for adoption of bylaws aside from the boundary issues. Montgomery confirms M. Payne's concern for passage of bylaws and suggests amending the bylaws later "to accommodate boundary changes so as not to hold up the passage of our by laws."

The motion is defeated and the proposed bylaws are rejected.

Counters to the Proposed Bylaws

A version of Payne's proposed bylaws had been distributed and discussed preliminarily by a few key grassroots leaders before the meeting, and there had been discussion about drafting a series of amendments. After Payne's presentation, and after his demonstrated resistance to facilitating the distribution of the proposed bylaws in the neighborhood, the grassroots leaders launched a concerted amendment-drafting effort. Several informal meetings were held in which a small group of residents and leaders came together to review the proposed bylaws point by point and to draft a set of sixteen amendments.

At the next meeting of the East End Area Council (May 2, 1994), Fritz, the principal architect of the amendments, made a polite attempt to present them for discussion. His efforts were rejected by the developer-controlled council and yet another Bylaws Committee was formed. At this point, the developers had become so frustrated by the grassroots resistance to their bylaws that they were willing to hand the bylaws revision back to the community. This committee was chaired by Fritz, who succeeded, through a series of informal, but very structured, breakfast meetings that included a strong committee of leaders and residents, in drafting a new set of bylaws. The meetings were held at someone's house. Everyone brought a contribution and the homey atmosphere helped the group work. After a series of weekly meetings, a set of bylaws that resembled the original 1989 set, was drafted and distributed. But to hand a project to a committee is not to sanction the committee's work.

This time the developer-controlled area council did not even attempt to examine the new bylaws. Rather, it dismissed the "grassroots bylaws" literally as "garbage," as ungrammatical and totally unacceptable. It managed to create yet a third Bylaws Committee, this time headed by a presumably neutral party, but actually a property owner and nonresident clearly in the developers' camp. This person was assigned to settle the discrepancies—especially the boundary issues—in the two sets of bylaws. What the third chair of the third Bylaws Committee didn't realize was that boundaries were always being contested as a manifestation of local-level factionalism and class interests.

Discussion

Bylaws change the meaning of community and how it is practiced. At first, I was quite surprised by the prevalence of bylaws and by the constant reference to them until I realized that both are products of and reactions to colonialism. Bylaws are invoked only in situations of class conflict and power struggles. The East End way of doing things, the informal way, would not involve bylaws. We can see in the description of the meeting an imposition of the colonizer's values in a way that insults and denigrates East Enders. Criticisms of the community's bylaws are criticisms of East Enders.

Control tactics not only are evident in the entire colonial discourse, they also are symbolic of the larger controls exercised by the colonizer as a landlord and as a person who provides jobs for people by hiring them on a temporary or part-time basis. The subtext of the colonial discourse communicates the speaker's presumed superiority and the listeners' (East Enders') inferiority.[4]

Resisting Colonialism: Using Power to the Advantage of the Community

Resisting colonialism—the takeover of the community by outsiders—is a key, if not the key, aspect of practicing community in the East End. East End leaders resist colonialism in a variety of ways: by remaining silent and withholding information and by keeping projects alive in the face of constant undermining and sabotage by developers. The establishment of the Pendleton Heritage Center Board as an independent board was itself an act of resistance to the colonial agendas of the developers. At the time the group was considering forming a board, there was considerable discussion about its relationship to a developer-controlled East End Area Council. Some old-timers consistently argued that everything in the community should come under the Area Council. Others worried that giving primacy to the Council was fine as long as the Council was controlled by East Enders.

With a developer-controlled Community Council, however, grass-roots leaders needed to create new ways of working in the community to ensure that the projects would remain under community control. Interacting with power elites on city committees that require community representation is one way East Enders have of resisting colonialism. Incorporating outsiders onto community boards is another way. In one sense, the ways of resisting colonialism are all related to one another; in another sense, the forms of resistance can be understood to be very different and dependent on the particular source of power and the particular contexts within which power is being exercised.

City Committees

Elite members of the greater Cincinnati community are key players in community planning and economic development in the city. They sit on important community development advisory boards; they donate enormous amounts of time and energy to meetings, subcommittees, making contacts, and all aspects of community preservation. Community residents and leaders interact with city elites in particular ways, all of which manifests subtle power relations. Elite members are not a homogeneous group; they range from corporate executives and their wives, some of whom consider themselves to be and, indeed, are real activists, to citizens in the Greater Cincinnati community. Wherever they originate, they are part of a group of powerful "others" from the perspective of real East Enders, especially grassroots leaders. The most sophisticated of the grassroots leaders realize that, without these powerful "others," the community has very little chance of surviving, much less of being revitalized in a way that maintains a place for real East Enders.

I was introduced to "them" at City Hall at my first encounter with a committee of the Riverfront Advisory Council. The RAC is an officially designated citizen advisory group to the city manager. This particular committee, the Plan Group of the RAC, had an imposing composition—prominent citizens, wives of corporate executives, and professionals with experience and expertise in architecture, engineering, and construction. The group met regularly in a very large conference room in City Hall with an oversized conference table and room for an audience to observe the discussion. I began attending the committee meetings in the winter of 1992. At first I sat in the audience, away from the conference table. I wanted just to observe. The conference table and the people sitting around it were somewhat intimidating. Men and women were wearing three-piece suits that looked like they had been purchased in the most elegant of Cincinnati's stores. They sat with leather-bound daily calendars and very thick file folders. City staff people had a somewhat rumpled appearance, but they, too, were dressed in suits. One or two East Enders dressed up; others wore regular East End clothes: pants, T-shirts in summer, sweatshirts in winter. Including me, there were five of us in all. We brought breakfast rolls and coffee from the bakery across the street. RAC members look annoyed at the noise produced by the white bakery bags when we extracted the rolls. They were not eating or drinking anything—not even coffee. "I eat breakfast at home," one woman remarked.

The tension in the room was very apparent. East Enders did not trust "the city" or the elites. The elites are committed to preserving the community, but they have their own ideas about what preserving community means and how it should be done. One or two of the East Enders were quite outspoken; the others were more reluctant to speak. After each meeting, one East Ender consistently complained to me that her comments were never recorded in the minutes. Another grassroots leader repeated over and over: "I speak from the heart, but they don't understand my heart."

What exactly is this "heart"? On one level, it is a metaphor for commitment to community, to maintaining it, to building and rebuilding existing institutions in revitalized form; on another level, it is a view about ways of doing things, about how things are accomplished in communities; on still another level, it is a statement about powerlessness, the kind of powerlessness that manifests a strong sense of commitment to what ought to be done in the community, but without the political or the financial resources to accomplish what needs to be done. The priorities of the heart are not commercial, profit-making, and tax-generating priorities, for the building and maintaining of the community in the form of a heritage center and housing for senior citizens is really an investment in future generations of East Enders.

The heart is not understood by corporate culture, for it represents a way of doing things that is very personal and that often values consensus building over getting the task done. At the same time, the negotiation of the hegemonic system—the use of the power structure to garner resources for community projects—is always critical, whether the powerful are being asked to testify before City Council or whether a corporate executive paves the way for the release of funds to the community. Community leaders must work with representatives of the hegemonic system (the power structure). At the same time, the clash between hegemonic and grassroots culture is always there as a fact to be dealt with, a force to contend with, an ever-present tension and conflict.

But it's how the linkages are forged that enable community leaders to work with the power structure—what keeps them connected, oiled, and working—requires teamwork, a delicate balancing of community agendas in the broadest sense. Some powerful people try to build bridges and smooth over deep-rooted conflicts between factions by denying, or at least downplaying the existence of factions. This has its merits, especially when it is task oriented. The grassroots, on the other hand, sees the factions clearly, feels the put-downs and the power plays. Real East

Enders experience patronizing, discriminatory behavior along with the crass power plays. The following is an example of a very positive collaboration between local Cincinnati elites and East End leaders.

TUESDAY, AUGUST 28, 1994:
HUMAN SERVICES COMMITTEE MEETING, CITY HALL

Donald Compton, the former chairman of the RAC Plan Group and the de facto chair of the Plan Implementation Team, indicates that he will introduce the Pendleton Heritage Center project according to the East End Community Development Plan. He weighs his words carefully and speaks slowly and softly. He is very rational, very clear, and very calm. He is impressive. He indicates that he would like a community person to summarize the Pendleton Heritage Center's progress and planning. The chair of the Pendleton Heritage Center Board, Doris Sells, does so with aplomb, speaking of the project as close to her heart and pulling a snapshot of the Pendleton Building from her purse. At this point, there are no new monies coming to the project. Madeline Payne, the president of the East End Area Council, had just received a letter indicating that the Pendleton Heritage Center project had been turned down as a Community Budget Request (CBR).

Despite this setback, the Pendleton Heritage Center presentation is very positive. Everyone wants to get something going, even if the entire building cannot be renovated at one time. A few telephones and a conference room would open the building and create activity. Such activity would, in turn, create positive energy in the community by attracting more residents to meetings and thereby create a greater sense of community involvement. For a long time, the Pendleton project was held up by the fact that it had no sewer hookup. A few strategic calls to the head of the Metropolitan Sewer District resulted in a promise that the sewers for the PHC would be finished in the next four months. This was, in fact, accomplished in the early part of 1995.

Outsiders and Community Boards

One of the most effective ways that community leaders have of resisting colonialism is by incorporating trusted outsiders into the community— on community boards and subcommittees and in informal groups. These outsiders include attorneys, professors, university students, planners, and professional advocates who are experienced community organizers. Each of these outsiders enters the community on a different premise, interacts in different contexts, and thus interfaces with those East Enders who are practicing community in different ways. Outsiders each have different relationships with East End residents and leaders. The power relations are different, but there always are power relations.

THE ROLE OF ATTORNEYS AS ADVOCATES IN THE EAST END

Attorneys play extremely important and varied roles in the East End. In most circumstances, in order to function well and retain the trust of East End leaders, they must function on a *pro bono* basis or be paid by another agency, such as Legal Aid.

One of the most important roles for attorneys is to provide legal advice to nonprofit corporations. They facilitate and file the papers for the establishment of nonprofit corporations; they anticipate legal issues such as liability and they provide legal advice on a variety of issues ranging from real estate law to lease arrangements. Attorneys also fight for community projects, especially housing projects, that are being sabotaged by developers. Were it not for the patience and skilled commitment of a few attorneys, there might be no affordable housing in the East End.

PROFESSIONAL ADVOCATES AND COMMUNITY ORGANIZERS

Professional advocates include people who work in social service agencies or consulting firms and who are paid to act as advocates on community projects, housing, health, and other needed services. Negotiating with the city bureaucracy and outside funding agencies is a special skill of professional advocates; so, too, is community organizing of an informal sort. Any East Ender's trip to City Hall, whether the purpose is to meet with a particular person—usually a member of City Council—or to attend a committee meeting or hearing, is strengthened by the presence of advocates. A City Council member will be much more likely to spend time listening to an East End leader if an advocate is present.

Advocates provide general support, legitimacy, and confirmation for community leaders, but they also function best when they perform the tasks that need to be done: writing minutes, typing reports, writing grants, and finding consultants and technical support people.

EAST END ADVOCATES

In the fall of 1995, the professional advocates, attorneys, researchers, and citizen elites came together to form a group that came to be known as the East End Advocates. Two powerful sentiments, one positive, the other less so, united the group from the outset: (1) a strong sense of commitment to maintaining and revitalizing the East End as a community for East Enders in accordance with the East End Plan; and (2) a strong sense of frustration that the community leaders were divided and that the years spent working to preserve the community by advocates and East End leaders alike were in danger of being wasted if some strategies were not developed to determine how advocates' time could be spent most effectively.

Each of the East End advocates had devoted countless hours of work toward these efforts, albeit in different capacities and from some very different perspectives. For example, while all of the advocates had already spent years working in the East End, some did so as Appalachians and African Americans devoted to the maintenance and preservation of their own culture; others did so as citizens devoted to democratic, participatory government. As a researcher/advocate, I had an ongoing cultural analysis to share with the group.

Among the agencies represented around the advocates' table were the UAC, Associated Neighborhood Practice of Hamilton County, Saint Andrew Social Services, the Evangelical Ministry, Christian Church Cathedral, and Research Associates, Inc. There were two attorneys, one who worked for the Legal Aid Society and the other who worked for a private law firm. Researchers included one faculty member from the University of Cincinnati and one from Chatfield College in Brown County, Ohio. Citizen elites included a retired executive and several women who had been active in many civic organizations and projects.

The precipitating event for the formation of the group was the floundering of the East End Riverfront Community Urban Redevelopment Corporation (described in Chapter 9). Meetings were not being held and, consequently, projects were not being developed. Without projects in which the board was actively engaged (that is, not a past or completed project such as Kelly's Landing), the nonprofit status of the board would not be renewed. Much to the frustration of one of the attorneys, the IRS repeatedly refused to grant nonprofit status (501[C][3]). Without a nonprofit designation in the form of an identification number, monies could not be used by the board. That is, for the development corporation to develop projects, another nonprofit group would have to be used as fiscal agent.

Advocates needed to gather around the same table, in part to support one another, but, more important, to communicate to one another in ways that were not possible in a community setting. The actions of community leaders, for example, could be analyzed in these meetings. While there was never any discussion about colonialism per se or resisting colonialism, there was recognition that advocates were vital partners in maintaining the East End for East Enders.

At first I was reluctant to participate in a group that excluded East End residents and leaders. It became clear, however, that a new context was needed for communicating among the different kinds of advocates, some of whom did not feel comfortable talking directly to East Enders, or who truly did not understand what was going on. I was assigned the task of community liaison by the East End advocates. That is, it was my job to keep community residents and leaders informed and to be the conduit for community input.

As a team of advocates, our primary goal in 1996 was to work on several fronts to rebuild East End institutions. Shoring up the development corporation so that it could create affordable housing, new and rehabbed, owner occupied, and rental units, was one example. The other was to work toward securing the Pendleton Heritage Center as a home for community groups. The Pendleton would provide an office for the development corporation, for example, as well as a permanent meeting place. These were some of the connections between various kinds of institution building. The expansion of the development corporation and Heritage Center boards to include a broader base of East Enders as well as to include outsiders with specific kinds of expertise (real estate and banking) was seen as an essential part of community preservation and revitalization.

One result of the East End Advocates' coordination of efforts was the staffing of the EERCURC board by ANP. Minutes were written and typed. The board was expanded and community-organizing efforts succeeded in increasing resident participation. The hiring of a consultant to oversee projects and secure funding for ongoing projects was also accomplished using grant monies from the Catholic Archdiocese. The East End needed a full-time community organizer to ensure broad-based community participation in projects. The advocates made plans to secure funding for the position.

The advocates' efforts intensified in the spring of 1996, when it became clear that the colonialists (developers) were continuing their efforts to sabotage community projects by spreading the rumor to key city and agency people that the Pendleton Heritage Center was of interest to only a few East End leaders and was not of broad interest to the community. When the East End Advocates learned of this rumor, efforts were stepped up to bring out the residents to meet with foundation representatives to discuss Heritage Center funding. These community organizing efforts were quite successful, and, in addition to communicating crucial information to the community about the Heritage Center, the large gathering of residents resulted in adding new East End members to the EERCURC board. In fact, this gathering, which occurred on June 4, 1996, was one of the largest gatherings of East End residents that I had seen in a long time. People who had been active in the community in previous years, but who had been driven away from meetings by developers' control tactics, returned to support the Pendleton. A retelling of the history of the building, a sharing of East Enders' childhood experiences playing pool and gathering at dances in the Pendleton Building further solidified the importance of the Pendleton as a community building and center of East End social life.

After the grant proposal was submitted to the foundation, one of the advocates received a call from a foundation staff member asking whether a copy of the grant could be shared with a city staffer. The advocate refused because she knew quite clearly that the proposal would go directly from the city into the hands of the developers.

RELATIONSHIPS BETWEEN ADVOCATES AND REAL EAST ENDERS

The relationships between advocates and East End leaders are always delicate. Advocates can be and are, in fact, dismissed by community groups. More often, advocates leave the community to spend their time in other endeavors, in other neighborhoods, for example. Sometimes outsiders quite unknowingly get caught in internal factions and become targets in the midst of interpersonal conflicts and personal power struggles. Sometimes outsiders alienate themselves for reasons of naïveté. Sometimes outsiders want a role in the community, but feel useless—or bow out for a time. In addition to keeping the advocates in communication with one another, the added goal of the East End Advocates was to keep people involved and keep people with power, resources, and skills in positions to play effective roles in the community.

The East End Advocates did provide the context and support to convince a very effective member of the citizen elite to return to chairing the Plan Implementation Team. His return was important not only because of his extensive and long-term knowledge of the plan and the planning process, but also because he was task-oriented and a very effective bridge builder among the various constituencies and stakeholders in the city and in the community.

For real East Enders, becoming too close to even very trusted outsiders can be very costly. Rejection and ostracism by the community in the form of dismissal from community boards is one possible outcome. Fear or, rather, worry about offending outsiders can also be taken to extremes.

Scenario: Alliance with Professionals as Resistance to Colonialism

During one health center board meeting three center staff members, who normally attend board meetings but who are not part of the board of trustees, were asked by the vice-president of the board (a real East Ender whom other East Enders view as self-interested) to leave the room while the board deliberated a difficult decision regarding the new health center. "We need to discuss this just among ourselves," he said. Everyone agreed, and the three staff members exited. The discussion that ensued was indeed calm and peaceful as some of the pressure to come to a decision was, at least momentarily, set aside. Board members who were reluctant to speak earlier or who were reluctant to ask questions for fear of appearing not to understand spoke up very freely. The issues, with accompanying tables and numbers, had, in fact, been presented rather quickly by a staffer. He was a very fast talker, not because he wanted to confuse or mystify anyone, but because he was very familiar with the technical issues involved, and because, in his enthusiasm, he managed to fill the room with words. The combination of his rapid-fire speech and his close relationship to one of the professionals with whom he had clearly spent hours discussing the matter overwhelmed the board members (including me). We simply had not spent as much time on the issue as had the staff.

The decisions being requested from the board were very serious ones. The removal of the staff members did, in fact, take some of the pressure off the decision-making process and, since the board members felt comfortable discussing points of confusion, within a relatively short period of time, the decision was finalized. The staff then returned to the room and the meeting was adjourned shortly thereafter.

One week later, the president of the board, who had not been present at the previous meeting, castigated the board in a very agitated and vehement manner for excluding these trusted staff members. He went on for ten minutes or more talking about how important these people were to the health center, how the center would be nothing without them, how they were a part of "us," and so on. His face became very red, to the point that the staff members repeatedly tried to assure him that they did not, in fact, feel excluded. Approximately one week later, this time at an informal gathering, the president became agitated once again. He insisted that such an exclusion would never, ever happen again if he could help it.

What was going on here? Why was so much tension produced by such a seemingly minor event? I asked the president to explain his reading of the situation to me in more depth. Did he think the vice-president had a motive other than that of facilitating the discussion and, ultimately, a decision?

"He wants to control the board. He wants power," I was told quite clearly. "He wants to be president. He insulted our staff!" When I thought about it, I realized there was logic to this argument.

When I described the situation to another East Ender, she concurred with the president's interpretation of the situation. She also added that getting upset was the wrong thing to do, because it only showed that the vice-president could easily get the president's goat.

As I thought about it, I could see the elements of control present in the act of excluding the staff members. I could also see that the exercise of power within a group of East Enders who were loyal to their president required the vice-president to go out of his way to cater to other board members. I began also to understand that such adamant castigation of the board did not win any favors and that to become close enough to outsiders to regard them as insiders could be costly to any local leader.

12 | THE FLOOD OF '97

$\mathcal{A}$s this book was sitting on the copyeditor's desk, the 1997 flood hit Cincinnati—the worst in forty-three years.

On Wednesday, March 5, 1997, the Ohio River crested at 64.7 feet. Downtown Cincinnatians were told to stay north of 3rd Street. East End Cincinnatians kept watching the river—anxiously, but with the knowledge that they had been through floods before. I began to see just how fortunate the hillside people were. Knowing in the abstract that social stratification follows the topography is one thing; seeing the devastation created by the river in a poor community on the floodplain is quite another. From the university and from many other "hill" locations, one would not realize that much of the region was under water and that any semblance of normal life would not resume for many weeks. By Friday, March 7, the waters had fallen enough so that the cleanup could begin.

East Enders take pride in coping with the river's power. Kim and Marcy carry garbage bags full of mud from Megan and James Strong's basement. Kim is their daughter and Marcy is their niece. They soon look like the bags they are carrying, they joke. "The dryer is gone," Kim announces.

James and Megan's yellow house sits in the East End's midsection on the north side of Eastern Avenue. Next door is their son Mick's house, and across the street is their daughter Ann's house. Marcy lives in the Betz Flats, the newly rehabbed apartment building diagonally across from James and Megan's. All of the basements, including that of the Betz Flats, are flooded. Pumps and labor are being shared.

Figure 23. Flood Collage

The men are at the docks cleaning out the boats that sank during the storm. "This is almost a ritual," says one leader. "If you sink your boat, you know where it's at. It's better than tying it and worrying about its breaking loose because of the fast-moving current."

The health center is giving tetanus shots to everyone in the neighborhood. "You need to get one, too," Megan admonishes me. "You're down here breathin' the stuff." I ask her whether James is okay. I had been told by Robbie that he took to bed just as the river was cresting.

"It's really rough when you can't help," James told me yesterday. Instead of probing his feelings, I said, "Look at all the help you have here." He is surrounded by family—in addition to his wife, he has sons, daughters, nieces and nephews, grandchildren, and other East Enders who check on him daily. His depression is very visible though. Robbie explains that James's depression is understandable if you consider that this is the first time in his adult life that he is not leading the flood cleanup. As the head of a large East End family, James is constantly called on by his grown children to help in times of crisis. He is a wise and calm man who has family and community as highest priorities. Now he is physically unable to help. He suffers from heart disease and other ailments, including arthritis, that make it difficult for him to move, much less to negotiate the steep basement stairs. Kim and Marcy keep dragging the bags and use a dolly to haul them to a dumpster provided by the city.

At the end of the first day of cleanup, Kim nods wearily as we sit around the Strongs' dining room table. There is barely room to sit with all of the boxes under and around it. The living room is barely recognizable. It looks more like a storage room with boxes piled to the ceiling. Everything—years of family memories—has been taken out of the basement.

"You are getting older," Kim says, hugging her dad. "Not old," she emphasizes, "just older."

Kim had a hard time convincing James and Megan to leave as the waters were rising. No heat, no water, and no electricity, except for ceiling lights, made their house cold and without functioning toilets. For people in their late seventies to live under these conditions was simply not safe. But James and Megan did not want Kim and her young daughter to have to stay by themselves upstairs in their flooded house.

After Marcy agreed to stay in the house with Kim, Megan and James went to stay with their grandson in Mount Washington. Eva, another daughter, chauffeurs them back and forth daily. They spend their days in their East End dining room that is now equipped with a kerosene heater. When Eva calls to arrange a time to pick them up at night, James and Megan negotiate as late a time as possible, and they leave reluctantly.

Vultures Are Descending on the Neighborhood

Robbie, Kim, and I walk from James and Megan's house across the street to see a barge that has become entangled in the trees that normally stand in back yards between the houses and the riverbank. It is amazing to see the barge so close to houses and trees. The barge momentarily distracts everyone from the drudgery of the flood cleanup.

As we are peering at the barge, a stranger, a man about thirty-five, drives up in a four-wheel-drive vehicle. After announcing that he is not a vulture but a "Christian man," he proceeds to offer "very good prices" for cleaning and power washing basements and houses.

Chuck, Ann Strong's boyfriend, who, Megan tells me is not a "river person," but is doing very well in this flood, politely tells the man that there are plenty of people in the East End to help and that if he is not offering his help for free, he is not needed. Kim and Marcy are polite to him as he hands each person, including me, a business card and a flyer.

Chuck is walking around in rubber boots helping all of the immediate neighbors pump and clean. He explains that it is essential to keep the water moving; otherwise, the mud cakes and dries. Robbie says that the streets should really be hosed as the water goes down before they become impossible to clean.

On Tuesday Robbie had called early in the morning to tell me that Kim had asked her to see about getting a portable toilet for "that part of the neighborhood." It's a rather densely populated part of the neighborhood, by East End standards, at least. There are houses on both sides of Eastern Avenue along with the thirteen units in the Betz Flats. The next morning, Kim called Robbie again to ask if she had a kerosene stove. "I could tell she was cold by the way she talked; her teeth were chattering," Robbie told me with great concern in her voice. I told her, "I don't have a kerosene stove, but I do have blankets and some warm clothes." Since no portable toilets were available for donation, Robbie was collecting money to pay the $100 rental fee. Missy, a former East Ender who now manages Robbie's apartment building in Mount Washington, gave her $10, and Robbie said she was going to call a few other people. It sounded to me as if a Cincinnati neighborhood had suddenly turned into a Third World country. And quickly, too. I started thinking about the potential for typhoid and cholera epidemics. In the last century, these had been common occurrences along the river.

Robbie and I talked several times that day. She knows my teaching schedule, so she called late in the afternoon, after classes were over. She explained that her nephew would be meeting the fellow with the portable toilet early the next morning. I told her it would be fine if she wanted to stop by my house that night. She called again around 9:00 that evening to say she had just finished bingo in Oakley and would stop by.

Many shelters had been set up in churches and schools throughout the Ohio Valley, but it quickly became clear that no one was feeding and clothing people who hadn't been forced to leave their homes and go to the shelters.

During the flood cleanup I received a call from state senator Jessica Allen, who had formerly worked for a county agency in the East End. She had spent years working with neighborhood leaders on a variety of projects, from housing to community organizing. She knew the community well. In her capacity as state senator, she had spent part of the day attending hearings on flood relief with the lieutenant governor, the mayor of Cincinnati, and Vice-President Al Gore. She, too, was upset: "Who is helping the people in the East End is what I want to know."

"As far as I can tell, no one yet—at least no one from the outside," I said, relating the portable toilet story (this came to be called the neighborhood "porta potty" story).

"What do people need?" she asked.

"Everything," I replied. "Food, warm clothes, blankets, cleaning supplies."

Jessica was upset about the insensitive, bureaucratic attitude toward people living in the floodplain. She told me that the bureaucrats wanted to move people off the river. I noted that they did not realize how important the river was as a source of livelihood and identity. Access to boat docks is critical to East End life and livelihood. Though an outsider dares not use the term "river rat," East Enders identify as river rats.

"I will relate [the river's importance to those] at the hearing in Columbus. Please let people in the East End know I care."

Practicing Community

The *Cincinnati Enquirer* has a photo of Robbie hugging Megan Strong. The caption, which is one of many referring to flood relief, talks about help from fellow community residents. Such help is the essence of practicing community. Megan, who is a tiny seventy-eight-year-old woman, looks so small next to Robbie, fifty-one, but her presence looms quite large in the East End in general and in her family in particular.

Kim is upset because—so intense has been her involvement with the flood cleanup—she has forgotten her daughter Lisa's ninth birthday. She mentions this as we are sitting around her dining room table several days after the fact. It's cold, but the kerosene stove is doing its job.

One day, Kim takes off her mud-covered shoes to go into the grocery store in Mount Washington to buy lunch meat. A customer keeps staring at her and then asks, "Were you in the flood?"

Kim says, "Why? Do I look that bad?" Robbie remarks, "She should have said, 'These are the clothes I wear when I sit with my tin cup and beg.'"

People's shoes are indeed wet and covered with mud. Shoes are much needed—many pairs. Kim and Robbie survey the shoe sizes within a three-block radius after a wealthy woman from a hillside neighborhood offers to donate fifty pairs of shoes. Just in case the offer falls through, Robbie and Kim do not tell the residents of the offer. They simply explain that they are doing a survey of shoe sizes so as not to

```
┌─────────────────────────────────────────┐
│                                           │
│   FURNITURE,  CLOTHING                    │
│        GIVE - AWAY                         │
│   FOR THE 1997 FLOOD                       │
│    VICTIMS OF THE                          │
│        EAST END                            │
│                                            │
│   SATURDAY, MAY 17, 1997                   │
│      9:00 a.m.  Until                      │
│                                            │
│            AT THE                          │
│     MT. CARMEL                             │
│   BAPTIST CHURCH                           │
│     3101 EASTERN AVENUE                    │
│                                            │
└─────────────────────────────────────────┘
```

Figure 24. "Give-Away" Flyer

raise expectations. Before the middle of March, sixty-five pairs of new shoes, including a size 16EEE for a very large man in the neighborhood, are delivered to the Strongs' house for distribution in the East End. The shoes are described to me as "good shoes, Reeboks and Converse."

After that, I begin talking to neighbors and friends, who proceed to bring me boxes of "stuff"—linens, clothes, shoes. Many people had things to contribute but were being turned away from churches.

A new neighbor is particularly generous, and one day around the middle of March I make the first of two trips to the East End to deliver her donations, but as I approach the underpass at Delta, I see a police blockade. How will I get through? Fortunately, I see Joe, the officer who gives the monthly police reports at the EEAC. He recognizes the car and waves me through.

The next day, it is not so easy. I am stopped by an unfamiliar officer.

"I'm just delivering food and clothes," I inform him with as much authority in my voice as I can muster.

"Where to?" he challenges.

"To the twenty-four hundred block." I have taken on the East End habit of identifying blocks.

"Go on," he grumbles reluctantly. I breathe a sigh of relief, realizing how close I have come to being turned away. As a white woman, I am lucky; an elderly black colleague and lifelong community organizer does not have as much luck with these white male officers. Not only is he turned away; he is almost arrested. The newspapers have been full of warnings about looters, and the police are determined to let only East Enders through.

The skill with which Robbie has mastered the bureaucracy of flood relief is truly impressive. She urges East Enders to register with the Federal Emergency Management Agency (FEMA) by using the 800 numbers. She then urges everyone to go to the senior citizens' center at Lunken Airport, where FEMA has set up its flood relief headquarters.

Not surprisingly, East Enders are reluctant to ask outsiders for help. Many people tell me that help has not been available in the past; why seek it now?

The Aftermath of the Flood

"We've had the high water; now comes the hell."

Robbie is in tears at the PHC meetings on Thursday, March 13: "You have to be crude and rude down here to get anything done."

She is despondent because one-third of the houses on Worth, a street that runs between Eastern Avenue and the river, just west of Delta, have been condemned. Mrs. Kimball's house, across from the old Highland School, has also been tagged. "Where do you go when you leave home if there is nowhere to go? There's no price you can put on a home. Chris Wool hasn't had a drink in twenty-five years; he's been drinking since 8:00 this morning." Joe Costello's house has been condemned; he had just put $17,000 into it.

Robbie and Kim have been delivering cleaning supplies to East Enders. City staffers distribute supplies from LeBlond Recreation Center. They are maintaining the pattern of householding—a community practice that is now accentuated by the crisis of the flood. When A. K. Jones, a developer, takes cleaning supplies, he is depriving the group. Robbie is furious because she knows he can pay for his own supplies.

Monday, March 17

I have never seen so many people at an EEAC meeting. The large room on the uppermost floor of LeBlond is packed. The room is very hot.

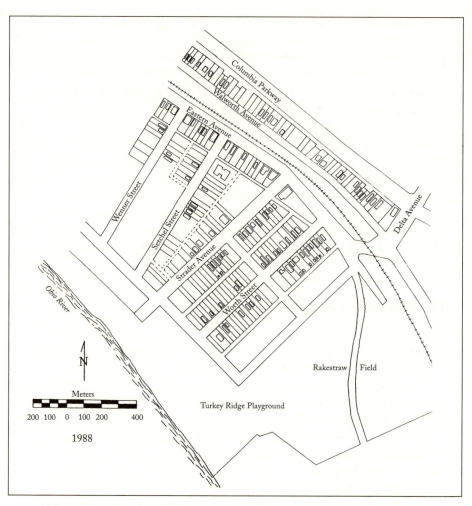

Map 8. East End Area: Wenner, Strader, Worth

People wearing T-shirts are fanning themselves. East Enders have come because they are really angry. Homes have been torn down. Flood relief is slow in coming.

Elizabeth Jones, a developer, presides. She stands during the entire meeting with one shoe in her hand. She uses it like a gavel when there is the least bit of rumbling from the floor. "Order," she shouts, banging the shoe on the table. "We must have order. People must be heard!"

"True enough," I think to myself, "but must you be so authoritarian?"

An East Ender remarks, "I knew she was bossy, but does she have to act like a dictator?"

The service providers and city, state, and county bureaucrats take their turns along with FEMA. There is someone from almost every segment of city government, or so it seems—Buildings and Inspections, Relocation, Neighborhood Services, Consumer Services, to name a few. There are also service providers: the Red Cross and the Linwood Baptist Church, which has been collecting clothing and distributing it throughout the community. The bureaucrats can easily be picked out of the crowd because they are the only people wearing suits and dresses.

In most instances, there is much talk, but very little action or concrete help or advice. Passing the buck from one level of government to another seems to be the order of the day.

The developers issue surveys to see who wants to stay in or leave the East End. They are collecting information about where to buy next. They glory in the demolition of houses. They argue vehemently with grassroots leaders, who are working outside of the Community Council to bring building supplies into the neighborhood.

Wednesday, March 19

Emergency EEAC Meeting

"We did catch the city in a couple of lies, which was fun."

The meeting is packed.

"Elizabeth Jones had a sore throat, so she didn't do a whole lot of talking—weren't we blessed."

Again, dozens of East Enders show up.

"I don't know who was on the spot more, FEMA or Building and Inspections."

James Strong is arguing with the building inspector. No more buildings are coming down for at least thirty days.

The child of the Legal Aid lawyer attending the emergency EEAC meeting draws a house with blue water running through it. A sun with a sad face looks down on the scene.

Elizabeth Jones ignores James Strong's raised hand as she closes the questions and cuts him off as he tries to speak. Kim and Robbie get out of their chairs.

"There is a plot against Worth Street. The damn crane fell and put a hole in Sam Donald's house."

Two City of Cincinnati employees are given baskets as thanks for their work in helping flood victims. They went out of their way and worked long hours. Amy Lane, an East Ender, also wants to be thanked. "You're an East Ender, I'm an East Ender. We know what we are supposed to do. You've been through it before."

The virtually instant organization of community work in flood relief is natural. Everyone knows what to do. Work tasks and equipment are shared among adult workers. The elderly are not allowed to work.

Monday, March 24

Robbie: "They've condemned a couple more. Kim and I are going to go to Strader tonight. Christ Hospital is donating 110 Easter baskets. Kim and I are going to deliver 60 baskets. I'm glad people are thinking about the kids."

Chris Wool has been scared into having his house torn down. He was told that it would be free if the city took the house down immediately; if they had to come back later, it would cost $3,000. Sam Donald says he could have repaired Chris's house. People are contacting attorneys.

A graduate student calls to tell me that his mother, a schoolteacher near Dayton, has a group of students who want to donate school supplies. The supplies go through Robbie to the Strongs for distribution. "School supplies, book bags—You never saw so many happy kids—this was something that was finally for them."

James is still depressed. Robbie says, "James is in his bed more than I have ever seen him. James has still got a lot to say and a lot to do. I sure don't want him to give up now."

James is worried about the medical tests he had just before the flood. He came through the tests nicely. He said the tests weren't as hard, and he didn't have to lie still as long. He doesn't really talk about the tests, but he has not gotten back all of the results.

"I think he's more worried about Megan. She's still making them trips up and down the steps. He wants to help—we keep trying to convince him that we're going to fix up the camp upriver. If they could see the camp coming back, they would be a lot better. You can't have 'em both depressed. It's gettin' me depressed."

The flood has taken a heavy toll on the East End, but not in the usual, expected ways. Flood damage is bad enough, but damage to the entire community, its identity, its social structure, its heritage, its self-esteem, is worse.

Week 10

A university student who is in the National Guard comes to talk to me. Post-traumatic stress is palpable in her, as it is still in many East Enders.

Kim and Robbie go to lower Delta and see Chris Wool sitting on the bleachers looking at his torn-down house. The Red Cross stupidly gave him cleaning supplies.

Three more houses are condemned on Worth Street—the City of Cincinnati came in Saturday morning and told people they had to take the houses down. Robbie got there just after they knocked down Chris Wool's house. She couldn't even talk to Karen, his wife. The city denied them due process. Chris and Karen were told no help would come from FEMA or the Red Cross. Chris's brother Karl has a house next door. The city tagged his house while he was in Jackson, Ohio. Karl had made a phone call to Channel 9. Robbie goes through the house with a building inspector. Karl was born in this house thirty-five years ago.

Robbie tells Channel 9 everything "I'm doing, what I know how to do." Karl Wool decided to take tags off houses and declare no more houses condemned for thirty days. This was a bold move for a neighborhood resident.

Jessica Allen, the state senator, holds two meetings in which she claims the federal government does not want to give assistance—wants to turn the East End and other flooded areas along the river into green space. People are saying that the dam was opened on purpose.

Right now it would be dangerous for a city worker to go into the East End and tag a building. "All we want are some solid answers that do not change hour to hour."

Kim is so mad at the Red Cross it's unreal. No one from Wenner to Worth had anything to eat for several days immediately after the flood. The Red Cross did not bring any food. The Red Cross is not welcome in the East End.

Elizabeth Jones is telling people that there is free plywood and drywall.

Robbie: "This is our family and we don't care what Recreation [the City Department of Recreation is setting up a flood relief center] thinks. Me and Kim been Butch Cassidy and the Sundance Kid."

James Strong is starting to get a little bit better. "If we can get his house back in order and get his stuff out of his living room, he will be about 1,000 percent better."

Robbie sees Elaine—"We loaded her up with cleaning supplies."

Kim and Robbie are still giving out cleaning supplies and food. At

Rakestraw (another Department of Recreation facility east of LeBlond), kids play softball, life goes on.

"We stopped to deliver to this one house on Kellog—these brooms and mops are only good for a once-over. People were tired of spending money on cleaning supplies like Janet Carol Hammond right across from LeBlond. Leslie loaded her up right then."

Postflood work is never-ending. It is almost as relentless as the flood itself. Kim picks Robbie up one Saturday morning. They work all day on the cleanup. They wake up early on Sunday to pick up where they left off.

The flood cleanup is still not finished in June.

Stresses of the Flood

Robbie: "I came home just in time to slap the lady upstairs. I have seen her slap Kenny before. Madeline opened the door and asked if I would come in. Heard Kenny say 'No, Mom'—it sounds like Kenny bounced off the wall. I get upstairs and Amy's cryin'—'Don't, Mommy.' Kenny tried to run to me. I backhanded her and asked if she liked how it felt. I called 241-kids."

Mothers abusing children is not at all common in the East End.

Lisa is mad at Robbie for taking her mother, Kim, away from her to work on flood relief. Kim explains that people need help. "I've cried a lot this weekend."

Karl Wool is telling Kim: "People tellin' me I'm nothin' but trash—we're the recyclable kind, we come back."

As always, East End humor saves people from utter despair. Kim Strong refers to Robbie as her boss. Kim went back to work at her job today.

Stress and Its Positives in the Aftermath

EERCURC gets to work to help with the rebuilding. More and more of the "young people," that is, people in their thirties and forties, come to EERCURC and Pendleton meetings.

Crises do have a way of bringing people out and pulling people together.

But the personal costs are yet to come. At the end of April, I get a late-night phone call from Aunt Emma, an East Ender elder who is a grandmother and highly respected member of the community. She tells me that Betty Ann, a woman in her late thirties and lifelong East End resident, is severely depressed and is threatening to kill herself. She goes on to tell me that, in addition to the stress of the flood, Betty Ann's daughter Beth's tenth birthday has compounded Betty Ann's fears and anxieties about her daughter's vulnerability to sexual abuse from Betty Ann's brother-in-law. Betty Ann was abused by him at age ten, as was Aunt Emma thirteen years earlier. Betty Ann and Aunt Emma are not his only victims.

I listen on the phone as Aunt Emma talks to Betty Ann—nonstop, relentless questions and urgings—cold logic and hot emotions. "Who will catch Beth's cap at her high school graduation? A bullet in your head will ricochet right to Beth. You will not be there to protect her."

Aunt Emma is keeping Betty Ann in her apartment.

"I want to go home," says Betty Ann over and over.

"You are home now," says Aunt Emma. "This is your home. You are home," she repeats. She also repeats the cap and gown example. They stay up most of the night, as they do for three consecutive nights. I urge Aunt Emma to call 911 or the mobile crisis unit, which will come to her apartment. I do this knowing quite well that she won't. Outsiders are not called upon when it comes to mental health. "Betty Ann will think I think she is crazy."

Betty Ann is also complaining of severe stomach pain and is not eating. Aunt Emma worries and worries. She convinces Betty Ann to go to Christ Hospital nuclear medicine for tests. Betty Ann resists calling her doctor for the results and tells Aunt Emma that quick results are bad news.

Aunt Emma is even more worried about the possibility of cancer. She's very anxious and tearful. The tests come back negative, I find out from the family doctor. A great relief. I call Betty Ann's mother and father.

Betty Ann is now on Tagamet.

By the middle of May, Betty Ann's house is almost back to normal, but she and Aunt Emma remain haunted by Betty Ann's abusive brother-in-law, who is still free to violate yet more East End women. To call in the authorities on an East Ender *and* a family member is a double taboo.

The flood renders East Enders vulnerable—but only temporarily. That one man can inflict a flood of abuse on several generations of East End women is a terrifying form of vulnerability that will not recede as easily or as quickly as the March floodwaters.

13 | PRACTICING COMMUNITY, CULTURE, AND CLASS

> "Community" is one of those words—like "culture," "myth," "ritual," "symbol"—bandied around in ordinary, everyday speech, apparently readily intelligible to speaker and listener, which, when imported into the discourse of social science, however, causes immense difficulty. (Cohen 1985)

"Community" is indeed a commonly used word, but does anyone know what it means? In real communities, residents live community every day—practicing the day-to-day tasks of maintaining elders and children and knitting the strands of kinship and community networks. Policymakers and others in positions of power turn to social scientists to understand community as a concept and as a reality. Whether policymakers actually listen to social scientists is another issue entirely.

I once attended a conference on good government where several of us researchers and advocates told the city manager that community councils did not necessarily represent the community, on the face of it, an obvious point if one acknowledges that all localities, especially those in the process of economic development, are factionalized to some degree. All communities in Cincinnati operate several nonprofit boards that may work either in opposition to or in conjunction with community councils. These nonprofits include neighborhood development corporations, health centers, and education centers. The officials in City Hall, both elected and appointed, ignore the fact that there may be numerous groups that operate in communities and use community councils as their point of contact with the city. Some might argue that the city government sets up structures to prevent community councils from representing communities, all for the convenience of "good government." Others might say that, by ignoring alternative community institutions, the city is simply acting as an agent of colonialism. Still others might say that bureaucracies and bureaucrats do what is easiest and most convenient.

In the East End, community as any kind of meaningful reality must be tied to class, but not in any simple way—not, unfortunately in a way that can immediately be plugged into a formula or used in a cookbook fashion. Community must be understood in terms of patterns and practices of class that anthropologists have conventionally called "culture": livelihood patterns and practices, including but not confined to the informal economy as well as patterns of exchange and elaborate systems of equivalencies. These are not patterns in the rigid, lockstep sense of pattern, but, rather, patterns, such as householding, that change, not just with the seasons, but with the vagaries of bureaucratic power structures and daily life in the East End—layoffs, crises, illnesses, gas station closings.

The pattern of householding described in Chapter 6 is extremely important for the practice and maintenance of community. The exchanges manifested in the East End's pattern of householding illustrate clearly that community is not confined to a bounded geographic area, but that geographic place—the locale of the East End, especially its place along the river—is the key reference point for community.

Local culture and local knowledge are affected by as much as they are a part of the larger regional and national culture. Relationships between community leaders and city officials, attorneys, university professors, and professional advocates are strong, but too much contact with outsiders can cause problems for East End leaders. East End leaders who get too much attention from these "insider-outsiders" run the risk of alienating themselves from East Enders who still find themselves confined to relationships with other working-class people. The identity issues for East End leaders are serious in this regard; even speech patterns change to become "bidialectical," speaking a more standard English to outsiders than would normally be the case at home or in the community.

Language patterns and practices are complicated; the discourses of class are many and include everyday, ordinary language as well as essays, poetry, speeches—oral as well as written. The eloquence and quick ability of East Enders to speak extemporaneously and without a text would put a lot of college professors to shame. The recording and transcribing of East Enders' speeches is necessary to preserve these very precious cultural resources. East End patterns of communication must be examined, including shouting across alleys and wide streets and mutterings under one's breath.

The textures of class and community, uses of space and place, sounds, rhythms of life, make up the very fabric of community. Attachment to place and the ways in which individuals and groups are attached to place are themselves a phenomenon of class. When the class composition of a geographical place changes, so will the community and its culture. Class culture includes, most broadly, the East End ways of negotiating everyday life—daily interactions, shared living places, horn honking on Eastern Avenue, and those very dangerous U-turns that real East Enders make at rush hour. These are small, seemingly insignificant bits of East End culture; they are, however, important markers of community and class culture.

Real East Enders feel that they belong in and to the community and that the community belongs to East Enders. A history of class and the sense of common heritage are key elements of East Enders' sense of community; the longevity of families in the East End is very deep—seven generations, in many cases. Memories of family members, events, vacations are extremely important.

The question of boundaries and the ways East Enders conceptualize their importance are functions of class and longevity in the community. To many lifelong East Enders, the East End is the place where real East Enders feel familiar and comfortable, where "we played as children, where Mrs. Wilson's store used to be, where the best boat dock was." Places associated with memorable activities are the markers of familiarity and the seats of class culture. Those who must draw precise boundary lines are not lifelong East Enders; they are outsiders. The fact that real East Enders can name every house number and every family is notable. The history of each dwelling is important; it presents a vision as well as a memory.

Marginality and Community

Fragmentation is a fact of life in a modern postindustrial state, especially at its margins. The power structure creates fragmentation in order to intensify marginalization in working-class communities. Social services are fragmented; so are legal services and education. People must seek these services outside the community in unfamiliar and alienating (impersonal) places that are large and bureaucratic. In the East End, health care is the exception, since the East End Health Center delivers care that is more personalized and more coordinated than in most urban areas. The one sure thing is uncertainty. Uncertainty is a fact of life—uncertainty about the very existence of the East End as East Enders have known it.

In the absence of long-term and secure work for steady wages, does community take on a more important role as a focus of identity? This is a complicated matter. On the one hand, people spend more time in the community when they are not working. On the other, the pull to leave the community in search of work, in the South, for example, is also present. East Enders have relatives in Florida, Texas, and other parts of the South. When winters are harsh and construction work is scarce or impossible to perform in snow and rain, the temptation to move south grows stronger. Young adults may move back to Kentucky or Tennessee, where resources are more plentiful than they are in the city.[1]

Working-class communities all over the world attract expatriates who are marginal to their own cultures; the East End is no exception. Colonialism and noblesse oblige operate with expatriates at the lead. In a postmodern era, one would expect an increase in the numbers of expatriates, who then further fragment—indeed, rip apart—the fabric of a community. They do this by pretending to practice community. In the East End, the expatriates chip away at the community in the name of community; they sit on community boards, they ask questions, and they filibuster with seemingly infinite patience and endurance.

In order to demonstrate the nature of fragmentation in practice, I have used narrative clips: East Enders' written or spoken forms of narration that are short and focused on a particular issue. These include essays, speeches, and poems. Admittedly, these narratives do not tell the whole story, but what is most clear is that no one, not even the anthropologist, could tell the whole story, for it is too fragmented, disjointed, and contradictory. The important thing to recognize about the narrative clips is that, even though they are written by individuals and are indeed often written in a very personal style, they are not individualistic or idiosyncratic. The views expressed are views that are part and parcel of practicing community.[2]

A colleague asked me whether there will be an East End for "real" East Enders in twenty years. I responded with uncertainty. Crystal balls are hard to come by. What is certain is that the marginality of the working class will not disappear; it will probably become more elaborate, if there is such a thing as an elaboration of marginality.

[Marginal] "hillbillies" are disturbing to the urban consciousness. They confuse boundaries of "us" and "them" and they muddle universalizing standards of propriety, deference and power.[3]

POSTSCRIPT: AN ESSAY ON THEORY AND PRACTICE

*W*riting this book in the late nineties presents some special challenges, theoretical and practical. How much explicit theory should be in an ethnography about community? How much personal detail told to me in strict confidence and trust can be published? Some ethnographic facts are unpublishable.

After I wrote the body of the text, I realized that the writing itself created a need for more reading and rereading. I felt that I had to reread contemporary theory, cultural studies, postmodern writing—Bauman, Geertz, Crapanzano, Foucault, Giddens, Bourdieu, to name a few—and engage it at a different level than I had when I started out to write this book. Several other literatures found their way onto my list of "must reads": the literature of community organizing, such as the works of Saul Alinsky; the fiction of the American South, including William Faulkner; and the literature of the working class. The novels of Appalachia—Jessie Stuart's work and especially Lee Smith's *Saving Grace*—capture the lives, motivations, feelings, and lifestyles of the working class. The jarring and grim qualities of lives portrayed in the clinical case histories in Chapter 8 of this book can be understood, at least in part, in the cultures of rural Appalachian religious fundamentalism, especially the cultural construction of spirituality and gender, male and female. The powerlessness of young men, the power of alcohol and snake handling along with the necessary support roles of women and the demands of children are woven in Smith's novel in the story told by Grace, a preacher's daughter. The grimness of poverty combined with the generosity of the community puts a shiny patina on an otherwise rather desperate set of circumstances.

Dialogue with Theorists Pure and Practical

The purpose of this dialogue is to draw out some key elements of theory and practice and their relationships, that is, to use theory to reflect on practice and vice versa. But which theory to choose—from which genres, however blurred? Serendipity strikes at odd times and in odd places when it comes to choosing theory. Often an event in the community—a celebration, a crisis, a funeral, a birth—will trigger thoughts that lead to certain kinds of reading, on postmodernism, on European and Latin American immigrants as working-class people dealing with many of the same kinds of struggles as those of East Enders. In the meantime, other events occur in the community and these become filtered through different sets of questions. This sense of starting and stopping with different ideas is both a disconcerting and a rewarding aspect of doing fieldwork at home. An ethnography as broadly based as this one presumably could have endless theoretical inputs and, thus, endless dialogues.

Theoretical and practical stances in the postmodern world are packaged in many ways—in the literature of the social sciences, in literature and literary theory, and in the literature of community organizing and advocacy, to name a few. I do not try to cover or even to touch upon many major theoretical streams of the twentieth century; I merely want to try to further the argument that theory and practice cannot be separated and that they serve one another in many unanticipated ways.

I have purposely reserved this dialogue for a postscript because I want to isolate and emphasize some of the ways in which theory and practice interact. While theory permeates and guides the ethnography all along, it is here that I want to make some theoretical concerns explicit. This postscript also brings out and engages some East End ethnography that has not been presented in the main body of the text.

My project here is to use practical knowledge of how things work in the East End community—and also how they don't work—to reflect on the nature of theory and practice and on the relationships between them. By "theory" I simply mean the kinds of questions and orientations—ideas, concepts, constructs—that attempt to uncover or explain the various layers of social life and trajectories of culture in communities like the East End. Questions range from the nature and importance of culture itself to the nature of class, community, and individual identities to the concept of practice to the nature of power and colonialism.

On the practical side, the questions are many. Why did this meeting work or not work so well? Why did a community leader take a certain position or identify and support someone or some issue in one context and not in another? The complex, dynamic relationships between those with certain kinds of power and those without all involve relationships between practice and theory.

By "practice" here I mean the practical realities—the day-to-day structures and agents, large and small, of the world economy, the city, the community, and the family. I also include a whole host of dispositions, actions, representations that make up the strategies for coping with and reproducing these structures. What it means to be a real East Ender can be translated to mean how to carry out the practical, daily tasks of living in ways that are consistent with East End culture and class. Practicing community requires such consistency.

Practice, Advocacy, and Theory

Thinking about the linkages between practice, advocacy, and theory requires a consideration—or, rather, a reconsideration of key underlying themes in the ethnography of the East End: concepts of the other, marginality, temporality, spatiality, modernity, and the relationships between the psychological and the social aspects of culture. These themes are intrinsic parts of "practicing community." In a community where the personal and the political are so intertwined, some thought must be given to the relationship between the psychological, the social, and the political. The psychological costs as well as the benefits of commitment to the community can be great.[1]

Major postmodern thinkers, among them Bauman (1989, 1991), Giddens (1990), Lyotard (1984), Foucault, and Derrida, have all dealt with these issues of modernity and postmodernity, albeit not in specific ethnographic contexts. This book, then, in part constitutes a critique of modernity.[2] Insofar as colonialism, racism, and classism are part of modernity, the critique is rather elaborate and, some might say, harsh.

In reaction to these multiple "isms," East Enders change positions politically, socially, and psychologically. Examples include not only dialect switching, but changing ethical, political, and moral positions depending on the context. A black leader in an all-white environment will speak one way; in an environment that includes other blacks, but also trustworthy whites, her language will change to include some elements of the former position but not all of them. Similarly, a grassroots leader may take one position in the community, where residents and advocates are present, but he may voice an entirely different position at City Hall or in the media when no other grassroots people are present.

In some contexts, tension and conflict are tolerable; in fact, their presence is exhilarating, an assertion of local power and autonomy. In other contexts, conflict is not at all productive; it is destructive, devastating, gut wrenching. People threaten to exit and they do; people cry and shout; communication among leaders who were close friends grinds to a halt. These horrible roadblocks to the practice of community combine with the capricious ways of City Hall and the tenacious ways of developers to create feelings of fragmentation, frustration, anger, and debilitation. Depending on the issue and how much support comes from other sources, usually outsiders—lawyers, advocates, researchers, and city officials—the pieces can gradually be put back together, at least temporarily. When things are going well, a person who is often ambivalent about taking on a strong leadership role will jump at the chance. When things are not going well, a person capable of strong leadership may take a leave of absence.

Surprises are constant in the East End. One community leader who is normally inclusive and encouraging of cooperative relationships on community boards will take a strong stance against a formerly trusted friend and fellow resident to the point of exclusion. Why? The relationship among the psychological, the social, and the political must be considered here, along with a combination of other factors, including race, ability to tolerate conflict, sexual orientation, and age. However competent a leader may be, he or she must not cross the line to the outside. Too much recognition from outsiders can ruin the career of a grassroots leader, even if he or she rejects notoriety and shares credit. Competition among leaders and discussions about who gets credit for community work are constant.

These issues concerning the fluidity and changeability of positions and practices relate in turn to Foucault's discussion of power/knowledge configurations.[3] For Foucault, who is writing against a great deal of conventional social theory, including many brands of Marxism, the idea of practice is central. Local practices—what Foucault calls the "essentially local character of criticism"—are one expression of the importance of practice, for he is referring here, among other things, to local practices of resistance. These include criticisms of the power structure as well as actual stonewalling. Another point is Foucault's idea of "subjugated knowledge." Here Foucault is talking about the kind of knowledge that is, as he puts it, "a particular local, regional knowledge . . . which owes its force only to the harshness with which it is opposed by everything surrounding it."[4] This is precisely the kind of knowledge commanded by real East Enders. The overarching *habitus,* as Bourdieu would put it, remains a key part of practices of regulation, resistance, and representation.

In this framework, the perception of power dynamics, actual and potential, is as important as reality. Thus, for example, a community leader who takes charge and puts a floundering community board back on its feet can be perceived as taking over and denying not only credit but credibility to a leader who has been temporarily and legitimately absent. If the absent leader is black and the take-charge leader is white, there can be over- and undertones of racism as well. That this kind of situation can be described as "damned if you do and damned if you don't" does not diminish the importance of local power perceptions and dynamics. Practicing community is difficult under such circumstances, which themselves grow out of the divide-and-conquer strategies of colonialists.

Representation and perception, then, can change the practice of community, especially at the local level. A person who is a strong leader can be removed from the center of local politics in a very short time. The divide-and-conquer strategies of colonialists do not enhance social solidarity and the practice of community.

The whole issue of how community institutions are created, maintained, revitalized, and reproduced must be questioned in creative ways. Practices of resistance and representation do not necessarily replicate anything that remotely resembles what went before. The creative practices of institution building, while very difficult, are just that, creative and inventive of new structures that build on the old but do not replicate them. The Pendleton Heritage Center is one example. The new health center is another. The idea of a heritage center is not unique by any means, but it is new for the East End. As a community-preserving institution that provides a home for East End boards and organizations, it is a threat to economic development of the conventional, market-driven sort. In March 1996, the president of the Community Council, a developer and real estate agent, announced that she saw no problem in running the Community Council out of her home, including keeping all the files, correspondence, and so on, in filing cabinets there. The control value of this tactic was not lost on the grassroots leaders. The building of the new health center has met with less opposition from developers, in part because it is being constructed in a location outside of the development plan area. It is also protected somewhat from colonialist sabotage because it is part of a larger umbrella organization, the Cincinnati Health Network, a consortium of federally funded community health centers.

New representations and new structures must be created to maintain place. New institutions may mean new forms and representations of leadership and of community itself. Or the presence of new institutions may mean a redefining of community and of practicing community with a reduced or different sense of attachment to place. East Enders are spreading themselves throughout the greater Cincinnati area at the same time that community institutions are reaching outside the community. What replaces attachment to place? Perhaps an increased sense of attachment to class or religion, race, or some combination. Perhaps there is no replacement.

The health center is in the process of transformation into a new structure. It used to be called the East End Community Health Center. Now it is simply called the East End Health Center. I attended the meeting in which the board of the health center decided to remove the word "Community." The fear was that to leave "community" in the name would be to discourage patients from outside "the community" from using the health center. Absent from the discussion was any notion that the inclusion of the word "community" might provide insiders and outsiders alike with a sense of belonging. Multiple sources of identity or shifting sources of identity depend on context, in this case, contexts that are constantly changing. Derrida's concept of *différance* is useful here because it opens the idea of reinterpreted identities, that is, identities that are never really fixed and immutable.[5]

Some East End examples of identities undergoing almost constant transformation immediately come to mind. A grassroots leader, Doris, is chair of one board and sits on a second. When she is criticized by one grassroots leader for siding with two other leaders, she disclaims identity as a member of the second board. She does this positively by saying she is most concerned about the work of the board she chairs. Thus she deflects the accusations and remains polite to the person from whom she is receiving criticism. In the presence of a third grassroots leader, however, she is ready to go after her critic, that is, to remove her critic from any leadership roles in the community at large. Doris recognizes and values the fact that her critic is a good worker and feels perfectly comfortable exploiting her labors on behalf of the Pendleton, which she, Doris, claims as her own.

The exercise of power at the community level is very personal. Outsiders in power contribute to the local power dynamics without intending to do so. Unknowingly, yuppies in minivans define the positive features of being an East Ender, that is, attachment to place and family, and family as a metaphor for community. As outsiders become residents and infiltrate the leadership structure, they tend to marginalize real East Enders—by their manners of speech, their clothing, their lifestyles, and their imposition of power and control.

Colonialism and Boundaries

The reason it is almost impossible for any two East Enders to agree on boundaries is that space is socially and culturally constituted; depending on a person's experience (personal history, family history) in the community, boundaries will be perceived differently. But the fact that houses are being torn down constantly, that new, not necessarily affordable, ones are being built where old memory-filled apartment buildings and stores used to be, means that space is being transformed constantly by the market. Time is thus an important element in the perception of space. Depending upon where and when a person and a person's family enters the process in time, that person's understanding of space will be different. Memories, stories, and family photos portray people *in situ*, in the community, on porches, streets, and in alleys.

Over time, the East End has gotten smaller, taken over by other constituencies that have renamed and, by doing so, claimed space that was originally part of the East End. The appropriated space is now defined by the power structure as Columbia Tusculum, a gentrified community that is said to be better than the East End. The distance between East Enders and the power structure grows greater, renders East Enders as "others," and thereby changes East Enders' original identity as people belonging to a large, and prominently situated, geographic area.

To create a "colonized other" in the midst of the "West" and moreover in the midst of a midwestern city is part of a process of what used to be called internal colonialism but is now referred to simply as colonialism.[6] One of the hallmarks of local colonialism (as I have called it) in the East End is the presumption on the part of the colonizers (developers, slum landlords) that they (often regarded as the other by the East Enders) are indeed residents of the East End. Clearly, they are stakeholders, but their claims to authenticity as East Enders are questionable at best.

I have used two kinds of colonial discourses here: those of the colonizers and those of the colonized. The discourses of the colonized take the form of poetry and narratives, those of the colonizers are monologues; these are patronizing, classist monologues that operate in a manner that parallels racism in its derogatory, distancing, quite frankly high-and-mighty tone. To use Edward Said's (1978) term, these developers have "orientalized" the East Enders as inferior and always in need of help, which comes in some form of domination.[7]

Time

> To substitute strategy for the rule is to reintroduce time, with its rhythm, its orientation, its irreversibility. (Bourdieu 1977: 9)

Things take a very long time to accomplish in the East End. Affordable housing in the East End takes longer to bring on-line than it does even in neighborhoods that are perceived by the power structure to be poorer, more complex, and more conflict ridden. This explains Paul Silver's statement at the Lewiston ribbon cutting that "we thought Over-the-Rhine was bad." Elders, in particular, feel a sense that time is running out, or that more should have been accomplished by now, considering not only the time that has elapsed, but the time East Enders have spent in meetings, hearings, and informal discussions. Time is a powerful local phenomenon, an intrinsic part of memory. Doris worries that she will not see the Pendleton completed in her lifetime.

Time in various dimensions and time considerations are inherent parts of practicing community, for to control time, to use it wisely, to not let those in positions of power impose time limitations is a topic of much discussion. "Why should we hurry up and wait?" is a question often spoken by East End leaders when they feel pushed by slow-moving city bureaucracies. At the same time, the sense of urgency, the sense that time is critical is always a subtext. Yet there is also the understanding that trying to move too fast, to have too many meetings in too short a time frame, will make things too intense, cause conflict and burnout, cause people to resign from community boards.

Seasonality is one ingredient of time. In spring and summer, when it is hot, when the outdoors beckon for leisure and recreation—boating, camping, time in the park—fighting City Hall takes a much lower priority, and there is a sense that some downtime is necessary—that time would be better spent resting and relaxing to refresh everyone for the hard work ahead. Fall is a time for beginning; spring is the end of the work season.

There are definite rhythms to practicing community; I am just beginning to understand them. These rhythms, of course, are alterable and changing. They are irregular. Meetings will be canceled on account of illness or bad weather. Rescheduling occurs, but not always right away. A phone call appears one day on my machine requesting my presence two weeks hence.

But time can also be used to the advantage of practicing community. Placing the East End Heritage Exhibit in the Mount Carmel Baptist Church during its anniversary celebration was very desirable and, in fact, worked to enhance empowerment. But the timing and spacing of the exhibit had to be carefully orchestrated using the intricacies of local knowledge and local practice. The exhibit was to be in the church, not exactly as background, but as an enhancement, subordinate to the anniversary. This was made clear in the discussion of a reception for the exhibit. The church had its own set of ceremonies and receptions, including food.

The exhibit became subsumed by the anniversary. This did not lessen its importance; it merely placed it in a different context—a not-uncontested one. People in the congregation began to ask why there were so many pictures of particular families—other people's families from the church congregation, but not their own. When an East End leader and prominent member of the congregation reminded other churchgoers that for six months she had stood up on Sunday at services and requested family pictures for the exhibit, her voice fell on deaf ears.

Was there something wrong with the timing here, or was it that many East Enders had to experience the exhibit before pictures would be offered? Should there have been several people of different ages and genders requesting materials for the exhibit? Should there have been a second phase to the exhibit—a kind of rolling or rotating set of photos—so that more residents could be included?

Kinship

In the East End, the practice of kinship is even more important than its official forms. Bourdieu writes of "practicing kinship": "Marriage provides a good opportunity for observing what in practice separates official kinship, single and immutable, defined once and for all by the norms of genealogical protocol, from practical kinship, whose boundaries and definitions are as many and as varied as its users and the occasions on which it is used."[8] In part, the practice of kinship is a function of East

Enders' distrust of the official system of foster care, health care, and social services. In part, it is a function of what all cultures do to reproduce themselves. Real East Enders look out for the children of real East Enders—and their grandchildren, for that matter. The prevalence of informal adoptions is difficult to calculate, but it is certainly higher than the untutored in East End ways would expect. To adopt a child is only one way to practice kinship. Other ways include a whole range of informal arrangements from temporary child foster care to blended households consisting of several unrelated adults of different generations and associated children.

Bourdieu also states clearly that the "ethnologist is in a particularly bad position to detect the distinction between official and practical kinship: as his dealings with kinship (at least, the kinship of others) are restricted to cognitive uses."[9] But advocacy reveals practical workings more quickly than would any form of so-called pure research. When the ethnologist is asked to be an advocate, "the group's official account of itself"[10] is not nearly as relevant to the situation as the practical workings of unofficial, practical kinship in daily life.

I was once asked to write a letter of support for a young mother whose ex-husband was fighting for the custody of one of her children. His argument was that she had moved recently, thereby creating an unstable situation for the child. The fact that she had moved back to her community of origin, where her entire extended family resided, and the fact that she had also created unofficial kin in the process of her move back would not have been nearly as clearly understood or articulated by me had I not been asked to write the letter to the judge. The unofficial kin network provides not only caretakers for her two children from different fathers, but playmates who are the unofficial kin of the child care provider. These kinds of practical kin relations are very common; they are practiced continuously, albeit in forms that change and transform themselves with circumstances. The corollary to this is that two systems, for example, two extended families, that look officially identical (that is, genealogically identical) may function very differently, depending on how kinship is practiced.

Habitus, Culture, and Practice

The structures constitutive of a particular type of environment (e.g., the material conditions of existence characteristic of a class condition) produce *habitus,* systems of durable, transposable *dispositions*

(. . . a way of being, a habitual state . . . a predisposition, tendency, propensity, or inclination). (Bourdieu 1977: 72)

For Bourdieu, what he calls structures (what Marx would call the forces and relations of production) produce culture (or *habitus*), which we can take to be a durable phenomenon that is passed on from one generation to another, but that does not die with individuals. All of those predispositions (cultural ways of being, thinking, acting) function as principles of generation and structuring. To translate and interpret these predispositions in ways relevant to East Enders, class conditions produce culturally organized and understood ways of doing things that structure the everyday practices, activities, forms of expression, representations of everyday life in the East End. All of the accepted ways of doing things, the practices associated with family and community together are dictated not by rules but by experience and by circumstances.

If we deconstruct what Bourdieu is saying, dispositions are "principles of the generation and structures of practices and representations which can be objectively 'regulated' and 'regular' without in any way being the product of obedience to rules . . . collectively orchestrated without being the product of the orchestrating action of a conductor."[11] In other words, there are patterns to the practices and representations, but these are not centrally controlled. These patterns are culturally shaped, but since East Enders' dispositions, inclinations, and strategies are flexible and changing, there is no rigidity to them and, internally at least, there is no hierarchical structure.

The absence of hierarchy troubles outsiders greatly, especially those who want to control the affairs of the community. The Plan Implementation Team, for example, was originally set up as an autonomous body that would advise both the city and its departments and the East End Area Council. The developers, however, after succeeding in gaining control of the Community Council, went to great lengths to place the Implementation Team under the council. They did this initially by bringing up the issue at every Implementation Team meeting. For a long time, they (the developers) met with great resistance from several sides, from advocates, from grassroots leaders, and from the elites. Over time, however, the developers managed to restructure the Implementation Team both by placing it under the East End Area Council and by summarily dismissing all of the advocates. As one of the very committed elites put it: "They have emasculated the Implementation Team."

Viewing culture as *habitus* is simultaneously a looser and a more powerful way of viewing culture and its patterns—more powerful because it can accommodate strategies and change. It also allows for a core of dispositions and meanings to emerge. In the East End, for example, the inclination to help other East Enders and the importance of family can be said to be part of a core of dispositions, but these inclinations can take many forms, including unofficial kin, for example, and the exclusion of official kin. I know sisters who do not speak to one another.

On another level of practice and practicality, it is precisely this flexibility of dispositions that the power structure has such difficulty understanding. In fact, it is part of the ethnocentrism of the hegemonic system—the need to see everything in hierarchically orchestrated terms.

There are many ways of talking about *habitus* (Bourdieu 1977: 78, 79): "The habitus, the durably instilled generated principle of regulated improvisations . . . The habitus is the universalizing mediation which causes an individual agent's practices, without either explicit reason or signifying intent, to be none the less 'sensible' and 'reasonable.'" [12] In other words, the *habitus* filters out or eliminates the non-sensible, the unreasonable, and, one would hope, the insane.

> One of the fundamental effects of the orchestration of habitus is the production of a common sense world endowed with the *objectivity* secured by consensus on the meanings of practices and the world, in other words the harmonization of agents' experiences and the continuous reinforcement that each of them receives from the expression, individual or collective . . . improvised or programmed (common . . . sayings) of similar or identical experiences. The homogeneity of habitus . . . is what causes practices and works to be immediately intelligible and foreseeable, and hence taken for granted. (Bourdieu 1977: 80)

In other words, *habitus* brings about the common understanding that this is the way we do things here. [13] This notion is very close to Geertz's common sense as cultural system. The experiences can be as commonplace and as positive as sitting in your grandmother's kitchen snapping green beans or sitting on a concrete bench and watching kids play in the pool at the recreation center, or as negative as the experience of rape as a young teenager or abuse by an alcoholic husband.

Class Culture

> How can we live without our lives? How will we know it's us without our past? (Steinbeck 1976: 114)

If you're in trouble or hurt or need—go to poor people. They're the only ones that'll help—the only ones. (Ibid.: 483)

What do we mean by class culture and how does it relate to practicing community? Working-class culture is many layered, multidimensional, and constantly changing. On the one hand, class culture has ties to a locality, but it is not confined to a single locale. Ties to place, in this case, the East End, are very important both as a source of identity and a locality within which daily life occurs. People who no longer live in the East End still identify themselves as East Enders. The power of place, that is, the ways in which a given locale figures importantly in the lives of working-class people, is significant, both because the place comes to be regarded as one's own common property, and because memory, experience, and history are all rooted in a particular place.

Practices of helping, sharing, trading, resisting reveal the dynamics of working-class culture. A notion of people first prevails, not in the superficial ways that politicians mean this, but in the deep, concrete sense that the needs of the young and the old must be met before one's own and before the externally imposed obligations of school or job. Thus, we see the giving of time, money, and resources to the community by those who can least afford to give.

The essential humanism of working-class culture cannot be overemphasized. The priorities placed on human dignity, the understanding of fragility and vulnerability, and the basic sensitivity to human needs is striking. Close intergenerational ties operate on a community-wide basis. Being there has become a cliché—but it, too, is multilayered and multidimensional. It means being physically present when needed, but it also means being there philosophically and symbolically. Usually this means sacrificing time, savings, and opportunity. Being there does not always work in practice. A leader apologizes for not following through on one of her many obligations as a member of an important community board by saying: "There are three things that's botherin' me: my job, my child, and my health." She says this very matter-of-factly. Knowing that one of her children has a serious drug problem and that another has great difficulties holding down a job, I begin to wonder how she managed to show up for the meeting at all.

The phrase "struggles for empowerment, identity, and control" slips easily off the pens of academics, but the actual day-to-day struggle that is so essential for maintaining a person's and a family's identity and control over life patterns is grueling, frustrating, and anger producing. I have often wondered how East Enders can stand the insults, the time wasting, the put-downs, the provocations from those with wealth and power while living in small and noisy spaces, while taking care of elderly relatives, and while realizing that market forces are larger and more powerful than the community itself.

The cultural construction of marginality has two views, one from the top down, the other from the bottom up. Both views are predicated on differences, mostly negatively valued between people of different classes with differential amounts of power, autonomy, and control. These differences form the basis for colonial practices and for resisting colonialism. While the power structure sees East Enders as exotic, dangerous, unwashed, and illiterate, East Enders not only struggle daily to resist these stereotypes, they reject the property-based, greed-based inhumane practices of people in power. This is not rationalization. It represents other priorities: family and community, rejection of the measuring rod of money. The East End belongs to East Enders—all East Enders—thus, the power of the young teen's poem (see Chapter 1) about the destruction of community, not just her community, but that of all East End teens, their children, and, indeed, of all East Enders, past, present, and future. The poetry of planning reinforces the negativity of commodification and, at the same time, asserts the strength and resilience of working-class cultures. This East End working-class notion of common property is foreign to the power structure, however.

The essence of practicing community in the East End is to claim ownership of the community, not in an exclusive, property-based sense that keeps people out, but in an inclusive sense that invites others in, in a way that ensures a place for East Enders to enjoy the river, the streets, and the people. Symbolically, the East End is more than a place; it is an identity that confers a sense of belonging, regardless of whether a person currently lives in the East End. This identity rests on a sense of community as common property with a sense of the past as well as a sense of the future. Continuities between the past, the present, and the future are important both symbolically and practically. These continuities are the threads of identity that are woven from memories of work, of family, of neighborhood goings-on.

Practicing community in the context of working-class culture is about power relations, struggles for autonomy and control over life and livelihood, struggles for resources, and struggles for ownership of place.

EPILOGUE

These are practices that ensure presence and agency in a hostile world where economic exploitation and social domination are all too common features. But, as the debilitating effects of global restructuring lay waste to national and local economies, we notice everywhere a resurgence of collective sentiments. These sentiments may not always succeed in staving off existing patterns of domination, but they foreground a sense of purpose that refuses to be silenced. (Lustiger-Thaler and Salee 1994: x)

Community practices at the local level offer new patterns of intervention which challenge the policy orientations of a State increasingly bent on accommodating market imperatives. (Ibid.: xvii–xviii)

On November 11, 1996, *The Cincinnati Enquirer* published a feature article with the following headline: "East End: Development Turns Tide on Makeup of Ohio River Neighborhood." In this article, two things are assumed. The first is that the community has been dying a slow death since the 1937 flood; the death of the community is, therefore, imminent. The second is that East Enders have no right to views of the river. As one developer put it: "Why should they [poor renters] be enjoying that river view when they are on the dole?" This marks the beginning of a whole series of wrong notions and contradictions about the East End and East Enders.

The East End community is indeed a poor, racially integrated, working-class neighborhood, spread out below Columbia Parkway from downtown to Delta Avenue. This is the East End Plan area, that is, the part of the East End chosen to be the focus of a community development plan passed by the City Council in 1992. The plan area is not the entire East End by any means, for the East End historically extends east to the edge of Fairfax and north to Kroger Avenue in Mount Lookout. The yuppie neighborhood that is now called Columbia Tusculum historically has always been part of the East End. One of the best ways to claim a neighborhood and take away its heritage is to rename it.

The community is by no means dead, however. Among the many things that the *Enquirer* reporter does not understand is the fact that community grassroots leaders, in concert with the 1992 development plan and guidelines and with local citizen elites, researchers, and advocates, have been fighting to preserve, maintain, and revitalize the East End for East Enders, many of whose children are seventh-generation East Enders. Now that the Community Council (the EEAC) is completely controlled by developers, the struggles to maintain the East End for East Enders take place in three arenas, all of which are resident-controlled nonprofit organizations: the Pendleton Heritage Center Board, the East End Community Health Center Board, and the East End Riverfront Community Urban Redevelopment Corporation. Evidence of neighborhood life is very visible. A new health center is growing daily on the corner of Carole and Eastern Avenue in the Upper East End. The first eleven units of new affordable rental housing (the Lewiston Townhomes) were opened in spring 1995. The Pendleton Heritage Center Board of Trustees and Members is a strong and committed grassroots organization that is waiting for the city to release the allocated funds for the rehab of the historic red-brick building that is known in the neighborhood as the old Pendleton carbarn. An experienced fundraiser is on board. EERCURC is planning several affordable housing projects in cooperation with a neighborhood-controlled board, the support of a local bank, and *pro bono* legal advice from a prominent law firm.

When the developer quoted in the story denies longtime East End residents a right to river views because they (presumably) are on the dole, he reveals his ignorance of the fact that fewer than one-third of East Enders receive any form of public assistance as well as his lack of any sense that East Enders are human beings with rights.

The neighborhood did not start to die in 1937 with the flood. It grew steadily to a population of fifteen thousand in 1975. East Enders know how to cope with floods of many varieties; East Enders cannot control the flooding of the housing market, however. East Enders cannot control rising taxes. This is why the Development Corporation and the Housing Preservation Board are necessary, vital institutions. This is why the PHC, which will provide offices for these institutions, is so critical.

When the city passed the plan to control development and maintain a place for East Enders in the East End, it made a commitment to the community. If the city can support (that is, subsidize) market-rate housing, it can also support affordable housing and other vital institutions.

There is room in the East End for all, but if the city succumbs to the pressures from developers to erase the existing community, it will not be the floods that wipe out real East Enders, but the powers that be.

NOTES

Prologue

1. See Batteau (1983, 1990); Ergood and Kuhre (1991); Obermiller (1996); Borman and Obermiller (1994); Obermiller and Philliber (1987).

2. There is an extensive and now classic literature on the nature and importance of community, beginning with Redfield (1964, 1973 [1960]). See Arensberg (1961), Arensberg and Kimball (1940), and Bott (1957) on the nature of small cultural units, Cohen (1982 and especially 1985) on the symbolic construction of community.

3. See Castells (1978, 1980, 1983); Eames, Edwin, and Goode (1977); Dirks, Ely, and Ortner (1994, especially the Introduction); Lazarus-Black and Hirsch (1994); and Joyce (1995, especially the Introduction).

4. See Tice and Billings (1991); Philliber and McCoy (1981); Turner and Cabbell (1985).

5. Writing of the period between 1880 and 1914, Zane Miller says: "Irish and Negroes shared the Ohio River Bottoms with whole sale houses and factories" (1968: 4). Miller remarks a bit later while referring to the same period, "Sicilians and Syrians/Lebanese shared the lower East End with Irish and Southern Whites" (1968: 13). Writing of the Circle along the Ohio River, Miller says: "The Circle's population was diverse, composed chiefly of recent arrivals in Cincinnati. They constituted an incongruous crowd of Negroes and Whites from the South plus a diminishing complement of Irish and German immigrants" (1968: 13). Of the East End Miller says: "Conditions in the East End slums were not much better. People could be found living in 'dreary rat holes,' ten, fifteen, and thirty feet underground, which were small,

dark, unventilated, wet, dreary dungeons" (1968: 17). Miller summarizes the features of the Circle, an area of impoverished people, of which the East End was a part: "Variety, instability, and disorder characterized the Circle in the new and divided metropolis. Its business districts were a curious amalgam of new and old, containing virtually every kind of enterprise represented in the city. Its residential section, aged and decrepit, housed members of every national, racial, religious—and almost every occupational—group. Their horizons were circumscribed by poverty and ignorance, and their lives revolved about the institutions in their home neighborhood. They led a harrowing existence, threatened by destitution, disease, and violence and harassed by strange and unknown laws and ways of life" (1968: 24).

6. "In 1880 there were 13,562 Southerners in Cincinnati. In the next decade the city received 18,891 more from the same source. The figure rose to 26,434 in 1900 and 33,165 in 1910. More came from Kentucky than from any other single Southern state, though an increase in the numbers from the Deep South is discernable after 1900" (Miller 1968: 248).

7. Negative media images of working-class people, especially rurally-originated Southerners, Black and White, would be the subject of another book. Miller (1968) cites numerous "contemporary" sources for the late nineteenth and early twentieth centuries. My own files of *Cincinnati Post* and *Cincinnati Enquirer* articles is not much improved when it comes to stereotyping poor people negatively.

1. Guideposts

1. See Raymond Williams (1973).

2. There is a substantial and growing literature on the built environment. See Low (1993), Richardson (1989), Rodman (1992, 1993), Rodman and Cooper (1989), Rotenberg and McDonogh (1993), and Sieber (1993).

3. Dropout rates are extraordinarily high. In 1996, not a single East End child graduated from high school. See Timm (1994).

4. The analysis of family structure and social organization in the East End would provide a substantial elaboration of Bourdieu's (1977) concept of official (biological) and unofficial (practical) kin. See also Schneider (1979) and Schneider and Smith (1978).

5. See Arnow (1978); Gaventa (1980); Gaventa, Smith, and Willingham (1990); Giddens (1971); Lewis, Johnson, and Askins (1978); Maggard (1986); Nash and Fernández-Kelly (1983); and Ong (1991).

6. See Batteau (1983, 1990); Ergood and Kuhre (1991).

2. Community in Practice

1. See Maloney (1991).

2. See Crompton (1995); see also Anglin (1993). As Rosemary Crompton points out in a review of class theory: "Social class and inequality have been amongst the central topic areas within sociology" (1995: 43). While I would not attempt even to begin to review this literature, it is important to acknowledge some of the influences on my own thinking about class in the East End. As Crompton points out, Stark (1980) argues, like Thompson (1963), for a concept of class that focuses on relationships: "a class is not 'composed of' individuals; it is not a collection or aggregation of individuals. *Classes* (emphasis in original), like the social relations from which they arise, exist in an antagonistic and dependent relation to each other. Classes are constituted by these mutually antagonistic relations. In this sense . . . the object of study is not the elements themselves but the relations between them" (Stark 1980: 96–97). The critique of positivism, especially the work of Anthony Giddens in *The Class Structure of Advanced Societies* (1981), is very important, especially his point that class relationships are always being actively structured, created, and transformed. This is certainly an important concept in a community that is undergoing revitalization and rapid culture change. The critique of the notion that classes and stratification patterns are somehow part of an organic whole is also part of the critique of positivist functionalism. See also Bauman (1995).

3. The model can be characterized in a manner not unlike what Bauman sets forth (1995: 80): "The sought theory must assume instead that the social condition it intends to model is essentially and perpetually *unequilibrated* (emphasis in original): composed of elements with a degree of autonomy large enough to justify the view of totality as a kaleidoscopic—momentary and contingent—outcome of interaction." This, of course, is extreme, especially as Bauman elaborates it, because he describes a situation in which no patterns exist at all (Bauman 1995: 80–81): "The orderly, structured nature of totality cannot be taken for granted; nor can its pseudo-representational construction be seen as the purpose of theoretical activity. The randomness of the global outcome of uncoordinated activities cannot be treated as a departure from the pattern which the totality strives to maintain; any pattern that may temporarily emerge out of the random movements of autonomous agents is as haphazard and unmotivated as the one that could emerge in its place or the one bound to replace it, if also for a time only. All order that can be found is a local, emergent and transitory phenomenon; its nature can be best grasped by a metaphor of a whirlpool appearing in the flow of a river,

retaining its shape only for a relatively brief period . . . with the totality dissipated into a series of randomly emerging, shifting and evanescent islands of order, its temporal record cannot be linearly represented. Perpetual local transformations do not add up so as to prompt (much less to insure) in effect an increased homogeneity, rationality or organic systemness of the whole. The postmodern condition is a site of constant mobility and change, but no clear direction of development. The image of Brownian movement offers an apt metaphor for this aspect of postmodernity; each momentary state is neither a necessary effect of the preceding state nor the sufficient cause of the next one. . . . A sociology geared to the conditions of postmodernity ought to replace the category of society with that of *sociality* (emphasis in original); a category that tries to convey the processual modality of social reality, the dialectical play of randomness (who happens to show up at a meeting for example) and pattern (or, from the agent's point of view, of freedom and dependence); a category that refuses to take the structured character of the process for granted—which treats instead all found structures as emergent accomplishments."

4. See Redfield (1964); see also Park (1967).

5. See also Liebow (1967), Mollenkopf (1983), Mullings (1987), Peattie and Robbins (1984), Rollwagen (1980), Sennett (1970), Sennett and Cobb (1972), Suttles (1968), and Whyte (1948).

6. Nathan Glazer (1975: 197) has a set of very poignant comments on this literature, particularly with respect to advocacy, urban renewal, and community preservation: "The most influential single book on urban renewal was perhaps Herbert Gans's *The Urban Villagers* [1962], which told with controlled objectivity and yet with passion the story of the destruction, by urban renewal, of the West End of Boston, and in particular of its working-class, second-generation Italian community. The West End was not Greenwich Village, but it had an Italian community, cheap and small-scale housing, a pleasant site near downtown, the urban amenities of small stores and street life celebrated by Jane Jacobs in *The Death and Life of Great American Cities*."

7. See Newby et al. (1995).

8. See also Bourdieu (1987), Raymond Smith (1984, 1987), and Stark (1980).

9. According to E. P. Thompson (1963: 142): "By class I understand an historical phenomenon, unifying a number of disparate and seemingly unconnected events, both in the raw material of experience and in consciousness. I emphasize that it is an historical phenomenon. I do not see class as a 'structure,' nor even as a 'category,' but as something which in fact happens and can be shown to have happened in community relationships.

"More than this, the notion of class entails the notion of historical relationship. Like any other relationship, it is a fluency which evades analysis if we attempt to stop it dead at any given moment and anatomise its structure . . . The relationship must always be embodied in real people and in a real context. . . . Class happens when some men, as a result of common experiences (inherited or shared), feel and articulate the identity of their interests as between themselves, and as against other men whose interests are different from (and usually opposed to) theirs. The class experience is largely determined by the productive relations into which men are born—or enter involuntarily. Class consciousness is the way in which these experiences are handled in cultural terms: embodied in traditions, value-systems, ideas, and institutional forms . . . Consciousness of class arises in the same way in different times and places, but never in just the same way. . . . class is not this or that part of the machine, but the way the machine works once it is set in motion—not this and that interest, but the friction of interests—the movement itself, the heat, the thundering noise . . . When we speak of a class we are thinking of a very loosely defined body of people who share the same congeries of interests, social experiences, traditions and value systems, who have a disposition to behave as a class, to define themselves in their actions and their consciousness in relation to other groups of people in class ways. But class itself is not a thing, it is a happening."

3. Being a Real East Ender

1. See Bourdieu (1977). We have the kinship charts of some sixty families, the data from which will not be analyzed here. Urban kinship has received relatively little attention in the anthropological literature. There are some exceptions, however. See Firth (1956); Firth, Hubert, and Forge (1970); Rapp (1987); Stack (1974); Yanagisako (1977, 1978); and Young and Willmott (1962).

4. East End Textures

1. Despite the widely held notion of Appalachia as a white, Anglo-Saxon, Protestant enclave, African Americans have played a crucial role in the region's social and economic history, and they fought side by side with European immigrants and native mountaineers in the battles to unionize the coalfields. See Lewis (1987) and Turner and Cabbell (1985). See also Manning-Miller (1993), Gaventa (1980), Gilkes (1983), and Gitlin and Hollander (1970).

2. See Collins (1968, 1990) and Stewart (1990).

3. The pattern of child care for grandchildren by grandmothers is very widespread in the East End. Children include official as well as unofficial kin. Mrs. Schiffer, deceased in 1996, took care of the grandchildren while her daughter worked. Mrs. Schiffer's children live in Amelia and Felicity, Ohio, two rural towns east of Cincinnati. Robbie Kale cares for her two grandchildren on a full-time basis while her daughter and son-in-law work. June Bogel lived for a while with her nephew and granddaughter. Her grandchildren visit regularly. These visits are not brief. They can last anywhere from a few days to a few weeks. She raised one of her granddaughters. Betsy O'Malley's grandson has lived with her for a few years. He wants to finish school in Cincinnati rather than in Kentucky, where his mother lives. Amy Lane is very close to her sister's grandchildren. She takes care of small children in her home. Mrs. Williams cares for a neighborhood boy who calls her and her husband Grandma and Grandpa. She has become very close to the single mother of these two boys. Phyllis Potter's grandchildren are in and out of her house all the time. Dottie Walters' children, grandchildren, and great-grandchildren visit regularly. "Kids come down almost every day." Dottie's older sister took her in after their mother died. Dottie was sixteen. Two of her grandchildren live with her.

5. Fieldwork at Home

1. See Fisher and Foster (1979). See also Foster, Robinson, and Fisher (1978).

2. See Jackson (1987). See also Hastrup and Elsass (1990), Maybury-Lewis (1985), Messerschmidt (1981), Obermiller (1996), Obermiller and Philliber (1987), Paine (1985), and Sansom (1985).

3. Two graduate students have written M.A. theses based on East End data; see Jared (1993) and Zaylor (1996).

4. See Jones (1972, 1987), Leacock (1987), Rodman (1992, 1993), and Rodman and Cooper (1989).

5. Our findings were not at all inconsistent with those of "The East End Community Report." They were arrived at and presented very differently, however, very informally, throughout the research process.

6. Among the more amazing ones we heard during our fieldwork was the story of a family that descended from the Hatfields of Hatfield and McCoy fame. The Hatfields are reputed to have owned the land on which Westminster Abbey now sits. The family is large, extended, and famous and had an enormous impact on the community once its members migrated to and settled in the rural parts of Appalachian Kentucky.

6. The Cultural Economy of the East End

1. See Halperin (1990).

2. See Halperin (1994a).

3. Batteau (1983); Precourt (1983: 91).

4. Billings, Blee, and Swanson (1986); Eller (1982).

5. Halperin (1990, 1994a).

6. Dow (1977: 111), following Ferman and Ferman (1973: 3), has referred to the informal economy as "the *irregular economy*, defined simply as any 'work that is unrecorded and unmeasured by any private or public monitoring agency and which entails a cash exchange' . . . As Ferman and Ferman explain, some of this work is criminal . . . but most is not. The bulk of it might more correctly be termed *extralegal*, rather than *criminal*, in that its illegality stems from the fact that people who engage in such work ignore administrative codes both by failing to report taxable income and by failing to obtain the licensing necessary to legitimize the work" (emphasis in original). I have written about the informal economy in rural Appalachia using a cross-cultural frame (see Halperin and Sturdevant 1990). See also Hannerz (1980), Harding and Jenkins (1989), Shraff (1987), and Young and Willmott (1957).

7. See Clarke-Ekong (in press).

8. Halperin (1990).

7. Community Planning

1. All of the poems in this chapter were written by Eileen Waters.

2. See Halperin (1994b).

3. The Plan Group is a subcommittee of the RAC, which is the citizens' group assigned to give advice to the city about planning along the riverfront.

4. Eminent domain is still an issue.

5. The ANP is an agency whose mission is to help low-income residents with housing problems, including assistance with heating, insulation, and relocation.

6. A reference to the East End's shabby exterior.

7. These mental health issues are explored in Chapter 8.

8. It was also in this period that the poem about the Pendleton Building was written (see beginning of Chapter 10).

8. Health, Culture, and Practicing Community

1. Reiter (1995) has argued that there are similarities in the symptom patterns of "nerves," *ataques de nervios,* and *susto* because they arise out of similar socioeconomic circumstances in situations of rapid culture change.

2. See Janzen (1978).

3. See Fuller (1992).

4. "Nerves" resembles other culture-bound syndromes around the world, that is, those prevalent in populations undergoing rapid culture change, rural-to-urban migration, and varying degrees of so-called modernization. See Davis and Low (1989), Simons and Hughes (1985), and Van Schaik (1988, 1989).

5. See Reiter (1995).

9. Contested Territory

1. She is referring to the East End Community Report discussed at length in Chapter 5.

10. The Heritage Center Comes of Age

1. This poem was written by Eileen Waters.

11. Local Colonialism and the Politics of Factionalism

1. See also Lewis, Johnson, and Askins (1978: 2).

2. See also Eller (1982), Giardina (1987), and Lewis (1987).

3. See Bhabha's (1994) discussion of colonialism.

4. See Klor de Alva (1995).

13. Practicing Community, Culture, and Class

1. Anglin (1993: 263) has suggested for rural southern Appalachia that "regional culture [is] a force that informs the construction of class consciousness, gender relations, and community life. In this reading, regional culture is not construed in simple terms as the locus of folk ideology or a set of doctrinal structures underwritten by traditional authority. Rather, regional culture encompasses material resources, systems of kin/community ties, and

pragmatic information about how to live in specific settings, in addition to perspectives on what is a life well-lived. It reflects a particular history and set of socioeconomic conditions, and is the means by which individuals come to terms with, or contest, these particularities.

"This approach stands in contrast with prevailing schools of thought that have either romanticized Appalachian culture or dismissed it as the locus of exploitative policies imposed by agents of industrial capitalism."

2. Banks, Billings, and Tice (1993) discuss postmodernism and Appalachian studies. See also Fisher (1993: 290–291) and Waller (1988).

3. Lowenhaupt-Singh (1993: 7).

Postscript

1. A fuller explication of these psychological costs and benefits is being drafted for the sequel to this book. The sequel, tentatively titled *Subtle Boundaries,* is an exploration of boundaries of race, gender, class, self, and "other."

2. My hope is that by dealing with a specific ethnographic context, it will be possible to diminish some of the blatant ethnocentrism of postmodern thought.

3. Foucault (1977, 1980).

4. Foucault (1980: 82).

5. ". . . one can extend to the system of signs in general what Saussure says of language: 'Language is necessary for speech to be intelligible and to produce all its effects; but speech is necessary for language to be established . . .' There is a circle here, for if one rigorously distinguishes language and speech, code and message, schema and usage, etc., and if one wishes to do justice to the two postulates thus enunciated, one does not know where to begin, nor how something can begin in general, be it language or speech. Therefore, one has to admit, before any dissociation of language and speech, code and message, etc. (and everything that goes along with such a dissociation), a systematic production of differences, the *production* of a system of differences—a *différance*—within whose effects one eventually, by abstraction and according to determined motivations, will be able to demarcate a linguistics of language and a linguistics of speech, etc." (Derrida 1981: 28).

"The term *différance,* which Derrida introduces here, alludes to this undecidable, nonsynthetic alternation between the perspectives of structure and event. The verb *différer* means to differ and to defer. *Différance* sounds exactly the same as *différence,* but the ending *ance,* which is used to produce verbal nouns, makes it a new form meaning 'difference-differing-deferring.' *Différance* thus designates both a 'passive' difference already in place as the condition of signification and an act of differing which produces differences" (Jonathan Culler, 1982 : 96 –97).

6. See Stavenhagen (1968).

7. See Bhabha (1990), Crapanzano (1992), Dirks (1992b), "Introduction" in Prakash (1995), and Said (1978, 1993).

8. Bourdieu (1977: 34).

9. Ibid.: 37.

10. Ibid.

11. Ibid.: 72.

12. Ibid.: 78, 79.

13. See Bourdieu (1977: 81): "The habitus is precisely this immanent law . . . laid down by each agent by his earliest upbringing, which is the precondition not only for the coordination of practices but also for practices of co-ordination, since the corrections and adjustments the agents themselves consciously carry out presuppose their mastery of a common code and since undertakings of collective mobilization cannot succeed without a minimum of concordance between the habitus of the mobilizing agents (e.g. prophet, party leader, etc.) and the dispositions of those whose aspirations and world view they express." Bourdieu is really talking about a superorganic concept of culture here: "So it is because they are the product of dispositions which, being the same internalization of the same objective structures, are objectively concerted that the practices of the members of the same group or, in a differentiated society, the same class are endowed with an objective meaning that is at once unitary and systematic, transcending subjective intentions and conscious projects whether individual or collective" (1977: 81).

He underlines the relationship between structure and agency here: "In fact it is their present and past positions in the social structure that biological individuals carry with them, at all times and in all places, in the form of dispositions which are so many ranks of *social position*" (p. 82).

He summarizes (p. 82): "In short, the habitus, the product of history, produces individual and collective practices . . . The system of dispositions—a past which survives in the present and tends to perpetuate itself into the future by making itself present in practices structured according to its principles is the principle of the continuity and regularity which objectivity discerns in the social world without being able to give them a rational basis."

The past is part of the present and the future in the East End: "Habitus, understood as a system of lasting, transposable dispositions which, integrating past experiences, function at every moment as a *matrix of perceptions, appreciations, and actions* and makes possible the achievement of infinitely diversified tasks" (p. 82).

"Because the habitus is an endless capacity to engender products— thoughts, perceptions, expressions, actions—whose limits are set by the historically and socially striated conditions of its production, the conditioned and conditional freedom it secures is as remote from a creation of unpredictable novelty as it is from a simple, mechanical reproduction of the initial conditionings" (p. 95).

BIBLIOGRAPHY

Alinsky, Saul D.
1989 *Reveille for Radicals.* New York: Vintage Books.

Anglin, Mary K.
1993 "Engendering the Struggle: Women's Labor and Traditions of Resistance in Rural Southern Appalachia." In *Fighting Back in Appalachia: Traditions of Resistance and Change,* edited by Stephen L. Fisher, pp. 263–281. Philadelphia: Temple University Press.

Arensberg, Conrad M.
1961 "The Community As Object and Sample." *American Anthropologist* 63: 241–264.

Arensberg, Conrad M., and S. T. Kimball
1940 *Family and Community in Ireland.* London: Peter Smith.

Arnow, Harriet
1978 *The Dollmaker.* New York: Macmillan.

Banks, Alan, Dwight Billings, and Karen Tice
1993 "Appalachian Studies, Resistance and Post-Modernism." In *Fighting Back in Appalachia,* edited by Stephen L. Fisher, pp. 283–301. Philadelphia: Temple University Press.

Batteau, Allen W.
1983 *Appalachia and America: Autonomy and Regional Dependence.* Lexington: University Press of Kentucky.
1990 *The Invention of Appalachia.* Tucson: University of Arizona Press.

Bauman, Zygmunt

1989 *Modernity and the Holocaust.* Cambridge: Polity Press.

1991 *Modernity and Ambivalence.* Cambridge: Polity Press.

1995 "Sociology and Postmodernity." In *Class,* edited by Patrick Joyce, pp. 74–83. Oxford: Oxford University Press.

Bhabha, Homi K.

1994 *The Location of Culture.* London and New York: Routledge.

Bhabha, Homi K., ed.

1990 *Nation and Narration.* London and New York: Routledge.

Billings, Dwight B., Kathleen Blee, and Louis Swanson

1986 "Culture, Family, and Community in Preindustrial Appalachia." *Appalachian Journal* 13: 154–170.

Borman, Kathryn M., and Phillip J. Obermiller, eds.

1994 *From Mountain to Metropolis: Appalachian Migrants in American Cities.* Westport, Conn.: Bergin & Garvey.

Bott, Elizabeth

1957 *Family and Social Network: Roles, Norms and External Relationships in Ordinary Families.* London: Tavistock.

Bourdieu, Pierre

1977 *An Outline of Practice.* Translated by Richard Nice. Cambridge and New York: Cambridge University Press.

1987 "What Makes a Social Class?" *Berkeley Journal of Sociology* 22: 1–18.

Castells, Manuel

1978 *City, Class and Power.* London: Macmillan.

1980 *The Urban Question: A Marxist Approach.* Translated by Alan Sheridan. Cambridge, Mass.: MIT Press.

1983 *The City and the Grassroots.* London: Edward Arnold.

Clarke-Ekong, Sheila

In press "Out of Sight: Working Women Who Stay Invisible." In *Women in the Informal Sector: Case Studies and Theoretical Approaches,* edited by Tamar Diana Wilson and Judith E. Marti. Albany: State University of New York Press.

Clifford, James

1986 "Introduction: Partial Truths." In *Writing Culture: The Poetics and Politics of Ethnography: A School of American Research Advanced Seminar,* edited by James Clifford and George E. Marcus, pp. 1–26. Berkeley and Los Angeles: University of California Press.

Clifford, James, and George E. Marcus, eds.

1986   *Writing Culture: The Poetics and Politics of Ethnography: A School of Ameri-can Research Advanced Seminar.* Berkeley and Los Angeles: University of California Press.

Cohen, Anthony P.

1982   *Belonging: Identity and Social Organization in British Rural Cultures.* St. John's, Newfoundland: Institute of Social Science Research.

1985   *The Symbolic Construction of Community.* London and New York: Tavistock.

Collins, Patricia Hill

1968   "Learning from the Outsider within: the Sociological Significance of Black Feminist Thought." *Social Problems* 33(6): 14–32.

1990   *Black Feminist Thought.* New York: Routledge.

Crapanzano, Vincent

1992   *Hermes' Dilemma and Hamlet's Desire: On the Epistemology of Interpretation.* Cambridge, Mass.: Harvard University Press.

Crompton, Rosemary

1995   "The Development of the Classical Inheritance." In *Class,* edited by Patrick Joyce. Oxford: Oxford University Press.

Culler, Jonathan D.

1982   *On Deconstruction: Theory and Criticism after Structuralism.* Ithaca, N.Y.: Cornell University Press.

Davis, Dona L., and Setha Low

1989   *Gender, Health, and Illness: The Case of Nerves.* New York: Hemisphere.

Derrida, Jacques

1977   *Of Grammatology.* Translated by Gayatri Chakravorty Spivak. Baltimore: Johns Hopkins University Press.

1978   *Writing and Difference.* Translated by Alan Bass. London: Routledge and Kegan Paul.

1981   *Positions.* Translated by Alan Bass. Chicago: University of Chicago Press.

Dirks, Nicholas B.

1992a   *Colonialism and Culture.* Ann Arbor: University of Michigan Press.

1992b   "Introduction: Colonialism and Culture." In *Colonialism and Culture,* edited by Nicholas Dirks, pp. 1–25. Ann Arbor: University of Michigan Press.

Dirks, Nicholas B., Geoff Ely, and Sherry B. Ortner

1994   *Culture/Power/History.* Princeton: Princeton University Press.

Dow, Leslie M., Jr.

1977 "High Weeds in Detroit: The Irregular Economy among a Network of Appalachian Migrants." *Urban Anthropology* 6: 111–128.

Eames, Edwin, and Judith Granich Goode, eds.

1977 *Anthropology of the City: An Introduction to Urban Anthropology.* Englewood Cliffs, N.J.: Prentice-Hall.

Eller, Ronald D.

1982 *Miners, Millhands, and Mountaineers: Industrialization of the Appalachian South, 1880–1930.* Knoxville: University of Tennessee Press.

Ergood, Bruce, and Bruce E. Kuhre, eds.

1991 *Appalachia: Social Context Past and Present.* 3d ed. Dubuque, Ia.: Kendall/Hunt.

Ferman, Patricia, and Louis Ferman

1973 "The Structural Underpinning of the Irregular Economy." *Poverty and Human Resources Abstracts* 8: 3–17.

Firth, Raymond

1956 *Two Studies of Kinship in London.* London: Athlone Press.

Firth, Raymond, Jane Hubert, and A. Forge

1970 *Families and Their Relatives.* London: Routledge and Kegan Paul.

Fisher, Stephen L., ed.

1993 *Fighting Back in Appalachia.* Philadelphia: Temple University Press.

Fisher, Steve, and Jim Foster

1979 "Models for Furthering Revolutionary Praxis in Appalachia." *Appalachian Journal* 6: 170–194.

Foster, Jim, Steve Robinson, and Steve Fisher

1978 "Class, Political Consciousness, and Destructive Power: A Strategy for Change in Appalachia." *Appalachian Journal* 5: 290–311.

Foucault, Michel

1977 *Discipline and Punishment.* London: Allen Lane.

1980 *Power/Knowledge: Selected Interviews and Other Writings, 1972–1977.* Edited by Colin Gordon. Translated by Colin Gordon et al. New York: Pantheon Books.

Fuller, Nancy J.

1992 "The Museum As a Vehicle for Community Empowerment: The Ak-Chin Indian Community Ecomuseum Project." In *Museums and Communities: The Politics of Public Culture,* edited by Ivan Karp, Christine

Mullen Kreamer, and Steven D. Lavine, pp. 327–366. Washington, D.C.: Smithsonian Institution Press.

Gans, Herbert J.

1962   *The Urban Villagers*. New York: Free Press.

García Canclini, Néstor

1993   *Transforming Modernity: Popular Culture in Mexico*. Translated by Lidia Lozano. Austin: University of Texas Press.

Gaventa, John

1980   *Power and Powerlessness: Quiescence and Rebellion in an Appalachian Valley*. Urbana: University of Illinois Press.

Gaventa, John, Barbara E. Smith, and Alex Willingham, eds.

1990   *Communities in Economic Crisis: Appalachia and the South*. Philadelphia: Temple University Press.

Geertz, Clifford

1983   *Local Knowledge: Further Essays in Interpretive Anthropology*. New York: Basic Books.

Giardina, Denise

1987   *Storming Heaven: A Novel*. New York: Norton.

Giddens, Anthony

1971   *Capitalism and Modern Social Theory*. Cambridge: Cambridge University Press.

1973   *The Class Structure of the Advanced Societies*. London: Hutchinson.

1990   *The Consequences of Modernity*. Cambridge: Polity Press.

1991   *Modernity and Self Identity*. Cambridge: Polity Press.

1994   "Living in a Post-traditional Society." In *Reflexivity and Its Doubles: Structures, Aesthetics and Community*, edited by U. Beck, A. Giddens, and S. Lash. Cambridge: Polity Press.

Gilkes, Cheryl

1983   "From Slavery to Social Welfare: Racism and the Control of Black Women." In *Class, Race, and Sex*, edited by Hanna Lessinger and Amy Swerdlow, pp. 288–300. Boston: Hall.

Gitlin, Todd, and Nanci Hollander

1970   *Uptown: Poor Whites in Chicago*. New York: Harper & Row.

Glazer, Nathan

1975   "For White and Black, Community Control is the Issue." In *Metropolitan Communities*, edited by Joseph Bensman and Arthur Vidich, pp. 197–212. New York: New York Times Co.

Halperin, Rhoda H.

1990 *The Livelihood of Kin: Making Ends Meet "the Kentucky Way."* Austin: University of Texas Press.

1994a *Cultural Economies Past and Present.* Austin: University of Texas Press.

1994b "Appalachians in Cities: Issues and Challenges for Research." In *From Mountain to Metropolis: Appalachian Migrants in American Cities,* edited by Kathryn M. Borman and Phillip J. Obermiller, pp. 181–198. Westport, Conn.: Bergin & Garvey.

Halperin, Rhoda H., and Sara Sturdevant

1990 "A Cross-Cultural Treatment of the Informal Economy." In *Perspectives on the Informal Economy,* edited by M. Estellie Smith, pp. 295–310. New York: University Press of America.

Hannerz, U.

1980 *Exploring the City: Inquiries towards an Urban Anthropology.* New York: Columbia University Press.

Harding, P., and R. Jenkins.

1989 *The Myth of the Hidden Economy: Towards a New Understanding of Informal Economic Activity.* Milton Keynes: Open University Press.

Hastrup, Kristen, and Peter Elsass

1990 "Anthropological Advocacy, a Contradiction in Terms?" *Current Anthropology* 31(3): 301–311.

Herzfeld, Michael

1987 *Anthropology through the Looking Glass: Critical Ethnography in the Margins of Europe.* Cambridge: Cambridge University Press.

Jackson, Anthony, ed.

1987 *Anthropology at Home. ASA Monographs 25.* London: Tavistock.

Jacobs, Jane

1961 *The Death and Life of Great American Cities.* New York: Random House.

Janzen, John

1978 *The Quest for Therapy in Lower Zaire.* Berkeley and Los Angeles: University of California Press.

Jared, Sherry

1993 "Household versus Social Network: Life Courses of Urban Appalachian Women." M.A. thesis, University of Cincinnati.

Jones, Delmos J.

1972 "Incipient Organizations and Organizational Failures in an Urban Ghetto." *Urban Anthropology* 1: 51–67.

1987   "The 'Community' and Organizations in the Community." In *Cities of the United States: Studies in Urban Anthropology*, edited by Leith Mullings, pp. 99–121. New York: Columbia University Press.

Joyce, Patrick, ed.
1995   *Class*. Oxford: Oxford University Press.

Klor de Alva, Jorge
1995   "The Postcolonization of the (Latin) American Experience: A Reconsideration of 'Colonialism,' 'Postcolonialism,' and 'Mestizaje.'" In *After Colonialism: Imperial Histories and Postcolonial Displacements*, edited by Gyan Prakash, pp. 241–275. Princeton: Princeton University Press.

Lash, Scott, and John Urry
1987   *The End of Organized Capitalism*. Cambridge: Polity Press.
1994   *Economies of Signs and Space*. London: Sage.

Lazarus-Black, Mindie, and Susan F. Hirsch
1994   *Contested States: Law, Hegemony and Resistance*. New York: Routledge.

Leacock, Eleanor
1987   "Theory and Ethics in Applied Urban Anthropology." In *Cities of the United States: Studies in Urban Anthropology*, edited by Leith Mullings, pp. 317–336. New York: Columbia University Press.

Leeds, Anthony
1973   "Locality Power in Relation to Supralocal Power Institutions." In *Urban Anthropology: Cross-Cultural Studies of Urbanization*, edited by Aidan Southall, pp. 15–41. New York: Oxford University Press.
1980   "Towns and Villages in Society: Hierarchies of Order and Cause," in *Cities in a Larger Context*, edited by Thomas W. Collins. Athens: University of Georgia Press.

Lewis, Helen M., Linda Johnson, and Donald Askins, eds.
1978   *Colonialism in Modern America: The Appalachian Case*. Boone, N.C.: Appalachian Consortium Press.

Lewis, Ronald L.
1987   *Black Coal Miners in America: Race, Class, and Community Conflict, 1780–1980*. Lexington: University Press of Kentucky.

Liebow, Elliot
1967   *Tally's Corner: A Study of Negro Streetcorner Men*. Boston: Little, Brown.

Low, Setha
1993   "Cultural Meaning of the Plaza: The History of the Spanish American Gridplan-Plaza Urban Design." In *The Cultural Meaning of Urban Space*,

edited by Robert Rotenberg and Gary McDonogh, pp. 75–94. Westport, Conn.: Bergin & Garvey.

Lowenhaupt-Singh, Anna

1993   *In the Realm of the Diamond Queen.* Princeton, N.J.: Princeton University Press.

Lustiger-Thaler, Henri, and Daniel Salee

1994   "The Quest for a Politically Effective Language of Everyday Life." In *Artful Practices: The Political Economy of Everyday Life,* edited by Henri Lustiger-Thaler and Daniel Salee. New York: Black Rose Books.

Lyotard, Jean François

1984   *The Postmodern Condition: A Report of Knowledge.* Manchester: Manchester University Press.

Maggard, Sally Ward

1986   "Class and Gender: New Theoretical Priorities in Appalachian Studies." In *The Impact of Institutions in Appalachia: Proceedings of the Eighth Annual Appalachian Studies Conference,* edited by Jim Lloyd and Anne G. Campbell. Boone, N.C.: Appalachian Consortium Press.

Maloney, Michael

1991   *The East End Community Report.* Cincinnati: Legal Aid Society and Urban Appalachian Council.

Manning-Miller, Don

1993   "Racism and Organizing in Appalachia." In *Fighting Back in Appalachia: Traditions of Resistance and Change,* edited by Stephen L. Fisher, pp. 57–68. Philadelphia: Temple University Press.

Maybury-Lewis, David

1985   "A Special Sort of Pleading—Anthropology at the Service of Ethnic Groups." In *Advocacy and Anthropology: First Encounters,* edited by Robert Paine. St. John's, Newfoundland: Institute of Social and Economic Research, Memorial University of Newfoundland.

Messerschmidt, Donald A.

1981   "On Anthropology 'at Home.'" In *Anthropologists at Home in North America: Methods and Issues in the Study of One's Society,* edited by Donald A. Messerschmidt, pp. 3–14. New York: Cambridge University Press.

Miller, Zane

1968   *Boss Cox's Cincinnati.* New York: Columbia University.

Mollenkopf, John H.

1983   *The Contested City.* Princeton, N.J.: Princeton University Press.

Mullings, Leith
1987 "Introduction: Urban Anthropology and U.S. Cities." In *Cities of the United States: Studies in Urban Anthropology,* edited by Leith Mullings, pp. 1–18. New York: Columbia University Press.

Nash, June, and M. Patricia Fernández-Kelly, eds.
1983 *Women, Men, and the International Division of Labor.* Albany: State University of New York Press.

Newby, Howard, et al.
1995 "An Inheritance Reaffirmed: Weber." In, *Class,* edited by Patrick Joyce, pp. 55–64. Oxford: Oxford University Press.

Obermiller, Phillip J.
1996 *Down Home, Downtown: Urban Appalachians Today.* Dubuque, Ia.: Kendall/Hunt.

Obermiller, Phillip J., and W. Philliber, eds.
1987 *Too Few Tomorrows: Urban Appalachians in the 1980s.* Boone, N.C.: Appalachian Consortium Press.

Ong, A.
1991 "The Gender and Labour Politics of Postmodernity." *Annual Review of Anthropology* 20: 279–307.

Paine, Robert, ed.
1985 *Advocacy and Anthropology: First Encounters.* St. John's, Newfoundland: Institute of Social and Economic Research, Memorial University of Newfoundland.

Park, R. E.
1967 "The City: Suggestions for the Investigation of Human Behavior in an Urban Environment." In *The City,* edited by R. E. Park, E. W. Burgess, and R. D. McKenzie. Chicago: University of Chicago Press.

Paul, Benjamin, ed.
1955 *Health, Culture and Community: Case Studies of Public Reactions to Health Programs.* With Walter Miller. New York: Russell Sage Foundation.

Peattie, Lisa Redfield, and Edward Robbins
1984 "Anthropological Approaches to the City." In *Cities of the Mind: Images and Themes of the City in the Social Sciences,* edited by Lloyd Rodwin and Robert M. Hollister, pp. 83–95. New York: Plenum Press.

Philliber, William W., and Clyde B. McCoy, eds.
1981 *The Invisible Minority: Urban Appalachians.* Lexington: University Press of Kentucky.

Polanyi, Karl

1944   *The Great Transformation.* New York: Holt, Rinehart & Winston.

Prakash, Gyan

1995   "Introduction: After Colonialism." In *After Colonialism: Imperial Histories and Postcolonial Displacements,* edited by Gyan Prakash, pp. 3–17. Princeton, N.J.: Princeton University Press.

Precourt, Walter

1983   "The Image of Appalachian Poverty." In *Appalachia and America: Autonomy and Regional Dependence,* edited by Alan Batteau. Lexington: University of Kentucky Press.

Rapp, Rayna

1987   "Urban Kinship in Contemporary America: Families, Classes and Ideology." In *Cities of the United States: Studies in Urban Anthropology,* edited by Leith Mullings, pp. 219–242. New York: Columbia University Press.

Redfield, Robert

1964   *The Folk Culture of Yucatan.* Chicago: University of Chicago Press.

1973   [1960] *The Little Community.* Chicago: University of Chicago Press.

Reiter, Jennifer L.

1995   "A Comparative Study of Culture-Bound Syndromes: Ataques de Nervios, Nerves, and Susto." M.A. thesis, University of Cincinnati.

Richardson, Miles

1989   "Place and Culture: Two Disciplines, Two Concepts, Two Images of Christ and a Single Goal." In *The Power of Place,* edited by John A. Agnew and James S. Duncan, pp. 140–156. Boston: Unwin.

Rodman, Margaret

1992   "Empowering Place: Multilocality and Multivocality." *American Anthropologist* 94(3): 640–656.

1993   "Beyond Built Form and Culture in the Anthropological Study of Residential Community Spaces." In *The Cultural Meaning of Urban Space,* edited by Robert Rotenberg and Gary McDonogh, pp. 123–138. Westport, Conn.: Bergin & Garvey.

Rodman, Margaret, and Matthew Cooper

1989   "The Sociocultural Production of Urban Space: Building a Fully Accessible Toronto Housing Cooperative," *City and Society* 3(1): 9–22.

Rollwagen, Jack R.

1980   "Evolutionary Perspective in the Study of Urban Anthropology." In *Cities in a Larger Context,* edited by Thomas Collins, pp. 123–140. Southern Anthropological Society Proceedings, no. 14. Athens: University of Georgia Press.

Rotenberg, Robert, and Gary McDonogh, eds.
1993   *The Cultural Meaning of Urban Space.* Westport, Conn.: Bergin & Garvey.

Said, Edward W.
1978   *Orientalism.* New York: Random House.
1993   *Culture and Imperialism.* New York: Alfred A. Knopf.

Sansom, Basil
1985   "Canons of Anthropology?" In *Advocacy and Anthropology: First Encounters,* edited by Robert Paine. St. John's, Newfoundland: Institute of Social and Economic Research, Memorial University of Newfoundland.

Schneider, David M.
1979   "Kinship, Community, and Locality in American Culture." In *Kinship and Communities,* edited by A. J. Lichtman and J. R. Challinor, pp. 155–174. Washington, D.C.: Smithsonian Institution Press.

Schneider, David, and Raymond T. Smith
1978   *Class Difference in American Kinship.* Ann Arbor: University of Michigan Press.

Sennett, Richard
1970   *Families against the City.* Cambridge, Mass.: Harvard University Press.

Sennett, Richard, and Jonathan Cobb
1972   *The Hidden Injuries of Class.* New York: Knopf.

Shraff, Jagna
1987   "The Underground Economy of a Poor Neighborhood." In *Cities of the United States: Studies in Urban Anthropology,* edited by Leith Mullings, pp. 20–50. New York: Columbia University Press.

Sieber, R. Timothy
1993   "Public Access on the Urban Waterfront: A Question of Vision." In *The Cultural Meaning of Urban Space,* edited by Robert Rotenberg and Gary McDonogh, pp. 123–138. Westport, Conn.: Bergin & Garvey.

Simons, Ronald C., and Charles C. Hughes, eds.
1985   *The Culture-Bound Syndromes: Folk Illnesses of Psychiatric and Anthropological Interest.* Boston: D. Reidel.

Smith, Lee
1995   *Saving Grace.* New York: G. P. Putnam's Sons.

Smith, Raymond T.

1984　"Anthropology and the Concept of Social Class." *Annual Review of Anthropology* 13: 467–494.

1987　"Kinship and Class in Chicago." In *Cities of the United States: Studies in Urban Anthropology,* edited by Leith Mullings, pp. 292–316. New York: Columbia University Press.

Stack, Carol

1974　*All Our Kin: Strategies for Survival in a Black Community.* New York: Harper and Row.

Stark, David

1980　"Class, Struggle, and the Labour Process." *Theory and Society* 9(1): 96–97.

Stavenhagen, Rodolfo

1968　*Clases, colonialismo y acculturación; Ensayo sobre un sistema de relaciones interétnicas en Mesoamérica.* Guatemala City: Editorial J. de Pineda Ibarra, Ministerio de Educación.

Steinbeck, John

1976　*The Grapes of Wrath.* Penguin Books.

Stewart, Kathleen C.

1990　"Backtalking the Wilderness: 'Appalachian' Engenderings." In *Uncertain Terms: Negotiating Gender in American Culture,* edited by Faye Ginsburg and Anna L. Tsing. Boston: Beacon Press.

1991　"On the Politics of Cultural Theory: A Case for 'Contaminated' Cultural Critique." *Social Research* 58: 395–412.

Susser, Ida

1986　"Political Activity among Working Class Women in a U.S. City." *American Ethnologist* 13(1): 108–117.

Suttles, G.

1968　*The Social Order of the Slum.* Chicago: University of Chicago Press.

Thomas, Nicholas

1994　*Colonialism's Culture: Anthropology, Travel, and Government.* Cambridge: Polity Press.

Thompson, E. P.

1963　*The Making of the English Working Class.* New York: Pantheon Books.

Tice, Karen W., and Dwight B. Billings

1991　"Appalachian Culture and Resistance." *Journal of Progressive Human Services* 2: 1–18.

Timm, Patricia
1994   "Early School Leaving: An Analysis across Three Generations of Urban Appalachian Women." Ph.D. dissertation, University of Cincinnati.

Turner, William H., and Edward J. Cabbell, eds.
1985   *Blacks in Appalachia.* Lexington: University Press of Kentucky.

Van Schaik, Eileen
1988   "The Social Context of 'Nerves' in Eastern Kentucky." In *Appalachian Mental Health,* edited by Susan Emley Keefe, pp. 81–100. Lexington: University Press of Kentucky.
1989   "Paradigms Underlying the Study of Nerves As a Popular Illness Term in Eastern Kentucky." *Medical Anthropology* 11: 15–28.

Walker, Alice
1982   *The Color Purple.* New York: Pocket Books.

Waller, Altina L.
1988   *Feud: Hatfields, McCoys, and Social Change in Appalachia, 1860–1900.* Chapel Hill: University of North Carolina Press.

West, Cornel
1993   *Race Matters.* Boston: Beacon Press.

Whyte, W.
1948   *Street Corner Society.* Chicago: University of Chicago Press.

Williams, Raymond
1973   *The Country and the City.* New York: Oxford University Press.

Yanagisako, Sylvia J.
1977   "Women-Centered Kin Networks in Urban, Bilateral Kinship." *American Ethnologist* 4(2): 207–226.
1978   "Variance in American Kinship: Implications for Cultural Analysis." *American Ethnologist* 5: 15–29.

Young, Michael, and Peter Willmott
1957   *Family and Kinship in East London.* London: Tavistock.
1962   *Family and Kinship in East London.* Harmondsworth: Penguin.

Zaylor, Andrea
1996   "Community-generated Representation: An Urban Appalachian Heritage Exhibit." M.A. thesis, University of Cincinnati.

AUTHOR INDEX

SUBJECT INDEX

Board of Health, 83
Brill family, 208–209
Broadway Street, 46

California, Ohio, 49, 53, 66, 70, 266
Carl Street, 83
Carnegie Library, 244
Carter family, 195–198
cash, shortage of, 63
Catholic Archdiocese, 275
Central Psychiatric Clinic, 209
Channel 9, 289
Chatfield College, 274
Children's Protective Services, 197, 207
churches; ministries and, 29; Saint Simon's, 108; Saint Steven's, 74, 106, 230. *See also* Mount Carmel Baptist Church; Saint Rose Catholic Church
Church family, 50–57, 85, 133, 138, 184, 224
Cincinnati, city of, 10, 270; power structure in, 39
Cincinnatians, 1
Cincinnati Buildings and Inspections Department, 24, 287
Cincinnati Consumer Services, 287
Cincinnati Department of Public Works, 203
Cincinnati Enquirer, 89, 283, 311–312
Cincinnati Gas and Electric Company, 63, 232, 243
Cincinnati Health Department, 24
Cincinnati Health Network, 302
Cincinnati Neighborhood Services, 287
Cincinnati Office of Research, Evaluation and Budget (REB), 242
Cincinnati Park Board, 174, 182
Cincinnati public schools, 132
Cincinnati Reds, 235
Cincinnati Water Works, 28

City Council (of Cincinnati), 24, 31, 33, 82, 93, 120–121, 154–155, 158–159, 161–165, 180
—and eminent domain, 161–162, 218, 220, 223–224, 233–234, 237, 260, 266, 271, 273
—and inclusion of East Enders in planning, 173
—and Information Committee, 163
—presented with summary of grassroots leaders' efforts, 182
City Hall, 16, 21, 32, 34, 44–45, 69, 73, 76, 98, 100, 118, 143, 144, 155–156, 159, 163, 173, 185, 217, 229, 230, 252, 270, 273, 292, 300, 304
City Manager, 158, 241–245
City Planning Department, 20, 24, 33, 35, 158, 160, 220
Clark, Peter, Academy, 64, 66
class, 1, 47, 79, 248, 317n9; and community, 43; language of, 40–41, 293; power, 43; relations, 40; solidarity, 42; tensions within, 41
class culture, 2, 43, 292–296, 308–309
Collins Avenue, 14, 68
colonialism, 6, 251–278; in Appalachia, 251, 253; and boundaries, 256; and bylaws, 256–262; discourse of, 252, 263, 269, 304; local, 252–254, 261, 303–304; power dynamics of, 253–254; resistance to, in East End, 254, 269, 277–278, 310. *See also* power structure
colonialists, 21, 195, 261, 303
Columbia Parkway, 13–14, 23, 28, 107, 232, 266, 286, 311
Columbia Parkway Trust, 168, 170–172
Columbia Tusculum area, 12, 35, 70, 100, 107, 163, 168, 170, 172, 265–266, 283, 303, 312
Columbia Tusculum Community Council, 159

floods, 13, 27, 47, 279–291; of 1937, 312; of 1945, 46; of 1997, 77, 279–291. *See also* Ohio River
Ford family, 63–64
Fourth Street, 46

gas station, 30, 83
gender, 49–71, 149, 248. *See also* family; householding
General Equivalency Diploma, 62
gentrification in Columbia Tusculum, 12
"Gigantic Eastern Avenue Sale" flyer, 11
Gladstone Avenue, 79
grandmothers, 29, 87. *See also* elders
grassroots organizations, 113, 270. *See also* East End Area Council; East End Community Health Center; East End Riverfront Community Urban Redevelopment Corporation; Pendleton Heritage Center

habitus, 301, 306–308, 323–324n13
Hamersville, Ohio, 206
Hamilton County, 162, 241, 274
Hammond family, 51, 53, 65, 66, 290
Harrison, Ohio, 203
Head Start Program, 104, 244
health and illness, 186–216
—abortion, 201
—abuse, 205–206, 291
—accidents, 214
—AIDS, 21
—alcohol, 75, 187, 200, 203, 205–208, 215
—Alzheimer's, 29, 188, 211–213, 216
—anxiety, 207
—asthma, 200, 203, 205
—Attention Deficit Disorder, 200, 206, 215
—back pain, 205, 207
—birth control, 203, 206, 215

—black lung disease, 203
—cardiac seizure, 206
—childcare and, 215–216
—Chronic Obstructive Pulmonary Disease, 198, 205
—and culture, 186
—depression, 199, 203, 207, 213–214, 288, 291
—diabetes, 198, 200, 214
—domestic violence and, 205–206
—drugs, 202
—dyslexia, 206
—East End Syndrome ("nerves"), 187, 203, 205, 215, 321nn8.1,8.4
—elderly and convalescent care, 188
—epilepsy, 206
—headaches, 206
—high blood pressure, 214
—HIV, 82, 199, 208
—holistic approach to, 186
—hypertension, 200
—illness patterns, 214
—liver disease, 203, 205
—low self-esteem, 206, 208
—medical card and, 202
—obesity, 200
—peptic ulcer, 207
—practical kinship and, 202
—pregnancy, 78, 187–188, 200, 202, 208, 211
—renal disease, 198–199
—respiratory illness, 203
—rural to urban migration and, 187, 205
—safe sex, 215
—and scarcity of affordable housing, 200
—social services and, 216
—SSDI and, 147, 187, 206
—stress, 202–203, 213, 290
—substance abuse, 75, 200, 202, 205
—suicide, 188, 209
—tuberculosis, 81
—vision problems, 203, 204

—and Recipe for Success, 165–166
—resistance to, 164, 168
—river and, 167
—and Riverfront Advisory Council, 156, 158–159, 163
—and social stratification, 167
—tension surrounding, 157
—texts, 155, 167, 180
—traffic and, 167, 174
—and trust between city and community, 157; poem, 168–169
Pleasant Ridge neighborhood, 66
poems: cooperation with city and developers, 176–178; "East End Rap," 156–157; empowerment, 178–180; power relations, 168–172; traffic, 175–176
poetry and class, 177
positivism, critique of, 316n2
postmodernism, 109
Pothandler's Flea Market, 62
power, 248, 309
power relations: complexity of, in East End, 253–254, 270–272; and language use, 256, 267; race and gender in, 43; unequal, 2. *See also* colonialism; poetry and class
power structure, 3, 15; assumptions on part of, 10; and fragmentation, 294–295; reflected in plan, 154; working class and, 12. *See also* poems; power structures
practicing community, xi–xii, 310. *See also* community; East End; East Enders
—and Bourdieu, 307
—class and, 39, 294
—example of, 55–56
—and joking, 75
—persistent efforts of East Enders, 5
—themes central to, 34
—through therapy, 96
—work and, 12
—working class structures and, 2

pregnancy, 78, 187–188, 200, 202, 208, 211
Price Hill neighborhood, 49, 53, 58
psychological services, 32–33

Queen Cafe, 191–192

race, 84, 147, 248; and memories of elderly, 86; prejudice and, 26
Rakestraw Field, 286, 290
Recipe for Success, 24
Recipe for Successful Implementation, 25, 121, 165–166, 180–182, 233
recreation, 27
Recreation Center, 33
Recreation Department, 27, 31
Red Cross, 101, 287–288
Reed family, 205–206
research, 103; and advocacy, 103, 108, 113, 123, 274, 317n6; collaborative nature of, 119–120; and dissonant voices, 113; qualitative and quantitative data in, 104, 115; questions, 115; team, multi-cultural, 104; and theory, 299–303; timing of, 103; training for, 104–105
Research Associates, Inc., 274
river bottoms, 66
River Inn, 37–38, 66, 98, 101, 106–107, 131–132, 148, 213
Riverfront Advisory Council (RAC), 23–24, 33, 110, 154, 156–157, 158, 163–165, 174, 182, 184, 233, 245, 261, 270, 272
Robertson family, 132–134, 136–138
Robert's Rules of Order, 256, 260
Rookwood Underpass, 11
Rosin family, 203–204

safety concerns, 36
Saint Andrew Social Services, 274
Saint Rose Catholic Church, 14, 27–29, 35, 38, 68, 86, 92, 106, 175
Saint Steven's Church, 74, 106, 230